MODERN
FIRST EDITIONS

MODERN
FIRST EDITIONS
Their Value to Collectors
JOSEPH CONNOLLY

ORBIS · LONDON

By the Same Author:

Collecting Modern First Editions (1977)
P. G. Wodehouse: An Illustrated Biography (1979)
Jerome K. Jerome: A Critical Biography (1982)

for my son Charles,
in the year of his birth –
1984
2nd issue, 1st thus

© 1984 by Joseph Connolly
First published in Great Britain by
Orbis Publishing Limited, London 1984
Reprinted 1985

Printed in Great Britain
ISBN 0-85613-657-3

Set by August Filmsetting, Haydock, St. Helens

Contents

Photographs appear between pages 64 and 65, 160 and 161, and 224 and 225.

'My father knows a man who's got a book written by some old geezer round about Julius Caesar's time, and says it's worth about a hundred pounds.'

'Who says – Julius Caesar?'

'No, you clodpoll! My father says. It's a rare first edition, you see.'

'What's the good of telling me all this? I haven't got anything written about Julius Caesar's time. Except, of course, my Latin book. They're always saying what sort of a time he had in that.'

'Oh no, that's no good at all. I'm talking about valuable first editions that collectors go in for when they're about a hundred years old – the books, I mean – not the collectors.'

'I bet my Latin book's not far short of a hundred, anyway,' Jennings maintained. 'It's terribly dog-eared; and what's more, I'm pretty sure it's got "first edition" printed inside. There are only about two like it in the whole school; apart from me and Venables, everyone else has got much newer ones.'

'Don't be a coot, Jennings! You're not going to tell me that your Latin book is really valuable!'

Jennings' voice rose in exasperation. 'But you great bazooka, Darbi – it was you who just said it *was*! When I thought I hadn't got an ancient priceless book, you told me how rare they were. Now I find I *have* got one you tell me they're no good. Make your mind up, for goodness' sake! You can't have it both ways!'

From *Jennings and Darbishire*
by Anthony Buckeridge

Introduction

Maybe it is because of the arrival of 1984, and that so much attention has been focused by the media upon one book by Orwell, that there has been an explosion of interest too in the general subject of collecting modern first editions – the writers, the values, the rarity, the values, the dust-wrappers, the values and the values. Certainly, media attention has been fierce. And much of what has been written has been valuable, stimulating, vital and true; much more, of course, has been utter bilge. I, anyway, am delighted to be back on this theme in so auspicious a year, and – as one might have expected of 1984 – very much has changed.

Apart from, I believe, Bauhaus art and artefacts and Oriental porcelain, rare books – and in particular modern first editions – have shown a more dramatic rise in values than anything else in the last five years. But this has been a *proportionate* rise, you understand, which makes at least some of them still affordable, and a cracking good investment to boot. Unfortunately, people like chartered accountants and inflation-hedgers have twigged to this truth, and through their advice to clients books at auction regularly top their estimates, sometimes by several hundred per cent. So why aren't the money-on-the-shelf, salt-it-away boys more interested in a Mondrian painting, or a nice bit of T'ang? Because such trinkets can fetch half a million up, while the rarest book in *this* book would fetch £10000, tops; and most are in the £5–£200 class, which is altogether different. Alas, alas – the bibliophile *does* have to be better heeled these days; but knowledge can still go a very long way and mouth-watering bargains are still a possibility. My first piece of advice, therefore – nowadays more than ever – is to know your subject (authors, imprints, dates, values) as thoroughly as possible. This way you will almost certainly be better briefed than a bookseller (his knowledge has to be extremely wide-ranging, and is therefore spread far thinner) or an auctioneer – and, with a bit of luck, the other bidders as well. This book, of course, will not make you an expert, for as always there can be no substitute for experience and 'feel' (don't ask me to explain 'feel': as the word suggests, it is tangible but elusive, like style – and, like style, you know it when it's there) but at least you will be aware of what is available, and the *area* of price you might be expected to pay.

Values

This leads us to the world of values, what a book's worth. I get asked this a lot – what a book's worth – and it's a fiendishly difficult question to answer, often, because in a sense *all* values are arbitrary and mutually agreed levels, reflecting current demand and scarcity. As ever, then, a book is worth whatever a collector is prepared to pay for it. To make this clearer, if a collector has all the volumes in Powell's Dance to the Music of Time sequence, fine in dust-wrapper, save one, he will be willing to pay over the odds to secure a clean copy; conversely, it would be quite unscrupulous and wrong of a dealer to boost the price in the light of the facts, and we may only hope that such never happens. In this book, one will find the sort of price that the missing volume *should* be, irrespective of the personal mania of the collector in question. The truth should be underlined at this point that the values quoted in the text refer to the current retail price of a good copy in the dust-wrapper (unless the dust-wrapper is impossibly scarce, in which case I usually say so). A very scarce dust-wrapper (*Brighton Rock*, say) could enhance the value of the book several fold; but I shall go further into this ever more important issue later on.

What, then, the collector might wish to know, if one wants to *sell* some items? How much should one expect? Well first of all it must be remembered that a dealer will buy only what he wants (if he has no Robert Graves customers, he will not buy Robert Graves; if he has two copies of *The Sea, the Sea* he will not buy a third) and the price he will offer will be in direct proportion to the price he knows he can eventually achieve. Many central London dealers, for instance, might find some of the valuations contained in this book on the low side, for they know that by picking up the phone to New York (or Dallas, or Tokyo, or even somewhere in England) they could quote prices far higher, and get them. Small country booksellers, on the other hand, might see the valuations as ludicrously exaggerated, for they too know their market. Either way, though, book dealers are a pretty honest and straightforward breed, and although they will not turn from a bargain if it comes their way (and nor will they cease to bore people about their brilliance in spotting it for months to come) they are not averse to paying the right price for the right book – indeed, they are eager to do so. Yes, but what *is* the right price? Well, the economic truth is that if a dealer owns a shop, the overheads of this shop (rates, rent, staff, insurance, phone, electricity, stationery, tea-bags, claret, Valium, etc) will dictate that he offers 50% of the eventual retail price, maximum. Which, I know, seems immoral – and if the hundred per cent mark-up were clear profit, so it would be. But life is not like that. In short, then, if you sell to a dealer a first edition for £5, do not feel cheated to see it on his shelf at £10 or £12. If, however, he has marked it up to £50, you might do well to request a quiet word. But, I stress that this is unlikely, for booksellers are not after a quick buck, but a fair and reasonable profit. If a quick buck *were* the objective, there are far more leisurely and lucrative occupations (rat-catching comes to mind).

If you are the proud possessor of a copy of my *Collecting Modern First Editions* (Studio Vista 1977 – now fetching £40 a throw and rising; I *told* you to look after it) you will be aware that prices have taken a very dramatic upswing indeed. Examples:

Richard Adams
Watership Down 1977 value: up to £50; 1984 up to £200
W.H. Auden
Poems (1928) 1977 value: up to £2000; 1984 up to £10 000
Roald Dahl
The Gremlins 1977 value: up to £10; 1984 up to £150
Agatha Christie
The Mysterious Affair at Styles 1977 value: up to £50; 1984 up to £1,000
Len Deighton

The Ipcress file 1977 value: up to £10; 1984 up to £80
Ian Fleming
Casino Royale 1977 value: up to £50; 1984 up to £750
John Fowles
The Collector 1977 value: up to £20; 1984 up to £250
William Golding
Lord of the Flies 1977 value: up to £35; 1984 up to £750
Ted Hughes
The Hawk in the Rain 1977 value: up to £30; 1984 up to £125
P.G. Wodehouse
Mike 1977 value: up to £30; 1984 up to £250

Dramatic indeed – plenty more shocks and surprises in the body of the text –
but what will also be observed is that these rises have been by no means
consistent. Some authors, some books, have risen in value quite as one would
have expected, in line with inflation and a relatively reduced availability;
others have rocketed, blinding us with their lights. A lot of this is to do with
the investment market already discussed and a lot more, maybe, is to do with
the fact that many collectors are now openly enthusiastic about authors once
thought of as only popular (and therefore second-rate) and entertaining
(and therefore not 'serious'). The really big rises in interest and value have
been with the very popular writers of crime and suspense – Fleming,
Christie, Chandler, Francis, Le Carré, etc – and with the one great popular
humorist, P.G. Wodehouse. On publication of *Collecting Modern First Editions*
I was criticized in some quarters for even *including* this lot, let alone
squandering space on them. Times change.

Will the values hold? Generally, yes. Too many people have invested too
much money for them not to. People will always wish to collect literature,
and the first edition is usually more elusive than any other, and hence more
desirable.

Taste and Choice
The first edition world is subject to the vagaries of taste and fashion, as is any
other, and swings have been known. Priestley seems popular again,
Rosamond Lehmann is back with a bang. Snow has woken up, and Pritchett
is sleeping – along with Solzhenitsyn and Yevtushenko – while Pasternak is
past. P.D. James and Barbara Pym have come in from nowhere. There is no
guarantee that all of this will remain – indeed, I should be more inclined to
guarantee further shifting – but this element of collecting, too, has its
intrinsic fascination. How much, for instance, will the recent crop of 'Best of
. . .' lists influence collecting tastes? Certainly, many of the authors on these
lists are to be found within this book – but those such as Golding and
Murdoch have anyway been collected for decades. The lists might turn
people's attention to the younger writers, though; it remains to be seen.

And what of the much-vaunted Booker McConnell prize? This prize – just
upped to £15 000 in order to pip Betty Trask – only recently became a
glamorous media event, and its annual appearance really does seem to sell
books and create celebrities. It was not always so. Many of the short-listed

Introduction

authors of past years are quite unknown today; indeed, quite a few of the winners are not collected at all.

The Nobel Prize for Literature – possibly because it is international – does not generate the same excitement, although it is seen to be the crowning achievement for a writer, and the prize money can amount to anything between £100 000 and £200 000. Since the Nobel was first implemented in 1901, seventy-eight awards have been made, sometimes jointly. Occasionally no prize was awarded in a given year, and twice it was declined – in 1958 by Boris Pasternak, and in 1964 by Jean-Paul Sartre. Its history, I think, might be worth a glance. Writers of the following nationalities have won the prize once: Columbian, Hungarian, Guatemalan, Japanese, Australian, Yugoslavian, Finnish, Israeli, Icelandic, Belgian, Yiddish and Hindu. (The last two are a language and a religion, I know, but as such are billed Isaac Bashevis Singer and Rabindranath Tagore.) The Swiss and the Greeks have won the prize on two occasions each, while the Poles, the Norwegians, the Danes and the Irish have three wins each to their credit. Italy, Spain and Russia have all won four times, and then comes England with five. Sweden pips us with six (it is a Swedish prize) and then come Germany and the United States with seven wins apiece. Towering above everyone is France, whose national writers have been awarded the prize no less than eleven times since its inception. So much for nationality. If we are discussing languages, then the English language comes out on top with eighteen winners (in order of receipt): Kipling, Tagore, Yeats, Shaw, Sinclair Lewis, Galsworthy, Eugene O'Neill, Pearl S. Buck, Eliot, Faulkner, Churchill, Hemingway, Steinbeck, Beckett, Patrick White, Saul Bellow and William Golding. Even here, there are one or two surprises.

I shall now list in their entirety the Booker Prize winners to date, and I shall follow it up with the Book Marketing Council's 1984 'Best Novels of Our Time' and round off with 'The Best of British Authors' and 'The Best of Young British Novelists'. It seems that if these lists are studied (though not too seriously) and kept up to date in future editions of this book, a correlation might be drawn between this world of promotion and razzmatazz and that of collecting. Many of the following authors, as I say, have been collected for ever, but a few names on the Booker list and – more likely – more than a few of the 'Young British Novelists' might prompt a fresh collector's evaluation; seven of them are already included in this book. Read them – and the others – and back your own judgment. And while you are about it – unless you feel too choked by lists to go on – you might look at Anthony Burgess's *Ninety-nine Novels: the best in English since 1939* (Allison & Busby 1984). This (very personal) view might also open out some new collecting avenues.

The Booker McConnell Prize

1969   P.H. Newby   *Something to Answer*   Faber
1970   Bernice Rubens   *The Elected Member*   Eyre & Spottiswoode
1971   V.S. Naipaul   *In a Free State*   Deutsch
1972   John Berger   *G*   Weidenfeld
1973   J.G. Farrell   *The Siege of Krishnapur*   Weidenfeld
1974   Nadine Gordimer   *The Conservationist*   Cape

1975 Ruth Prawer Jhabvala   *Heat and Dust*   Murray
1976 David Storey   *Saville*   Cape
1977 Paul Scott   *Staying On*   Heinemann
1978 Iris Murdoch   *The Sea, the Sea*   Chatto
1979 Penelope Fitzgerald   *Offshore*   Collins
1980 William Golding   *Rites of Passage*   Faber
1981 Salman Rushdie   *Midnight's Children*   Cape
1982 Thomas Keneally   *Schindler's Ark*   Hodder
1983 J.M. Coetzee   *Life and Times of Michael K*   Secker

'The Best Novels of Our Time'
(All of the following may be referred to within this book for publication details, except the Compton-Burnett.)
Kingsley Amis   *Take a Girl Like You*
Saul Bellow   *Herzog*
Ivy Compton-Burnett   *Manservant and Maidservant*   (Gollancz 1947)
William Golding   *Lord of the Flies*
Graham Greene   *The Honorary Consul*
Iris Murdoch   *The Sea, the Sea*
Vladimir Nabokov   *Lolita*
George Orwell   *Animal Farm*
Anthony Powell   *A Dance to the Music of Time*   (series of 12)
J.D. Salinger   *Catcher in the Rye*
Paul Scott   *The Raj Quartet* and *Staying On*   (5 books)
Elizabeth Taylor   *Angel*
Evelyn Waugh   *Sword of Honour*   (trilogy)

'Best of British Authors'
Beryl Bainbridge
John Betjeman
Malcolm Bradbury
Anthony Burgess
Margaret Drabble
Lawrence Durrell
John Fowles
Leon Garfield
William Golding
Graham Greene
Ted Hughes
John le Carré
Laurie Lee
Rosamond Lehmann
Iris Murdoch
V.S. Naipaul
V.S. Pritchett
Rosemary Sutcliff
Laurens van der Post
Rebecca West

Introduction

'Best of Young British Novelists'
Martin Amis
Pat Barker
Julian Barnes
Ursula Bentley
William Boyd
Buchi Emecheta
Maggie Gee
Kazuo Ishiguro
Alan Judd
Adam Mars-Jones
Ian McEwan
Shiva Naipaul
Philip Norman
Christopher Priest
Salman Rushdie
Lisa St Aubin de Teran
Clive Sinclair
Graham Swift
Rose Tremain
A.N. Wilson

It is silly putting authors into football teams, I know, but it might provide a stimulus for a younger collector. Is anyone collecting *all* the Booker winners, say? That might be a curiosity in years to come. Or how about gathering all those 'Best Novels'? Expensive business, that. It is already interesting to note, though, that out of the forty 'best' writers, there have been only two Booker winners. Such as John Fowles, Graham Greene and Margaret Drabble have never even been short-listed. What better time to remind collectors again that they should always be guided by their own taste (and, of course, pocket) and not to be too influenced by the latest brouhaha in the media. As for the investors who buy fine copies of books they have never read and never intend to – they deserve to get burnt, but such are the curious workings of the Lord, that they rarely are – mainly because they buy at the very top end of the market: a fine first edition of *Prufrock*, say, will never go out of style, and its value will always rise.

But the rich gatherer (as opposed to collector) is prey to one side of the book trade that the more canny (and cost-conscious) among us is not: the manufactured rarity, the instantly valuable. This deserves analysis, but whether such analysis amounts to exposure in the eye of the collector must remain a personal conclusion. Although publishers and presses must be free to print whatever they want, and no one has to buy their output, it is true, I feel, that the myth on offer along with the artefact is misleading in the extreme: i.e. that if one buys an extravagantly produced 'first edition' at some giddy price, it will increase enormously in value because so few were printed. This *may* be true; it need not be.

I shall begin at the beginning. First editions – those which make up the bulk of this book – were never meant to be collected. They were printed for the larger part by a commercial publisher in the sort of quantity that he expected to sell at a price that covered outlay and showed a profit – just as trade publishing is conducted today. The first edition of an author's first book was not collected on publication. It was sold (largely to libraries) and, with a bit of luck, read. A reprint was a bonus, a paperback was another. A fine copy of the first in dust-wrapper, then, is difficult to acquire because the number that survive survive by accident. Many will have been lost, defaced, read to bits or – in the case of the public library copies – ritually destroyed upon acquisition. A genuine rarity, therefore, exists. The collector is eager to seek out a copy, which could take years, and is gratified by his eventual success. If the author becomes collected, this first book will probably be the scarcest, as the publisher was feeling his way with the lowest feasible print-run. As popularity grows, of course, so initial print-runs are increased, and the subsequent 'rarity' diminishes. The reason why, say, le Carré's *The Little Drummer Girl* is so easy to acquire in a first (although it has been reprinted) while *The Spy Who Came in from the Cold* is rare, is not because the former is so very recent, but because the first edition was fifty times larger. This is sensible. *All* le Carré collectors could add a mint copy of his latest work to their shelves at moderate cost, and would not expect it to soar in value; the *cumulative* value of the collection, however, is commensurately advanced.

All this contrasts markedly with the deliberately limited edition. For such a publication, the author must already be very well known *and* collected (otherwise no one would buy the thing) and yet by aiming at the few hundred – sometimes few dozen – collectors who can afford the book, the publisher is purposely excluding hundreds, maybe thousands, more. The idea is that instead of putting out, say, 6000 copies of a slim volume of verse at £6 or so – thus satisfying the collectors, the poetry lovers, the libraries, the schools and the impulse buyers, while at the same time profiting both the author and the publisher – only 200, maybe, would be printed, bound in ostrich or lizard or some other bizarre dead thing, at maybe £150 or £200 a time. This means that very few people will have the opportunity of adding this verse to their collections (assuming they could afford to; assuming they would wish to) and no one else at all will be able to read it. The author and publisher make the same amount of money as with trade publication, at the very least. And now the book is rare! Well, it is rare in that there are only 200 – but there will *always* be 200; none will get lost or defaced; and none, certainly, will be read to bits. They are unlikely even to see the light of day; I have seen dozens of the things in the recesses of collectors' drawers, wrapped in greaseproof paper. Sad, mean, and rather strange, it seems to me.

Certainly I am not censuring the private presses – many do very fine work indeed – and equally certainly I am not cautioning collectors against these items, for a collector, as I have maintained, should follow his or her own inclination. I am merely pointing out that it is not always true that such items are a sound investment, for like many artefacts manufactured for collectors' markets – commemorative plates, sets of medallions, official souvenirs – they can be damnably difficult to sell. Many hoarders, I think, forget that real value is value realized, and not a potential figure touted by interested parties.

Introduction

Last year, on the front page of *The Times*, an advertisement appeared exhorting us to 'imagine possessing your own private library of author-signed first editions', and beneath a photograph of something that resembled an opulently tooled hymnal, one read: 'Important new books by today's great writers in hand-signed First Editions that may well become tomorrow's collecting treasures.' Aside from confirming that 'today's great writers' (who include, we learn, Leon Uris, Irving Stone and Irwin Shaw, among many others) used neither foot nor mouth to sign the books on offer, this guff tells us nothing. It is true, of course, that they '*may well* become tomorrow's collecting treasures', but it is as well to be aware that they might equally well become Tuesday fortnight's whitest elephants, even if they are – as the advert tells us – 'illustrated with original art'. Only the taste and sense of the collector will determine whether or not he buys these things.

Another example: in 1977, Allen & Unwin published Tolkien's *The Silmarillion* for the very first time. Although it was quickly reprinted, a first edition ought now to be available at not more than £10, and any Tolkien collector would be pleased to have it. A different sort of person, however, would prefer a new edition of the same work put out five years later, in 1982, bound in leather at £75 – or, signed by Tolkien's *son*, £100. This is a thing that is bought to be treasured, and treasured it will be – but it will probably never be read, and in the future I doubt whether anyone would know what to do with the thing – except to give it away. Such objects are eternal gifts: they are given to people who treasure them until it is time to pass them on. Now there is nothing wrong with that; but collectors should remember that paper dust-wrappers are invariably far scarcer than leather bindings simply because they are flimsy and vulnerable and are not subject to the slavish veneration inspired by a bit of goatskin. Such upholstery is not the stuff of which 'important' collections are made. Although these volumes may be lovely to live with, fondle, and turn your neighbours Chartreuse-envious while soaring in value on account of their rarity, just bear in mind – it ain't necessarily so.

Condition

First, a short glossary. Different people say different things and mean the same.

The coloured piece of paper around the book
Publishers call it the dust-jacket.
Booksellers and collectors call it the dust-wrapper.
People call it the cover.

The cardboard bits
Publishers refer to the case.
Booksellers and collectors refer to the boards and the spine.
People refer to the cover.

The pieces of paper at the front of the book before the story
Publishers say prelims.
Booksellers and collectors say fixed endpaper, free endpaper, blank, half-title, title-page, verso of title-page.
People say the pieces of paper at the front of the book before the story.

Shiny soft covers on book with pages coming away from the spine
Publishers call it a perfect binding.
Booksellers and collectors call it a trade paperback.
People call it a Penguin (no disrespect to Penguin – people call *anything* not hardbound a Penguin).

A brief translation of terms used in bookseller's catalogues
MINT   means fine
FINE   means fine also
VERY GOOD   means good
GOOD   means not very good
GOOD +   means not very good also
GOOD −   means no good at all
FAIR   means filthy/atrocious
ONLY FAIR   means filthy/atrocious
READING COPY   means filthy/atrocious
WORKING COPY   means filthy/atrocious
SOME SCORING   means illegible/atrocious
GRUBBY   means dirty
HANDLED   means dirty
BUMPED   means has been tied up/dropped/thrown about
SOME LOOSE PAGES   means in its component parts
NEAT INSCRIPTION   means defaced endpaper
MENDED D/W   means Sellotaped tatters
1st THUS   means reprint

The best description to look for is FINE IN D/W. One cannot wish for better than this.

Condition is still, of course, all-important. It always was impossible to sell a bent, dog-eared, wrapper-less book with someone else's name inside, first edition or not. Now, however, there are increasing numbers of dealers reluctant to take on any first without a clean dust-wrapper – unless, of course, the book or the wrapper is exceptionally scarce, in which case both dealer and collector are very happy to see any copy at all. This new discernment is really attributable to the collector rather than the dealer. I suggested in *Collecting Modern First Editions* that the dust-wrapper was more than just a pretty appendage to the book, but rather an integral part of it (as much as the title-page) and others were making similar noises around the same time. Certainly today no one needs to be convinced of this truth – the dust-wrapper has become the major selling factor and *on average* accounts for

Condition

half the purchase price. In some cases, the dust-wrapper can be worth many times the value of the book, because it is so scarce. An example at random is *Brave New World* – a common book (£10) but rare in the dust-wrapper (up to £100). This said, it ought to be recorded that a lot of nonsense has been written about dust-wrappers lately, suggesting that any book is worth *far* more with the wrapper than without: the Huxley quoted is an exception.

The presence of the dust-wrapper seems to be of particular importance to collectors of crime and detective fiction, possibly because it is often the most attractive feature of the book. In order to forestall accusations of fanaticism, I defend collectors on the grounds that they well understand that the presence of the dust-wrapper does nothing to enhance the literary quality of the work, and is not at all necessary to a reading of the book. In order to render the book collectable, however, the wrapper really ought to be there. It's tricky defending the inherently indefensible: one either understands, or one does not – and in the latter case, one is probably not reading this book, and so I think I would do well to cease addressing a hypothetical sceptic. Some collectors, though, object even to a 'price-clipped' dust-wrapper – that is, an otherwise fine dust-wrapper, lacking the corner of the inside flap where once was printed the retail price. This really *is* indefensible, and I shall not even try to render it sane. More recent books, it might be noted in passing, are rarely clipped in this way. This, I think, is due to a combination of factors: purchasers are less coy, these days, about how much they paid for a book (even if it *is* destined for a present); and publishers now often have stickers on the flap, or on the rear of the wrapper, rendering it more convenient for them when they wish to double the price – and paving the way, I think, for the latest technological iniquity, the computer-readable 'bar-code'. This, I am afraid, is soon to be ubiquitous, a mandatory defacement upon the rear of each and every future dust-wrapper – assuming that the wrapper itself survives several recent publishing sallies into the paperback original (Philip Larkin's *Required Writing*, say), and the less popular laminated boards which are still more or less confined to the realm of children's books.

As to condition other than the dust-wrapper, it is succinct and true to say that the collector is searching simply for a copy of the first edition in a condition that comes as close as possible to the original published state. The list of things one does *not* want is as endless as it is obvious: a beige ring on the upper board, the result of a careless coffee mug (a surprisingly common scarring, this); names and inscriptions on the endpapers or title-page (with the exceptions of association or author's signatures, which I shall deal with next); a 'sprung' binding (limp, broken, or split); ex-library labels; faded or chipped lettering or gilding on the spine; folded or dog-eared pages; and, most important of all, the absence of any leaf or plate.

There are other aspects of condition, or state, which can make the book more desirable, because it is rendered unique. For instance, a first illustrated edition of *Old Possum's Book of Practical Cats*, fine in dust-wrapper, is a desirable item and worth forty or fifty pounds. If it were signed by Eliot, it could be worth £150. If it were *inscribed* by Eliot to Nicolas Bentley (who drew the pictures) it could be worth £500 upwards. If Bentley too had signed the book, and maybe drawn a cat on the endpaper, it could be worth . . . well, you get the idea. In each case, the book is unique, but on a rising scale of desirability and worth. Valuation becomes fairly arbitrary at this point, because by definition the volume becomes incomparable. The price may really be decided only between dealer and collector, but it's a pretty hit-and-miss affair.

For another instance, just a few years before he died, Fred Warburg asked me to value a first edition of *Animal Farm* in his possession. Warburg was the publisher, and this copy (as issued, in a fine dust-wrapper) was inscribed to him by George Orwell, and beneath his pseudonym, Orwell had added 'Eric Blair' in parentheses. Warburg's own signature was also in the book, and here – clearly – was a unique and valuable item. But how valuable was it? Very tricky. As I say, this was some years ago now, and I think I hazarded £500, which seemed a fairly round and sensibly large figure at the time (an ordinary first in wrapper in those days would have been worth about a tenner). Today I suppose the Warburg copy would fetch thousands – but how many thousands? I should bravely guess several.

Generally speaking, it is true to say that if a book is desirable at all in first edition, the presence of the author's signature will enhance the value. An inscription is better, particularly if the recipient is known in his or her own right, or else had some connection with the author. Just so there should be no doubt: a signed Graham Greene is very good; an inscribed Graham Greene to his milkman is better; and an inscribed Graham Greene to Evelyn Waugh is drool-making, and if buying it should involve the taking of a second mortgage on the house, there are many collectors who would not hesitate to do so – for what good is a house anyway, without books?

The other area of state whereby a book may differ from the general run of the first edition, and will be at least rare and at best unique, is that of the proof copy, by which is meant the paper-bound publisher's book-proof for use in-house and for pre-publication publicity purposes. (The lure of endless and writhing chains of galley-proofs has so far been resisted by the serious collector, but I maintain a vigilant watch; it can only be a short time before the emergence of rare Auden galleys, in a four-foot fine binding by Sangorski and Sutcliffe.) The book-proof itself is a physically unlovesome thing – it comprises the bare text (very often with misprints, due for correction) printed on proof (i.e. nasty) paper with sugar-paper wrappers – and it is avidly collected. The print run of a new John Fowles, say, might be 30 000; but more than 100 proofs are seldom printed: hence, rarity. Furthermore, they are not meant to be collected, or sold, or even to leave the publisher's office. (The manner in which they do is a closely guarded open secret.) What can render them more desirable is if, say, the author's name is misspelt on the wrapper (which happened, notably, to T.S. Eliot on a Faber proof, when he was chairman of the firm) or if the book has undergone a title-change between proof-stage and publication – anything, in short, that distinguishes it from the finished text. Much better, of course, if the proof bears autograph changes (preferably extensive) by the author in, presumably, his own copy of the uncorrected proof. A lot of collectors of these oddities often have the regular first edition alongside as well, which is an expensive and space-consuming way of going about things; but visually it breaks up the shelves, and saves the library from resembling a rummage shop or, worse, a publisher's office. A proof of a collectable first is *always* more expensive than the regular first; once again, whether one wants to own them – and whether one is willing to pay the price – is an entirely personal choice. A visit to a few editor's offices and newspaper buildings might restore proportion, though: here, proofs are treated with a healthy disrespect. I wonder for how much longer?

This Book

The foregoing, in conjunction with the text to follow, should arm you with the bare essentials. The rest you will get, if you have not already, from experience, and mistakes, and talking and listening, and bargains, and discoveries, and years. It's all great fun if you like that sort of thing – which, presumably, you do.

There have been a lot of changes since *Collecting Modern First Editions* in 1977. What follows, of course, is not a comprehensive list of every collected author: I doubt if there could ever be such a thing. I suppose every writer ever published is collected by someone, if only by the writer himself. The authors that follow are, I believe, those in whom there is most interest from *collectors today*. I italicize these two words, for it must be understood that this is no encyclopedia of twentieth-century literature – for that, seek elsewhere. Nor does it imply that every author included is great, and all those excluded are no good at all. There are quite a few fine authors who are not, and never have been, collected (I've included one or two of these because I think they should be) and it must be admitted that a very few writers who are avidly sought after are really quite dreadful. This, however, is the collectors' choice, and this book is to both reflect and stimulate the interests of the young collector today.

Most authors are listed in their entirety, except where they are known only for one or two highlights, or – in rare cases – where there are ample bibliographies elsewhere. Every title includes details of English and American publication (including relevant publishers and dates) and carries a separate valuation for each edition, the alphabetical key to which may be found after the Index. This valuation is the price a collector might have to pay for a good copy, in the dust-wrapper, unless otherwise stated. Standard biographies and bibliographies are recorded, as are films made from the author's works, their makers and dates. Those comparing the book with *Collecting Modern First Editions* will find, I hope, a clearer layout and immediately accessible valuations. They will also note that sixty-seven authors from that work are no longer listed, while there are forty-three brand-new entries. Some of those entries common to each book have been expanded to cover the author's entire output, replacing the short selection previously supplied, and all are updated to spring 1984. Many of the authors dropped were considered to be very fine indeed (and very much collected) but simply too early for the present brief of 'modern' – notably Hardy, Shaw,

Wilde, Wells and Yeats. There are in existence, of course, very full bibliographies of all these. Others were omitted because their original works were written in their own (foreign) language, and it was felt that lists of first editions in translation were of far less interest to the collector than books written and first published in the English language, although many notable foreign writers remain. More were dropped because interest has flagged. Such interest, of course, may easily and soon be revived. It will be interesting to see the shape of the next edition: how many of the new forty-three will have weathered the storm? There are very many new and young writers included now – some of whom had published nothing in 1977, when *Collecting Modern First Editions* was published. I watch with interest. It will be not only interesting but amusing to see how the 'Best of . . .' lists alter over the next year or two. Or are they regarded as static? Will they even be abandoned? I doubt it – they generate too much media attention for that.

Some good old bookshops have vanished, prices have risen very dramatically, and the rare has got rarer. Book collecting – first edition collecting – weathers all this. It has become even more worthwhile; and, most important, it remains very great fun. It is far more satisfying than collecting stamps, or porcelain, or anything I can think of. How long can one stare at a stamp? How long before a crackle-glaze fails to mesmerize? But books! Books are the beginning, the end, and most things in between. Go for them.

Index of Authors Listed

Larkin, Philip
Lawrence, D.H.
Lawrence, T.E.
Leacock, Stephen
Le Carré, John
Lee, Laurie
Lehmann, John
Lehmann, Rosamond
Lennon, John
Lessing, Doris
Lewis, C.S.
Lewis, Wyndham
Loos, Anita
Lovecraft, H.P.
Lowell, Robert
Lowry, Malcolm
Lurie, Alison

Macdonald, Ross
McEwan, Ian
MacInnes, Colin
MacNeice, Louis
Mailer, Norman
Manning, Olivia
Marcus, Frank
Marsh, Ngaio
Miller, Arthur
Miller, Henry
Milne, A.A.
Mitchell, Margaret
Mitford, Nancy
Monsarrat, Nicholas
Mortimer, John
Muldoon, Paul
Murdoch, Iris

Nabokov, Vladimir
Naipaul, V.S.
Nash, Ogden
Naughton, Bill

O'Brien, Edna
O'Brien, Flann
O'Casey, Sean
Orton, Joe
Orwell, George
Osborne, John
Owen, Wilfred

Parkinson, C. Northcote
Pasternak, Boris
Peake, Mervyn
Perelman, S.J.
Pinter, Harold
Plath, Sylvia
Potter, Stephen
Pound, Ezra
Powell, Anthony
Powys, J.C.
Powys, Llewelyn
Powys, T.F.
Priestley, J.B.
Puzo, Mario
Pym, Barbara
Pynchon, Thomas

Ransome, Arthur
Raven, Simon
Read, Herbert
Rhys, Jean
Richards, Frank
Rosenberg, Isaac
Rosten, Leo
Roth, Philip
Rushdie, Salman
Russell, Bertrand

Sagan, Françoise
Salinger, J.D.
Sandford, Jeremy
Sapper
Sassoon, Siegfried
Sayers, Dorothy L.
Scott, Paul
Searle, Ronald
Shaffer, Peter
Sharpe, Tom
Sillitoe, Alan
Simenon, Georges
Simon, Neil
Sitwell, Edith
Sitwell, Osbert
Sitwell, Sacheverell
Smith, Stevie
Snow, C.P.
Solzhenitsyn, Alexander
Spark, Muriel

Spender, Stephen
Steinbeck, John
Stevens, Wallace
Stewart, J.I.M.
Stoppard, Tom
Storey, David
Story, Jack Trevor
Strachey, Lytton
Styron, William
Swift, Graham
Symons, Julian

Taylor, Elizabeth
Tennant, Emma
Thomas, D.M.
Thomas, Dylan
Thomas, R.S.
Thurber, James
Tolkien, J.R.R.
Travers, P.L.
Trevor, William

Updike, John
Upward, Edward

Vidal, Gore
Vonnegut, Kurt Jnr

Wallace, Edgar
Waterhouse, Keith
Waugh, Evelyn
Wesker, Arnold
Wheatley, Dennis
White, Patrick
White, T.H.
Williams, Tennessee
Wilson, A.N.
Wilson, Angus
Wilson, Colin
Wodehouse, P.G.
Woolf, Leonard
Woolf, Virginia
Wyndham, John

Scale of Values Used Throughout the Book

A	up to £5
B	up to £10
C	up to £20
D	up to £30
E	up to £40
F	up to £50
G	up to £60
H	up to £80
I	up to £100
J	up to £125
K	up to £150
L	up to £200
M	up to £250
N	up to £300
O	up to £400
P	up to £500
Q	up to £750
R	up to £1000
S	up to £1500
T	up to £2000
U	up to £3000
V	up to £4000
W	up to £5000
X	up to £6000
Y	up to £7000
Z	up to £10 000

Adams, Richard Born in Berkshire, 1920.

The story of Adams – the civil servant who turned to writing late in life, mainly with a view to entertaining his own children – is now well known, and *Watership Down* appears to have a secure place in the ranks of modern classics. From the collector's point of view, *Watership Down* remains the only truly desirable item, for not only do its successors seem to have been printed in huge numbers in first edition (the first print run of *Watership Down* was only 2000 copies) but also because there is a feeling that Adams never equalled his inaugural and triumphant sally into the fantastic. *Watership Down*, then, is safe – despite all those who would rather die than be seen reading a fat kiddies' book about talking rabbits.

1	**Watership Down** (novel)	Rex Collings 1972	L
		Macmillan (NY) 1974	D
2	**Shardik** (novel)	Lane 1974	B
		Simon & Schuster 1975	B
3	**Nature Through the Seasons** (non-fiction)	Kestrel 1975	A
		Simon & Schuster 1975	A
4	**The Tyger Voyage** (illustrated)	Cape 1976	A
		Knopf 1976	A
5	**The Ship's Cat** (illustrated)	Cape 1977	A
		Knopf 1977	A
6	**The Plague Dogs** (novel)	Lane 1977	A
		Knopf 1978	A
7	**Nature Day and Night** (non-fiction)	Kestrel 1978	A
		Viking 1978	A
8	**The Girl in a Swing** (novel)	Knopf 1980	B
		Lane 1980	A

Review copies of the Lane edition were hurriedly recalled, some material removed, and then reissued. Some slipped through, though, and one of these or the Knopf edition would be preferable.

The *visible* differences between the first and second issues of the Lane edition are that the title page of the first bears the words 'Allen Lane' (the second does not) and that throughout the novel the *name* of the heroine has been changed.

9	**The Iron Wolf and Other Stories**	Lane 1980	A

Film:
Watership Down CIC1978

Albee, Edward   Born in Washington D.C. 1928.

In Britain, interest in Albee has rather waned since the days of glory in the sixties, as is reflected in the fact that Cape no longer publishes in this country. *Who's Afraid of Virginia Woolf?*, however, remains a classic, and with so powerful a film in existence, it is difficult to see how it will not remain so, for the vision of a quivering Elizabeth Taylor spitting and shrieking gin-sodden hysteria remains ever frightful. Without question the highlight, then, and still an undervalued book.

1	**The Zoo Story, The Death of Bessie Smith, The Sandbox: Three Plays**	Coward McCann (NY) 1960	C
2	**The Zoo Story**	*Evergreen Review* March–April 1960	B
3	**Fam and Yam**	Dramatists Play Service (NY) 1961	B
4	**The American Dream**	Coward McCann (NY) 1961	B
5	**Who's Afraid of Virginia Woolf?**	Atheneum 1962	D
		Cape 1964	B
6	**The Zoo Story and Other Plays** (same as 1)	Cape 1962	B
7	**The Ballad of the Sad Café**	Atheneum 1963	B
		Cape 1965	A
8	**Tiny Alice**	Atheneum 1965	B
		Cape 1966	A
9	**Malcolm**	Atheneum 1966	B
		Cape 1967	A
10	**A Delicate Balance**	Atheneum 1966	B
		Cape 1968	A
11	**Box** and **Quotations from Chairman Mao Tse-Tung**	Atheneum 1969 Cape 1970	B A
12	**All Over**	Atheneum 1971	B
		Cape 1972	A
13	**Seascape**	Atheneum 1975	A
		Cape 1976	A
14	**Counting the Ways** and **Listening: Two Plays**	Atheneum 1977	A
15	**The Lady from Dubuque**	Atheneum 1980	A

Films:
Who's Afraid of Virginia Woolf? Warner Bros 1965
A Delicate Balance Seven Keys 1974

Bibliography:
Charles Green **Edward Albee: An Annotated Bibliography 1968–1977** AMS Press (NY) 1980

Aldiss, Brian W. Born in Norfolk, England, 1925.

Although primarily a writer of science fiction – and hence avidly collected by SF buffs – Aldiss's reputation as a 'serious' novelist has continued to climb, not least, perhaps, when the arrival of the year 1984 caused much attention to be given to speculative and prophetic fiction. Aldiss's sally into cheekiness (the Horatio Stubbs trilogy) has its admirers, too, though Weidenfeld only acquired the first of the trio when a shocked Hutchinson turned down the novel at book-proof stage.

1	**The Brightfount Diaries** (novel)	Faber 1955	D
2	**Space, Time and Nathaniel** (stories)	Faber 1957	C
3	**Non-Stop** (novel)	Faber 1958	C
4	**Starship** (same as 3)	Criterion (NY) 1959	B
5	**Vanguard from Alpha** (novel)	Ace (NY) 1959	B
6	**No Time Like Tomorrow** (stories)	NAL (NY) 1959	B
7	**The Canopy of Time** (stories)	Faber 1959	B
8	**Bow Down to Nul** (novel)	Ace 1960	B
9	**Galaxies Like Grains of Sand** (novel)	NAL 1960	B
10	**Equator** (novel)	Digit 1961	B
11	**The Interpreter** (novel)	Digit 1961	B
12	**The Male Response** (novel)	Beacon Press, Boston 1961	B
		Dobson 1963	B
13	**The Primal Urge** (novel)	Ballantine (NY) 1961	B
		Sphere 1967	A
14	**Hothouse** (novel)	Faber 1962	B
15	**The Long Aftermath of Earth** (same as 14)	NAL 1962	A
16	**The Airs of Earth** (stories)	Faber 1963	B
17	**Starswarm** (stories)	NAL 1964	B
18	**The Dark Light Years** (novel)	Faber 1964	B
		NAL 1964	B
19	**Greybeard** (novel)	Faber 1964	B
		Harcourt Brace 1964	B
20	**Best SF Stories of Brian Aldiss** (rev. ed. 1971)	Faber 1965	B
21	**Earthworks** (novel)	Faber 1965	B
		Doubleday 1966	B
22	**Who Can Replace a Man?** (same as 20)	Harcourt Brace 1966	A
23	**The Saliva Tree and Other Strange Growths** (stories)	Faber 1966	B
24	**Cities and Stones: A Traveller's Jugoslavia** (non-fiction)	Faber 1966	B
25	**An Age** (novel)	Faber 1967	B

26 **Cryptozoic** (same as 25)	Doubleday 1968	B
27 **Report on Probability A** (novel)	Faber 1968	B
	Doubleday 1968	B
28 **A Brian Aldiss Omnibus** (stories)	Sidgwick & Jackson 1969	A
29 **Intangibles Inc. and Other Stories**	Faber 1969	A
30 **Barefoot in the Head** (novel)	Faber 1969	A
	Doubleday 1970	A
31 **Neanderthal Planet** (stories)	Avon (NY) 1970	B
32 **The Shape of Further Things** (non-fiction)	Faber 1970	B
	Doubleday 1971	B
33 **The Hand-Reared Boy** (novel)	Weidenfeld 1970	B
	McCann 1970	B
34 **A Soldier Erect** (novel)	Weidenfeld 1971	B
	McCann 1971	B
35 **The Moment of Eclipse** (stories)	Faber 1971	A
	Doubleday 1971	A
36 **Brian Aldiss Omnibus 2**	Sidgwick & Jackson 1971	A
37 **The Comic Inferno** (stories)	Daw Books 1972	A
38 **The Book of Brian Aldiss** (same as 37)	NEL 1973	A
39 **Frankenstein Unbound** (novel)	Cape 1973	A
	Random House 1974	A
40 **Billion Year Spree: The History of Science Fiction**	Weidenfeld 1973	B
	Doubleday 1973	B
41 **The Eighty Minute Hour** (novel)	Cape 1974	A
	Doubleday 1974	A
42 **The Malacia Tapestry** (novel)	Cape 1976	A
	Harper 1977	A
43 **Brothers of the Head** (novel)	Pierrot 1977 (UK & US)	A
44 **Last Orders and Other Stories**	Cape 1977	A
45 **Enemies of the System: A Tale of Homo Uniformis** (novel)	Cape 1978	A
	Harper & Row 1978	A
46 **A Rude Awakening** (novel)	Weidenfeld 1978	B
With 33 and 34, this completes the trilogy of Horatio Stubbs novels.	Random House 1979	B
47 **New Arrivals, Old Encounters** (essays)	Cape 1979	A
	Harper 1979	A
48 **This World and Nearer Ones: Essays Exploring the Familiar**	Weidenfeld 1979	A
	Kent State 1981	A
49 **Pile** (illustrated)	Cape 1979	A
50 **Life in the West** (novel)	Weidenfeld 1980	A
51 **Moreau's Other Island** (novel)	Cape 1980	A
52 **An Island Called Moreau** (same as 51)	Simon & Schuster 1981	A

53 **Helliconia Spring** (novel)	Cape 1982	A
	Atheneum 1982	A
54 **Helliconia Summer** (novel)	Cape 1983	A
	Atheneum 1983	A

Amis, Kingsley   Born in London, 1922.

Kingsley Amis once told me the very interesting truth behind the marketing of his first and most famous novel, *Lucky Jim*. While delighted that Gollancz had accepted the novel for publication, he groaned with despair when he learned that the publisher (Victor Gollancz himself, in those days) intended to publish in the early days of January. 'But *nobody*,' protested Amis, 'publishes novels in January.' 'Precisely, my boy,' returned Gollancz. Large media coverage was thereby assured, but the scheme was not yet played out, for although it is true that the book was successful from the first, during the successive printing, Gollancz would periodically (about every thousand copies or so) halt the presses, and insert news of a further impression upon the verso of the title page. Thus, within a couple of years of publication, *Lucky Jim* was in its twelfth 'impression', having in fact sold about twelve thousand copies – a success, of course, but less than the *first* print run of an Amis novel in the nineteen-eighties.

Lucky Jim remains a deathless classic, and without question one of the most important post-war novels, whatever the Book Marketing lists say. Amis, though, has never been content to rest upon this one considerable laurel, but has consistently produced very fine books ever since, among the best being *Ending Up* and *Jake's Thing*.

Amis is now seen to be one of the handful of best contemporary writers, and although he has been collected for many years, his books remain undervalued, for it is still possible to pick up many Amis 1sts for under £10, while a new novel might be published at little less than nine. I think this situation will not last for long.

1 **Bright November** (verse)	Fortune Press 1947	I
Mint copy should be unopened and in d/w. Copies with grey boards are apparently of later issue. Very scarce.		
2 **A Frame of Mind** (verse)	Reading School of	H
Early and privately printed – hence very scarce – only 150 copies.	Art 1953	
3 **Lucky Jim** (novel)	Gollancz 1953	J
Very scarce, and a keystone to any collection of fiction. Green boards with yellow Gollancz house-style d/w.	Doubleday 1954	H
4 **Fantasy Poets No. 22** (verse)	Fantasy Press 1954	E
A fairly fragile item, and hard to find.		
5 **That Uncertain Feeling** (novel)	Gollancz 1955	D
Red boards, house-style d/w.	Harcourt Brace 1956	C

Amis, K.

6 **A Case of Samples: Poems**   Gollancz 1956   **F**
1946–1956   Harcourt Brace 1957   **E**
In print a very short time, surprisingly
never reissued, and always a very
difficult book to find.

7 **Socialism and the Intellectuals**   Fabian Society 1957   **D**
Fabian Tract No. 304. A very
interesting, but ephemeral, item. As it is
just a 13-page pamphlet, there are very
few remaining in a condition
acceptable to collectors, hence the grade.

8 **I Like It Here** (novel)   Gollancz 1958   **C**
Standard Gollancz production.   Harcourt Brace 1958   **C**

9 **Take a Girl Like You** (novel)   Gollancz 1960   **D**
Standard Gollancz production.   Harcourt Brace 1961   **C**

10 **New Maps of Hell: A Survey of**   Harcourt Brace 1960   **D**
Science Fiction   Gollancz 1961   **D**
According to the d/w of Gollancz
edition, the American edition preceded
for 'technical reasons'. This is the only
Amis to be published in America first.
Both editions are scarce.

11 **My Enemy's Enemy** (stories)   Gollancz 1962   **C**
Usual Gollancz production, but never   Harcourt Brace 1963   **C**
as easy to find as the novels of this
period.

12 **The Evans Country** (verse)   Fantasy Press 1962   **E**
Grey wraps, lettered in black and red.
A slim pamphlet, and scarce.

13 **One Fat Englishman** (novel)   Gollancz 1963   **C**
Standard Gollancz production. Not   Harcourt Brace 1964   **C**
difficult.

14 **The Egyptologists** (novel) (with   Cape 1965   **B**
Robert Conquest)   Random House 1966   **B**
The beginning of Amis's association
with Cape, and his first photographic,
laminated d/w! Not too difficult.

15 **The James Bond Dossier**   Cape 1965   **B**
Appropriately, the d/w reproduces   NAL 1965   **B**
excerpts of Richard Chopping's Bond
wrappers, and the book is published by
Fleming's own publishers. Not very
difficult, despite being sought by both
Amis and Fleming collectors.

16 **The Anti-Death League** (novel)   Gollancz 1966   **C**
Although the first Gollancz Amis to   Harcourt Brace 1966   **C**
break with house style, the last Amis for
Gollancz. Photographic d/w much like

Raymond Hawkey's designs for the
early Deightons (q.v.). Not too difficult.

17	**A Look Round the Estate: Poems 1957–1967**	Cape 1967 Harcourt Brace 1968	C C

Green boards with white spine. Green,
black and white d/w. This slim volume
was reprinted soon after publication,
and the 1st is quite difficult.

18	**Colonel Sun: A James Bond Adventure**	Cape 1968 Harper 1968	B B

By 'Robert Markham' – the most un-
secret pseudonym in the world. See
essay in 22. A similar situation to 15,
this – a novel wanted by Amis and
Fleming collectors, this time with a
'Choppingesque' d/w, but quite easy to
find – and only £1 if, perchance, the
vendor does not know of Markham's
true identity.

19	**Lucky Jim's Politics**	Conservative Centre 1968	C

A scarce, ephemeral item, but a pretty
counterpart to 7.

20	**I Want It Now** (novel)	Cape 1968 Harcourt Brace 1969	B B

Blue boards, laminated, photographic
d/w. Quite easy.

21	**The Green Man** (novel)	Cape 1969 Harcourt Brace 1970	B B

Blue boards, laminated, photographic
d/w. Quite easy.

22	**What Became of Jane Austen? and Other Questions**	Cape 1970 Harcourt Brace 1971	B B

Amis's only book of essays. Not too
difficult.

23	**Girl, 20** (novel)	Cape 1971 Harcourt Brace 1972	B B

Black boards, laminated, photographic
d/w. A pushover.

24	**On Drink**	Cape 1972 Harcourt Brace 1973	B B

Boards, aptly, are wine-coloured.
Laminated, photographic d/w featuring
Kingsley tippling. Was reprinted very
quickly.

25	**Dear Illusion** (story)	Covent Garden Press 1972	B

Mustard wrpps. Limited edition of
600–100 numbered and signed (D).
Quite difficult now.

26	**The Riverside Villas Murder** (novel)	Cape 1973 Harcourt Brace 1973	B B

Green boards, laminated, photographic
d/w. Easy.

27 **Ending Up** (novel) Easy to find at present, but destined to become a highlight of his work.	Cape 1974 Harcourt Brace 1974	B B
28 **Rudyard Kipling and His World** (biog.) One of the well-known series. Easy.	Thames & Hudson 1975 Scribner 1975	B B
29 **The Alteration** (novel) Olive boards – d/w with rather '*Woman's Own*' artwork.	Cape 1976 Viking Press 1977	A A
30 **Harold's Years** A collection of articles from many hands, originally printed in the *New Statesman* and the *Spectator*, all written during the Downing Street reign of Sir Harold Wilson – then Mr, now Lord. K.A. edits and provides a six-page introduction. Brown paper-covered boards, gold blocked, with white d/w bearing a caricature of Wilson by Marc.	Quartet 1977	A
31 **The New Oxford Book of Light Verse** Chosen and edited by K.A., with a 16-page introduction. Dark blue cloth, blocked in gold, in Oxford house style. The d/w reproduces Gregory's good old 'Boulter's Lock – Sunday Afternoon', which can always be depended upon at times like this.	OUP 1978	B
32 **The Darkwater Hall Mystery** (story) This Sherlock Holmes spoof was first published in a reduced form in *Playboy* (May 1978) and this expanded version constitutes first book publication. An edition of only 165 copies, however, so many Amis collectors will have to go without. 35 pages in beautifully marbled wrappers, a thin cream label on the spine.	Tragara Press (Edinburgh) 1978	F
33 **Jake's Thing** (novel) Lucky Jim lives – under a slightly altered name. Here – in his first novel for his new publisher, Hutchinson – Amis writes of an ageing don whose name is Jake (James, Jim) Richardson (Dickson, Dixon) and who is in search of his lost libido. Mainstream Amis. Mid-blue paper-covered boards,	Hutchinson 1978 Viking 1979	B B

blocked in silver, and cream laminated
d/w with a cartoon by Quentin Blake.

34 **The Faber Popular Reciter**   Faber 1978   A
An anthology of learn-it-by-heart and
read-it-out-loud poems, edited by K.A.
and with a four-page introduction.
Published simultaneously in hard and
paperback, with a bright red and white
cover.

35 **Collected Poems 1944–1979**   Hutchinson 1979   A
His first 'collected', and dedicated to   Viking 1980   A
John Betjeman. Tan boards, gold
blocked, typographic cream d/w,
lettered in khaki and black.

36 **An Arts Policy?** (lecture)   Centre for Policy   A
An expanded version of a lecture   Studies 1979
delivered that year. Stiff paper
wrappers.

37 **Russian Hide-and-Seek** (novel)   Hutchinson 1980   A
While the title page announces the
above, the d/w reads *Russian Hide &*
Seek, rather inconsistently. Anyway,
same blue boards as 33, and lettered in
silver again. Crimson d/w, with blue
and white typography.

38 **Collected Short Stories**   Hutchinson 1980   A
A vastly entertaining collection,
including the *Playboy* version of 32, and
many more. As Amis says in the
introduction (recalling to me the
throwaway genius of P.G. Wodehouse)
'These are nearly all the short stories I
have ever published; I omit The Sacred
Rhino of Uganda as uncharacteristic.'
Cream boards, silver blocked. Orange,
gold and white laminated
typographical d/w.

39 **The Golden Age of Science Fiction**   Hutchinson 1981   A
An anthology of all his favourites,
selected and introduced by K.A. Grey
boards, lettered in red. The d/w lists
the authors included in brown, on a
light yellow background.

40 **Every Day Drinking**   Hutchinson 1983   A
The Amis pun will be seen in the title.
Paperback-size collection of boozy
articles originally published in the *Daily*
Express. Not a seminal work – although,

Amis, K.

as usual, very entertaining and
informative. Black boards lettered in
gold. Black d/w lettered in red and
yellow, and bearing a terribly good
caricature of K.A. by Marc (see 30).
The book is illustrated by Merrily
Harpur.

Films:
Lucky Jim British Lion 1957   **Only Two Can Play** British Lion 1961
(*That Uncertain Feeling*)   **Take a Girl Like You** Columbia 1971

Bibliography:
Jack Benoit Gohn **Kingsley Amis: A Checklist** Kent State University
Press 1976. Kingsley Amis has also edited a number of publications, most
notably the **Spectrum** volumes, with Robert Conquest. The first was
published by Gollancz in 1961 (Harcourt Brace 1962) and should be
Grade B. The subsequent volumes are Grade A, except perhaps
Spectrum IV, which contains a discussion between Amis, Brian Aldiss
and C.S. Lewis. Amis has also edited **G. K. Chesterton: Selected
Stories**, Faber 1972, and **Tennyson**, Penguin 1973. Both should be
Grade A.   Also worth having are his contributions to **Penguin Modern
Poets 2**, Penguin 1962 – difficult now, but Grade A – **G. K. Chesterton:
A Century Appraisal**, Elek 1974, and **Bookmarks**, Cape 1975 –
containing a short essay on Amis's reading tastes.

Amis, Martin   Born in Oxford, 1949.

Some people still refer to him as the son of Kingsley Amis, but many of the
younger generation see Kingsley only as Martin's father. Certainly, in the
decade since his first novel, Martin Amis has established himself in the
forefront of the younger novelists and journalists, and has repudiated critics
who suggested at the time that had he not been who he was, he would not be
in print at all. This is now seen to be unjust and ridiculous, for although
many may not warm to the subject matter, frankness and obsessions of
Martin Amis's fiction, the power and skill are undeniable, the dialogue and
observation accurate and seductive.

Younger collectors identify with this sort of fiction, and I predict a sharp
rise of interest soon, with the inevitable and commensurate increasing
scarcity and prices. At the moment, very good value.

1	**The Rachel Papers** (novel)	Cape 1973	B
		Knopf 1974	B
2	**Dead Babies** (novel)	Cape 1975	B
	The title was much disliked, and the	Knopf 1976	B
	book was reissued in 1977 by Triad as		
	Dark Secrets.		

3 **Success** (novel)	Cape 1978	A
4 **Other People** (novel)	Cape 1981	A
	Viking 1981	A
5 **Invasion of the Space Invaders**	Hutchinson 1982	A

5 **Invasion of the Space Invaders**
A non-fiction popular paperback,
illustrated by Martin's brother, Philip.

Asimov, Isaac   Born in Russia, 1920. Naturalized American, 1928.

Although often applied to this author or that, Asimov may safely be said to be prolific. Beneath is listed only his fictional work – a sizeable enough *œuvre*, and usually of most interest to collectors. No bibliographies quite agree upon how many non-fiction works he has written in addition, but the general consensus seems to be around the hundred mark. A lot of these are deeply serious and technical, some of the *titles* stretching to three or four lines.

As in the last edition, then, this book contents itself with listing just the fiction to date.

1 **Pebble in the Sky** (novel)	Doubleday 1950	C
	Sidgwick & Jackson 1968	B
2 **I, Robot** (stories)	Gnome Press 1950	C
	Grayson 1952	C
3 **The Stars, Like Dust** (novel)	Doubleday 1951	C
4 **Foundation** (novel)	Gnome Press 1951	C
	Weidenfeld 1953	C
5 **Foundation and Empire** (novel)	Gnome Press 1952	C
6 **The Currents of Space** (novel)	Doubleday 1952	C
	Boardman 1955	B
7 **Second Foundation** (novel)	Gnome Press 1953	C
8 **The Caves of Steel** (novel)	Doubleday 1954	C
	Boardman 1954	C
9 **The End of Eternity** (novel)	Doubleday 1955	C
10 **The Martian Way and Other Stories**	Doubleday 1955	C
	Dobson 1964	B
11 **The Naked Sun** (novel)	Doubleday 1957	C
	Joseph 1958	B
12 **Earth Is Room Enough** (stories)	Doubleday 1957	B
13 **Nine Tomorrows: Tales of the Near Future**	Doubleday 1959	B
	Dobson 1963	B
14 **The Rest of the Robots** (stories plus 8 and 11)	Doubleday 1964	B
	Dobson 1967	B
15 **Fantastic Voyage** (novel)	Houghton Mifflin 1966	B
	Dobson 1966	A
16 **Through a Glass, Clearly** (stories)	New English Library 1967	A

Asimov

17 **A Whiff of Death** (novel)	Walker 1968	A
	Gollancz 1968	A
18 **Asimov's Mysteries** (stories)	Doubleday 1968	A
	Rapp & Whiting 1968	A
19 **Nightfall and Other Stories**	Doubleday 1969	A
	Rapp & Whiting 1969	A
20 **The Gods Themselves** (novel)	Doubleday 1972	A
	Gollancz 1972	A
21 **The Early Asimov** (stories)	Doubleday 1972	A
22 **The Best of Isaac Asimov** (stories)	Sidgwick & Jackson 1973	A
	Doubleday 1974	A
23 **Tales of the Black Widowers** (stories)	Doubleday 1974	A
	Gollancz 1975	A
24 **Buy Jupiter and Other Stories**	Doubleday 1975	A
	Gollancz 1976	A
25 **Authorised Murder** (novel)	Doubleday 1976	A
	Gollancz 1976	A
26 **The Bicentennial Man and Other Stories**	Doubleday 1976	A
	Gollancz 1977	A
27 **More Tales of the Black Widowers** (stories)	Doubleday 1976	A
	Gollancz 1977	A
28 **Murder at the Aba** (novel)	Doubleday 1976	A
29 **The Key Word and Other Mysteries**	Walker (US) 1977	A
30 **The Casebook of the Black Widowers** (stories)	Doubleday 1980	A
	Gollancz 1980	A
31 **Robots of Dawn** (novel)	Doubleday 1983	A
	Gollancz 1984	A

Asimov has also published six juveniles under the pseudonym of Paul French:

David Starr: Space Ranger	Doubleday 1952	D
Lucky Starr and the Pirates of the Asteroids	Doubleday 1954	C
Lucky Starr and the Oceans of Venus	Doubleday 1954	C
Lucky Starr and the Big Sun of Mercury	Doubleday 1956	B
Lucky Starr and the Moons of Jupiter	Doubleday 1957	B
Lucky Starr and the Rings of Saturn	Doubleday 1958	B

These were published in England – under Asimov's real name – by NEL in 1972–73.

Auden, W.H.   Born in York, England, 1907. Died 1973.

Although Auden is still very much collected, the enthusiasm that was detectable in the mid-seventies has somewhat declined. The rare and early remains sought-after and expensive, though, as is shown by the recent auction price achieved for his first book – the little orange-wrapped *Poems*, hand printed by Spender in 1928: £6000.

The voice of Auden will always be with us – perhaps not only because of the greatness of his work, but also because Auden himself – his face, his voice – is so intensely *memorable*.

It has been necessary to limit the list that follows to books and pamphlets written by Auden and published by commercial English and American publishers, and those he edited and translated that seem to be most pertinent to his *œuvre*. However, an excellent bibliography of Auden exists: *W.H. Auden: A Bibliography 1924–1969* (University Press of Virginia, 2nd ed. 1972). This contains everything – including contributions to periodicals – within 420 pages. The 1st edition of this work, incidentally, is desirable in that Auden wrote the intro., though as it was published in 1964, it is not of such practical use as the current edition.

1 **Poems**   SHS 1928   **X–Z**
Spender hand-printed this little volume in Frognal, Hampstead, in an edition of less than thirty. No collector has any hope of finding one, unless one of the known owners decides to sell, but the price could easily be £6000 or more. It is one of the legendary 1sts of the century. Three facsimiles of the book have been published, however, and one of these might be an acceptable substitute:
University Microfilms Xerox 1960
University of Cincinnati Library 1964 (limited to 500 copies)
Ilkley Literature Festival 1973
The Cincinnati facsimile is cloth-bound, with an introduction by Spender, but the Ilkley copy is faithful to the orange wrpps, reproduces the erratum slip for the first time, and has a separate foreword by B.C. Bloomfield, Auden's bibliographer.

2 **Poems**   Faber 1930   **J**
This wrappered volume, his first with Faber, is scarce.

3 **The Orators: An English Study** Black boards. Scarce. Grade I if in the cream and blue d/w.	Faber 1932	**F**
4 **The Dance of Death** Green printed boards with d/w of identical design.	Faber 1933	**G**
5 **Poems** Dark orange boards, cream d/w. Contains *The Orators* and *The Dance of* *Death*.	Random House 1934	**D**
6 **The Dog Beneath the Skin** (play) (with C. Isherwood) Red cloth, yellow d/w.	Faber 1935 Random House 1935	**E** **D**
7 **The Ascent of F6** (play) (with C. Isherwood) Blue cloth, cream d/w.	Faber 1936 Random House 1937	**E** **D**
8 **Look, Stranger!** (verse) Grey boards, yellow d/w. The title was invented by Faber and called by Auden 'bloody'. He chose the title of the American edition – see 9.	Faber 1936	**G**
9 **On This Island** (verse) Same as 8. Brown cloth, cream d/w.	Random House 1937	**E**
10 **Spain** (poem) Eight-page pamphlet in red wrpps. Scarce and unreprinted since 1942.	Faber 1937	**F**
11 **Letters from Iceland** (with Louis MacNeice) Lime boards with photographic d/w.	Faber 1937 Random House 1937	**E** **E**
12 **Selected Poems** Faber Library series, with usual green cloth.	Faber 1938	**C**
13 **On the Frontier** (play) (with C. Isherwood) Red cloth, cream d/w.	Faber 1938 Random House 1939	**C** **C**
14 **Education Today and Tomorrow** (essay) (with T.C. Worsley) Day to Day Pamphlets No. 40. Reddish wrpps. Scarce – Auden does not 'remember the pamphlet, or how it came to be written'.	Hogarth Press 1939	**E**
15 **Journey to a War** (prose) (with C. Isherwood) Black boards, cream d/w. Scarce. Reissued in Faber Paper Covered Editions 1973 with new intros by Auden and Isherwood.	Faber 1939 Random House 1939	**E** **D**

16	**Another Time** (verse) Reddish boards, cream d/w. Faber ed.: red boards, red d/w.	Random House 1940 Faber 1940	D D
17	**Some Poems** Pink paper boards, pale blue d/w.	Faber 1940	C
18	**The Double Man** (verse) Brown cloth, cream d/w. Scarce.	Random House 1941	F
19	**New Year Letter** (verse) Same as 18. Grey cloth, orange d/w.	Faber 1941	D
20	**For the Time Being** (verse) White and mauve boards, grey d/w. Faber ed.: orange cloth, cream d/w.	Random House 1944 Faber 1945	D C
21	**The Collected Poetry** Bluish cloth, pink d/w.	Random House 1945	C
22	**The Age of Anxiety** (verse) Bluish cloth, cream d/w. Faber ed.: green cloth, blue d/w.	Random House 1947 Faber 1948	C C
23	**Collected Shorter Poems 1930–1944** Bright blue cloth, yellow d/w.	Faber 1950	C
24	**The Enchafèd Flood** (verse) Dark green boards, grey d/w. Faber ed.: blue cloth, white d/w.	Random House 1950 Faber 1951	D D
25	**Nones** (verse) Dark blue and grey boards, grey d/w. Faber ed.: blue cloth, orange d/w.	Random House 1951 Faber 1952	D D
26	**Mountains** Ariel Poem, in pink envelope.	Faber 1954	B
27	**The Shield of Achilles** (verse) Orange and black boards, cream d/w. Faber ed.: wine cloth, yellow d/w.	Random House 1955 Faber 1955	D C
28	**The Magic Flute** (libretto trans.) (with C. Kallman) Black, pink and grey boards, white d/w. Faber ed.: grey cloth, green d/w.	Random House 1956 Faber 1957	C C
29	**Making, Knowing and Judging** (lecture) 18-page pamphlet in grey wrpps. Scarce.	OUP 1956	C
30	**W.H. Auden: A Selection by the Author** Penguin paperback, originally published at 3/6d.	Penguin 1958	A
31	**Selected Poetry of W.H. Auden** American edition of 30. Blue cloth, white d/w.	Modern Library 1959	A
32	**Homage to Clio** (verse) Black and orange cloth, cream d/w. Faber ed.: wine cloth, green d/w.	Random House 1960 Faber 1960	C C

Auden

33	**The Dyer's Hand** First book of essays. Green cloth, grey d/w. Faber ed.: green cloth, light green d/w.	Random House 1962 Faber 1963	C C
34	**Selected Essays** Shiny perfect binding.	Faber 1964	B
35	**About the House** (verse) Black and grey boards, white d/w. Faber ed.: blue cloth, green and purple d/w.	Random House 1965 Faber 1966	C C
36	**Collected Shorter Poems 1927–1957** Blue cloth, black and yellow d/w. RH ed.: orange and green boards with black and yellow d/w.	Faber 1966 Random House 1967	C C
37	**Selected Poems** Shiny tan and blue perfect binding.	Faber 1968	A
38	**Collected Longer Poems** Blue cloth, grey and orange d/w. RH ed.: orange and green boards with yellow and orange d/w.	Faber 1968 Random House 1969	C C
39	**Secondary Worlds** (T.S. Eliot Memorial Lectures) Red cloth, white d/w. RH ed.: grey and orange boards, violet and yellow d/w.	Faber 1969 Random House 1969	C B
40	**City Without Walls** (verse) Black cloth, cream d/w.	Faber 1969 Random House 1970	C C
41	**A Certain World** A Commonplace book. Fine Faber typography on English d/w.	Viking 1970 Faber 1971	C C
42	**Academic Graffiti** (clerihews) Red cloth, white d/w. Auden's 'Old Possum'.	Faber 1971 Random House 1972	A A
43	**Epistle to a Godson** (verse) Brown and cream boards, beige and blue d/w.	Faber 1972 Random House 1972	B B
44	**Forewords and Afterwords** Second volume of essays – see 33.	Viking 1973 Faber 1973	C C
45	**Auden/Moore: Poems and Lithographs** Catalogue of a fine exhibition. Wrpps.	British Museum 1974	B
46	**Thank You, Fog** (verse) Posthumous publication. Fine Faber typography on d/w, and photo of Auden on rear.	Faber 1974 Random House 1974	B B
47	**Collected Poems**	Faber 1976 Random House 1976	B B
48	**The English Auden: Poems, Essays, & Dramatic Writings 1927–1939**	Faber 1977 Random House 1978	B B

Auden was also the editor of many
works. A selection appears below.

The Poet's Tongue (2 vols)	Bell 1935	**F**
(with John Garrett)		
Scarce.		
The Oxford Book of Light Verse	OUP 1938	**C**
Poets of the English Language	Viking Press 1950	**E**
(5 vols)	Eyre & Spottiswoode 1952	**E**
An Elizabethan Song Book	Doubleday 1955	**C**
	Faber 1957	**C**
The Faber Book of Modern American Verse	Faber 1956	**C**
Selected Writings of Sydney Smith	Farrar Straus 1956	**C**
	Faber 1957	**C**
Van Gogh: A Self-Portrait	New York Graphic Society 1961	**D**
	Thames & Hudson 1961	**C**
The Viking Book of Aphorisms	Viking 1962	**C**
The Faber Book of Aphorisms	Faber 1965	**C**
A Choice of de la Mare's Verse	Faber 1963	**A**
Selected Poems, by Louis MacNeice	Faber 1964	**A**
Nineteenth Century British Minor Poets	Delacorte 1966	**B**
	Faber 1967	**B**
G.K. Chesterton: A Selection from his Non-Fiction Prose	Faber 1970	**B**
A Choice of Dryden's Verse	Faber 1973	**A**
George Herbert	Penguin 1973	**A**

Ayckbourn, Alan   Born in Hampstead, London, 1939.

Possibly because his output is so enormous, or possibly because he writes only comedy (the British adore comedy, but rarely see fit to promote its creator to the ranks of the artists who make them cry) Ayckbourn has not been seen to be the highly talented and important playwright that he is. Quite apart from the fact that his plays are intensely funny, and allow for such good acting from his favourite stable of performers, his understanding and wielding of stagecraft can sometimes be nothing short of phenomenal, as seen in the *Norman Conquests* trilogy, where we the audience can be in three places at once, as it were, and the deviousness, vanity, hypocrisy and sheer lunacy of these prime examples of the British middle class is magnified and enhanced that we might relish it all the more. And being British, and middle class, we adore it.

Ayckbourn is really not at all collected at the moment, but he should be, and he will be, I think.

Ayckbourn

1	**Relatively Speaking**	Evans 1968	**A**
		French (US) 1968	**A**
2	**Ernie's Incredible Illucinations** Included in *Playbill One*, edited by Alan Durband. There were three volumes in this series of non-net paperbacks intended for schools.	Hutchinson Educational 1969	**A**
3	**Countdown** Included in an anthology of plays entitled *We Who Are About To . . .*	Methuen 1970	**A**
4	**How the Other Half Loves**	French (US) 1972	**A**
		Evans (UK) 1972	**A**
5	**Time and Time Again**	French (UK & US) 1973	**A**
6	**Absurd Person Singular**	French (UK & US) 1974	**A**
7	**The Norman Conquests** A hardcover edition – Ayckbourn's first – was published in the same year by Chatto & Windus.	French (UK & US) 1975	**A**
8	**Absent Friends**	French (UK & US) 1975	**A**
9	**Bedroom Farce**	French (UK & US) 1977	**A**
10	**Three Plays** Includes 6, 8 and 9.	Chatto & Windus 1977	**B**
		Grove Press 1979	**B**
11	**Just Between Ourselves**	French (UK & US) 1978	**A**
12	**Ten Times Table**	French (UK & US) 1978	**A**
13	**Joking Apart**	French (UK & US) 1979	**A**
14	**Confusions** Includes *Mother Figure, Drinking Companion, Between Mouthfuls, Gosforth's Fete*, and *A Talk in the Park*.	French (UK & US) 1979	**B**
15	**Joking Apart** Includes 13, 11 and 12.	Chatto & Windus 1979	**B**
16	**Sisterly Feelings**	French (UK & US) 1981	**A**
17	**Taking Steps** 16 and 17 were published together in hardcover by Chatto and Windus in the same year.	French (UK & US) 1981	**A**
18	**Suburban Strains**	French (UK & US) 1982	**A**

The book that gives considerable insight into the way that
Ayckbourn's singular mind works is:
Ian Watson **Conversations with Ayckbourn**
Macdonald Futura 1981

Bainbridge, Beryl   Born in Liverpool, 1934.

A regular producer of very slim, dextrous novels, all respectfully received
and underlining her position of Middle C and main string at Duckworth's
Old Piano Factory. Not a huge noise with collectors, but still pursued, her
first couple of novels remaining obstinately difficult to track down.

1	**A Weekend with Claude** (novel)	Hutchinson 1967	E
2	**Another Part of the Wood** (novel)	Hutchinson 1968	D
3	**Harriet Said . . .** (novel)	Duckworth 1972	C
		Braziller 1972	B
4	**The Dressmaker** (novel)	Duckworth 1973	B
5	**The Secret Glass** (same as 4)	Braziller 1974	B
6	**The Bottle Factory Outing** (novel)	Duckworth 1974	B
		Braziller 1974	B
7	**Sweet William** (novel)	Duckworth 1975	B
		Braziller 1975	B
8	**A Quiet Life** (novel)	Duckworth 1976	A
		Braziller 1977	A
9	**Injury Time** (novel)	Duckworth 1977	A
		Braziller 1977	A
10	**Young Adolf** (novel)	Duckworth 1978	A
		Braziller 1979	A
11	**Winter Garden** (novel)	Duckworth 1980	A
		Braziller 1981	A
12	**A Weekend with Claude** (novel)	Duckworth 1981	A
	A reissue of her first book.	Braziller 1982	A
13	**English Journey** (non-fiction)	BBC/Duckworth 1984	B

Film:
Sweet William ITC 1980

Ballard, J.G.   Born in Shanghai, China, 1930. British.

An author of serious, and rather disturbing fiction, difficult to categorize, for
there is more in the books than 'science fiction' implies. Ballard's own words
make it clearer: he says he is more concerned with inner space than outer
space.
   Of middling interest to collectors, but high on the list of those who
specialize in SF.

1	**The Wind from Nowhere** (novel)	Berkley (NY) 1962	D
2	**The Voices of Time and Other Stories**	Berkley 1962	D
3	**Billenium and Other Stories**	Berkley 1962	D
4	**The Drowned World** (novel)	Berkley 1962	D
		Gollancz 1963	C
5	**The Four-Dimensional Nightmare** (stories)	Gollancz 1963	B
6	**Passport to Eternity and Other Stories**	Berkley 1963	C
7	**The Terminal Beach** (stories)	Gollancz 1964	B
8	**The Drought** (novel)	Cape 1965	B
9	**The Crystal World** (novel)	Cape 1966	B
		Farrar Straus 1966	B
10	**The Disaster Area** (stories)	Cape 1967	B
11	**The Day of Forever** (stories)	Panther 1968	A
12	**The Overloaded Man** (stories)	Panther 1968	A
13	**The Atrocity Exhibition** (novel)	Cape 1970	B
14	**Vermilion Sands** (stories)	Berkley 1971	B
		Cape 1973	B
15	**Crash!** (novel)	Cape 1973	C
		Farrar Straus 1973	C
16	**Concrete Island** (novel)	Cape 1974	A
		Farrar Straus 1974	A
17	**High Rise** (novel)	Cape 1975	A
18	**Low-Flying Aircraft** (stories)	Cape 1976	A
19	**The Best of J.G. Ballard**	Sidgwick & Jackson 1977	A
20	**The Unlimited Dream Company** (novel)	Cape 1979	A
		Holt Rinehart 1979	A
21	**The Venus Hunters** (stories)	Granada 1980	A
22	**Hello America** (novel)	Cape 1981	A
23	**Myths of the Near Future** (stories)	Cape 1982	A

Banks, Lynne Reid   Born in London, 1929.

Author of upwards of a dozen works, though still notable for *The L-Shaped Room* and its two successors, which form the trilogy.

1	**The L-Shaped Room** (novel)	Chatto & Windus 1960	D
		Simon & Schuster 1962	C
2	**The Backward Shadow** (novel)	Chatto & Windus 1970	B
		Simon & Schuster 1970	A

3 **Two Is Lonely** (novel)	Chatto & Windus	A
These three form a trilogy: 1 is in itself a	1974	
milestone, and a desirable work.	Simon & Schuster	A
	1974	

Film:
The L-Shaped Room British Lion 1962

Barstow, Stan   Born in Yorkshire, 1928.

Perhaps superfluous to note that Barstow was born in Yorkshire, as it courses through his work like the Ouse. The bite, tenacity and freshness have much in common with John Braine, so it must be Yorkshire that does it. *A Kind of Loving* (like *Room at the Top*) still has the power to make you wince at the truth of it, the grinding power surviving in the novel after nearly a quarter of a century ('No smoking in the bedroom, please, Victor'), the film ('Sometimes I love 'er and sometimes I hate t'bloody sight of 'er') and the TV adaptation ('You do love me, Vic – don't you?').

1 **A Kind of Loving** (novel)	Joseph 1960	C
	Doubleday 1961	B
2 **The Desperadoes** (stories)	Joseph 1961	B
3 **Ask Me Tomorrow** (novel)	Joseph 1962	B
4 **Joby** (novel)	Joseph 1964	B
5 **The Watchers on the Shore** (novel)	Joseph 1966	B
6 **Ask Me Tomorrow** (play)	French 1966	A
With Alfred Bradley.		
7 **A Raging Calm** (novel)	Joseph 1968	A
Published in America as *The Hidden Part*.	Coward McCann 1969	A
8 **A Kind of Loving** (screenplay)	Blackie 1970	B
9 **A Season with Eros** (stories)	Joseph 1971	A
10 **Stringer's Last Stand** (play)	French 1972	A
11 **The Right True End** (novel)	Joseph 1976	A
With 1 and 5, this forms the Vic Brown Trilogy.		
12 **A Casual Acquaintance and Other Stories**	Longman 1976	A
Edited by Marilyn Davies.		
13 **Joby** (play)	Blackie 1977	A
14 **An Enemy of the People** (play)	Calder 1977	A
Adaptation of Ibsen.		
15 **A Brother's Tale** (novel)	Joseph 1980	A
16 **A Kind of Loving: The Vic Brown Trilogy**	Joseph 1982	B
Includes 1, 5 and 11.		

17 **The Glad Eye** (novel)   Joseph 1984   **A**

Film:
A Kind of Loving   Anglo-Amalgamated 1962

Beckett, Samuel   Born near Dublin, 1906.

Still very highly regarded by collectors, despite his not having produced a major work for a very long time. It would indeed be a joy to hear of a forthcoming full-length novel, or a three-acter coming to the Royal Court. In the meantime, we must content ourselves with Calder's occasional residua, ends and odds. While a total understanding of Beckett's later snippets might sometimes seem elusive, at least Calder leaves nothing to chance in the way of legibility, the slim volumes being printed in ever huger typefaces, rivalling the old Large Print books. It could be that they feel this grand, spacious layout reflects well the sparseness of Beckett's prose, or it could be a way of stretching twenty pages of typescript to forty pages of print, in order to part justify the five pounds fifty.

I believe the later, and more usual, Beckett works to be still undervalued, for he remains the most inventive and exciting person working in the theatre – indeed, the only one concerned with pushing back the barriers ever further.

In the list that follows, I have recorded the first editions in the English language, but as the French-language edition precedes many of these, the following bibliography should be consulted for the fullest information:
Raymond Federman and John Fletcher *Samuel Beckett, His Works And His Critics: An Essay in Bibliography* University of California Press, Berkeley 1970.

1 **Our Exagmination Round His Factification for Incamination of Work in Progress**	Shakespeare & Co. (Paris) 1929	**M**
	Faber 1936	**H**
Cont. Dante . . . Bruno . . . Vico . . . Joyce. By S.B. All very scarce.	New Directions 1939	**H**
2 **Whoroscope** (verse) Beckett's first separately published work. Limited to 300 copies, 100 signed. Wrpps. Very scarce.	Hours Press (Paris) 1930	**(Q) O**
3 **Proust** Very scarce.	Chatto & Windus 1931	**K**
	Grove Press 1957	**K**
4 **More Pricks than Kicks** (texts) Very scarce.	Chatto & Windus 1934	**N**
	Grove Press 1970	**N**
5 **Echo's Bones** (verse) Very scarce.	Europa Press (Paris) 1935	**M**
6 **Murphy** (novel) Scarce.	Routledge 1938	**M**
	Grove Press 1957	**C**

7 **Molloy** (novel) (French-language ed. 1951 **K**)	Olympia Press (Paris) 1955	I
	Grove Press 1955	G
	Calder 1959	D
8 **Waiting for Godot** (play) (French-language ed. 1952 **L**)	Grove Press 1954	H
	Faber 1956	F
9 **Malone Dies** (Novel) (French-language ed. 1951 **H**)	Grove Press 1956	G
	Calder 1958	D
10 **All That Fall** (play)	Grove Press 1957	D
	Faber 1957	C
11 **Endgame** (play) (French-language ed. 1957 **F**)	Grove Press 1958	D
	Faber 1958	C
12 **The Unnamable** (French-language ed. 1953 **F**)	Grove Press 1958	D
	Calder 1959	C
13 **From an Abandoned Work** Wrpps.	Faber 1958	C
14 **Krapp's Last Tape** and **Embers** (plays) Wrpps.	Faber 1959	D
	Grove Press 1960	C
15 **Watt** (novel)	Olympia Press (Paris) 1953	H
	Grove Press 1959	D
	Calder 1963	C
16 **Poems in English**	Calder 1961	C
	Grove Press 1963	C
17 **Happy Days** (play)	Grove Press 1961	C
	Faber 1962	C
18 **Play and Two Short Pieces for Radio** (incl. *Words & Music* and *Cascando*)	Faber 1964	C
19 **How It Is** (novel) (French-language ed. 1961 **E**)	Grove Press 1964	C
	Calder 1964	C
20 **Imagination Dead Imagine** (text) (French-language ed. 1965 **D**)	Calder 1965	B
21 **Proust and Three Dialogues with Georges Duthuit**	Calder 1965	B
22 **Come and Go: Dramaticule**	Calder 1967	B
23 **Eh Joe and Other Writings** (play) Incl. *Act Without Words* II and *Film*.	Faber 1967	B
24 **No's Knife: Selected Shorter Prose 1945–1966** Incl. *Stories and Texts for Nothing, From an Abandoned Work, Imagination Dead Imagine, Enough* and *Ping*.	Calder 1967	B
25 **Film** (screenplay)	Grove Press 1969	C
	Faber 1972	B

26	**Breath and Other Shorts** Incl. *Come and Go, Act Without Words* I and II, *From an Abandoned Work*.	Faber 1971	B
27	**Lessness** (story) (French-language ed. 1969 **C**)	Calder 1971	B
28	**First Love** (story) (French-language ed. 1970 **C**)	Calder 1973 Grove Press 1974	B B
29	**The Lost Ones** (story) (French-language ed. 1971 **C**)	Calder 1972	B
30	**Not I** (play)	Faber 1973	B
31	**The North** Limited to 137 numbered and signed copies.	Enitharmon Press 1973	J
32	**Mercier and Camier** (novel) (French-language ed. 1970 **C–D**)	Calder 1974 Grove Press 1975	B B
33	**Footfalls** (play)	Faber 1976	A
34	**That Time** (play)	Faber 1976	A
35	**For to End Yet Again, and Other** **Fizzles** Published as **Fizzles** by Grove Press in 1977 **A**	Calder 1977	A
36	**Collected Poems in English and** **French**	Calder 1977	B
37	**Four Novellas**	Calder 1977	A
38	**Ends and Odds** (plays) Incl. 30, 33, 34.	Grove Press 1977 Faber 1977	A A
39	**Six Residua** (reprinted pieces)	Calder 1978	A
40	**All Strange Away** (prose) First published in a limited edition illustrated by Edward Gorey in 1976 by the Gotham Book Mart **G**.	Calder 1979	A
41	**Company** (prose) Translated by S.B. from his *Compagnie*, Editions de Minuit, 1979.	Grove Press 1980 Calder 1980	A A
42	**Rockaby and Other Short Pieces** Contains *Rockaby, Ohio Impromptu, All* *Strange Away* and *A Piece of Monologue*.	Grove Press 1981	A
43	**Ill Seen Ill Said** (prose)	Grove Press 1981 Calder 1982	A A
44	**Three Occasional Pieces** (plays)	Faber 1982	A
45	**Worstward Ho** (prose)	Calder 1983	A
46	**Collected Shorter Plays**	Faber 1983	A
47	**Disjecta: Miscellaneous Writings** **and Dramatic Fragments**	Calder 1984	A
48	**Collected Shorter Prose 1945–1980**	Calder 1984	B
49	**Collected Poems 1930–1978**	Calder 1984	B

Beckett translated the following:

Anthology of Mexican Poetry	Indiana University, Bloomington 1958	D
	Thames & Hudson 1959 Ed. by Octavio Paz.	D

Robert Pinget **The Old Tune** in:		
Robert Pinget **Three Plays**	Hill & Wang (NY) 1966	B
Robert Pinget **Plays**	Calder 1966	B
Guillaume Apollinaire **Zone**	Calder 1972	A
	Dolmen Press 1972	A

Samuel Beckett: An Exhibition
(Turret Books 1971) is also a useful
book to the collector.

Film:
Film Evergreen Theatre Inc. 1965

A fine biography has been published, which could well prove to be
definitive:
Deirdre Bair **Samuel Beckett: A Biography** Cape 1978
(Beckett refused to co-operate with the writing of this book, has refused to
read it, and wishes his friends to ignore it.)

Behan, Brendan Born in Dublin, 1923. Died 1964.

Still underrated by collectors, and therefore still undervalued – even *Borstal Boy*. Behan is best remembered for his somewhat unconventional – that is to say, drunken – lifestyle, rather than for his books and plays, which are really very good.

1	**The Quare Fellow** (play)	Methuen 1956	E
2	**The Hostage** (play)	Methuen 1958	D
	These two plays pub. in America in one vol.	Grove Press 1964	B
3	**Borstal Boy**	Knopf 1957	D
		Hutchinson 1958	D
4	**Brendan Behan's Island** (non-fiction)	Hutchinson 1962	C
		Geis 1962	C
5	**Hold Your Hour and Have Another**	Hutchinson 1963	C
		Little Brown 1964	C
6	**Brendan Behan's New York**	Hutchinson 1964	C
		Geis 1964	C
7	**The Scarperer** (novel)	Doubleday 1964	C
		Hutchinson 1966	C
8	**Confessions of an Irish Rebel**	Hutchinson 1965	B
		Geis 1966	B

Behan

9	**Borstal Boy** (play)	Random House (NY) 1971	**B**
10	**Richard's Cork Leg** (play)	Methuen 1973	**A**
		Grove Press 1974	**A**
11	**After the Wake: Uncollected Prose** First published in Ireland, and then by Allison & Busby in UK, and by Devin in US.	O'Brien Press 1983	**B**

Film:
The Quare Fellow British Lion 1962

Bellow, Saul   Born in Canada, 1915. American.

Bellow's reputation, always high, rose considerably after his winning the Nobel Prize in 1976. He publishes rarely, and his prestige and following are now such that heavy press coverage is assured each time, and hence large first print runs. Only the first couple of Bellow's books are difficult to acquire, which is why it might seem that the body of his *œuvre* is underpriced: it is just that they are easy to find. As a bookseller, I find that most later Bellows (even good ones in d/w) stay on the shelves interminably, either because the initiated already have them, or because the tyro is deeply suspicious of the low prices.

1	**Dangling Man** (novel)	Vanguard Press 1944	**O**
		Lehmann 1946	**J**
2	**The Victim** (novel)	Vanguard Press 1945	**L**
		Lehmann 1948	**H**
3	**The Adventures of Augie March** (novel)	Viking 1953	**E**
		Weidenfeld 1954	**C**
4	**Seize the Day, with Three Short Stories and a One Act Play**	Viking 1956	**D**
		Weidenfeld 1957	**C**
5	**Henderson the Rain King** (novel)	Viking Press 1959	**C**
		Weidenfeld 1959	**B**
6	**Herzog** (novel)	Viking 1964	**C**
		Weidenfeld 1965	**B**
7	**The Last Analysis** (play)	Viking 1965	**B**
		Weidenfeld 1966	**B**
8	**Mosby's Memoirs and Other Stories**	Viking 1968	**B**
		Weidenfeld 1969	**A**
9	**Mr Sammler's Planet** (novel)	Viking 1970	**B**
		Weidenfeld 1970	**A**
10	**Humboldt's Gift** (novel)	Viking 1975	**B**
		Alison Press/ Secker & Warburg 1975	**A**
11	**To Jerusalem and Back** (non-fiction)	Viking 1976	**B**
		Secker & Warburg 1976	**A**

12 **The Nobel Lecture**	US Information Service, Stockholm 1977	E
13 **The Dean's December** (novel)	Harper 1982	B
	Secker & Warburg 1982	B
14 **Him with His Foot in His Mouth and Other Stories**	Harper 1984	B
	Secker & Warburg 1984	B

Bennett, Alan   Born in Yorkshire, 1934.

Bennett is a very funny and a very clever playwright, one of our most accurately observant living writers, and very much neglected by collectors; thus the prices are low. Although known as a TV face as actor and comedian, he has never been tempted to continue to cash in on the early (and easier) satire, but has continued to produce high quality, witty plays, TV possibly being his most successful medium.

1 **Beyond the Fringe** (play)	Souvenir Press 1962	C
	Random House 1963	B
2 **Forty Years On** (play)	Faber 1969	C
3 **Getting On** (play)	Faber 1972	A
4 **Habeas Corpus** (play)	Faber 1973	A
5 **The Old Country** (play)	Faber 1978	A
6 **Enjoy** (play)	Faber 1980	A
7 **Office Suite**	Faber 1981	A

Includes *Green Forms* and *A Visit From Miss Prothero.*

Bentley, E.C.   Born 1875. Died 1956.

Famous for having written an excellent detective novel, and for having invented a rather silly four line poem form, which he christened with his middle name, Clerihew. Example:

Miss Dorothy Sayers
Never cared about the Himalayas.
The height that gave her a thrill
Was Primrose Hill.

Britain has taken the clerihew to its heart, and the first complete collection of the things was recently published. Although Bentley wrote other books, then, here are the two highlights:

1 **Trent's Last Case**	Nelson 1913	E

Bentley

2 **The Complete Clerihews** OUP 1981 **A**
Illustrated by Nicolas Bentley, G.K.
Chesterton, Victor Reinganum and E.C.
Bentley.

Film:
Trent's Last Case 20th Century Fox 1929 British Lion 1950

Berger, John Born in London, 1926.

Berger has been publishing for some time, but his popularity is quite recent, as is seen by the number of his old works that have now been reissued in paperback. Most collectors will go for the novels, but the art criticism is worth investigating, and it has a much kinder reception these days – it was not in keeping with the times in the nineteen-fifties to champion realism. Many are stimulated and amused by Berger's strength in his convictions, and by his facility to express them.

1	**A Painter of Our Time** (novel)	Secker & Warburg 1958	**D**
		Simon & Schuster 1959	**C**
2	**Permanent Red: Essays in Seeing**	Methuen 1960	**C**
3	**The Foot of Clive** (novel)	Methuen 1962	**C**
4	**Corker's Freedom** (novel)	Methuen 1964	**C**
5	**The Success and Failure of Picasso**	Penguin 1965	**A**
6	**A Fortunate Man: The Story of a Country Doctor** (photo-documentary)	Lane 1967 Holt Rinehart 1967	**B** **B**
7	**Art in Revolution** (non-fiction)	Weidenfeld 1969 Pantheon 1969	**B** **B**
8	**The Moment of Cubism and Other Essays**	Weidenfeld 1969 Pantheon 1969	**B** **B**
9	**The Look of Things: Selected Essays and Articles**	Penguin 1971 Viking 1974	**A** **A**
10	**Ways of Seeing** (art)	Penguin 1972 Viking 1973	**A** **A**
11	**G** (novel)	Weidenfield 1972 Viking 1972	**C** **C**
12	**A Seventh Man** (photo-documentary)	Penguin 1975	**A**
13	**Pig Earth** (novel)	Writers & Readers 1979 Pantheon 1980	**A** **A**
14	**About Looking** (art)	Writers & Readers 1980 Pantheon 1980	**A** **A**

52

Berryman, John Born in Oklahoma, 1914. Died 1972.

A much respected American poet, whose reputation now seems totally secure. A very difficult poet to collect, however, as his books, for some reason or another (it happens with some authors, for no *apparent* reason) very rarely turn up in the bookshops – even the English editions. Still, worth pursuing.

1	**Five American Poets** With others.	New Directions (NY) 1940	G
2	**Poems**	New Directions 1942	L
3	**The Dispossessed** (verse)	Sloane (NY) 1948	J
4	**Stephen Crane** (criticism)	Sloane 1950	E
		Methuen 1951	D
5	**Homage to Mistress Bradstreet** (verse)	Farrar Straus (NY) 1956	G
	The Amer. ed. is just the title poem, whereas the Faber ed. includes a selection from 3 and 6.	Faber 1959	D
6	**His Thoughts Made Pockets & The Plane Buckt**	Frederick (NY) 1958	H
7	**77 Dream Songs** (verse)	Farrar Straus 1964	E
		Faber 1964	C
8	**Berryman's Sonnets** (verse)	Farrar Straus 1967	D
		Faber 1968	C
9	**Short Poems** The same as the Eng. ed. of 5, without the title poem, but with one new poem.	Farrar Straus 1967	C
10	**His Toy, His Dream, His Rest** (verse)	Farrar Straus 1968 Faber 1969	E C
11	**Love and Fame** (verse)	Farrar Straus 1970	C
		Faber 1971	B
12	**Delusions, etc.** (verse)	Farrar Straus 1972	C
		Faber 1972	B
13	**Selected Poems 1938–1968**	Faber 1972	A
14	**Recovery** (novel)	Farrar Straus 1973	C
		Faber 1973	B
15	**The Freedom of the Poet** (essays)	Farrar Straus 1977	C
		Faber 1977	B
16	**Henry's Fate** (verse)	Farrar Straus 1977	C
		Faber 1978	B

Biography:
John Haffenden **The Life of John Berryman** Routledge 1982

Betjeman, John Born in Highgate, London, 1906. Died 1984.

As famous, British and indestructible as Harrods, and just as full of scrumptious things, Sir John had utterly perfected his persona; he was the epitome of old, slightly distrait 'sorft' and lovable man of letters, from the woolliness of the cardigan to the teddy by the bed. Defender of Victoriana, Metroland and homely English values. How much was he laughing, or did he merely marvel? Betjeman kept us guessing, and we loved him dearly. It is difficult to say his name without smiling fondly.

His poetry is becoming discernibly scarcer. There has been a definite surge in interest among younger collectors as well as the diehard loyalists. Only the later, commoner items come up with any regularity now, but even these can be elusive as most are reprinted within the year of publication, and the firsts seem to go to ground.

Latterly, Betjeman went in for the signed, limited edition in a fairly big way, Murray usually doing such an edition simultaneously with the 1st, though never announcing it. For instance, *A Nip in the Air* was also published in a limited edition of 175 copies on handmade paper, signed by the author, and bound in yellow buckram. These appreciate in value very quickly, not least of the reasons being the very low limitation, though the published price is generally quite steep. Blond reissued *Ghastly Good Taste* in a revised edition in 1970. The pink-boarded trade edition was everywhere, but 200 were quarter-bound in leather, cloth-slipcased, numbered and signed by the author.

1 **Mount Zion** (verse)　　　　　　　James Press 1931　　　**N**
As with all major writers' first works,
very scarce, and expensive.

2 **Ghastly Good Taste** (architecture)　Chapman & Hall 1933　**F**
Worth buying for the title alone, this
really is a fine item. Small format with
pink boards and the famous 'gatefold'
at the rear. Ensure that this is present.

3 **Devon** (architecture)　　　　　　　Architectural Press　**E**
A rare book.　　　　　　　　　　　　1936

4 **Continual Dew: A Little Book of**　Murray 1937　　　　**F**
Bourgeois Verse
The first of a lifelong partnership with
John Murray. A charming production,
the black boards featuring mock brass
hinges and rustic lettering. The title is
illustrated on the t/p by a dripping tap,
and the book has India paper inserts,
decorated by Osbert Lancaster. A fine
item, and quite scarce.

5 **An Oxford University Chest**   J. Miles 1938   **G**
A larger-format book; though recently
reissued in facsimile, the 1st remains
scarce.

6 **A Handbook on Paint**   Silicate Paint Co.   **H**
A very curious little item that has just   J.B. Orr & Co. Ltd
come to my notice. It looks like a King   1939
Penguin, and contains two essays – one
by J.B., 'Colour and the Interior
Decorator', and the other by Hugh
Casson. Very scarce, unusual, and
desirable.

7 **Antiquarian Prejudice** (essay)   Hogarth Press 1939   **C**
Scarce, and made doubly so by
Hogarth collectors.

8 **Old Light for New Chancels** (verse)   Murray 1940   **D**
First of the paperback-size Murray
books, with paper label on blue boards.

9 **Vintage London** (architecture)   Collins 1942   **C**
Pleasing large, slim volume with
tipped-in colour plates.

10 **English Cities and Small Towns**   Collins 1943   **B**
(architecture)
In the Britain in Pictures series, and
one of the two or three sought by
collectors (other than collectors of the
whole series, who invariably collect
King Penguins as well). Pleasant
production.

11 **John Piper** (art)   Penguin 1944   **C**
Wrappered booklet in 'Modern
Painters' series.

12 **New Bats in Old Belfries** (verse)   Murray 1945   **C**
Small, slim volume. Red boards with
paper label on front. White d/w with
red printed design.

13 **Slick, but Not Streamlined: Poems**   Doubleday (NY) 1947   **D**
and Short Pieces
Only 1,750 copies printed, and edited
by W.H. Auden – hence the scarcity.
Black cloth, with our dripping tap
again (see 4).

14 **Murray's Buckinghamshire**   Murray 1948   **C**
Architectural Guide
With John Piper – see 10.

15 **Selected Poems**   Murray 1948   **B**
Ed. by John Sparrow. Red boards,
white paper label.

16	**Murray's Berkshire Architectural Guide** As 13.	Murray 1949	C
17	**Murray's Shropshire Architectural Guide** As 13.	Murray 1951	C
18	**First and Last Loves** (essays) Illustrated and d/w by John Piper (see 10). White boards, decorated in pale blue.	Murray 1952	C
19	**A Few Late Chrysanthemums** (verse) Blue cloth, yellow paper label on front, yellow d/w.	Murray 1954	C
20	**Poems in the Porch** Wrappered pamphlet, illus. by John Piper. Take care with this one, as the verso will always read 'First published in 1954 by SPCK', whereas t/p itself may bear a different date. They must agree.	SPCK 1954	B
21	**The English Town in the Last Hundred Years** Architectural work.	CUP 1956	C
22	**Collins Guide to English Parish Churches**	Collins 1958 Obolensky 1959	B B
23	**Collected Poems** Edited by Earl of Birkenhead. White boards, brown d/w.	Murray 1958	B
24	**Summoned by Bells** (verse autobiog.) Green diamond-paned boards, beige d/w.	Murray 1960 Houghton Mifflin 1960	B B
25	**A Ring of Bells** Edited by Irene Slade, being excerpts of 23, intended for children. d/w by Ardizzone.	Murray 1963 Houghton Mifflin 1963	B A
26	**English Churches** (architecture) With Basil Clarke.	Studio Vista 1964	B
27	**Cornwall** Only Faber Betjeman.	Faber 1965	C
28	**High and Low** (verse) Yellow cloth, pink d/w.	Murray 1966 Houghton Mifflin 1967	B A
29	**London's Historic Railway Stations** Pictorial. Photographic d/w.	Murray 1972	B
30	**A Pictorial History of English Architecture**	Murray 1972 Macmillan (US) 1972	B B

Fine book, but thousands upon thousands printed for a certain Book Club, so it is not at all difficult.

31	**A Nip in the Air** (verse)	Murray 1974	A
	Yellow cloth, green d/w.		
32	**Archie and the Strict Baptists**	Murray 1977	A
	Large format, jolly juvenile, with coloured illustrations.	Lippincott 1978	A
33	**The Best of Betjeman**	Murray 1978	A
	An anthology, selected by John Guest.		
34	**Church Poems**	Murray 1981	A
	A collection of all the church poems, illustrated by John Piper.		
35	**Uncollected Poems**	Murray 1982	B
	A late vintage, discovered by Bevis Hillier while researching his forthcoming biography of J.B. Hillier contributes a foreword.		

Bowen, Elizabeth   Born in Dublin, 1899. Died 1973.

Very much collected, and very much read. Very difficult to assemble a complete collection here, as the same few tend to keep coming up.

1	**Encounters: Stories**	Sidgwick & Jackson 1923	H
		Boni & Liveright 1926	D
2	**Ann Lee's and Other Stories**	Sidgwick & Jackson 1926	G
		Boni & Liveright 1926	D
3	**The Hotel** (novel)	Constable 1927	G
		Dial Press 1928	D
4	**The Last September** (novel)	Constable 1929	E
		Dial Press 1929	C
5	**Joining Charles and Other Stories**	Constable 1929	E
		Dial Press 1929	C
6	**Friends and Relations** (novel)	Constable 1931	E
		Dial Press 1931	C
7	**To the North** (novel)	Gollancz 1932	D
		Knopf 1933	C
8	**The Cat Jumps and Other Stories**	Gollancz 1934	E
9	**The House in Paris** (novel)	Gollancz 1935	D
		Knopf 1936	C
10	**The Death of the Heart** (novel)	Gollancz 1938	C
		Knopf 1939	B

57

Bowen

11 **Look at All Those Roses** (stories)	Gollancz 1941	C
	Knopf 1941	B
12 **Bowen's Court** (non-fiction)	Longman 1942	C
	Knopf 1942	B
13 **English Novelists** (non-fiction)	Collins 1942	B
	Hastings House 1942	A
14 **Seven Winters** (non-fiction)	Cuala Press, Dublin 1942	E
	Longman 1943	B
	Knopf 1943	A
15 **The Demon Lover and Other Stories**	Cape 1945	C
16 **Ivy Gripped the Steps and Other Stories** (same as 15)	Knopf 1946	B
17 **Selected Stories**	Fridberg, Dublin 1946	B
18 **Anthony Trollope: A New Judgement**	OUP (UK & US) 1946	B
19 **Why Do I Write?: An Exchange of Views Between Elizabeth Bowen, Graham Greene, and V. S. Pritchett**	Marshall 1948	C
20 **The Heat of the Day** (novel)	Cape 1949	B
	Knopf 1949	B
21 **Collected Impressions**	Longman 1950	B
	Knopf 1950	B
22 **The Shelbourne** (non-fiction)	Harrap 1951	C
23 **The Shelbourne Hotel** (same as 22)	Knopf 1951	B
24 **A World of Love** (novel)	Cape 1955	B
	Knopf 1955	A
25 **Stories**	Knopf 1959	B
26 **A Time in Rome** (non-fiction)	Longman 1960	B
	Knopf 1960	B
27 **Afterthought: Pieces About Writing**	Longman 1962	B
	Knopf 1962	B
28 **The Little Girls** (novel)	Cape 1964	B
	Knopf 1964	B
29 **A Day in the Dark and Other Stories**	Cape 1965	B
30 **The Good Tiger** (juvenile)	Knopf 1965	B
	Cape 1970	B
31 **Eva Trout** (novel)	Knopf 1968	B
	Cape 1969	B
32 **Pictures and Conversations**	Knopf 1975	B
33 **The Collected Stories**	Cape 1981	B
	Random House 1982	B

Elizabeth Bowen also edited the
following two important works:

The Faber Book of Modern Stories	Faber 1937	**B**
Stories (by Katherine Mansfield)	Knopf 1956	**C**
34 Short Stories (same as above)	Collins 1957	**C**

Boyd, William Born in Gold Coast (Ghana), 1952. British.

One of the new crop of novelists who, unlike their forbears, do not seem in the least bit angry. It seems a good time to start collecting Boyd, before he has published very much. One fellow, who had just bought and enjoyed *An Ice-cream War* has come into my shop every week since, asking if I have 'any early Boyds' which – as you will see when you peruse the ensuing bibliography – is faintly ridiculous.

1	**A Good Man in Africa** (novel)	Hamilton 1981	**C**
		Morrow 1982	**B**
2	**On the Yankee Station** (stories)	Hamilton 1981	**B**
3	**An Ice-cream War** (novel)	Hamilton 1983	**A**
		Morrow 1983	**A**

Bradbury, Malcolm Born in Yorkshire, 1932.

Bradbury maintains the balance between being an academic and a novelist by continuing to lecture, and publishing works of literary criticism in between his (very occasional) novels. Although his latest was shortlisted for the Booker Prize, it is still *The History Man* for which he is known, not least because of the haunting images of the television adaptation – the gum-chewing indecency of Howard Kirk, the hot coolness of Flora Beniform. One of the few identifiable 'seventies' books, and well worth having as a landmark in a collection of fiction, even if you don't collect Bradbury. Which you should: he's very good.

1	**Eating People is Wrong** (novel)	Secker & Warburg 1959	**C**
		Knopf 1960	**B**
2	**How to Have Class in a Classless Society**	Parrish 1960	**C**
3	**All Dressed Up and Nowhere to Go**	Parrish 1962	**C**
4	**Evelyn Waugh** (Writers & Critics Series)	Oliver & Boyd 1964	**C**
5	**Stepping Westward** (novel)	Secker & Warburg 1965	**C**
		Houghton Mifflin 1966	**B**
6	**What is a Novel?**	Arnold 1969	**B**

Bradbury, M.

7	**The Social Context of Modern English Literature**	Blackwell 1971	**B**
		Schocken 1971	**B**
8	**Possibilities: Essays on the State of the Novel**	OUP 1973	**B**
9	**The History Man** (novel)	Secker & Warburg 1975	**C**
		Houghton Mifflin 1976	**B**
10	**Who Do You Think You Are** (stories)	Secker & Warburg 1976	**A**
11	**Saul Bellow** (criticism) In the Contemporary Writers series.	Methuen 1982	**A**
12	**The Modern American Novel** (criticism)	OUP 1983	**A**
13	**Rates of Exchange** (novel)	Secker 1983	**B**
		Knopf 1983	**A**

Bradbury, Ray   Born in Illinois, 1920. American.

The early works remain highly popular with collectors, and have risen fairly sharply in price. In my experience, however, only the absolutely dedicated are in pursuit of a complete Bradbury collection, some contenting themselves with just his representative highlight, *Fahrenheit 451*.

1	**Dark Carnival** (stories)	Arkham House 1947	**I**
		Hamish Hamilton 1948	**G**
2	**The Meadow** (play) In *Best One-Act Plays of 1947–48*.	Dodd Mead (NY) 1948	**C**
3	**The Martian Chronicles** (stories)	Doubleday (NY) 1950	**F**
4	**The Illustrated Man** (stories)	Doubleday 1951	**E**
		Hart-Davis 1952	**D**
5	**The Golden Apples of the Sun** (stories)	Doubleday 1953	**E**
		Hart-Davis 1953	**D**
6	**Fahrenheit 451** (novel)	Ballantine (NY) 1953	**I**
		Hart-Davis 1954	**G**
7	**Switch on the Night** (juvenile)	Pantheon (NY) 1955	**E**
		Hart-Davis 1955	**D**
8	**The October Country** (stories)	Ballantine 1955	**D**
		Hart-Davis 1956	**C**
9	**Dandelion Wine** (stories)	Doubleday 1957	**D**
		Hart-Davis 1957	**C**
10	**A Medicine for Melancholy** (stories)	Doubleday 1959	**D**
11	**The Day It Rained Forever** (same as 10)	Hart-Davis 1959	**C**
12	**R is for Rocket** (juvenile)	Doubleday 1962	**D**
		Hart-Davis 1968	**B**
13	**Something Wicked This Way Comes** (novel)	Simon & Schuster 1962	**D**
		Hart-Davis 1963	**C**

14 **The Anthem Sprinters and Other Antics** (play)	Dial Press 1963	C
15 **The Machineries of Joy: Short Stories**	Simon & Schuster 1964 Hart-Davis 1964	C B
16 **The Vintage Bradbury** (stories)	Random House (NY) 1965	B
17 **The Autumn People** (stories)	Ballantine 1965	C
18 **Tomorrow Midnight** (stories)	Ballantine 1966	C
19 **The Day It Rained Forever** (play)	French (NY) 1966	B
20 **The Pedestrian** (play)	French (NY) 1966	B
21 **S is for Space** (juvenile)	Doubleday 1966 Hart-Davis 1968	C B
22 **I Sing the Body Electric!** (stories)	Knopf 1969 Hart-Davis 1970	B A
23 **The Wonderful Ice-Cream Suit and Other Plays** Incl. **The Veldt** and **To the Chicago Abyss.**	Bantam 1972 Hart-Davis 1973	B A
24 **The Halloween Tree** (novel)	Knopf 1972 Hart-Davis 1973	B A
25 **When Elephants Last in the Dooryard Bloomed: Celebrations for Almost any Day of the Year** (verse)	Knopf 1972 Hart-Davis 1975	C B
26 **The Small Assassin** (stories)	NEL (NY) 1973	B
27 **Mars and the Mind of Man** (non-fiction)	Harper 1973	B
28 **Pillar of Fire and Other Plays for Today, Tomorrow, and Beyond Tomorrow**	Bantam 1975	B
29 **Long After Midnight** (stories)	Hart-Davis 1977	B
30 **Where Robot Mice and Robot Men Run Round in Robot Towns: New Poems Both Light and Dark**	Knopf 1977 Granada 1979	B A
31 **The Mummies of Guanajuato** (non-fiction)	Abrams 1978	B
32 **The Stories of Ray Bradbury**	Knopf 1980	B
33 **The Ghosts of Forever** (non-fiction)	Rizzoli 1981	B
34 **The Complete Poems of Ray Bradbury**	Ballantine 1982	B

Films:
The Beast from 20,000 Fathoms Warner Bros 1953 (*The Foghorn* – story)   **Fahrenheit 451** United Artists 1966   **The Illustrated Man** Warner Bros 1968

Braine, John   Born in Yorkshire, 1922.

A consistent, always readable, and professional author, and one of our best storytellers. Of course, *Room at the Top* will always be the highlight (it is his best book) but many of the later books have been underrated perhaps partly because of the fame of the first – books such as, say, *The Crying Game*. Other than *Room at the Top*, then, easy to gather, and low in price.

1	**Room at the Top** (novel)	Eyre & Spottiswoode 1957	E
		Houghton Mifflin 1957	C
2	**The Vodi** (novel)	Eyre & Spottiswoode 1959	B
3	**From the Hand of the Hunter** (same as 2)	Houghton Mifflin 1960	A
4	**Life at the Top** (novel) Sequel to 1.	Eyre & Spottiswoode 1962	B
		Houghton Mifflin 1962	A
5	**The Jealous God** (novel)	Eyre & Spottiswoode 1965	A
		Houghton Mifflin 1965	A
6	**The Crying Game** (novel)	Eyre & Spottiswoode 1968	A
		Houghton Mifflin 1968	A
7	**Stay with Me till Morning** (novel)	Eyre & Spottiswoode 1970	A
8	**The View from Tower Hill** (same as 7)	Coward McCann (NY) 1971	A
9	**The Queen of a Distant Country** (novel)	Methuen 1972	A
		Coward McCann 1973	A
10	**Writing a novel** (non-fiction) The US edition includes some additional manuscript material on *Room at the Top*.	Eyre Methuen 1974	A
		McGraw Hill 1975	A
11	**The Pious Agent** (novel)	Eyre Methuen 1975	A
		Atheneum 1976	A
12	**Waiting for Sheila** (novel)	Eyre Methuen 1976	A
		Methuen Inc. 1976	A
13	**Finger of Fire** (novel) A sequel to 11.	Eyre Methuen 1977	A
14	**J. B. Priestley** (biography)	Weidenfeld 1978	A
		Barnes & Noble 1979	A
15	**One and Last Love** (novel)	Eyre Methuen 1981	A
16	**The Two of Us** (novel) A sequel to 7.	Eyre Methuen 1984	A

Films:
Room at the Top British Lion 1958   **Life at the Top** British Lion 1965

The following checklist has been
published:
Dale Salwak **John Braine & John**
Wain: A Reference Guide   Hall (US) 1979

Braithwaite, E.R.   Born in British Guiana (Guyana), 1922.

Still notable for his novel about black-white relations in a London school,
filmed memorably, if with perhaps more than a suspicion of sentiment, and a
rather haunting Lulu of a song.

To Sir, With Love   Bodley Head 1959   C

Film:
To Sir, With Love Columbia 1966

Brooke, Rupert   Born in Rugby, 1887. Died 1915.

As with all the war poets, killed so young, a great deal of the *œuvre* is
posthumous, collected, and recollected. The very early publications –
brought out when Brooke was still a schoolboy – are of legendary rarity, and
therefore would command a massive price. As will be seen from the ensuing
checklist, Brooke is not an author one has any hope of assembling in full, but
a fair idea of availability and price should be achieved.

1 **The Pyramids**	Rugby Press 1904	S
2 **The Bastille**	Rugby Press 1905	R
3 **Prize Compositions**	Rugby Press 1905	Q
4 **Poems 1911**	Sidgwick & Jackson 1911	J
5 **1914 and Other Poems** An American edition seems to have been printed by Doubleday in 1915 for copyright reasons only, and never published.	Sidgwick & Jackson 1914	H
6 **1914: Five Sonnets**	Sidgwick & Jackson 1915	G
7 **The Collected Poems of Rupert Brooke**	Lane (NY) 1915	F
	Sidgwick & Jackson 1918	F
8 **Lithuania** (drama)	Chicago Little Theatre 1915	J
	Sidgwick & Jackson 1935	E

9	**Letters from America**	Scribner 1916	E
		Sidgwick & Jackson 1916	D
10	**John Webster** (drama)	Lane 1916	E
		Sidgwick & Jackson 1916	D
11	**Selected Poems**	Sidgwick & Jackson 1917	D
12	**The Complete Poems of Rupert Brooke**	Sidgwick & Jackson 1932	C
13	**Twenty Poems**	Sidgwick & Jackson 1935	C
14	**The Poetical Works of Rupert Brooke**	Faber 1946	B
15	**Democracy and the Arts**	Hart-Davis 1946	B
16	**The Prose of Rupert Brooke**	Sidgwick & Jackson 1956	B
17	**The Letters of Rupert Brooke**	Faber 1968	C

For fullest information on Brooke, see the following:

Christopher Hassall **Rupert Brooke: A Biography**	Faber 1964
Geoffrey Keynes **Rupert Brooke: A Bibliography**	Soho Bibliographies, Hart-Davis 1959

Buckeridge, Anthony Born in London, 1912.

Now as far as I know, Buckeridge is not collected at all. This is a grave miscarriage of justice, at the least. As Richmal Crompton's *William* books have been collected for years, and Frank Richards' *Bunter* books have been collected for decades (both of which appeared in the first edition of this book) I think it is time to include the other great fictional schoolboy and – in my opinion – the best.

Here is a complete listing. All bar the last were published by Collins, who should pull themselves together and get them back into print again, pronto.

1	**Jennings Goes to School**	1950	B
2	**Jennings Follows a Clue**	1951	A
3	**Jennings' Little Hut**	1951	A
4	**Jennings and Darbishire**	1952	A
5	**Jennings' Diary**	1953	A
6	**According to Jennings**	1954	A
7	**Our Friend Jennings**	1955	A
8	**Thanks to Jennings**	1957	A
9	**Take Jennings, for Instance**	1958	A
10	**Jennings, as Usual**	1959	A

Fowles's first four books

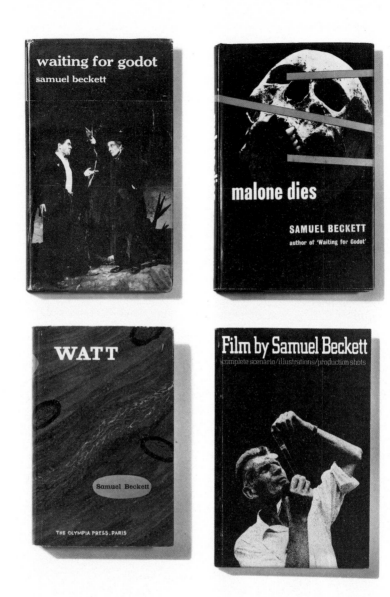

Four spare and distinctive works by Samuel Beckett

A scarce pseudonymous Anthony Burgess, Amis's first and famous novel, the first
English edition of Donleavy's first novel, and the autobiography of Britain's
noisiest Crisp

The first and the first illustrated editions of Old Possum, and a brace from the late, lamented Laureate

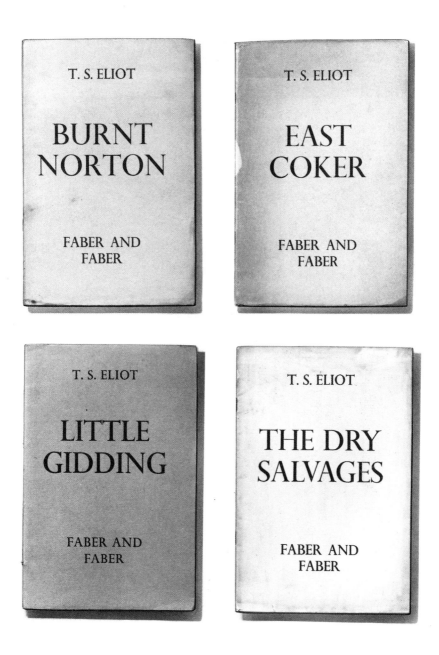

The Four Quartets, in their original separate editions

A neat companion to the Greenes' *Bedside* book might be *The Book of Bond* by Bill Tanner (Kingsley Amis). Beneath are the two Bond books to follow on directly from the inaugural *Casino Royale*

Deighton's first three novels, comprising the 'Secret Files' – all with dust-wrappers
by Raymond Hawkey

A scarce Waugh, a representative Green in a John Piper dust-wrapper, a Greene with a film tie-in wrapper, and the English first edition of Bellow's first novel

11	**The Trouble with Jennings**	1960	A
12	**Just Like Jennings**	1961	A
13	**Leave It to Jennings**	1963	A
14	**Jennings, of Course!**	1964	A
15	**Especially Jennings!**	1965	A
16	**Jennings Abounding**	1967	A
17	**Jennings in Particular**	1968	A
18	**Trust Jennings!**	1969	A
19	**The Jennings Report**	1970	A
20	**Typically Jennings!**	1971	A
21	**Speaking of Jennings**	1973	A
22	**Jennings at Large**	1977	A

This was a paperback 'Armada' original.

Buckeridge has also published the following, all from the Lutterworth Press:

A Funny Thing Happened!	1953	A
Rex Milligan's Busy Term	1953	A
Rex Milligan Raises the Roof	1955	A
Rex Milligan Holds Forth	1955	A
Rex Milligan Reporting	1961	A

Burgess, Anthony   Born in Manchester, 1917.

How does he do it? All those Sunday reviews, non-fiction commissions, television adaptations, anthologies, biographies – oh yes, and novels. Amazing. The only man possibly more awe-inspiring is John Mortimer, who seems to have time to be a practising barrister as well. And Burgess is never put down for being so prolific (in general, we tend to distrust prolific writers) simply because the quality remains fine. It is notable that a recent (and very long) novel was praised as highly as anything he had ever done (*Earthly Powers*) and that when rush publication of Burgess's list of 99 novels of our time is announced, we all want to hear it. And he didn't even include himself – which will annoy Burgess fanatics everywhere, for I have found that it is the nature of the true Burgess devotee to feel hard pressed to include anyone *other* than Burgess on any list of favourites, and although he has not yet published his own ninety-ninth book, rest assured: he is working on it.

1	**Time for a Tiger** (novel)	Heinemann 1956	I
2	**English Literature: A Survey for Students**	Longman 1958	E

Pseud. John Burgess Wilson.

3	**The Enemy in the Blanket** (novel)	Heinemann 1958	E
4	**Beds in the East** (novel)	Heinemann 1959	E

This, together with 1 and 3, forms the Malayan Trilogy.

5 **The Right to an Answer** (novel)	Heinemann 1960	D
	Norton 1961	C
6 **The Doctor is Sick** (novel)	Heinemann 1960	C
	Norton 1966	B
7 **The Worm and the Ring** (novel) Suppressed book.	Heinemann 1961	J
8 **Devil of a State** (novel)	Heinemann 1961	B
	Norton 1962	A
9 **One Hand Clapping** (novel) Pseud. Joseph Kell.	Davies 1961	I
	Knopf 1971	C
10 **A Clockwork Orange** (novel)	Heinemann 1962	H
	Norton 1963	F
11 **The Wanting Seed** (novel)	Heinemann 1962	C
	Norton 1963	B
12 **Honey for the Bears** (novel)	Heinemann 1963	C
	Norton 1964	B
13 **Inside Mr Enderby** (novel) Pseud. Joseph Kell.	Heinemann 1963	I
14 **The Novel Today** (non-fiction)	Longman 1963	C
15 **Nothing Like the Sun: A Story of Shakespeare's Love-Life**	Heinemann 1964	B
	Norton 1964	A
16 **The Eve of Saint Venus** (novel)	Sidgwick & Jackson 1964	B
	Norton 1967	A
17 **Languages Made Plain** (non-fiction)	English Universities Press 1964	B
	Crowell 1965	B
18 **The Long Day Wanes** (incl. 1, 3 and 4)	Norton 1965	B
19 **A Vision of Battlements** (novel)	Sidgwick & Jackson 1965	B
	Norton 1966	A
20 **Here Comes Everybody: An Introduction to James Joyce for the Ordinary Reader**	Faber 1965	C
21 **Re Joyce** (same as 20)	Norton 1965	B
22 **Tremor of Intent** (novel)	Heinemann 1966	B
	Norton 1966	A
23 **The Novel Now** (non-fiction)	Faber 1967	B
	Norton 1967	A
24 **Enderby Outside** (novel)	Heinemann 1968	C
25 **Enderby** (incl. 13 and 24)	Norton 1968	B
26 **Urgent Copy: Literary Studies**	Cape 1968	B
	Norton 1969	A
27 **Shakespeare** (non-fiction)	Cape 1970	B
	Knopf 1971	A
28 **MF** (novel)	Cape 1971	A
	Knopf 1971	A

29	**Joysprick: An Introduction to the Language of James Joyce**	Deutsch 1972	C
30	**Napoleon Symphony** (novel)	Cape 1974	A
		Knopf 1974	A
31	**The Clockwork Testament: or, Enderby's End** (novel)	Hart-Davis MacGibbon 1974	B
		Knopf	A
32	**Moses: A Narrative** (prose)	Dempsey & Squires 1976	A
33	**A Long Trip to Teatime** (prose)	Dempsey & Squires 1976	A
34	**Beard's Roman Women** (novel)	McGraw Hill 1976	A
		Hutchinson 1977	A
35	**Abba Abba** (novel)	Faber 1977	A
		Little Brown 1977	A
36	**Ernest Hemingway and His World** (biography)	Thames & Hudson 1978	B
		Scribner 1978	A
37	**1985** (novel)	Hutchinson 1978	B
		Little Brown 1978	A
38	**The Land Where Ice-cream Grows** (juvenile)	Benn 1979	A
		Doubleday 1979	A
39	**Man of Nazareth** (adaptation)	McGraw Hill 1979	A
		Magnum 1980	A
40	**Earthly Powers** (novel)	Hutchinson 1980	B
		Simon & Schuster 1980	B
41	**On Going to Bed** (anthology) Edited and introduced by A.B.	Deutsch 1982	A
42	**The End of the World News** (novel)	Hutchinson 1982	A
		McGraw Hill 1983	A
43	**This Man and His Music** (non-fiction)	Hutchinson 1982	A
		McGraw Hill 1983	A
44	**Ninety-nine Novels: The Best in English Since 1939**	Allison & Busby 1984	A
		Simon & Schuster 1984	A
45	**Enderby's Dark Lady** (novel)	Hutchinson 1984	B
		McGraw Hill 1984	B

Burgess has also edited and translated a number of works. For complete details, see:

Paul W. Boytinck **Anthony Burgess: A Bibliography**   West 1978

Film:
A Clockwork Orange Warner Bros 1971

Burroughs, Edgar Rice   Born in America, 1875. Died 1950.

Creator of the deathless Tarzan of the apes, and of the equally deathless grunt: 'Me Tarzan – you Jane.'

There were very many Tarzan books. I list here the first of them, which is very scarce and expensive. Subsequent titles, though, should be in the £5–£20 class.

Tarzan of the Apes	McClurg (Chicago) 1914	**P**

Films:
Dozens and dozens of films were made, *based* upon the original Tarzan character.

Burroughs, William S.   Born in Missouri, 1914.

There is a rise in interest in this sort of writer who, in the sixties – along with the Beat Poets – was seen to be the last word, and then rather languished in the seventies when books concerning drug-ridden nomads seemed to have a reduced appeal. The up-and-coming generation, however – too young for this sort of thing in the sixties – now appear to have quite an appetite for it.

1 **Junk** (novel) Pseud. William Lee.	Ace (NY) 1953	**J**
Junkie	Ace 1964	**D**
	NEL 1966	**C**
2 **The Naked Lunch** (novel) In Amer. and Eng. eds, no *The* in title.	Olympia Press (Paris) 1959	**D**
	Grove Press 1962	**C**
	Calder 1964	**B**
3 **The Exterminator** (verse) With Brion Gysin.	Auerhahn Press (San Francisco) 1960	**C**
4 **Minutes to Go:Poems** With others.	Two Cities (Paris) 1960	**D**
	Beach Books (San Francisco) 1968	**C**
5 **The Soft Machine** (novel)	Olympia Press (Paris) 1961	**D**
	Grove Press 1966	**C**
	Calder 1968	**B**
6 **The Ticket That Exploded** (novel)	Olympia Press 1962	**D**
	Grove Press 1967	**C**
	Calder 1968	**B**

7 **Dead Fingers Talk** (novel)	Olympia Press (Paris) 1963	D
	Calder 1964	B
8 **The Yage Letters** With Allen Ginsberg.	City Lights (San Francisco) 1963	E
9 **Nova Express** (novel)	Grove Press 1964	C
	Cape 1966	B
10 **Time** (verse)	C Press (NY) 1965	D
11 **Valentine Day's Reading** (verse)	American Theatre for Poets (NY) 1965	D
12 **APO-33: A Metabolic Regulator**	Beach Books (San Francisco) 1966	D
13 **So Who Owns Death TV** With Claude Pelieu and Carl Weissner.	Beach Books 1967	D
14 **The Job: Interviews with William Burroughs** French-language ed.: Belfond, Paris 1969.	Grove Press 1970 Cape 1970	C B
15 **The Third Mind** (non-fiction)	Grove Press 1970	C
16 **The Last Words of Dutch Schultz** (filmscript)	Cape 1970 Viking 1975	C B
17 **The Wild Boys: A Book of the Dead** (novel)	Grove Press 1971 Calder 1972	C B
18 **Exterminator** (novel)	Viking 1974 Calder 1974	C B
19 **White Subway**	Aloes Books 1974	D
20 **Port of Saints** (prose)	Covent Garden Press 1975	C
	Blue Wind Press (US) 1980	B
21 **Short Novels**	Calder 1978	B
22 **Blade Runner: A Movie** (novel)	Blue Wind Press 1979	C
23 **Ah Pook is Here and Other Texts**	Calder 1982	B
24 **Cities of the Red Night: A Boy's Book** (novel)	Holt Rinehart 1981 Calder 1981	B A

Camus, Albert Born in Algeria, 1913. Died 1960. French.

Camus – although still very much read – is not strongly collected in Britain, as is often true with modern work appearing in translation, for all the true firsts are, of course, French. For this reason, I am listing only his first and most interesting work, and although this too is just the first *English* edition, it has points that make it very desirable in its own right, as will be seen below.

The Outsider   Hamilton 1946   **D**
Though first published as *L'Etranger* in
France in 1942, this English edition is of
great interest to collectors, as it is
translated by Stuart Gilbert, introduced
by Cyril Connolly, and has a d/w by
Edward Bawden. It is also, of course, the
first appearance of Camus in English.
Very undervalued, however. It must
soon be worth much more. The Knopf
edition is entitled *The Stranger*.

Film:
The Outsider Paramount 1968

Canetti, Elias   Born in Bulgaria, 1905.

Always very much more appreciated in Europe than in Britain, Canetti's
winning of the Nobel Prize in 1981 brought him to a wider audience as Cape
rushed back into print his best known work, hailing it (rightly) as a
masterpiece, many cynically wondering why such a masterpiece had been
allowed to go out of print in the first place.

Although Canetti has written quite a few books of importance (such as
Crowds and Power) I record here his highlight which was also, incidentally, his
first book and his only novel. It was originally published in German in 1935
(firsts of this edition have fetched up to £300) and was put out in this country
after the war, in a translation by C.V. Wedgwood 'under the personal
supervision of the author' as the title page records.

Auto da Fe (novel)   Cape 1946   **H**
The book went into several impressions
in its first year, and it is scarce.

Capote, Truman   Born in New Orleans, 1924.

Admired and read in Great Britain, rather than collected and still known
chiefly for *Breakfast at Tiffany's* – a short story spun out into a full-length
feature film. A cute, sentimental film with the stars of the moment, the title
confusing everyone in this country because we had never *heard* of Tiffany's –
unless it was somewhere you bought lamps – and on learning that it was a
jeweller the breakfast bit became odd, but the early sixties had a great
appetite for whimsy on this sort of scale, and it seems a strange highlight from
an author capable of such power, as exemplified in *In Cold Blood*, something
of a *cause célèbre* at the time.

1	**Other Voices, Other Rooms** (novel)	Random House (NY) 1948	E
		Heinemann 1948	B
2	**A Tree of Night and Other Stories**	Random House 1949	D
3	**Local Color** (non-fiction)	Random House 1950	C
4	**The Grass Harp** (novel)	Random House 1951	C
		Heinemann 1952	B
5	**The Grass Harp** (play)	Random House 1952	C
6	**The Muses Are Heard: An Account**	Random House 1956	C
7	**Breakfast at Tiffany's** (stories)	Random House 1958	F
		Heinemann 1959	D
8	**Observations**	Simon & Schuster 1959	E
	With Richard Avedon.	Weidenfeld 1959	D
9	**Selected Writings**	Modern Library (NY) 1963	C
		Hamilton 1963	B
10	**A Christmas Memory** (story)	Random House 1966	C
11	**In Cold Blood: A True Account of a Multiple Murder and Its Consequences**	Random House 1966	C
		Hamilton 1966	A
12	**House of Flowers** (play)	Random House 1968	B
13	**The Thanksgiving Visitor** (play)	Random House 1968	B
		Hamilton 1969	A
14	**The Dogs Bark: Public People and Private Places**	Random House 1973	B
		Weidenfeld 1974	A
15	**Then It All Came Down: Criminal Justice Today Discussed by Police, Criminals and Correcting Officers With Comments by Truman Capote**	Random House 1976	B
16	**Music for Chameleons** (essays)	Random House 1980	B
		Hamilton 1981	A
17	**One Christmas** (novel)	Random House 1982	B
		Hamilton 1983	A

Films:
Breakfast at Tiffany's Paramount 1961   **In Cold Blood** Columbia 1968

Carter, Angela   Born in London, 1940.

A sleeper. Angela Carter has been publishing steadily since the mid-sixties, well reviewed and building up a following. Quite recently – largely through her being brought to wider audiences in the influential Virago paperbacks – she became one of the authors to watch. Soon, people will be asking booksellers for the new Carter, and expect them to know who they mean.

Which, knowing booksellers, is expecting a lot – but the point being made here is that Angela Carter's reputation – that is, *Carter's* reputation – seems sound, and although the early work is not common, it might not be too late to assemble a collection at not too horrific a cost. Buy now – while stocks last.

1	**Shadow Dance** (novel)	Heinemann 1966	G
2	**Honeybuzzard** (same as 1)	Simon & Schuster 1966	D
3	**The Magic Toyshop** (novel)	Heinemann 1967	E
		Simon & Schuster 1968	B
4	**Several Perceptions** (novel)	Heinemann 1968	D
		Simon & Schuster 1968	B
5	**Heroes and Villains** (novel)	Heinemann 1969	C
		Simon & Schuster 1969	B
6	**Miss Z, The Dark Young Lady** (juvenile)	Heinemann 1970	C
		Simon & Schuster 1970	C
7	**Love** (novel)	Hart-Davis 1970	B
8	**The Donkey Prince** (juvenile)	Simon & Schuster 1970	B
9	**The Infernal Desire Machines of Doctor Hoffman** (novel)	Hart-Davis 1972	B
10	**The War of Dreams** (same as 9)	Harcourt Brace 1974	B
11	**Fireworks** (stories)	Quartet 1974	B
		Harper & Row 1981	A
12	**The Passion of New Eve** (novel)	Gollancz 1977	B
		Harcourt Brace	B
13	**Comic and Curious Cats** Illus. Martin Leman.	Gollancz 1979	B
		Crown 1979	B
14	**The Sadeian Women** (non-fiction)	Virago 1979	A
		Pantheon 1979	A
15	**The Bloody Chamber** (novel)	Gollancz 1979	B
		Harper 1980	B
16	**Sleeping Beauty and Other Favourite Fairy Tales**	Gollancz 1983	A
17	**Come Unto These Yellow Sands** (four radio plays)	Bloodaxe Books 1983	B

Chandler, Raymond   Born in Chicago, 1888. Died 1959.

Still extremely popular with collectors – and not just the collectors of exclusively detective fiction. Chandler is even now much imitated, but the McCoy is still the *real* thing. Memories of the films linger, of course – even recent miscasting does nothing to diminish the originals, underlining as the recent efforts do the perfection of Bogart in the part (the word 'hero' would not be appropriate).

Strange books, really, to have come from an American who attended an English public school (Dulwich College; his contemporary there, P.G. Wodehouse, must have pleasd the Board of Governors rather better). But it is the characteristic hard-edged humour and blunt strength of Chandler's prose that readers go back to, hearing Bogart chewing the lines.

1	**The Big Sleep** (novel)	Knopf 1939	R
		Hamilton 1939	P
2	**Farewell, My Lovely** (novel)	Knopf 1940	Q
		Hamilton 1940	N
3	**The High Window** (novel)	Knopf 1942	M
		Hamilton 1943	K
4	**The Lady in the Lake** (novel)	Knopf 1943	L
		Hamilton 1944	I
5	**Five Murderers** (stories) This, along with 6 and 7, was published in wrappers.	Avon (NY) 1944	H
6	**Five Sinister Characters** (stories)	Avon 1945	H
7	**The Finger Man** (stories)	Avon 1946	H
8	**The Little Sister** (novel)	Knopf 1949	J
		Hamilton 1949	H
9	**Trouble is My Business** (stories)	Penguin 1950	D
		Houghton Mifflin 1951	D
10	**The Simple Art of Murder** (miscellany)	Houghton Mifflin 1950	E
		Hamilton 1950	D
11	**The Long Goodbye** (novel)	Hamilton 1953	F
		Houghton Mifflin 1953	E
12	**Playback** (novel)	Houghton Mifflin 1958	E
		Hamilton 1958	D
13	**Raymond Chandler Speaking** (non-fiction)	Houghton Mifflin 1962	D
		Hamilton 1962	C
14	**Killer in the Rain** (stories)	Houghton Mifflin 1964	E
		Hamilton 1964	D
15	**The Smell of Fear** (stories)	Hamilton 1965	C
16	**The Blue Dahlia** (screenplay)	S. Illinois University Press 1976	C
		Elm Tree 1976	B
17	**The Notebooks of Raymond Chandler**	Ecco Press 1976	B
		Weidenfeld 1977	A
18	**The Selected Letters of Raymond Chandler**	Cape 1981	B

Films:
The Big Sleep Warner Bros 1946   **The Falcon Takes Over** (*Farewell,*

My Lovely) RKO 1942   **Murder, My Sweet** (*Farewell, My Lovely*) RKO
1944   **Lady in the Lake** MGM 1946   **The Brasher Doubloon** (*The
High Window*) 20th Century Fox 1947   **Marlowe** (*The Little Sister*)
MGM 1969   **The Long Goodbye** United Artists 1973   **Farewell, My
Lovely** Fox-Rank 1975   **The Big Sleep** ITC 1978

Charteris, Leslie   Born in Singapore, 1907. Pseudonym for Leslie Charles Bowyer Yin.

The Saint has been around for over fifty years, but his heyday in Britain was
without doubt the sixties, when the television series brought us Roger
Moore's interpretation of Simon Templar.

Few people are after a complete Charteris collection, a couple of representative Saint titles contenting most. Below I list Charteris first book, and the
first to feature Templar. Each of these is rather expensive, but later titles can
be acquired pretty cheaply.

1 **X Esquire**	Ward Lock 1927	G
2 **Enter the Saint** (3 novelettes)	Hodder & Stoughton 1930	G

Films:
The Saint in New York RKO 1938   **The Saint's Vacation** (*Getaway*)
RKO 1941   **The Saint Meets the Tiger** (*Meet the Tiger*) Republic 1943

Cheever, John   Born in Massachusetts, 1912.

Very little is known of Cheever in this country, and until recently his *name*
was quite unknown. Now something of a cult, and collected by the younger
set, mainly, who might be surprised to learn that he is over seventy years old.
His acute observations of middle-class America do have an appeal, and
although his acknowledged highlight is *Bullet Park* (indeed, it is often difficult
to recall any other title) I have yet to discover anyone who particularly
admires it, the consensus of opinion being that Cheever's stories work far
better than his novels. It has been virtually impossible, until now, to even
find out just how much he has published, and so there follows here a
complete checklist.

1 **The Way Some People Live: A Book** of Stories	Random House 1943	H
2 **The Enormous Radio and Other** Stories	Funk & Wagnall 1953	F
3 **Stories** (with others)	Farrar Straus 1956	E
4 **A Book of Stories** (same as 3)	Gollancz 1957	C
5 **The Wapshot Chronicle** (novel)	Harper Row 1957	D
	Gollancz 1957	C

6 **The Housebreaker of Shady Hill** **and Other Stories**	Harper Row 1958 Gollancz 1959	D C
7 **Some People, Places and Things** **that Will Not Appear in My Next Novel** (stories)	Harper Row 1961 Gollancz 1961	D C
8 **The Wapshot Scandal** (novel)	Harper Row 1964 Gollancz 1964	C C
9 **The Brigadier and the Golf Widow** (stories)	Harper Row 1964 Gollancz 1965	C C
10 **Bullet Park** (novel)	Knopf 1969 Cape 1969	C C
11 **The World of Apples** (stories)	Knopf 1973 Cape 1974	C B
12 **Falconer** (novel)	Knopf 1977 Cape 1977	C B
13 **The Stories of John Cheever**	Knopf 1978 Cape 1979	B B
14 **Oh What a Paradise It Seems** (novel)	Knopf 1982 Cape 1982	B B

Chesterton, G.K. Born in London, 1874. Died 1936.

Chesterton was extremely prolific, and a very entertaining author. It must be admitted, though, that an awful lot of his books would nowadays be wanted *only* by the collector for the sake of completeness, for he did put out a lot of very topical, religious and rhetorical literature that admirers of his poetry, say, or of the Father Brown stories would hardly warm to. This tends to be reflected in prices, of course. It is perfectly possible to build up a fairly large collection of first editions by Chesterton, or Wells or Shaw, none of which anyone particularly wants, none of which will you read, and all of which the bookseller will be pleased to be shot of. With the gems, though, the story is rather different. There follows, therefore, a list of his best-known works, and those which are probably the most desirable as 1st editions. Fuller information might very well be required, however – particularly for his very many non-fiction works – and for this I refer you to: John Sullivan *G. K. Chesterton: A Bibliography* University of London Press 1958

1 **The Napoleon of Notting Hill**	Bodley Head 1904	F
2 **The Man Who was Thursday**	Arrowsmith 1908	E
3 **The Innocence of Father Brown**	Cassell 1911	G
4 **Manalive**	Nelson 1912	E
5 **The Flying Inn**	Methuen 1914	F
6 **The Wisdom of Father Brown**	Cassell 1914	E
7 **The Man Who Knew Too Much**	Cassell 1922	E
8 **The Incredulity of Father Brown**	Cassell 1926	D
9 **The Collected Poems of G. K.** **Chesterton**	Palmer 1927	C

10	**The Secret of Father Brown**	Cassell 1927	**D**
11	**The Scandal of Father Brown**	Cassell 1935	**C**
12	**Autobiography**	Hutchinson 1936	**B**

Films:
Father Brown, Detective Paramount 1935 (*The Wisdom of Father Brown*) **Father Brown** Columbia 1954 (based on the Father Brown stories)

Christie, Agatha   Born in Devon, 1890. Died 1976.

The late 'Queen of Crime' has become one of the most avidly pursued of all English authors. This said, it must be noted that her later books are still around in droves (as is reflected in the prices) and without the all-important dust-wrappers are more or less unsaleable. But the early titles! The following values might well dizzy the unwary, but the true collector would stop at nothing to acquire fine copies; he might even be driven to murder.

1	**The Mysterious Affair at Styles** (novel)	Lane (US) 1920	**R**
		Lane (UK) 1921	**Q**
2	**The Secret Adversary** (novel)	Lane 1922	**O**
		Dodd Mead 1922	**M**
3	**Murder on the Links** (novel)	Lane 1923	**N**
		Dodd Mead 1923	**K**
4	**The Man in the Brown Suit** (novel)	Lane 1924	**M**
		Dodd Mead 1924	**K**
5	**Poirot Investigates** (stories)	Lane 1924	**N**
		Dodd Mead 1925	**K**
6	**The Secret of Chimneys** (novel)	Lane 1925	**M**
		Dodd Mead 1925	**K**
7	**The Road of Dreams** (verse)	Bles 1925	**K**
8	**The Murder of Roger Ackroyd** (novel)	Collins 1926	**N**
		Dodd Mead 1926	**K**
9	**The Big Four** (novel)	Collins 1927	**K**
		Dodd Mead 1927	**H**
10	**The Mystery of the Blue Train** (novel)	Collins 1928	**K**
		Dodd Mead 1928	**H**
11	**The Seven Dials Mystery** (novel)	Collins 1929	**K**
		Dodd Mead 1929	**H**
12	**Partners in Crime** (stories)	Collins 1929	**I**
		Dodd Mead 1929	**H**
13	**The Underdog** (story) With *Blackman's Wood* by E. Phillips Oppenheim.	Reader's Library 1929	**H**
14	**The Murder at the Vicarage** (novel)	Collins 1130	**K**
		Dodd Mead 1930	**I**

15 **The Mysterious Mr Quin** (stories)	Collins 1930	I
	Dodd Mead 1930	H
16 **Giant's Bread** (novel)	Collins 1930	G
As Mary Westmacott.	Doubleday 1930	D
17 **The Sittaford Mystery** (novel)	Collins 1931	H
18 **The Murder at Hazelmoor**	Dodd Mead 1931	F
(same as 17)		
19 **Peril at End House** (novel)	Collins 1932	H
	Dodd Mead 1932	F
20 **The Thirteen Problems** (stories)	Collins 1932	G
21 **The Tuesday Club Murders** (same	Dodd Mead 1933	E
as 20)		
22 **Lord Edgware Dies** (novel)	Collins 1933	H
23 **Thirteen at Dinner** (same as 22)	Dodd Mead 1933	F
24 **The Hound of Death and Other**	Odhams 1933	C
Stories		
25 **Parker Pyne Investigates** (stories)	Collins 1934	G
26 **Mr Parker Pyne, Detective** (same	Dodd Mead 1934	E
as 25)		
27 **The Listerdale Mystery and**	Collins 1934	G
Other Stories		
28 **Black Coffee** (play)	Ashley 1934	F
29 **Why Didn't They Ask Evans?**	Collins 1934	I
(novel)		
30 **Murder on the Orient Express**	Collins 1934	M
(novel)		
31 **Murder on the Calais Coach** (same	Dodd Mead 1934	I
as 30)		
32 **Murder in Three Acts** (novel)	Dodd Mead 1934	H
33 **Unfinished Portrait** (novel)	Collins 1934	G
As Mary Westmacott.	Doubleday 1934	D
34 **Boomerang Clue** (same as 29)	Dodd Mead 1935	E
35 **Three Act Tragedy** (same as 32)	Collins 1935	E
36 **Death in the Clouds** (novel)	Collins 1935	H
37 **Death in the Air** (same as 36)	Dodd Mead 1935	F
38 **The A.B.C. Murders: A New**	Collins 1936	H
Poirot Mystery	Dodd Mead 1936	G
39 **Cards on the Table** (novel)	Collins 1936	H
	Dodd Mead 1936	G
40 **Murder in Mesopotamia** (novel)	Collins 1936	H
	Dodd Mead 1936	G
41 **Murder in the Mews and Other**	Collins 1937	H
Stories		
42 **Dead Man's Mirror and Other**	Dodd Mead 1937	G
Stories (same as 41)		
43 **Death on the Nile** (novel)	Collins 1937	H
	Dodd Mead 1938	G
44 **Dumb Witness** (novel)	Collins 1937	H

45	**Poirot Loses a Client** (same as 44)	Dodd Mead 1937	G
46	**Appointment With Death: A Poirot Mystery**	Collins 1938 Dodd Mead 1938	H G
47	**The Regatta Mystery and Other Stories**	Dodd Mead 1939	E
48	**Hercule Poirot's Christmas** (novel)	Collins 1939	I
49	**Murder for Christmas: A Poirot Story** (same as 48)	Dodd Mead 1939	G
50	**Murder Is Easy** (novel)	Collins 1939	H
51	**Easy to Kill** (same as 50)	Dodd Mead 1939	G
52	**Ten Little Niggers** (novel)	Collins 1939	M
53	**And Then There were None** (same as 52)	Dodd Mead 1940	K
54	**One, Two, Buckle My Shoe** (novel)	Collins 1940	G
55	**Sad Cypress** (novel)	Collins 1940 Dodd Mead 1940	G F
56	**The Patriotic Murders** (same as 54)	Dodd Mead 1941	D
57	**Evil Under the Sun** (novel)	Collins 1941 Dodd Mead 1941	G F
58	**N or M?** (novel)	Collins 1941 Dodd Mead 1941	G F
59	**The Body in the Library** (novel)	Collins 1942 Dodd Mead 1942	G F
60	**The Moving Finger** (novel)	Dodd Mead 1942 Collins 1943	F E
61	**Five Little Pigs** (novel)	Collins 1942	F
62	**Murder in Retrospect** (same as 61)	Dodd Mead 1942	E
63	**Death Comes as the End** (novel)	Dodd Mead 1942 Collins 1945	F E
64	**Towards Zero** (novel)	Collins 1944 Dodd Mead 1944	F E
65	**Absent in the Spring** (novel) As Mary Westmacott.	Collins 1944 Farrar & Rinehart (NY) 1944	D C
66	**Ten Little Niggers** (play)	French 1944	E
67	**Sparkling Cyanide** (novel)	Collins 1945	F
68	**Remembered Death** (same as 67)	Dodd Mead 1945	D
69	**Appointment with Death** (play)	French 1945	D
70	**The Hollow** (novel)	Collins 1946 Dodd Mead 1946	E D
71	**Come Tell Me How You Live** (travel)	Collins 1946 Dodd Mead 1946	D C
72	**Ten Little Indians** (play) (same as 66)	French (NY) 1946	B
73	**Murder on the Nile** (play)	French 1946 French (NY) 1946	B B

74	**The Labours of Hercules: Short Stories**	Collins 1947	D
75	**Labors of Hercules** (same as 74)	Dodd Mead 1947	C
76	**Taken at the Flood** (novel)	Collins 1948	D
77	**There Is a Tide . . .** (same as 76)	Dodd Mead 1948	C
78	**The Rose and the Yew Tree** (novel) As Mary Westmacott.	Heinemann 1948 Rinehart 1948	C B
79	**Witness for the Prosecution** (stories)	Dodd Mead 1948	D
80	**Crooked House** (novel)	Collins 1949 Dodd Mead 1949	D C
81	**A Murder is Announced** (novel)	Collins 1950 Dodd Mead 1950	D C
82	**Three Blind Mice and Other Stories**	Dodd Mead 1950	C
83	**Under Dog and Other Stories**	Dodd Mead 1951	C
84	**They Came to Baghdad** (novel)	Collins 1951 Dodd Mead 1951	D C
85	**The Hollow** (play)	French 1952 French (NY) 1952	B B
86	**They Do It with Mirrors** (novel)	Collins 1952	C
87	**Murder with Mirrors** (same as 86)	Dodd Mead 1952	B
88	**Mrs McGinty's Dead** (novel)	Collins 1952 Dodd Mead 1952	C B
89	**A Daughter's a Daughter** (novel) As Mary Westmacott.	Heinemann 1952	C
90	**After the Funeral** (novel)	Collins 1953	C
91	**Funerals Are Fatal** (same as 90)	Dodd Mead 1953	B
92	**A Pocket Full of Rye** (novel)	Collins 1953 Dodd Mead 1954	C B
93	**Witness for the Prosecution** (play)	French 1954 French (NY) 1954	B B
94	**Destination Unknown** (novel)	Collins 1954	C
95	**So Many Steps to Death** (same as 94)	Dodd Mead 1955	B
96	**Hickory, Dickory, Dock** (novel)	Collins 1955	C
97	**Hickory, Dickory, Death** (same as 96)	Dodd Mead 1955	B
98	**The Mousetrap** (play)	French 1956 French (NY) 1956	J H
99	**Dead Man's Folly** (novel)	Collins 1956 Dodd Mead 1956	C B
100	**The Burden** (novel) As Mary Westmacott.	Heinemann 1956	C
101	**The Spider's Web** (play)	French 1957 French (NY) 1957	B B

Christie

102	**Towards Zero** (play)	French 1957	B
		Dramatists Play	
		Service 1957	B
103	**4.50 from Paddington** (novel)	Collins 1957	B
104	**What Mrs McGillicuddy Saw!**	Dodd Mead 1957	B
	(same as 103)		
105	**Verdict** (play)	French 1958	B
106	**The Unexpected Guest** (play)	French 1958	B
107	**Ordeal by Innocence** (novel)	Collins 1958	B
		Dodd Mead 1958	B
108	**Cat Among the Pigeons** (novel)	Collins 1959	B
		Dodd Mead 1959	B
109	**The Adventure of the Christmas Pudding** (stories)	Collins 1960	B
110	**Go Back for Murder** (play)	French 1960	B
	Adaptation of 61.		
111	**Double Sin and Other Stories**	Dodd Mead 1961	B
112	**13 for Luck** (stories)	Dodd Mead 1961	B
		Collins 1966	B
113	**The Pale Horse** (novel)	Collins 1961	B
		Dodd Mead 1962	A
114	**The Mirror Crack'd from Side to Side** (novel)	Collins 1962	B
115	**The Mirror Crack'd** (same as 114)	Dodd Mead 1963	A
116	**Rule of Three** (plays)	French 1963	B
	Cont. *Afternoon at the Seaside, The Patient* and *The Rats.*		
117	**The Clocks** (novel)	Collins 1963	B
		Dodd Mead 1964	A
118	**A Caribbean Mystery** (novel)	Collins 1964	B
		Dodd Mead 1965	A
119	**Star over Bethlehem and Other Stories**	Collins 1965	B
	As A.C. Mallowan.	Dodd Mead 1965	B
120	**Surprise! Surprise!** (stories)	Dodd Mead 1965	A
121	**13 Clues for Miss Marple** (stories)	Dodd Mead 1965	A
122	**At Bertram's Hotel** (novel)	Collins 1965	A
		Dodd Mead 1965	A
123	**Third Girl** (novel)	Collins 1966	A
		Dodd Mead 1967	A
124	**Endless Night** (novel)	Collins 1967	A
		Dodd Mead 1968	A
125	**By the Pricking of My Thumbs** (novel)	Collins 1968	A
		Dodd Mead 1968	A
126	**Passenger to Frankfurt** (novel)	Collins 1970	A
		Dodd Mead 1970	A
127	**Nemesis** (novel)	Collins 1971	A
		Dodd Mead 1971	A

128	**The Golden Ball and Other Stories**	Dodd Mead 1971	A
129	**Elephants Can Remember** (novel)	Collins 1972	A
		Dodd Mead 1972	A
130	**Postern of Fate** (novel)	Collins 1973	A
		Dodd Mead 1973	A
131	**Akhmaton** (play)	Collins 1973	A
		Dodd Mead 1973	A
132	**Poems**	Collins 1973	B
		Dodd Mead 1973	B
133	**Hercule Poirot's Early Cases** (stories)	Collins 1974	A
		Dodd Mead 1974	A
134	**Murder on Board: Three Complete Mystery Novels** Cont. **The Mystery of the Blue Train, Death in the Air, What Mrs McGillicuddy Saw!**	Dodd Mead 1974	B
135	**Curtain: Hercule Poirot's Last Case**	Collins 1975	B
		Dodd Mead 1975	A
136	**Sleeping Murder** (novel)	Collins 1976	A
		Dodd Mead 1976	A
137	**Miss Marple's Final Cases and Others** (stories)	Collins 1979	A
		Dodd Mead 1979	A
138	**Autobiography**	Collins 1979	B

Films:

Ten Little Niggers 20th Century Fox 1945 **Witness for the Prosecution** United Artists 1957 **The Spider's Web** United Artists 1960 **Murder She Said** (*4.50 from Paddington*) MGM 1961 **Murder Most Foul** (*Mrs McGinty's Dead*) MGM 1963 **Murder at the Gallop** (*After the Funeral*) MGM 1963 **Murder Ahoy** (based on Miss Marple) MGM 1964 **Ten Little Indians** (*Ten Little Niggers*) Associated British 1965 **The Alphabet Murders** (*The A.B.C. Murders*) MGM 1966 **Endless Night** British Lion 1971 **Murder on the Orient Express** EMI 1974 **Death on the Nile** EMI 1978 **Agatha** Columbia-EMI-Warner Brothers 1979 **Evil Under the Sun** Columbia 1981 **The Mirror Crack'd** EMI 1981

Clarke, Arthur C. Born in Somerset, 1917.

Arthur C. Clarke has published nearly thirty non-fiction works, in addition to his better-known novels and short stories. Space, as it were, does not allow me to list these, but below are the novels and stories in full.

| 1 | **Prelude to Space** (novel) | New World (NY) 1951 | D |
| | | Sidgwick & Jackson 1953 | C |

Clarke

2	**The Sands of Mars** (novel)	Sidgwick & Jackson 1951	C
		Gnome Press 1952	B
3	**Islands in the Sky** (novel)	Winston, Philadelphia 1952	C
		Sidgwick & Jackson 1952	B
4	**Against the Fall of Night** (novel)	Gnome Press 1953	C
5	**Childhood's End** (novel)	Ballantine 1953	C
		Sidgwick & Jackson 1954	B
6	**Expedition to Earth** (stories)	Ballantine 1953	C
		Sidgwick & Jackson 1954	B
7	**Earthlight** (novel)	Ballantine 1955	C
		Muller 1955	B
8	**The City and the Stars** (novel)	Harcourt Brace 1956	C
		Muller 1956	B
9	**Reach for Tomorrow** (stories)	Ballantine 1956	C
		Gollancz 1962	B
10	**Tales from the White Hart** (stories)	Ballantine 1957	C
		Sidgwick & Jackson 1972	B
11	**The Deep Range** (novel)	Harcourt Brace 1957	C
		Muller 1957	B
12	**The Other Side of the Sky** (stories)	Harcourt Brace 1958	C
		Gollancz 1961	B
13	**Across the Sea of Stars** (incl. 5, 7 and stories)	Harcourt Brace 1959	B
14	**A Fall of Moondust** (novel)	Harcourt Brace 1961	C
		Gollancz 1961	B
15	**From the Oceans, From the Stars** (incl. 11, 8 and stories)	Harcourt Brace 1962	B
16	**Tales of Ten Worlds** (stories)	Harcourt Brace 1962	C
		Gollancz 1963	B
17	**Dolphin Island** (novel)	Holt Rinehart 1963	C
		Gollancz 1963	B
18	**Glide Path** (novel)	Harcourt Brace 1963	C
		Sidgwick & Jackson 1969	A
19	**Prelude to Mars** (incl. 1, 2 and stories)	Harcourt Brace 1965	B
20	**An Arthur C. Clarke Omnibus** (incl. 1, 5 and 6)	Sidgwick & Jackson 1965	B
21	**The Nine Billion Names of God** (stories)	Harcourt Brace 1967	B
22	**2001: A Space Odyssey** (novel)	NAL 1968	D
		Hutchinson 1968	C

23 **An Arthur C. Clarke Second Omnibus** (incl. 2, 7 and 14)	Sidgwick & Jackson 1968	B
24 **The Lion of Comarre** (novel)	Harcourt Brace 1968	B
	Gollancz 1970	A
25 **A Meeting with Medusa** (stories)	Harcourt Brace 1972	B
26 **The Wind from the Sun** (stories)	Harcourt Brace 1972	B
	Gollancz 1972	A
27 **Of Time and Stars** (stories)	Gollancz 1972	A
28 **The Lost Worlds of 2001** (miscellany)	NAL 1972	B
	Sidgwick & Jackson 1972	B
29 **The Best of Arthur C. Clarke** (**1937–1971**)	Sidgwick & Jackson 1973	B
30 **Rendezvous with Rama** (novel)	Harcourt Brace 1973	A
	Gollancz 1973	A
31 **Imperial Earth** (novel)	Gollancz 1975	A
	Harcourt Brace 1976	A
32 **The Fountains of Paradise** (novel)	Gollancz 1979	A
	Harcourt Brace 1979	A
33 **2010: Odyssey Two** (novel)	Granada 1982	B
	Ballantine 1982	B

Film:
2001: A Space Odyssey MGM 1968

Connolly, Cyril Born in Coventry, 1903. Died 1974.

At Eton with George Orwell, Anthony Powell, Henry Green and John Lehmann, and then later on to Balliol under Maurice Bowra, who dubbed Connolly 'the cleverest boy of his generation.' This is quite something to live up to, and there still seems to be a feeling abroad that Connolly did not. I believe this to be as unjust as it is illogical, for he failed to do only what others decided he should have done. In his own endeavours he was invariably successful – as Palinurus, as the founder and editor of *Horizon*, as novelist and critic – although it is true that in later life he observed that his position as star reviewer at *The Sunday Times* brought in far more money than would the writing of books, and therefore he no longer wrote books. This may be said to be a disappointing attitude for an artist, though it should be remembered that by then Connolly was no longer the coming young man of promise, but an established man of letters. First editions are becoming increasingly scarce, and for some reason or another are very rarely in truly fine condition (*Enemies of Promise* being particularly prone to shabbiness) and this would have gratified Connolly (he is still being *read*) and it also would have given him pause, for he was himself a passionate and devoted collector of modern firsts in fine state, most with a personal inscription from the author. There is a (probably apocryphal) story concerning Connolly hearing with great sadness that Huxley lay on his death bed, and rushing round in a taxi

clutching a *Brave New World* for inscription before Huxley could quite quit
this one.

His final 'Comment' in the last issue of *Horizon* (Nos. 120–121) is now in
the Oxford Dictionary of Quotations, and is worth repeating here: 'It is
closing time in the gardens of the West and from now on an artist will be
judged only by the resonance of his solitude or the quality of his despair.'

1 **The Rock Pool** (novel) This was his only novel, and is of course very scarce in the Paris and American editions.	Obelisk Press, Paris 1936 Scribner 1936 Hamilton 1947	N J E
2 **Enemies of Promise** Scarce.	Routledge 1938 Little Brown, Boston 1939	F D
3 **The Unquiet Grave** This, under the pseudonym Palinurus, is Connolly's masterpiece. This edition was limited to 1,000 copies, and is scarce. A revised edition was published the following year (1945) by Hamish Hamilton and by Harper in New York. The Hamilton edition has John Piper d/w, but is not too difficult (**C**).	Horizon 1944	H
4 **The Condemned Playground** (essays) Quite difficult, particularly in d/w.	Routledge 1945 Macmillan 1946	D D
5 **The Missing Diplomats** Wrpps, yellow d/w. This slight volume, about Burgess and Maclean, is quite scarce.	Queen Anne Press 1952	D
6 **Ideas and Places** Although fairly recent, a scarce item in its grey d/w.	Weidenfeld 1953 Harper 1953	D D
7 **Les Pavillons** With Jerome Zerbe. A large-format illustrated book with photographic d/w. Very difficult to find.	Macmillian (NY) 1962 Hamilton 1962	D D
8 **Bond Strikes Camp** This spoof of James Bond first appeared in the *London Magazine* for April 1963, the words 'Cyril Connolly' featuring strongly on its green wrappers. One might pick this up for pennies, but in a list, it would be Grade C. It is reprinted in 9.		
9 **Previous Convictions** A collection of pieces, mostly from *The* *Sunday Times*. Orange and grey d/w, not dissimilar in style to that of 6.	Hamilton 1963 Harper 1964	C C

10 **The Modern Movement: 100 Key**   Deutsch/Hamilton 1965   **E**
    Books from England, France and   Atheneum 1966   **E**
    America 1880–1950
    White d/w. This little book is of interest
    to book collectors, and is most useful as
    a small bibliography. In 1971 there was
    an exhibition based on this book at the
    University of Texas at Austin. The
    blue-wrapped catalogue is, apart
    from being a desirable and scarce
    Connolly item, a mine of bookish
    information, and reproduces much
    manuscript material.

11 **The Evening Colonnade**   Bruce & Watson 1973   **C**
    Connolly held a signing session in   Harcourt Brace 1975   **C**
    London on publication of this book, so
    it might be possible to find an
    autographed copy.

12 **A Romantic Friendship: The**   Constable 1975   **B**
    Letters of Cyril Connolly to Noel
    Blakiston
    Posthumously published.

13 **Journal and Memoir**   Collins 1983   **B**
    A journal kept by Connolly between   Ticknor & Fields 1984   **B**
    1927 and 1938, edited by David Pryce-
    Jones, who also contributes the memoir,
    with the full co-operation of Connolly's
    widow Mrs Deirdre Levi (she is now
    married to Peter Levi, the poet). The
    d/w bears a pastel drawing of Connolly
    by Augustus John.

Another item of note is:
Cyril Connolly: A Memoir by
Stephen Spender (Tragara Press 1978,
limited to 165 numbered copies). The
memoir first appeared in the *Times
Literary Supplement* (**D**).

Connolly edited the following:
Horizon Stories   Faber 1943   **C**
                                              Vanguard Press 1946   **B**
Great English Short Novels   Dial Press (NY) 1953   **C**
The Golden Horizon   Weidenfeld 1953   **C**
                                              University Books 1956   **B**

Connolly translated the following:
Vercors Put Out the Light   Macmillan 1944   **C**
This translation of *Le Silence de la mer*

was published in America by
Macmillan in the same year under the
more reasonable title *Silence of the Sea*.

Contributions include:

Essays in Leonard Russell **Press Gang!** and **Parody Party**, and	Hutchinson 1936 1937	C
an introduction to the first English edition of Albert Camus **The Outsider**	Hamilton 1946	D

Corvo, Baron   Born in London, 1860. Died 1913.

His real name was Frederick William Serafino Austin Lewis Mary Rolfe. A highly eccentric character who could not be blamed, one might think, for taking a pseudonym – maybe it was the *Mary* that convinced him – except that Baron Corvo always claimed that here was no pseudonym but a genuine title conferred upon him while he was living in Italy in the 1880s, by the Duchess Sforza-Cesarini.

Below I list some highlights of Corvo's work, but for complete bibliographical details, see: Cecil Woolf *A Bibliography of Baron Corvo, Frederick Rolfe* (Soho Bibliographies, Hart-Davis 1972)

1 **Stories Toto Told Me** This wrappered volume is Corvo's first book, and scarce.	Lane 1898	L
2 **Hadrian the Seventh** Probably Corvo's best-known work. He designed the patterned boards.	Chatto & Windus 1904 Knopf 1925	L L
3 **Don Tarquinio** Corvo designed the covers. Scarce.	Chatto & Windus 1905	K
4 **The Desire and Pursuit of the Whole** Although published 21 years after his death, this book has become one of his best-known works. The 1st Amer., though much later, is also interesting for the facts that the Foreword is by W.H. Auden, and the d/w is by Andy Warhol.	Cassell 1934 New Directions 1953	I E

Biography:
A.J.A. Symons **The Quest for Corvo** (Cassell 1934; Michigan State University 1955) **F, C**.

Crisp, Quentin Born in Sutton, 1908.

It's queer, but both the book and the television adaptation of *The Naked Civil Servant* remain intensely memorable. One could debate whether the book may be said to be truly seminal, but certainly it stands out as a landmark – as does Crisp himself, in his own words 'one of the stately homos of England'. Although he is the author of other diversions, such as *How to Have a Lifestyle* and *Love Made Easy*, I list here only the key work which is not, Crisp will be charmed to know, a common book.

The Naked Civil Servant	Cape 1968	**D**

Crispin, Edmund Born in Buckinghamshire, 1921. Died 1978.

He started life as Robert Bruce Montgomery, Oxford scholar, music teacher, and composer. He then became Edmund Crispin, highly successful author of detective fiction – the J.I.M. Stewart variety (literary and Varsity) not that of Mickey Spillane (blood, broads and booze).

The reason for the very long gap in the ensuing checklist (1953 until 1977) is that during this period Crispin chose to edit a series of short stories and to review other books, instead of writing his own, although he did return to fiction in 1977, the year before he died.

1	**The Case of the Gilded Fly** (novel)	Gollancz 1944	**I**
2	**Obsequies at Oxford** (same as 1)	Lippincott 1945	**G**
3	**Holy Disorders** (novel)	Gollancz 1946	**H**
		Lippincott 1946	**F**
4	**The Moving Toyshop** (novel)	Gollancz 1946	**G**
		Lippincott 1946	**E**
5	**Swan Song** (novel)	Gollancz 1947	**F**
6	**Dead as Dumb** (same as 5)	Lippincott 1947	**D**
7	**Love Lies Bleeding** (novel)	Gollancz 1948	**F**
		Lippincott 1948	**E**
8	**Buried for Pleasure** (novel)	Gollancz 1948	**E**
		Lippincott 1948	**D**
9	**Frequent Hearses** (novel)	Gollancz 1950	**D**
10	**Sudden Vengeance** (same as 9)	Dodd Mead 1950	**C**
11	**The Long Divorce** (novel)	Gollancz 1951	**D**
	This was reissued in 1952 by Spivak under the title *A Noose for Her*.	Dodd Mead 1951	**C**
12	**Beware of the Trains: 16 Stories**	Gollancz 1953	**D**
		Walker 1962	**B**
13	**The Glimpses of the Moon** (novel)	Gollancz 1977	**B**
		Walker 1978	**A**
14	**Fen Country** (stories)	Gollancz 1979	**B**

Crispin

Crispin edited the following:
Best SF (7 volumes, 1955–1970, Faber)   **Best Detective Stories**
(2 volumes, 1959 & 1964, Faber)   **Best Tales of Terror**
(2 volumes, 1962 & 1965, Faber)   **The Stars and Under:**
A Selection of Science Fiction (Faber 1968)   **Best Murder Stories 2**
(Faber 1973)   **Outwards from Earth: A Selection of Science**
Fiction (Faber 1974)

Crompton, Richmal   Born in Lancashire, 1890. Died 1969. Full name Richmal Crompton Lamburn.

The *William* books continue to be very popular with collectors, and are increasingly difficult to find. Indeed, although a few tie-in paperbacks were reissued to coincide with the television series, and the first three titles have just been republished in hardback, *any* copies are difficult to track down, and usually – as is common with popular literature – read to pieces. It is the later books that are the more entertaining, I think, as they are written *for* children, whereas the first few were written *about* children *for* adults, and hence tend towards condescension. All, except *, were published by Newnes.

1	**Just William**	1922	I
2	**More William**	1922	G
3	**William Again**	1923	F
4	**William the Fourth**	1924	F
5	**Still William**	1925	F
6	**William the Conqueror**	1926	E
7	**William in Trouble**	1927	E
8	**William the Outlaw**	1927	E
9	**William the Good**	1928	E
10	**William**	1929	E
11	**William the Bad**	1930	E
12	**William's Happy Days**	1930	E
13	**William's Crowded Hours**	1931	D
14	**William the Pirate**	1932	D
15	**William the Rebel**	1933	D
16	**William the Gangster**	1934	D
17	**William the Detective**	1935	D
18	**Sweet William**	1936	D
19	**William the Showman**	1937	D
20	**William the Dictator**	1938	D
21	**William and A.R.P.** (title later changed to *William's Bad Resolution*)	1939	D
22	**William and the Evacuees** (later title *William the Film Star*)	1940	D
23	**William Does His Bit**	1941	C

24	**William Carries On**	1942	C
25	**William and the Brains Trust**	1945	C
26	**Just William's Luck**	1948	C
27	**William the Bold**	1950	C
28	**William and the Tramp**	1952	C
29	**William and the Moon Rocket**	1954	C
30	**William and the Space Animal**	1956	C
31	**William's Television Show**	1958	C
32	**William the Explorer**	1960	B
33	**William's Treasure Trove**	1962	B
34	**William and the Witch**	1964	B
35	**William and the Ancient Briton***	1965	A
36	**William and the Monster***	1965	A
37	**William the Globetrotter***	1965	A
38	**William the Cannibal***	1965	A
39	**William and the Pop Singers**	1965	B
40	**William and the Masked Ranger**	1966	B
41	**William the Superman**	1968	B
42	**William the Lawless**	1970	B

The four marked * above were published by Mayfair.

Film:
Just William Associated British 1940

---

cummings, e.e. Born in Massachusetts, 1894. Died 1962.

People are uncertain as to whether or not they should continue to adhere to cummings's determined avoidance of the capital letter when printing his name, but most go along with it in (lower) case.

cummings published quite a few strictly limited editions and signed pamphlets which I have not been able to list within this book, though details of these may be found in: George J. Firmage *e.e. cummings: A Bibliography* (Wesleyan University Press 1960).

1	**The Enormous Room** (novel) The 1st Eng. has an Intro. by Robert Graves	Boni & Liveright 1922 Cape 1928	Q G
2	**Tulips and Chimneys** (verse)	Seltzer 1923	O
3	**XLI Poems**	Dial Press 1925	K
4	**Is 5** (verse)	Boni & Liveright 1926	J
5	**Him** (prose)	Boni & Liveright 1927	I
6	**Vi Va** (verse)	Liveright Inc. 1931	H
7	**Tom** (ballet) Limited to 1500 copies.	Arrow Editions (NY) 1935	H
8	**One Over Twenty** (verse)	Contemporary Poetry & Prose Editions, London 1936	G

9 **Collected Poems**	Harcourt Brace 1938	E
10 **One Times One** (verse)	Holt (NY) 1944	E
	Horizon 1947	D
11 **Santa Claus** (prose)	Holt 1946	E
12 **XAIRE** (verse)	OUP (NY) 1950	F
13 **i: Six Nonlectures**	Harvard University Press 1953	E
14 **Poems 1923–1954**	Harcourt Brace 1954	D
15 **95 Poems**	Harcourt Brace 1958	J
300 copies limited and signed, 5000 ordinary. (**D**)		
16 **100 Selected Poems**	Grove Press 1959	C
17 **Selected Poems**	Faber 1960	C
18 **73 Poems**	Faber 1964	C
19 **Collected Poems** (2 vols)	MacGibbon & Kee 1968	D
20 **Selected Letters**	Harcourt Brace 1969	C
	Deutsch 1972	C
21 **Complete Poems**	Harcourt Brace 1972	C
22 **Etcetera: The Unpublished Poems**	Norton 1984	C
23 **Hist Whist and Other Poems for Children**	Norton 1984	C

Dahl, Roald   Born in South Wales, 1916.

Dahl retains his reputation among children as being their *favourite* – and although children have a great deal of time too for *The Beano* and Enid Blyton, parents actually *approve* of Dahl, and hence he is almost unique in being bought by adults *and* read by the young. His adult stories too are excellent, though he has yet to equal his early successes of *Someone Like You* and – best of all – *Kiss Kiss*.

Vastly prolific nowadays, Dahl holds the record number of new publications since my last listing in 1977: no less than *fourteen* in seven years. The only authors who have approached that are Tolkien and Virginia Woolf, both of whom are dead.

1 **The Gremlins** (juvenile)	Random House 1943	K
This book is virtually unknown.	Collins 1944	K
2 **Over to You** (stories)	Reynal & Hitchcock	I
This first example of his masterly stories	1945	
is very scarce, and has been out-of-print	Hamilton 1947	H
for a long time.		
3 **Sometime Never** (novel)	Scribner 1948	H
Scarce.	Collins 1949	G
4 **Someone Like You** (stories)	Knopf 1953	F
Rare, but Michael Joseph reissued the	Secker & Warburg 1964	F
book in 1961, with two extra stories,		
and this may be found more easily.		

5 **Kiss, Kiss** (stories)   Knopf 1960   **D**
This must be Dahl's highlight. The great   Joseph 1960   **D**
success of this book prompted Joseph to
reissue 4 the following year (see above)
with a similar d/w – red and blue shapes
on a background of net curtain.

6 **James and the Giant Peach**   Knopf 1961   **D**
(juvenile)   Allen & Unwin 1967   **C**
Published in the usual way in America
in boards and d/w. Allen & Unwin
published it in laminated boards, rather
like the *Beano Book*. These shiny boards
have not stood the test of time, and it
will be hard to find good copies.

7 **Charlie and the Chocolate Factory**   Knopf 1964   **F**
(juvenile)   Allen & Unwin 1967   **C**
His best-known children's book.

8 **The Magic Finger** (juvenile)   Harper 1966   **C**
Less well known.   Allen & Unwin 1968   **B**

9 **Twenty-Nine Kisses**   Joseph 1969   **B**
As the title suggests, a collection of past
stories.

10 **Selected Stories**   Random House 1970   **A**
No new material.

11 **Fantastic Mr Fox** (juvenile)   Knopf 1970   **C**
Recent, though little known.   Allen & Unwin 1970   **B**

12 **Charlie and the Great Glass**   Knopf, 1972   **C**
Elevator (juvenile)   Allen & Unwin 1973   **B**
Successful, because of the word
'Charlie', though less successful in
England, because of the word
'Elevator'.

13 **Switch Bitch** (stories)   Knopf 1974   **B**
Only his third collection of stories, this   Joseph 1974   **B**
time on the theme of sex.

14 **Danny: The Champion of the**   Knopf 1975   **B**
World (juvenile)   Cape 1975   **B**

15 **The Wonderful Story of Henry**   Knopf 1977   **B**
Sugar (novel)   Cape 1977   **B**

16 **The Best of Roald Dahl**   Vintage (US) 1978   **B**

17 **The Enormous Crocodile** (juvenile)   Knopf 1978   **A**
Illus. Quentin Blake.   Cape 1978   **A**

18 **Tales of the Unexpected** (stories)   Joseph 1979   **A**
     Vintage 1979   **A**

19 **My Uncle Oswald** (novel)   Joseph 1979   **A**
     Knopf 1980   **A**

20 **More Tales of the Unexpected**   Joseph 1980   **A**
Including four new stories.

21	**The Twits** (juvenile)	Cape 1980	B
	Illus. Quentin Blake.	Knopf 1981	B
22	**George's Marvellous Medicine**	Cape 1981	A
	(juvenile)	Knopf 1982	A
	Illus. Quentin Blake.		
23	**Roald Dahl's Revolting Rhymes**	Cape 1982	B
	Illus. Quentin Blake.	Knopf 1983	B
24	**The BFG** (juvenile novel)	Cape 1982	A
		Farrar Straus 1982	A
25	**Dirty Beasts** (juvenile)	Cape 1983	A
	Illus. Rosemary Fawcett.	Farrar Straus 1983	A
26	**The Best of Roald Dahl** (stories)	Joseph 1983	A
27	**Roald Dahl's Book of Ghost Stories**	Cape 1983	A
	A misleading title; Dahl is merely the editor, and not the author, of these stories.		
28	**The Witches** (juvenile)	Cape 1983	A
	Illus. Quentin Blake.	Farrar Straus 1983	A

Films:
Willie Wonka and the Chocolate Factory Paramount 1971 (*Charlie and the Chocolate Factory*) Dahl wrote the screenplay for the above, as well as the screenplays for Ian Fleming's **You Only Live Twice** (United Artists 1965) and **Chitty-Chitty-Bang-Bang** (United Artists 1968). None has been published.

Davies, W.H.   Born in Monmouthshire, 1871. Died 1940.

The most famous tramp ever, mainly for his highlight, recorded below. Davies became a near-compulsive writer, publishing over fifty books in his lifetime, mostly verse.

The Autobiography of a Super-Tramp	Fifield 1908	F
	Knopf 1917	
Bernard Shaw wrote the Preface for this work, which helped a great deal to get it noticed and read. It has now become a classic, and is quite scarce.		

Day-Lewis, C.   Born in Ireland, 1904. Poet Laureate 1968. Died 1972.

Day-Lewis published about fifty books under his own name, occasionally omitting the hyphen, as well as the detective novels under the pseudonym Nicholas Blake. A checklist may be found in *The New Cambridge Bibliography of English Literature* vol. 4. For fuller details, an excellent bibliography is G.

Handley-Taylor and Timothy d'Arch Smith *C. Day-Lewis: The Poet Laureate* (St James Press 1968).

Apart from his translations of Virgil, Day-Lewis is probably best remembered for *The Poetic Image* Cape 1947; 1st Amer. Oxford 1947. This is Grade C.

Of late, the Blake novels have come to the fore, and these are listed below:

1	**A Question of Proof**	Collins 1935	N
		Harper 1935	L
2	**Thou Shell of Death**	Collins 1936	K
	The American edition omits *Thou* from the title.	Harper 1936	I
3	**There's Trouble Brewing**	Collins 1937	I
		Harper 1937	H
4	**The Beast Must Die**	Collins 1938	I
		Harper 1938	H
5	**The Smiler with the Knife**	Collins 1939	H
		Harper 1939	G
6	**Malice in Wonderland**	Collins 1940	H
7	**Summer Camp Mystery**	Harper 1940	G
	(Same as 6)		
8	**The Case of the Abominable Snowman**	Collins 1941	G
9	**Corpse in the Snowman**	Harper 1944	G
10	**Minute for Murder**	Collins 1947	F
		Harper 1948	E
11	**Head of a Traveller**	Collins 1949	F
		Harper 1949	E
12	**The Dreadful Hollow**	Collins 1953	E
		Harper 1953	D
13	**The Whisper in the Gloom**	Collins 1954	E
		Harper 1954	D
14	**A Tangled Web**	Collins 1956	E
		Harper 1956	D
15	**End of Chapter**	Collins 1957	E
		Harper 1957	D
16	**A Penknife in my Heart**	Collins 1958	E
		Harper 1958	D
17	**The Widow's Cruise**	Collins 1959	E
		Harper 1959	D
18	**The Worm of Death**	Collins 1961	D
		Harper 1961	C
19	**The Deadly Joker**	Collins 1963	D
		Harper 1963	C
20	**The Sad Variety**	Collins 1964	C
		Harper 1964	B

21	**The Morning after Death**	Collins 1966	C
		Harper 1966	B
22	**The Nicholas Blake Omnibus** (incl. Nos 4, 12 and 14)	Collins 1966	C
23	**The Private Wound**	Collins 1968	B
		Harper 1968	B

Film:
Que la Bête meure (Killer/This Man Must Die) La Boétie/Rizzoli 1969
(*The Beast Must Die*)

Deighton, Len   Born in London, 1929.

Deighton's name is now universally known, as is that of his first book *The Ipcress File*, filmed with great success two years after its launch. A first novel by an unknown author, it had a small run and is scarce. So are his ephemeral writings – the Dossiers, the cookbooks. Latterly, Deighton has published a lot of Second World War stuff – fiction and non-fiction – but it is still his spy novels for which people have the most affection. Initial print runs nowadays are very large, of course, and so recent titles should not be difficult to find. A certain sameness has become very evident in the design of Deighton d/ws – all being white with heavy black and red block lettering, this persisting even when he moved publishers recently from Cape to Hutchinson. Possibly they are executed at Deighton's request, but the following from a letter (received in the seventies in response to one from me) would seem to underline his appreciation of the early ones: 'I believe Mr Hawkey's dust jacket designs are well able to survive the test of time, in spite of the way each of them influenced jacket design and so produced many imitative jackets.'
But the eye-catching would appear to have replaced the subtle.

1	**The Ipcress File** (novel) Secret File No. 1. Very distinctive black and white photographic d/w, and orange boards. It is scarce.	Hodder & Stoughton 1962	H
		Simon & Schuster 1963	F
2	**Horse Under Water** (novel) Secret File No. 2. First book with Cape. The appearance is very similar to 1, though. Quite difficult.	Cape 1964	F
		Putnam 1958	D
3	**Funeral in Berlin** (novel) Secret File No. 3. Continuing the theme and design of 1 and 2, this forms a trilogy, in a sense.	Cape 1964	C
		Putnam 1965	C
4	**Action Cook Book: Len Deighton's Guide to Eating** Printed boards, text printed in comic-strip style. Another original design, and an attractive book. Because original	Cape 1965	D

owners used it, however, it is difficult to
find a nice copy.

5 **Où Est le Garlic; or, Len**   Penguin 1965   **B**
Deighton's French Cook Book
First published as a paperback, this was
as successful as his three Secret Files.
Although they were everywhere in
1965, I suspect that a clean copy of this
Penguin would be hard to find.

6 **Cookstrip Cook Book**   Geis (NY) 1966   **B**
This is the American edition of
No. 4.

7 **Billion Dollar Brain** (novel)   Cape 1966   **B**
Another superb Hawkey d/w, though   Putnam 1966   **B**
now appearing fearfully sixties, in its
silver and black shininess. The d/w
announced (on the front!) that the
book was to be filmed 'by the producers
of James Bond', and that *The New York
Times* described it as 'even better than
The Spy Who Came In from the Cold' (see
le Carré). The endpapers continue a
fine tradition with a very official
'Automath Statement'. (1's endpapers
were plain, but on 2's was printed a
crossword by Cape, and Gothic
German in negative for 3.)

8 **An Expensive Place to Die** (novel)   Cape 1967   **C**
The d/w is still by Hawkey, but in   Putnam 1967   **B**
colour for the first time, perhaps losing
some of its style. The endpapers here
are a trendy black and white Art
Nouveau, but the very special feature is
a very effectively produced TOP
SECRET buff wallet, with letters and
documents within – reminiscent of
Wheatley's Dossiers (see Wheatley).
Needless to say, a copy *must* have this
wallet.

9 **London Dossier** (non-fiction)   Penguin 1967   **B**
Deighton edited this volume. It is an   Cape 1967   **C**
interesting book, and now quite scarce.

10 **Only When I Larf** (novel)   Joseph 1968   **C**
This, the first trade edition, was
published simultaneously by Sphere in
paperback (**B**), the Joseph edition
being far scarcer. Both, however, were
preceded by a ring-bound limited

edition of only 150 copies, privately printed (**H**). Not published in America, perhaps because of the Cockney phoneticism of the title.

11	**Len Deighton's Continental Dossier** (non-fiction) A follow-up to 9, but very little known.	Joseph 1968	C
12	**Bomber** (novel) Deighton's longest book, and a change of style.	Cape 1970 Harper 1970	B B
13	**Declarations of War** (stories)	Cape 1971	C
14	**Close-Up** (novel) Unusual subject-matter for Deighton.	Cape 1972 Atheneum 1972	B B
15	**Spy Story** (novel) The triumphant return, with the title leaving nothing to doubt.	Cape 1974 Harcourt Brace 1974	B B
16	**Yesterday's Spy** (novel) A repeat of 15's success story in the bestseller charts, and a welcome change from black and red d/ws.	Cape 1975 Harcourt Brace 1975	B B
17	**Eleven Declarations of War** (stories) The same as 13.	Harcourt Brace 1975	B
18	**Twinkle, Twinkle, Little Spy** (novel)	Cape 1976 Harcourt Brace 1976	B B
19	**Fighter** (non-fiction) Subtitled *The True Story of the Battle of Britain*, this has an introduction by A.J.P. Taylor.	Cape 1977 Knopf 1978	B B
20	**Five Complete Novels** A fat omnibus – one of a series – containing 1, 3, 8, 16 and 18.	Collins 1978	B
21	**Airshipwreck** A landscape format book of rather bizarre photographs of, as the title suggests, wrecked airships. Already an elusive book.	Cape 1978 Holt Rinehart 1979	C C
22	**SS – GB** (novel) According to pre-publication announcements, this novel was originally to be called just SS, without the GB.	Cape 1978 Knopf 1979	B B
23	**Basic French Cooking** A reissue in one volume of the old cookbooks – and a very welcome one, for this can be *used*, while the originals remain annoyingly valuable.	Cape 1979	B

24 **Blitzkrieg** (non-fiction) Knopf, publishing the following year, missed out on the tie-in. As the Cape review slip said: 'to be published on Monday September 3, the 40th anniversary of Britain's declaration of war against Nazi Germany.'	Cape 1979 Knopf 1980	B B
25 **Battle of Britain** (non-fiction) A large format heavily illustrated book on a recurrent Deighton theme.	Cape 1980 Coward McCann 1980	B B
26 **XPD** (novel) The acronym means 'expedient demise'. No experiments with the d/w, however, for although this is Deighton's first book for Hutchinson, the design, colours and typeface are identical to 19 and 24.	Hutchinson 1981 Knopf 1981	B B
27 **Goodbye, Mickey Mouse** (novel) A novel, but maintaining Deighton's fierce interest in World War II's air battles.	Hutchinson 1982 Knopf 1982	B B
28 **Berlin Game** (novel) A return to home ground. Once again the blurb writer can refer to the 'master of the spy story'.	Hutchinson 1983 Knopf 1984	B B

Bibliography (forthcoming at time of writing)
Len Deighton: A Checklist 1962–1984 by Edward Milward-Oliver

Films:
The Ipcress File Rank 1964 **Funeral in Berlin** Paramount 1966 **Billion Dollar Brain** United Artists 1967 **Only When I Larf** Paramount 1969 **Spy Story** Gala 1976
Deighton wrote the screenplay for **Only When I Larf**, as well as that for **Oh! What a Lovely War**. Neither was published.
He also wrote the introduction to Arthur Conan Doyle **The Valley of Fear** (reissue of Sherlock Holmes stories; Murray/Cape 1974).

Delaney, Shelagh   Born in Lancashire, 1939.

Although she has published several books and plays, Delaney remains notable for one – an important work for collectors of modern drama, and a key of the late fifties and early sixties, made more so by the quality of the ensuing film, with the wonderful Rita Tushingham.

A Taste of Honey (play)	Methuen 1959 Grove Press 1959	C C

Delaney

Film:
A Taste of Honey British Lion 1961
She wrote the screenplay, with Tony Richardson. She also wrote the
screenplay for the film **Charlie Bubbles**, but neither was published.

De Teran, Lisa St Aubin   Born in London, 1953.

The youngest author in this book. It might be too early to tell whether she
will become a *collected* author, but the feel seems right, and this is the time to
gather in both her books, if you like her style. Her name, it must be said, is
less than catchy.

1 **Keepers of the House** (novel)	Cape 1982	B
2 **The Long Way Home** (same as 1)	Harper Row 1983	A
3 **The Slow Train to Milan** (novel)	Cape 1983	A
	Harper Row 1984	A

Donleavy, J.P.   Born in New York, 1926. Irish citizen, 1967.

Perhaps more read than collected, these days. His first book remains the
most important, but Donleavy is enjoyed with each new publication for his
ribaldry, wit and consonance.

1 **The Ginger Man** (novel)	Olympia Press	H
This is Donleavy's highlight.	(Paris) 1955	
	Spearman 1956	F
	McDowell Obolensky	D
	1958	
	1st complete ed.:	A
	Corgi 1963	
	Delacorte 1965	A
2 **Fairy Tales of New York** (play)	Penguin 1961	B
	Random House 1961	B
3 **The Ginger Man** (play)	Random House 1961	B
4 **What They Did in Dublin with the**	McGibbon & Kee 1962	A
Ginger Man (same as 3)		
5 **A Singular Man** (novel)	Little Brown, 1963	C
	Bodley Head 1964	C
6 **Meet My Maker the Mad Molecule**	Little Brown 1964	C
(stories)	Bodley Head 1965	B
7 **A Singular Man** (play)	Bodley Head 1965	B
8 **The Saddest Summer of Samuel S**	Delacorte 1966	B
(novel)	Eyre & Spottiswoode	A
	1967	
9 **The Beastly Beatitudes of**	Delacorte 1968	B
Balthazar B (novel)	Eyre & Spottiswoode	A
	1969	

10 **The Onion Eaters** (novel)	Delacorte 1971	**B**
	Eyre & Spottiswoode 1971	**A**
11 **The Plays of J. P. Donleavy** (incl. 3, 2, 7 and the play of 8)	Delacorte 1972	**B**
	Penguin 1974	**A**
12 **A Fairy Tale of New York** (novel)	Delacorte 1973	**B**
	Eyre Methuen 1973	**A**
13 **The Unexpurgated Code: A Complete Manual of Survival and Manners**	Delacorte 1975	**B**
	Wildwood House 1975	**A**
14 **The Destinies of D'Arcy Dancer Gentleman** (novel)	Delacorte 1977	**B**
	Lane 1978	**A**
15 **Schultz** (novel)	Delacorte 1979	**B**
	Lane 1980	**A**
16 **Leila** (novel) Sequel to 14.	Delacorte 1983	**B**
	Lane 1983	**A**

Douglas, Keith   Born in Tunbridge Wells, 1920. Died 1944.

Among the millions, many poets and artists were killed at the front during the Great War. During the Second World War, many more were to lose their lives. Keith Douglas was one of these.

Nothing was published during his lifetime. His war journals, entitled *Alamein to Zem-Zem*, were published in 1946. These contained a few poems, which were reprinted in:

1 **Collected Poems** This is scarce. Almost half the poems in the above were reprinted in:	Editions Poetry (London) 1951	**G**
2 **Selected Poems** This is edited and has an Introduction by Ted Hughes, and is also sought after by Hughes collectors.	Faber 1964	**C**
	Chilmark Press 1964	**C**
3 **Complete Poems**	OUP 1977	**C**

Biography:
Desmond Graham **Keith Douglas 1920–1944** OUP 1974

Doyle, Arthur Conan Born in Edinburgh, 1859. Died 1930.

All of Doyle's books are wanted by collectors, but there is no denying the supreme popularity of Mr Sherlock Holmes. It seems almost insolent to talk of Holmes being the most famous fictional character ever; it is very difficult to get one's mind around the fact that he *was* fictional, so great is the conspiracy to render him real, the latest example of note being H.R.F.

Doyle

Keating's *Sherlock Holmes and His World* (1979) in the famous Thames & Hudson biographical series.

A complete checklist of Conan Doyle may be found in *The New Cambridge Bibliography of English Literature* vol. 3, and some valuable information in: John Dickson Carr *The Life of Sir Arthur Conan Doyle* Murray 1949.

Below are all the Sherlock Holmes books.

1 **A Study in Scarlet**
The wrappered annual which ushered Holmes into the world is fantastically scarce. The book is also very scarce.

28th Beeton's Christmas Annual 1887   **V**

1st book form Ward Lock 1887   **Q**

2 **The Sign of Four**
Very, very scarce.

Lippincott's Magazine 1890   **N**

1st book form Blackett 1890   **O–P**

3 **The Adventures of Sherlock Holmes**
The Strand Magazine, which began in 1891, issued bound volumes of six months' issues, and Newnes (who owned the *Strand*) published the *Adventures* in a similar format – pale blue bevelled boards, with gold blocking. It is strange that there is so much difference between the prices of the bound magazines and the 1st book forms. This is true also of many of the following titles, but it is apparent now that bound *Strands* are not as common as they used to be, and a marked rise in price seems inevitable.

Strand Magazine 1891–92 (per volume)   **B**

1st book form Newnes 1892   **M–N**

4 **The Memoirs of Sherlock Holmes**
Same situation as in 3. Identical format, but in dark blue cloth.

Strand Magazine 1892–93 (per volume)   **B**

1st book form Newnes 1894   **M**

5 **The Hound of the Baskervilles**
Newnes ed. has an attractively decorated red cover.

Strand magazine 1901–02 (per volume)   **B–C**

1st book form Newnes 1902   **K**

6 **The Return of Sherlock Holmes**
The Newnes 1st is one of the most difficult to find. Blue cloth.

Strand Magazine 1903–04 (per volume)   **B–C**

1st book form Newnes 1905   **L–M**

7 **The Valley of Fear** 1st book in red cloth.	Strand Magazine 1914–15 (per volume)	B
	1st book form Smith, Elder 1915	I
8 **His Last Bow** These stories were scattered throughout *The Strand Magazine* over the period 1893–1917.	Murray 1917	H
9 **The Case-Book of Sherlock Holmes** These too were scattered in the *Strand* over many years.	Murray 1927	H

Films:
Sherlock Holmes films are too numerous to list here, but those based on
Conan Doyle's stories include: **The Return of Sherlock Holmes**
Paramount 1929 **The Sign of Four** Wide World 1932 **The Hound of
the Baskervilles** First Division 1932; 20th Century Fox 1939; United
Artists 1959 **A Study in Scarlet** Wide World 1933 **Sherlock
Holmes and the Voice of Terror** Universal 1942 (*His Last
Bow*) **Adventure of the Five Pips** Universal 1945 (*The Five Orange
Pips*) **The Man with the Twisted Lip** Gaumont 1951

There have been a vast number of books on Holmes, each specializing in
putting forward theories more fantastic than the last, and indicating flaws
in their predecessors' deductions, hopefully in the manner of the great
man himself. Two works that strike me as essential are: William S.
Baring-Gould (ed.) **The Annotated Sherlock Holmes** (2 vols) Murray
1968 Michael and Mollie Hardwick **The Sherlock Holmes
Companion** Murray 1962

Drabble, Margaret Born in Yorkshire, 1939.

Popular with readers and collectors from the beginning, Margaret Drabble
now paces her novels, interspersing them with non-fiction and editing. Her
current silence is due to her working on the new (and much-needed) edition
of The Oxford Companion to English Literature.

1 **A Summer Bird-Cage** (novel)	Weidenfeld 1963	E
	Morrow 1964	D
2 **The Garrick Year** (novel)	Weidenfeld 1964	D
	Morrow 1965	C
3 **The Millstone** (novel)	Weidenfeld 1965	C
	Morrow 1966	B
4 **Wordsworth** (non-fiction)	Evans 1966	B
5 **Jerusalem the Golden** (novel)	Weidenfeld 1967	C
	Morrow 1967	B

Drabble

6 **The Waterfall** (novel)	Weidenfeld 1969	B
	Knopf 1969	B
7 **The Needle's Eye** (novel)	Weidenfeld 1972	B
	Knopf 1972	A
8 **Virginia Woolf: A Personal Debt** (essay)	Aloe Editions 1973	D
9 **Arnold Bennett: A Biography**	Weidenfeld 1974	B
	Knopf 1974	B
10 **The Realms of Gold** (novel)	Weidenfeld 1975	A
	Knopf 1975	A
11 **The Genius of Thomas Hardy** (ed.)	Weidenfeld 1976	B
	Knopf 1976	B
12 **The Ice Age** (novel)	Weidenfeld 1977	A
	Knopf 1977	A
13 **For Queen and Country: Britain in the Victorian Age** (juvenile)	Deutsch 1978	B
	Seabury Press 1979	B
14 **A Writer's Britain: Landscape in Literature** (non-fiction)	Thames & Hudson 1979	B
	Knopf 1979	B
15 **The Middle Ground** (novel)	Weidenfeld 1980	A
	Knopf 1980	A

Film:
A Touch of Love British Lion 1969

Du Maurier, Daphne   Born in London, 1907.

Author of nearly forty books, only the highlights appealing to collectors. These appear below.

1 **The Loving Spirit** (novel) Her first book.	Heinemann 1931	D
	Doubleday 1931	D
2 **Jamaica Inn** (novel) Quite scarce.	Gollancz 1936	C
	Doubleday 1936	B
3 **Rebecca** (novel)	Gollancz 1938	C
	Doubleday 1938	B
4 **Frenchman's Creek** (novel)	Gollancz 1941	B
	Doubleday 1942	A
5 **The Breaking Point** (stories) Incl. 'The Birds'.	Gollancz 1959	B
	Doubleday 1959	A

Films:
There have been nine films made from Daphne du Maurier's books, four of which are listed above. **Jamaica Inn** Paramount 1939   **Rebecca** United Artists 1940   **Frenchman's Creek** Paramount 1944   **The Birds** Rank 1963

Dunn, Nell   Born in London, 1936.

Still notable for just two books, despite her triumphant return to the public eye with the very successful stage play *Steaming*, about ladies sweating in a sauna.

1 **Up the Junction** (stories)	MacGibbon & Kee 1963	B
	Lippincott 1966	B
2 **Poor Cow** (novel)	MacGibbon & Kee 1967	A
	Doubleday 1967	A

Films:
Poor Cow Warner Bros 1967   **Up the Junction** Paramount 1968

Durrell, Lawrence   Born in India, 1912. British.

At the time of writing, Durrell has just published the fourth in the series of five connected novels which he calls a 'quincunx', but which Faber are beginning to refer to as the Avignon Quintet, I suppose to bring the series more in line with the Alexandria Quartet. Certainly Faber's bindings and artwork have declined since then. All the vibrancy is gone now; no more two-coloured cloth cases with labels, lozenges and rich gold blocking. No more textured, unlaminated brightly coloured d/ws bearing sweeping Berthold Wolpe graphics. Just plain paper boards and watercoloured dust-wrappers. One particularly irritating inconsistency occurs with the presentation of *Sebastian*, the fourth and latest in the 'quincunx'. Pentagram's new 'ff' colophon was tolerated on *Constance*, but now we find the typeface and design of the preceding three volumes completely abandoned (despite the retention of David Gentleman watercolours) in order to bring it into the new 'house style'. This means that *every* new Faber novel will have its title and author set into a ruled box surmounted by the ubiquitous 'ff', the blurb appearing in another box on the d/w's rear, and only the depiction will differ from book to book. Wolpe's wonderful Albertus typeface has been forsaken for a slender Times Roman, and all scope for innovative design, it seems to me, has been subdued into a device and a formula. Sad.

Spirit of Place and Durrell's private correspondence with Henry Miller (see below) will fill in a good deal of biographical information. G.S. Fraser *Lawrence Durrell: A Study* Faber 1968 is also essential reading, and contains a bibliography by Alan G. Thomas.

1 **Quaint Fragment** (poems)	Cecil Press 1931	U

   Durrell says that this was never
   published; but Thomas (see above) says
   that several have passed through the

salerooms, though it is extremely scarce. Very difficult to grade such an item, as it would seem to be on a par with Auden's *Poems* (1928).

2 **Ten Poems**　　　　　　　　　　Caduceus Press 1932　　**Q–R**
Very limited, and very rare – the remaining stock having been destroyed in the Blitz. Again, difficult to grade.

3 **Bromo Bombasts**　　　　　　Caduceus Press 1933　　**Q**
This parody of Shaw's *Black Girl* is far more scarce than the original, and was limited to 100 copies.

4 **Transition** (poems)　　　　　Caduceus Press 1934　　**Q**
The same situation as 2.

5 **Pied Piper of Lovers** (novel)　Cassell 1935　　**Q**
The first commercially published work, with d/w by Nancy Myers, Durrell's first wife. Very scarce.

6 **Panic Spring** (novel)　　　　Faber 1937　　**O**
Although Durrell's first book with　Covici-Friede 1937　　**O**
Faber, it was published under the pseudonym Charles Norden at their request, because 5 had sold so badly. This item is very scarce. It was also the first Durrell book to be published in America.

7 **The Black Book** (novel)　　　Obelisk Press (Paris)　**N**
For the publication of the work in　1938
England, Durrell held a signing session　Dutton 1960　　**G**
in London, and so autographed copies　Faber 1973　　**B**
might turn up soon.

8 **A Private Country** (verse)　　Faber 1943　　**G**
Grey boards, grey d/w with red lettering. First poetry published by Faber, and scarce.

9 **Prospero's Cell** (non-fiction)　Faber 1945　　**E**
Although quite an early work, it seems　Dutton 1960　　**D**
to come up fairly often.

10 **Cities, Plains and People** (verse)　Faber 1946　　**E**
Quite scarce.

11 **Cefalû** (novel)　　　　　　Editions Poetry　　**E**
Scarce. It was apparently issued in both　(London) 1947
brown and green cloth, but either is particularly difficult in the d/w.

12 **On Seeming to Presume** (verse)　Faber 1948　　**C**
Red boards, with cream d/w printed in black and red.

13 **Sappho** (play)   Faber 1950   **D**
    Grey boards with purple d/w.   Dutton 1958   **C**

14 **Key to Modern Poetry** (lectures)   Nevill 1952   **E–F**
    This is particularly scarce, though quite
    recent.

15 **A Key to Modern British Poetry**   Oklahoma Press 1952   **D**
    (same as 14)

16 **Reflections on a Marine Venus**   Faber 1953   **E**
    (travel)   Dutton 1960   **D**
    Quite scarce.

17 Emmanuel Royidis **Pope Joan**   Verschoyle 1954   **D**
    Translated from the Greek by L.D.   Dutton 1961   **C**
    Quite scarce, particularly in the d/w.

18 **The Tree of Idleness** (verse)   Faber 1955   **D**
    Quite difficult, although there is an
    abundance of second impressions
    around!

19 **Selected Poems**   Faber 1956   **B**
        Grove Press 1956   **B**

20 **Bitter Lemons** (travel)   Faber 1957   **C**
    His best-known travel work, this book   Dutton 1958   **C**
    on Cyprus has become quite a classic.
    The d/w can be hard to find. Be careful
    of the Book Society editions, of which
    there are plenty around, as they are not
    the true 1st, although printed by Faber.

21 **Esprit de Corps** (stories)   Faber 1957   **C**
    The first of the Antrobus trilogy.   Dutton 1958   **B**

22 **Justine** (novel)   Faber 1957   **I**
    The 1st edition has always been very   Dutton 1957   **F**
    difficult, and many are the Alexandria
    Quartets lacking the first volume!
    Durrell says there were about '250
    errors which were put right in the 2nd'.
    An important work – see *Balthazar*,
    Mountolive and *Clea* below.

23 **White Eagles over Serbia** (novel)   Faber 1957   **E**
    Durrell thought it a detective story;   Criterion 1957   **D**
    Faber thought it a juvenile, and as such
    was it published. Quite scarce.

24 **The Dark Labyrinth** (same as 11)   Ace (NY) 1958   **B**
    Faber published it under this title in
    1961 (**B**).

25 **Balthazar** (novel)   Faber 1958   **F**
    The second of the Quartet.   Dutton 1958   **E**

26 **Mountolive** (novel)   Faber 1958   **E**
    The third of the Quartet.   Dutton 1959   **D**

27 **Stiff Upper Lip** (stories)	Faber 1958	C
The second of the Antrobus trilogy (see 21). Nicolas Bentley drew the pictures.	Dutton 1959	B
28 **Art and Outrage**	Putnam 1959	C
A correspondence about Henry Miller between Alfred Perles and Lawrence Durrell. Quite difficult.	Dutton 1960	B
29 **Clea** (novel)	Faber 1960	D
The completion of the Quartet. The four look dynamic together, with their bold, graphic d/ws – yellow, grey, green and off-white, respectively, with red and black designs and lettering.	Dutton 1960	C
30 **Collected Poems**	Faber 1960	B
	Dutton 1960	B
31 **The Alexandria Quartet**	Faber 1962	D
This one-volume edition was issued in an ordinary trade edition and one limited to 500 copies, signed by L.D. This is Grade **I**.	Dutton 1962	D
32 **Lawrence Durrell and Henry Miller: A Private Correspondence**	Dutton 1963	C
	Gaber 1963	C
33 **Beccafico Le Becfigue** (verse)	La Licorne (France)	H
Limited to 150 copies, signed.	1963	
34 **An Irish Faustus** (play)	Faber 1963	C
	Dutton 1964	B
35 **La Descente du Styx** (verse)	La Murène (France)	H
Limited to 250 copies, signed.	1964	
36 **Selected Poems 1935–1963**	Faber 1964	A
Paper-covered edition.		
37 **Acte** (play)	Faber 1965	C
	Dutton 1965	C
38 **Sauve Qui Peut** (stories)	Faber 1966	A
The final Antrobus (see 21 and 27). Nicolas Bentley drew the pictures. Remaindered in the seventies, and therefore abundant.	Dutton 1967	A
39 **The Ikons** (poems)	Faber 1966	C
	Dutton 1967	B
40 **Tunc** (novel)	Faber 1968	B
The first of the *Revolt of Aphrodite* duet.	Dutton 1968	B
41 **Spirit of Place** (travel)	Faber 1969	C
Essays edited by Alan G. Thomas.	Dutton 1969	B
42 **Nunquam** (novel)	Faber 1970	A
The completion of the duet (see 40).	Dutton 1970	A
43 **The Red Limbo Lingo** (poetry notebook)	Faber 1971	D
An unusual venture for Faber. Limited		

edition, 100 of which signed (**G**). Red
cloth in slipcase.

44 **On the Suchness of the Old Boy**　　Turret 1972　　　　　**E**
(verse)
Illustrated by Sappho Durrell. Limited.

45 **Vega and Other Poems**　　　　Faber 1973　　　　　**B**
Very quickly replaced by a paperback
edition, and may already prove quite
hard to find.

46 **The Big Supposer**　　　　　Abelard-Schuman 1973　**A**
A dialogue with Marc Alyn. First　　Grove Press 1974　　**A**
published in French as *Le Grand
Suppositoire* by Editions Pierre Belfond
(Paris) 1972.

47 **The Revolt of Aphrodite**　　　Faber 1974　　　　　**C**
40 and 42 in one volume.

48 **The Best of Antrobus**　　　　Faber 1974　　　　　**A**
A selection from 21, 27 and 38.

49 **Monsieur: or, The Prince of**　　Faber 1974　　　　　**B**
Darkness (novel)　　　　　Viking 1974　　　　**B**
The publication of this work saw a
signing session with Durrell in London,
so check title pages!

50 **Prospero's Cell**　　　　　　Faber 1975　　　　　**A**
A reissue of 9, with a new Preface.

51 **Sicilian Carousel** (travel)　　Faber 1977　　　　　**A**
Possibly the slightest of the travel　Viking 1977　　　　**A**
books.

52 **The Greek Islands** (travel)　　Faber 1978　　　　　**C**
A fine book, this. Large format, and　Viking 1978　　　　**C**
beautifully illustrated. Reprinted very
quickly.

53 **Livia or Buried Alive** (novel)　　Faber 1978　　　　　**A**
The second in the Avignon 'quincunx'.　Viking 1979　　　　**A**

54 **Collected Poems: 1931–1974**　　Faber 1980　　　　　**B**
　　　　　　　　　　　　Viking 1980　　　　**B**

55 **A Smile in the Mind's Eye** (essay)　Wildwood House　　**A**
An odd little essay, from an untypical　　1980
publisher.

56 **Literary Lifelines: The Richard**　Faber 1981　　　　　**B**
Aldington/Lawrence Durrell　　Viking 1981　　　　**B**
Correspondence (letters)

57 **Constance or Solitary Practices**　Faber 1982　　　　　**A**
(novel)　　　　　　　　Viking 1982　　　　**A**

58 **Sebastian or Ruling Passions**　Faber 1983　　　　　**A**
(novel)　　　　　　　　Viking 1984　　　　**A**

Film:

Justine 20th Century Fox 1969

Durrell

Durrell also edited many works, including, most notably: **A Henry Miller Reader** New Directions 1959 (**C**)   **The Best of Henry Miller** (same as above) Heinemann 1960 (**C**)   **New Poems 1963: A PEN Anthology** Hutchinson 1963 (**A**)   **Wordsworth** Penguin 1973 (**A**)

Eliot, T.S.   Born in St Louis, Missouri, 1888. Died 1965. British.

Although Eliot's reputation as a great poet is rock solid, I detect less interest in the collecting world, I suspect because most interested parties would by now have all the more available items, and cannot hope to find (or, having found, afford) the rarities. And yet a new and strange fame has landed rather awkwardly upon Eliot's shoulders. It was unthinkable a few years ago that *Old Possum* might be dramatized, let alone made into a musical – let alone a *hit* musical – but this has happened, and it has brought a new audience for the poet.

From the collector's point of view, the essential book is: Donald Gallup *T.S. Eliot: A Bibliography* Faber 1969. This extremely fine bibliography lists absolutely everything, though I must limit myself to a checklist of his books. He wrote many Introductions and the like, all of which are in Gallup.

1	**Prufrock and Other Observations**	Egoist Ltd 1917	**R**
2	**Ezra Pound: His Metric and Poetry**	Knopf (NY) 1917	**N**
	Published anonymously.		
3	**Poems**	Hogarth Press 1919	**M**
4	**Ara Vos Prec** (verse)	Ovid Press 1920 (unsigned)	**N**
		(signed)	**P**
5	**Poems** (same as 4)	Knopf 1920	**K**
6	**The Sacred Wood** (essays)	Methuen 1920	**F**
		Knopf 1921	**E**
7	**The Waste Land** (verse)	Boni & Liveright (NY) 1922	**L**
		Hogarth Press 1923	**L**
8	**Homage to John Dryden** (verse)	Hogarth Press 1924	**I**
9	**Poems 1909–1925**	Faber & Gwyer 1925	**H**
		Harcourt Brace 1932	**F**
10	**Journey of the Magi** (poem)	Faber & Gwyer 1927	**E**
	Faber ed.: 5000 copies printed. Rudge ed.: 27 copies printed.	Rudge 1927	**O**
11	**Shakespeare and the Stoicism of Seneca** (address)	OUP 1927	**E**
12	**A Song for Simeon** (poem)	Faber & Gwyer 1928	**D**
13	**For Lancelot Andrewes** (essays)	Faber & Gwyer 1928	**E**
		Doubleday 1929	**D**
14	**Dante** (essay)	Faber 1929	**E**

15 **Animula** (poem) 400 signed. (**I**)	Faber 1929	**D**
16 **Ash-Wednesday** (verse) Slightly preceded by limited, signed edition. (**J**)	Faber 1930 Putnam 1930	**F** **E**
17 **Anabasis: A Poem by St J. Perse** Translated by T.S.E.	Faber 1930 Harcourt Brace 1938 1st rev. eds Harcourt Brace 1949 Faber 1959	**G** **F** **D** **D**
18 **Marina** (poem)	Faber 1930	**D**
19 **Thoughts After Lambeth** (*Criterion* miscellany)	Faber 1931	**C**
20 **Triumphal March** (poem)	Faber 1931	**C**
21 **Charles Whibley: A Memoir**	OUP 1931	**E**
22 **Selected Essays 1917–1932**	Faber 1932 Harcourt Brace 1932	**E** **D**
23 **John Dryden: The Poet, the** **Dramatist, The Critic** (criticism)	Holliday (NY) 1932	**E**
24 **Sweeney Agonistes** (drama)	Faber 1932	**E**
25 **The Use of Poetry and the Use of** **Criticism**	Faber 1933 Harvard University Press 1933	**E** **D**
26 **After Strange Gods** (lectures)	Faber 1934 Harcourt Brace 1934	**F** **E**
27 **The Rock** (play)	Faber 1934 Harcourt Brace 1934	**C** **C**
28 **Elizabethan Essays**	Faber 1934	**C**
29 **Murder in the Cathedral** (play)	Goulden 1935 1st complete eds. Faber 1935 Harcourt Brace 1935	**I** **F** **E**
30 **Essays Ancient and Modern**	Faber 1936 Harcourt Brace 1936	**C** **C**
31 **Collected Poems 1909–1935** Cont. first appearance of *Burnt Norton*.	Faber 1936 Harcourt Brace 1936	**E** **D**
32 **The Family Reunion** (play)	Faber 1939 Harcourt Brace 1939	**C** **C**
33 **Old Possum's Book of Practical** **Cats** 1939 ed.: d/w by T.S.E. 1940 ed.: Nicolas Bentley drew the pictures.	Faber 1939 Harcourt Brace 1939 Illus. ed. Faber 1940	**I** **H** **F**
34 **The Idea of a Christian Society** (lectures)	Faber 1939 Harcourt Brace 1940	**C** **C**
35 **The Waste Land and Other Poems**	Faber 1940 Harcourt Brace 1955	**C** **B**
36 **East Coker** (poem) Published previously in *The New English*	Faber 1940	**C**

Weekly Easter no. of the same year.

37	**Burnt Norton** (poem) 1st separate ed. See 31.	Faber 1941	C
38	**Points of View** (essays) Contains no new material.	Faber 1941	B
39	**The Dry Salvages** (poem)	Faber 1941	C
40	**The Classics and the Man of Letters** (address)	OUP 1942	C
41	**The Music of Poetry** (lecture)	Jackson (Glasgow) 1942	F
42	**Little Gidding** (poem) This, with 36, 37 and 39, completes the *Four Quartets*.	Faber 1942	C
43	**Four Quartets**	Harcourt Brace 1943 Faber 1944	C C
44	**What is a Classic?** (address)	Faber 1945	C
45	**On Poetry** (address) 750 copies printed, and distributed gratis.	Concord (Massachusetts) 1947	G
46	**Milton** (lecture) 500 copies printed.	Cumberlege (London) 1947	F
47	**A Sermon** 300 copies printed, and distributed gratis.	CUP 1948	G
48	**Selected Poems**	Penguin 1948 Harcourt Brace 1967	A A
49	**Notes Towards the Definition of Culture**	Faber 1948 Harcourt Brace 1949	C C
50	**From Poe to Valéry** (lecture) 1500 copies printed for distribution to friends of publisher.	Harcourt Brace 1948	G
51	**The Undergraduate Poems** Unauthorized publication. 1000 copies printed.	Harvard Advocate, (Massachusetts) 1949	H
52	**The Aims of Poetic Drama**	Poets' Theatre Guild 1949	E
53	**The Cocktail Party** (play)	Faber 1950 Harcourt Brace 1950	C C
54	**Poetry and Drama** (lecture)	Cambridge (Massachusetts) 1951 Faber 1951	C B
55	**The Value and Use of Cathedrals in England Today**	Chichester 1952	G
56	**An Address to Members of the London Library** 500 copies printed.	London 1952	G
57	**The Complete Poems and Plays** (1909–1950)	Harcourt Brace 1952	C

58	**Selected Prose**	Penguin 1953	A
59	**American Literature and the American Language**	Washington University 1953	F
	500 copies printed.		
60	**The Three Voices of Poetry** (lecture)	NBL 1953	C
		CUP (US) 1954	B
61	**The Confidential Clerk** (play)	Faber 1954	C
		Harcourt Brace 1954	C
62	**Religious Drama: Mediaeval and Modern**	House of Books (NY) 1954	G
	326 copies printed. 300 numbered, 26 lettered and signed (**J**).		
63	**The Cultivation of Christmas Trees** (poem)	Faber 1954	B
		Farrar Straus 1956	B
	Illus. David Jones		
64	**The Literature of Politics** (address)	Conservative Centre 1955	C
65	**The Frontiers of Criticism** (lecture)	Minnesota 1956	C
	10,050 copies printed, and distributed gratis.		
66	**On Poetry and Poets** (essays)	Faber 1957	C
		Farrar Straus 1957	C
67	**The Elder Statesman** (play)	Faber 1959	C
		Farrar Straus 1959	C
68	**Geoffrey Faber 1889–1961** (memoir)	Faber 1961	I
	Limited to 100 copies, distributed gratis.		
69	**Collected Plays**	Faber 1962	C
70	**George Herbert** (essay)	NBL 1962	B
71	**Collected Poems 1909–1962**	Faber 1963	C
		Harcourt Brace 1963	C
72	**Knowledge and Experience in the Philosophy of F.H. Bradley**	Faber 1964	C
		Farrar Straus 1964	C
73	**To Criticize the Critic** (essays)	Faber 1965	C
		Farrar Straus 1965	C
74	**Poems Written in Early Youth**	Faber 1967	B
	Preceded only by a privately printed edition in 1950, which was limited to 12 copies (**R–S**).	Farrar Straus 1967	B
75	**The Complete Poems and Plays**	Faber 1968	C
76	**The Waste Land: A Facsimile and Transcript**	Faber 1971	C
		Harcourt Brace 1971	C

Eliot edited and introduced a vast number of books, a few of the more important being:

Ezra Pound: Selected Poems	Faber & Gwyer 1928	F

A Choice of Kipling's Verse	Faber 1941	**D**
	Scribner 1943	**D**
Introducing James Joyce	Faber 1942	**C**
Literary Essays of Ezra Pound	Faber 1954	**D**
	New Directions 1954	**D**

Film:
Murder in the Cathedral Film Traders 1951   T.S. Eliot and George Hoellering **The Film of Murder in the Cathedral** was published by Faber in 1952, and by Harcourt Brace in America in the same year (**B**).

Farrell, J.G.   Born in Liverpool, 1935. Died 1979.

The British, as has been seen very clearly in recent years, have a great affinity for books (and films) concerning India, and Farrell's prize-winning *The Siege of Krishnapur* brought him a much wider readership than formerly. Winning literary prizes, though, was not so glamorous a business ten years ago as it is today, and although Farrell's name became known, he did not become a star overnight as did, say, Salman Rushdie. The succeeding novels were extremely well received, although some say that at the time of his premature death Farrell had not yet reached the acme of his powers.

Although the following list is short, the early titles are not at all common.

1	**A Man from Elsewhere** (novel)	Hutchinson 1963	**F**
2	**The Lung** (novel)	Hutchinson 1965	**C**
3	**A Girl in the Head** (novel)	Cape 1967	**B**
		Harper 1969	**B**
4	**Troubles** (novel)	Cape 1970	**B**
		Knopf 1971	**B**
5	**The Siege of Krishnapur** (novel)	Weidenfeld 1973	**C**
		Harcourt Brace 1974	**B**
6	**The Singapore Grip** (novel)	Weidenfeld 1978	**B**
		Knopf 1979	**B**
7	**The Hill Station** (novel)	Weidenfeld 1981	**A**

Faulkner, William   Born in New Albany, Mississippi, 1867. Died 1962.

In America, Faulkner is hugely regarded – he has been since he was awarded the Nobel Prize in 1949 – and first editions change hands for fortunes. His reputation is high in Britain, too, but even English firsts are not easy to come by, and Faulkner is a difficult man to collect. It ought to be remembered (and this is true of all American literary lions) that the US 1sts are worth *very much* more than their English counterparts.

1	**The Marble Faun** (verse)	Privately printed 1924	**T**
2	**Soldier's Pay** (novel)	Liveright 1926	**Q**
		Chatto & Windus 1930	**K**

3 **Mosquitoes** (novel) A revised ed. was published by Garden City in 1937 (**H**), and in England by Chatto & Windus in 1964 (**C**).	Privately printed 1927	**Q**
4 **Sartoris** (novel)	Harcourt Brace 1929	**M**
	Chatto & Windus 1933	**J**
5 **The Sound and the Fury** (novel)	H. Smith 1929	**M**
	Chatto & Windus 1931	**J**
6 **As I Lay Dying** (novel)	H. Smith 1930	**L**
	Chatto & Windus 1935	**H**
7 **Sanctuary** (novel)	H. Smith 1930	**M**
	Chatto & Windus 1931	**I**
8 **These 13** (stories)	H. Smith 1930	**K**
	Chatto & Windus 1933	**H**
9 **Light in August** (novel)	Random House 1932	**M**
	Chatto & Windus 1933	**I**
10 **A Green Bough** (verse)	H. Smith 1933	**I**
11 **Doctor Martino and Other Stories**	H. Smith 1934	**M**
	Chatto & Windus 1934	**J**
12 **Pylon** (novel)	H. Smith 1935	**J**
	Chatto & Windus 1936	**H**
13 **Absalom, Absalom!** (novel)	Random House 1936	**H**
	Chatto & Windus 1937	**G**
14 **The Unvanquished** (novel)	Random House 1938	**H**
	Chatto & Windus 1938	**E**
15 **The Wild Palms** (stories)	Random House 1939	**H**
	Chatto & Windus 1939	**E**
16 **The Hamlet** (novel)	Random House 1940	**G**
	Chatto & Windus 1940	**E**
17 **Go Down, Moses** (novel)	Random House 1942	**G**
	Chatto & Windus 1942	**D**
18 **Intruder in the Dust** (novel)	Random House 1948	**G**
	Chatto & Windus 1949	**D**
19 **Knight's Gambit** (stories)	Random House 1949	**G**
	Chatto & Windus 1951	**D**
20 **Collected Stories**	Random House 1950	**E**
	Chatto & Windus 1951	**C**
21 **Requiem for a Nun** (novel)	Random House 1951	**E**
	Chatto & Windus 1953	**C**
22 **A Fable** (novel)	Random House 1954	**D**
	Chatto & Windus 1954	**B**
23 **Faulkner's Country** (stories)	Chatto & Windus 1955	**B**
24 **The Town** (novel)	Random House 1957	**E**
	Chatto & Windus 1958	**C**
25 **New Orleans Sketches**	Rutgers University Press 1958	**D**
	Sidgwick & Jackson 1959	**C**

26 **The Collected Stories** (3 vols)	Chatto & Windus 1958	**D**
27 **The Mansion** (novel)	Random House 1959	**D**
With 16 and 24, this forms a trilogy.	Chatto & Windus 1960	**C**
28 **The Reivers** (novel)	Random House 1962	**D**
	Chatto & Windus 1962	**C**
29 **Selected Short Stories**	Random House 1962	**C**
30 **Early Prose and Poetry**	Little Brown 1962	**C**
	Cape 1962	**C**
31 **Essays, Speeches, and Public**	Random House 1966	**B**
Letters	Chatto & Windus 1966	**B**

Films:
The Story of Temple Drake (*Sanctuary*) Paramount 1933
Intruder in the Dust MGM 1949 **The Long, Hot Summer** (*The Hamlet*) 20th Century Fox 1957 **The Tarnished Angels** (*Pylon*) United Artists 1957 **The Sound and the Fury** 20th Century Fox 1959 **Sanctuary** (based on *Requiem for a Nun* and *Sanctuary*) 20th Century Fox 1960 **The Reivers** Warner Bros 1969

Biography:
Joseph Blotner **Faulkner: A Biography** (2 vols) Chatto & Windus 1974

Ferlinghetti, Lawrence   Born in Yonkers, New York, 1919.

Not seriously collected in Britain, largely because so very few of his books have been published in the U.K., and hence the body of his work is very hard to come by. The Beats, however, have been revived by the younger generation.

1 **Pictures of the Gone World** (verse)	City Lights (San Francisco) 1955	**F**
2 **A Coney Island of the Mind** (verse)	New Directions (NY) 1958	**E**
3 **Tentative Description of a Dinner Given to Promote the Impeachment of President Eisenhower** (verse)	Golden Mountain (San Francisco) 1958	**C**
4 **Her** (novel)	New Directions 1960	**C**
	MacGibbon & Kee 1966	**B**
5 **One Thousand Fearful Words for Fidel Castro** (verse)	City Lights 1961	**C**
6 **Berlin** (verse)	Golden Mountain 1961	**C**
7 **Starting From San Francisco: Poems**	New Directions 1961	**C**
8 **Penguin Modern Poets** 5	Penguin 1963	**A**
With Allen Ginsberg and Gregory Corso.		

9 **Unfair Arguments with Existence** (plays) Incl. **The Soldiers of No Country, Three Thousand Red Ants, The Alligation, The Victims of Amnesia, Motherlode, The Customs Collector in Baggy Pants, The Nose of Sisyphus.**	New Directions 1963	**C**
10 **Routines** (plays)	New Directions 1964	**B**
11 **Where Is Vietnam?** (verse)	City Lights 1965	**B**
12 **To Fuck is to Love Again; Kyrie Eleison Kerista** (verse)	Fuck You Press (NY) 1965	**C**
13 **An Eye on the World: Selected Poems**	MacGibbon & Kee 1967	**B**
14 **After the Cry of the Birds** (verse)	Haslewood (San Francisco) 1967	**B**
15 **Moscow in the Wilderness, Segovia in the Snow** (verse)	Beach (San Francisco) 1967	**B**
16 **The Secret meaning of Things** (verse)	New Directions 1969	**B**
17 **Tyrannus Nix?** (verse)	New Directions 1969	**B**
18 **The Mexican Night** (travel)	New Directions 1970	**B**
19 **Back Roads to Far Places** (verse)	New Directions 1971	**B**
20 **Open Eye, Open Heart** (verse)	New Directions 1973	**B**
21 **Director of Alienation** (verse)	Main Street (US) 1976	**B**
22 **Who are We Now?** (verse)	New Directions 1976	**B**
23 **Northwest Ecolog** (verse)	City Lights 1978	**B**
24 **Landscapes of Living and Dying** (verse)	New Directions 1979	**B**
25 **Endless Life: Selected Poems**	New Directions 1981	**B**
26 **A Trip to Italy and France** (verse)	New Directions 1981	**B**

Ferlinghetti has also edited several works, and has translated Jacques Prévert **Selections from Paroles** City Lights 1958; Penguin 1963 (**B**).

Firbank, Ronald Born in London, 1886. Died 1926.

Had Firbank been born earlier, he most certainly would have been with Wilde and the Aesthetes. Osbert Sitwell tells us that Firbank wrote his books not in an exercise book, not on loose leaves, but upon an interminable succession of azure blue postcards. Any man so disposed would have been at no loss as to what he might do with a green carnation.

1 **Odette d'Antrevernes and A Study in Temperament** (stories)	Elkin Mathews 1905	**J**

Firbank

2	**Vainglory** (novel) Frontis. by Felicien Rops.	Grant Richards 1915	H
3	**Odette** (same as in 1)	Grant Richards 1916	F
4	**Inclinations**	Grant Richards 1916	H
5	**Caprice** Frontis. by Augustus John.	Grant Richards 1917	H
6	**Valmouth: A Romantic Novel** Frontis. by Augustus John.	Grant Richards 1919	H
7	**The Princess Zoubaroff: A Comedy**	Grant Richards 1920	H
8	**Santal** (story)	Grant Richards 1921	H
9	**The Flower Beneath the Foot** (biog.) Portraits by Augustus John and Wyndham Lewis.	Grant Richards 1923	G
10	**Prancing Nigger** (novel)	Brentano's (NY) 1924	I
11	**Sorrow in Sunlight** (same as 10)	Brentano's (UK) 1925	G
12	**Concerning the Eccentricities of** **Cardinal Pirelli** (novel) Portrait by Augustus John.	Grant Richards 1926	G
13	**The Artificial Princess** (novel)	Duckworth 1934	G

Details of the works may be found in: M.J. Benkowitz **A Bibliography of Ronald Firbank** Soho Bibliographies, Hart-Davis 1963   Brigid Brophy **Prancing Novelist: A Defence of Fiction in the Form of a Critical Biography in Praise of Ronald Firbank** Cape 1972; Barnes & Noble 1973.

Two of the several collected editions are: **The Collected Works of Ronald Firbank** (6 vols) Duckworth 1929. Intro. by Arthur Waley, with an essay by Osbert Sitwell   **Five Novels** (6, 10, 9, 13 and 12) Duckworth 1949. Intro. by Osbert Sitwell, portrait by Augustus John.

Fitzgerald, F. Scott   Born in Minnesota, 1896. Died 1940.

Admired in Britain, deified in the United States, and always remembered for *The Great Gatsby*, possibly his most *English* book. Certainly the elegant lushness recalls Waugh to me, and the very lavish film serves to crystallize various images – primarily, I think, that never-to-be-forgotten and delicious cascade of Turnbull & Asher shirts.

Collected editions and anthologies have been omitted.

1	**This Side of Paradise** (novel)	Scribner 1920	Q
		Grey Walls Press 1948	G
2	**Flappers and Philosophers** (stories)	Scribner 1920 Collins 1922	M J
3	**The Beautiful and Damned** (novel)	Scribner 1922 Collins 1922	K I
4	**Tales of the Jazz Age** (stories)	Scribner 1922 Collins 1923	I G

5 **The Great Gatsby** (novel)	Scribner 1925	M
	Chatto & Windus 1925	J
6 **All the Sad Young Men** (stories)	Scribner 1926	I
7 **John Jackson's Arcady** (stories)	Baker (NY) 1928	I
8 **Tender is the Night** (novel)	Scribner 1934	H
	Chatto & Windus 1934	G
9 **Taps at Reveille** (stories)	Scribner 1935	G
10 **The Last Tycoon** (unfinished novel)	Scribner 1941	H
	Grey Walls Press 1949	E
11 **The Crack-Up** (letters and essays)	New Directions 1945	E
	Grey Walls Press 1947	C
12 **Afternoon of an Author** (stories)	Scribner 1957	D
	Bodley Head 1958	C

Films:
The Great Gatsby Paramount 1949; Paramount 1974   **The Last Time I Saw Paris** MGM 1954 (*Babylon Revisited*: story) **Tender is the Night** 20th Century Fox 1962   **The Last Tycoon** Paramount 1976

Bibliography:
Charles E. Shane **Scott Fitzgerald** University of Minnesota American Authors Pamphlet

---

Fitzgerald, Penelope   Born in Lincoln, 1916.

Still a largely unrecognized writer, despite her having won several literary prizes, including the Booker. The novels should not be too hard to gather, but her first two books – both biographies – could be elusive. Unusual for a novelist to commence his or her writing career with non-fiction, but there is a notable precedent in Muriel Spark.

1 **Edward Burne-Jones: A Biography**	Joseph 1975	C
2 **The Knox Brothers** (biography)	Macmillan 1977	C
	Coward McCann 1977	C
3 **The Golden Child** (novel)	Duckworth 1977	C
	Scribner 1978	B
4 **The Bookshop** (novel)	Duckworth 1978	B
5 **Offshore** (novel)	Collins 1979	B
6 **Human Voices** (novel)	Collins 1980	B
7 **At Freddie's** (novel)	Collins 1982	B
	Godine 1983	B

Fleming, Ian   Born in London, 1908. Died 1964.

When I published *Collecting Modern First Editions* in 1977, I was aware of a slight air of disapproval in some quarters that I had seen fit to include (and at length, to boot) such popular authors as Fleming, Christie, Wodehouse, Deighton, etc. The collecting of modern first editions, it was felt then, should be a rather serious pursuit, concerned solely with the acquisition of lasting, serious fiction, and not at all with the business of gathering up all the latest fads, which any book loosely branded 'entertainment' was seen to be. And this view, I am delighted to report, is now seen to be hooey. The explosion of interest in our more popular writers – along with the commensurate and astonishing rises in values – surprised me only by its intensity, not by its coming. The truth is, of course, that all these people could really *write*; the fact that they chose to wield their art in order to thrill you, hold you in suspense or make you laugh in no way diminishes their capabilities. The trouble is, from the collector's point of view, that in 1977 few could believe that a secondhand James Bond book could have any value, whereas now the Bond books (and particularly *Casino Royale*) are *famous* for being hugely rare and expensive – so much so that people now have a rather too inflated idea of their value. True, *Casino Royale* remains a scarce and desirable book, but it is *not* worth £2000, as everyone seems to think it is. (This is because of an auction record of this figure reached last year for a copy inscribed by Fleming to his secretary whom apparently – it is almost too poetically splendid to record – he addressed as 'M'). Prices have risen dramatically, though, and show every indication of continuing to do so, not least because of vast interest in America, for although they were always keen, it would appear now that Sherlock Holmes shares his throne with Bond. Or Band, as they insist on saying.

Quite a lot has happened on the James Bond front. *Goldfinger* was included in Anthony Burgess's '99 Best Novels' – a highly suitable accolade, as Fleming's contemporaries and fellow writers have long appreciated his talent. Personally, I should have selected *Casino Royale* as the best novel, but *From Russia, with Love* as the best Bond book, which is not the same thing. The Bond phenomenon is always in the news, and the momentum of the films, together with the ersatz Gardner-Bonds, will ensure that the machine keeps on turning.

1 **Casino Royale** (Bond novel)	Cape 1953	**Q**
Black boards, as are all the Bond books, with red heart motif. Grey (gunmetal?) d/w, repeating heart motif, devised by I.F. This is the very first appearance of Bond, and it is very, very scarce. 4750 copies were printed of the 1st edition, many of these going to public libraries.	Macmillan 1954	**I**

2 **Live and Let Die** (Bond novel) Medallion motif on boards. Scarlet d/w with yellow lettering, devised by I.F. Very difficult.	Cape 1954 Macmillan 1955	**N** **H**
3 **Moonraker** (Bond novel) Silver titling on boards, yellow and orange flame design on d/w, with black lettering, devised by I.F. Very difficult.	Cape 1955 Macmillan 1955	**I** **F**
4 **Diamonds Are Forever** (Bond novel) Blind-stamped diamond-pane motif on boards. Black, tank, pink and white d/w lettered in black and white.	Cape 1956 Macmillan 1956	**G** **D**
5 **From Russia, with Love** (Bond novel) Gun and rose motif on boards, repeated on the superb Chopping d/w, depicting a sawn-off Smith and Wesson and a red rose against a pale wood ground. The famous stencil lettering appears to be inked onto the wood, but beneath the rose stem. This is the first of Richard Chopping's *trompe l'oeuil* d/ws, which continued, with the exception of 7, to the end of the Bond saga.	Cape 1957 Macmillan 1957	**G** **D**
6 **The Diamond Smugglers** (non-fiction) Black boards, red, black and grey d/w. Quite scarce.	Cape 1957 Macmillan 1958	**E** **C**
7 **Dr No** (Bond novel) Brown and black d/w with a girl's silhouette, repeated on boards. One feels Cape might have compared this d/w with that of 5, and recalled Chopping quickly!	Cape 1958 Macmillan 1958	**F** **C**
8 **Goldfinger** (Bond novel) Skull motif with gold coins on boards, repeated on Chopping d/w.	Cape 1959 Macmillan 1959	**E** **C**
9 **For Your Eyes Only** (Bond stories) Matisse-like eye motif on boards. Chopping d/w.	Cape 1960 Viking 1960	**E** **C**
10 **Thunderball** (Bond novel) Blind-stamped skeletal hand motif, repeated on Chopping d/w.	Cape 1961 Viking Press 1961	**C** **B**
11 **The Spy Who Loved Me** (Bond novel) Silver dagger motif on boards, repeated on Chopping d/w. t/p reads: by Ian Fleming with Vivienne Michel. This is	Cape 1962 Viking 1962	**C** **B**

not a genuine collaboration: Fleming
wrote this novel as Vivienne Michel in
the first person. Hence, the 'Spy' in the
title is none other than 007.

12	**On Her Majesty's Secret Service** (Bond novel)	Cape 1963 NAL 1963	**B** **A**

White gunsmoke motif on boards.
Chopping d/w.

12a	**On Her Majesty's Secret Service** (ltd ed.)	Cape 1963	**P**

Same motif on black boards, as in 12,
but with white vellum spine. Coloured
frontis. portrait of I.F. by Amherst
Villiers. t/p printed in red and black.
Verso of t/p reads: 'This special edition
is limited to 250 numbered copies only
for sale, each signed by the author.
Copy number . . .', followed by IF.'s
signature. As is apparent from the
limitation, this book is very, very
scarce.

13	**Thrilling Cities** (non-fiction)	Cape 1963 NAL 1964	**D** **C**

Grey mottled boards with white cloth
spine. Daliesque d/w by Paul Davis in
monochrome with shocking-pink spine
and lettering. Quite scarce.

14	**You Only Live Twice** (Bond novel)	Cape 1964 NAL 1964	**B** **C**

Chinese characters motif on boards.
Chopping d/w.

15	**Chitty-Chitty-Bang-Bang** (juveniles)	Cape 1964–5 (individually) (set) Random House 1964	**E** **I** **E–I**

There are three of these books, all
admirably illustrated by John
Burningham. The pictorial boards are
also by Burningham, the identical
designs being reproduced on the
laminated d/ws. The first has
'Adventure Number 1' within a red
disc on the cover (1964), the second
(1964) bears a turquoise disc reading
'Adventure Number 2', and the third
(1965) had Adventure Number 3 on a
lilac disc. They are very difficult,
particularly in fine condition – as is the
case with all children's books.

16	**The Man with the Golden Gun** (Bond novel)	Cape 1965 NAL 1965	**B** **A**

The only Bond to lack a motif on the
boards. The blurbs, which used to be

very newsy, have grown simpler now.
This one reads: The New James Bond.
Enough said. Chopping d/w.

17 **Ian Fleming Introduces Jamaica**   Deutsch 1965   **C**
(non-fiction)   Hawthorne 1965   **B**
Rust cloth, laminated photographic
d/w. Despite the two-inch-high
lettering of 'Ian Fleming' on the d/w, it
contains only an 11-page Intro. by him.
Nonetheless, a handsome book, with
many fine coloured photographs. The
second impression was remaindered,
but the 1st remains elusive.

18 **Octopussy** and **The Living**   Cape 1966   **B**
Daylights (Bond stories)   NAL 1966   **A**
Intended to be a sequel (i.e. a book of
short stories) to 9, but sadly, Fleming
died having completed only these two.
Chopping d/w.

In addition, there are the following
James Bond books NOT written by Ian
Fleming:

Robert Markham (Kingsley Amis)	Cape 1968	C
Colonel Sun	Harper 1968	B
John Gardner **Licence Renewed**	Putnam 1981	B
	Cape/Hodder 1981	A
John Gardner **For Special Services**	Coward McCann 1982	B
	Cape/Hodder 1982	A
John Gardner **Icebreaker**	Putnam 1983	B
	Cape/Hodder 1983	A
John Gardner **Role of Honour**	Putnam 1984	B
	Cape/Hodder 1984	A

Fleming's first appearance in print was   Cassell 1950   **D**
a contribution to **The Kemsley**
Manual of Journalism entitled
'Foreign News'

A James Bond story (*The Property of a*
Lady) appeared in **The Ivory**
Hammer: The Year at Sotheby's
Longman 1963

Fleming wrote introductions to the
following, all of which are scarce:
Herbert O. Yardley **The Education of**   Cape 1959   **F**
a Poker Player

Fleming

Donald Fish **Airline Detective**	Collins 1962	G
Hugh Edwards **All Night at Mr Stanyhurst's**	Cape 1963	E

Another item of interest to collectors:

Iain Campbell **Ian Fleming: A Catalogue of a Collection**	B

This is termed a preliminary to a bibliography, and is published by the author.

The essential sourcework on Fleming is still:

John Pearson **The Life of Ian Fleming**	Cape 1966	B
	McGraw Hill 1966	B

Pearson has also written the amusing, and very convincing:

James Bond: The Authorized Biography	Sidgwick & Jackson 1973	B
	Morrow 1973	B

Several books have been written about Bond, though the best is:

Kingsley Amis **The James Bond Dossier**	Cape 1965	C
	NAL 1965	B

Films:
Dr No United Artists 1962 **From Russia, with Love** United Artists 1963 **Goldfinger** United Artists 1963 **Thunderball** United Artists 1964 **You Only Live Twice** United Artists 1966 **Casino Royale** Columbia 1966 **Chitty-Chitty-Bang-Bang** United Artists 1968 **On Her Majesty's Secret Service** United Artists 1969 **Diamonds Are Forever** United Artists 1971 **Live and Let Die** United Artists 1974 **The Man with the Golden Gun** United Artists 1974 **The Spy Who Loved Me** United Artists 1977 **Moonraker** United Artists 1979 **For Your Eyes Only** United Artists 1981 **Octopussy** United Artists 1983 Also **Never Say Never Again**, based on *Thunderball*, 1983

Forester, C.S. Born in Cairo, 1899. Died 1966.

Apart from the Hornblower series, listed below, Forester is best remembered for *The African Queen*, everyone having seen the film and few realizing that Forester wrote it. One always recalls Bogart dragging that boat through the filthy swamp – two of the most disgusting moments being when he emerges from the silage covered in leeches, and when a still evangelical Katherine Hepburn pours all that whisky over the side. Horrific.

1	**A Pawn Among Kings** (novel)	Methuen 1924	H
	This is his first book. Scarce.		
2	**The African Queen** (novel)	Little Brown 1935	E
	Not a title always associated with	Heinemann 1935	D
	Forester, but a highlight of his work.		

Herewith follows the Hornblower
series, in entirety, but omitting
collections, anthologies, Omnibus
volumes and extracts – of which there
seem to have been an amazing number.

3	**Beat to Quarters**	Little Brown 1937	E
4	**The Happy Return**	Joseph 1937	D
	(same as 3)		
5	**A Ship of the Line**	Little Brown 1938	E
		Joseph 1938	D
6	**Flying Colours**	Little Brown 1938	E
		Joseph 1938	D
7	**To the Indies**	Little Brown 1940	D
8	**The Earthly Paradise**	Joseph 1940	C
	(same as 7)		
9	**Commodore Hornblower**	Little Brown 1945	D
10	**The Commodore** (same as 9)	Joseph 1945	C
11	**Lord Hornblower**	Little Brown 1946	C
		Joseph 1946	C
12	**Mr Midshipman Hornblower**	Little Brown 1950	C
		Joseph 1950	C
13	**Lieutenant Hornblower**	Grosset (NY) 1952	C
		Joseph 1952	B
14	**Hornblower and the Atropos**	Little Brown 1953	C
		Joseph 1953	B
15	**Admiral Hornblower in the West Indies**	Little Brown 1958	C
16	**Hornblower in the West Indies**	Joseph 1958	C
	(same as 15)		
17	**Hornblower and the Hotspur**	Little Brown 1962	C
		Joseph 1962	B
18	**Captain Hornblower R.N.**	Joseph 1965	C

Films:
The African Queen Romulus 1951   **Captain Hornblower RN**
Warner Bros 1951

Forster, E.M.   Born in London, 1879. Died 1970.

Although *A Passage to India* retains a secure place as a classic – as does, to a slightly lesser extent, *Howard's End* – Forster is now quite as famous for having been an artistically repressed homosexual, having endlessly and puzzlingly referred to 'personal relationships' in his books, feeling unable to be frank. The publication of *Maurice* in 1971 (the year after his death) made things clearer, but it seems extraordinary now that such a book should have been (voluntarily) suppressed for fifty-seven years after it was written. Unlike many such books, though, it does not end in sourness and despair, but happily – even in triumph.

1 **Where Angels Fear to Tread** (novel)	Blackwood 1905	M
	Knopf 1920	H
2 **The Longest Journey** (novel)	Blackwood 1907	K
	Knopf 1922	G
3 **A Room with a View** (novel)	Arnold 1908	J
	Putnam 1911	H
4 **Howard's End** (novel)	Arnold 1910	I
	Putnam 1910	G
5 **The Celestial Omnibus** (stories)	Sidgwick & Jackson 1911	H
	Knopf 1923	D
6 **The Story of the Siren**	Hogarth Press 1920	G
7 **Egypt** (non-fiction)	Labour Research Dept. 1920	H
8 **Alexandria** (history)	Whitehead Morris 1922	I
	Doubleday 1961	B
9 **Pharos and Pharillon** (essays)	Hogarth Press 1923	G
	Knopf 1923	D
10 **A Passage to India** (novel)	Arnold 1924	K
	Harcourt Brace 1924	H
11 **Anonymity** (essay)	Hogarth Press 1925	D
12 **Aspects of the Novel** (prose)	Arnold 1927	C
	Harcourt Brace 1927	B
13 **The Eternal Moment** (stories)	Sidgwick & Jackson 1928	D
	Harcourt Brace 1928	C
14 **A Letter to Madan Blanchard** (essay)	Hogarth Press 1931	B
	Harcourt Brace 1932	A
15 **Goldsworthy Lowes Dickinson**	Arnold 1934	B
	Harcourt Brace 1934	A
16 **Abinger Harvest** (essays)	Arnold 1936	C
	Harcourt Brace 1936	B
17 **What I Believe** (essay)	Hogarth Press 1939	B

18 **Reading as Usual** (lecture)	Tottenham Public Libraries 1939	B
19 **England's Pleasant Land** (prose)	Hogarth Press 1940	C
20 **Nordic Twilight** (essay)	Macmillan 1940	C
21 **Virginia Woolf** (lecture)	CUP 1942	D
	Harcourt Brace 1942	C
22 **The Development of English Prose** (lecture)	Jackson (Glasgow) 1945	D
23 **The Collected Tales**	Knopf 1947	C
24 **Collected Short Stories** (same as 23)	Sidgwick & Jackson 1948	C
25 **Two Cheers for Democracy** (essays)	Arnold 1951	B
	Harcourt Brace 1951	B
26 **Billy Budd** (libretto for Britten's opera)	Boosey & Hawkes 1951	C
27 **The Hill of Devi**	Arnold 1953	B
	Harcourt Brace 1953	B
28 **Marianne Thornton** (biography)	Arnold 1956	B
	Harcourt Brace 1956	B
29 **Maurice** (novel)	Arnold 1971	B
	Norton 1971	B
30 **The Life to Come** (stories)	Arnold 1972	B
	Norton 1973	B
31 **Selected Letters** (Volume 1)	Collins 1983	C
	Harvard University Press 1983	C
32 **Selected Letters** (Volume 2)	Collins 1984	C
	Harvard University Press 1984	C

There is now a standard, authorized biography: P.N. Furbank **E.M. Forster: A Life** (2 vols) Secker & Warburg 1977, 1978
Further bibliographical details may be found in: B.J. Kirkpatrick **A Bibliography of E.M. Forster** Soho bibliographies, Hart-Davis 1968

Forsyth, Frederick Born in England, 1939.

The sort of author they call 'bankable'. He has still only written four novels, but each of them has been a smash. He is collected, but everyone seems to have everything except maybe *The Day of the Jackal*, which is sought after with enthusiasm, and *The Biafra Story*, which is sought after with extreme reluctance; it is his first book, so what can you do? But no Forsyth fan would consider actually *reading* the thing.

1 **The Biafra Story** (non-fiction)	Penguin 1969	E
2 **The Day of the Jackal** (novel)	Hutchinson 1971	F
	Viking 1971	D

Forsyth

3	**The Odessa File** (novel)	Hutchinson 1972	C
		Viking 1972	B
4	**The Dogs of War** (novel)	Hutchinson 1974	B
		Viking 1974	B
5	**The Shepherd** (story)	Hutchinson 1975	A
		Viking 1976	A
6	**The Novels of Frederick Forsyth**	Hutchinson 1978	B
	Includes 2, 3 and 4.		
7	**The Devil's Alternative** (novel)	Hutchinson 1979	A
		Viking 1980	A
8	**No Comebacks** (stories)	Hutchinson 1982	A
		Viking 1982	A
9	**The Four Novels of Frederick Forsyth**	Hutchinson 1982	B
	Includes 2, 3, 4 and 7, together with a new intro.		

Films:
The Day of the Jackal Universal 1972   **The Odessa File** Columbia 1974   **The Dogs of War** United Artists 1980

Fowles, John   Born in Essex, 1926.

Fowles's reputation is secure, despite the publication of *Mantissa*, still largely due to *The Magus* and *The French Lieutenant's Woman* – the respect for the latter yet further enhanced by the recent and splendid film version, which succeeded with the apparently impossible – thanks in large part, of course, to Harold Pinter's screenplay. Prices for the known highlights continue to be very steep, but what can often dog a collection is the failure to secure *at the time* these photograph books that he has lately been given to publishing. They vanish so quickly, I can only assume that the print runs are low.

1	**The Collector** (novel)	Cape 1963	M
	Very distinctive in its 'Chopping-style' d/w by Tom Adams, which was used for both the English and American editions. It is interesting to note that the advance proof of the Cape edition was issued in the d/w, though in place of the quotation on the rear, there is an announcement of the sale of film rights, and that it has been 'sold to Little Brown . . . for a very big advance'. This on the proof of a yet-unpublished first novel! It is scarce, and getting more scarce each year.	Little Brown 1963	I

2 **The Aristos**   Little Brown 1964   **L**
Although the American edition   Cape 1965   **L**
precedes, either is desirable, and very
difficult. It is worth noting that the Pan
paperback edition (1968, **D**) is not a
straight reprint, but 'specially revised
for Pan by the author', and has a new
preface. This preface begins: 'This book
was first published against the advice of
almost everyone who read it. I was told
it would do my "image" no good.'

3 **The Magus** (novel)   Cape 1966   **G**
Another very fine d/w by Tom Adams   Little Brown 1966   **F**
for Fowles' longest book. Although it
used to be quite common, it is
becoming less so. A revised and
supplemented edition was published by
Cape in 1977 (**C**). In the seventies
Fowles signed quite a large number of
second impressions for the New Fiction
Society(**C**).

4 **The French Lieutenant's Woman**   Cape 1969   **F–G**
(novel)   Little Brown 1969   **F–G**
Superb d/w of gold engraved letters on
a claret stippled ground. Although
quite recent, quite elusive.

5 S. Baring-Gould **Mehalah**   Chatto & Windus 1969   **D**
Fowles wrote the Introduction to this
Landmark Library reissue.

6 **Poems**   Ecco Press (NY) 1973   **C**
Not published in England.

7 Sir A. Conan Doyle **The Hound of**   Murray/Cape 1974   **B**
the Baskervilles
Fowles wrote the Introduction to this
volume of the Collected Edition of
Sherlock Holmes.

8 Perrault **Cinderella**   Cape 1974   **E**
A large-format, thin shiny book,   Little Brown 1975   **E**
published in Britain at the very low
price of £1.25. Fowles translated the
original of 1697, and Sheilah Beckett
illustrated it.

9 **The Ebony Tower** (novellas)   Cape 1974   **D**
Handsome green d/w, the typography   Little Brown 1974   **C**
reminiscent of 4. This was reprinted
very quickly.

10 **Shipwreck** A slim, landscape volume of photographs of shipwrecks, with text by Fowles.	Cape 1974 Little Brown 1975	D C
11 **The Magus** (revised edition) 'This is not,' says Fowles, 'in any thematic sense, a new version of *The Magus*. It is rather more than a stylistic revision.' Purple and gold d/w reminiscent of 4.	Cape 1977 Little Brown 1977	C B
12 **Daniel Martin** (novel) A massive novel – the first for eight years. Green and gold d/w, similar in design to 11.	Cape 1977 Little Brown 1977	C B
13 **Islands** A landscape book of photographs by Fay Godwin, with a text by Fowles.	Cape 1978 Little Brown 1978	B B
14 **Conditional** A book of verse from a private press. Not published in UK.	Lord John Press (California) 1979	E
15 **The Tree** Another book of photographs (by Frank Horvat), the subject matter self- explanatory.	Aurum Press 1979 Little Brown 1979	B B
16 **The Enigma of Stonehenge** More photographs, this time by Barry Brukoff.	Cape 1980 Summit 1980	B B
17 **The Screenplay of the French Lieutenant's Woman** by Harold Pinter Fowles contributes a nine-page foreword.	Cape 1981 Little Brown 1981	B B
18 **Mantissa** (novel) A slight novel representing – shall we say? – a departure.	Cape 1982 Little Brown 1982	B B

An interview with John Fowles was included in Roy Newquist (ed.)
Counterpoint Allen & Unwin 1965, and one book has been written
about him: William J. Palmer **The Fiction of John Fowles** University
of Missouri Press (Columbia) 1974

Films:
The Collector British Lion 1964   **The Magus** 20th Century Fox
1969   **The French Lieutenant's Woman**   United Artists 1981

Francis, Dick   Born in Pembrokeshire, 1920.

Every single autumn, a new Dick Francis; every single autumn, a smash bestseller. Francis writes extremely well, and will soon, I think, feature on one or other of these interminable best of British something or others, for he really is several cuts above the run-of-the-mill thriller writer. This seems to have been appreciated by collectors for years, for the early titles remain obnoxiously stubborn; they simply *refuse* to be found.

1	**The Sport of Queens: The**	Joseph 1957	G
	Autobiography of Dick Francis	Harper 1969	D
2	**Dead Cert** (novel)	Joseph 1962	G
		Holt Rinehart 1962	D
3	**Nerve** (novel)	Joseph 1964	D
		Harper 1964	C
4	**For Kicks** (novel)	Joseph 1965	D
		Harper 1965	C
5	**Odds Against** (novel)	Joseph 1965	C
		Harper 1966	B
6	**Flying Finish** (novel)	Joseph 1966	C
		Harper 1967	B
7	**Blood Sport** (novel)	Joseph 1967	C
		Harper 1968	B
8	**Forfeit** (novel)	Joseph 1968	C
		Harper 1969	B
9	**Enquiry** (novel)	Joseph 1969	C
		Harper 1969	B
10	**Rat Race** (novel)	Joseph 1970	C
		Harper 1971	B
11	**Bonecrack** (novel)	Joseph 1971	B
		Harper 1972	A
12	**Smokescreen** (novel)	Joseph 1972	B
		Harper 1972	A
13	**Slay-Ride** (novel)	Joseph 1973	B
		Harper 1974	A
14	**Knock-Down** (novel)	Joseph 1974	B
		Harper 1975	A
15	**Across the Board**	Harper 1975	B
	(incl. 6, 7 and 9).		
16	**High Stakes** (novel)	Joseph 1975	B
		Harper 1976	A
17	**In the Frame** (novel)	Joseph 1976	B
		Harper 1977	A
18	**Risk** (novel)	Joseph 1977	B
		Harper 1978	A
19	**Trial Run** (novel)	Joseph 1978	B
		Harper 1979	A

Francis

20	**Whip Hand** (novel)	Joseph 1979	B
		Harper 1980	A
21	**Reflex** (novel)	Joseph 1980	B
		Putnam 1981	B
22	**Twice Shy** (novel)	Joseph 1981	B
		Putnam 1982	B
23	**Banker** (novel)	Joseph 1982	B
		Putnam 1983	B
24	**The Danger** (novel)	Joseph 1983	B
		Putnam 1984	B

Film:
Dead Cert United Artists 1974

Fraser, George Macdonald   Born in Carlisle, 1925.

Although his books – and in particular his *Flashman* books – sell very well on publication and in paperback, Fraser seems to be underrated by collectors (as opposed to *just* readers) and hence the books – although not common – are low in price. They are great fun, these *Flashman* books – and anyway, an author who can make a hero (kind of) out of the school bully in an essentially sentimental children's classic deserves considerable investigation.

Fraser has published four books in addition to the *Flashman* series listed below: *The General Danced at Dawn* (1970), *The Steel Bonnets* (non-fiction 1971), *McAuslan in the Rough* (1974) and *Mr American* (1980).

1	**Flashman** (novel)	Barrie & Jenkins 1969	C
2	**Royal Flash** (novel)	Barrie & Jenkins 1970	B
3	**Flash for Freedom** (novel)	Barrie & Jenkins 1971	B
4	**Flashman at the Charge** (novel)	Barrie & Jenkins 1973	B
5	**Flashman in the Great Game** (novel)	Barrie & Jenkins 1975	B
6	**Flashman's Lady** (novel)	Barrie & Jenkins 1977	A
7	**Flashman and the Redskins** (novel)	Collins 1982	A

Film:
Royal Flash Fox-Rank 1976

Frayn, Michael   Born in London, 1933.

Much loved by his peers, and a very well known name, but perhaps still underrated by the collectors. Not easy to find, of course, and the journalism and fiction is more sought after (and more elusive) than the plays.

1	**The Day of the Dog** (articles)	Collins 1962	B
		Doubleday 1963	A

2 **The Book of Fub** (articles)	Collins 1963	B
3 **Never Put Off to Gomorrah** (same as 2)	Pantheon (NY) 1964	A
4 **On the Outskirts** (articles)	Collins 1964	B
5 **The Tin Men** (novel)	Collins 1965	C
	Little Brown 1966	B
6 **The Russian Interpreter** (novel)	Collins 1966	C
	Viking 1966	B
7 **Towards the End of Morning** (novel)	Collins 1967	B
8 **Against Entropy** (same as 7)	Viking 1967	A
9 **At Bay in Gear Street** (articles)	Fontana 1967	A
10 **A Very Private Life** (novel)	Collins 1968	B
	Viking 1968	A
11 **The Two of Us** (play)	Fontana 1970	A
12 **Sweet Dreams** (novel)	Collins 1974	A
	Viking 1974	A
13 **Constructions** (philosophy)	Wildwood House 1974	A
14 **Alphabetical Order, Donkey's Years and Clouds** (plays)	Eyre Methuen 1977	A
15 **The Cherry Orchard** (play) Adaptation from Chekhov.	Eyre Methuen 1978	A
16 **The Fruits of Enlightenment** (play) Adaptation from Tolstoy.	Eyre Methuen 1979	A
17 **Make and Break** (play)	Eyre Methuen 1980	A
18 **Noises Off** (play)	Methuen 1982	A
19 **Benefactors** (play)	Methuen 1984	A

Frost, Robert   Born in San Francisco, 1874. Died 1963.

Frost is still the Grand Old Man of American poetry, and hugely respected and collected in that country. I am aware of few collectors in Britain – and indeed, it must be admitted that assembling Frost in any quantity here has never been an easy task, as so much was published only in America, and even then in limited and private press editions. In recognition of Frost's importance, however, there follows a listing of his commercially published works.

1 **A Boy's Will** (verse)	Holt 1913	J
2 **North of Boston** (verse)	Holt 1914	I
3 **Mountain Interval** (verse)	Holt 1916	H
4 **New Hampshire** (verse)	Holt 1923	F
5 **Selected Poems**	Heinemann 1923	D
6 **West-Running Brook** (verse)	Holt 1928	D
7 **Collected Poems**	Holt 1930	C
	Longman 1930	C
8 **The Lone Striker** (verse)	Holt 1933	C

9 **A Further Range** (verse)	Holt 1936	C
	Cape 1937	B
10 **From Snow to Snow** (verse)	Holt 1936	B
11 **A Witness Tree** (verse)	Holt 1942	B
	Cape 1943	B
12 **A Masque of Reason** (verse)	Holt 1945	B
	Cape 1948	B
13 **Steeple Bush** (verse)	Holt 1947	B
14 **A Masque of Mercy** (verse)	Holt 1947	B
15 **In the Clearing** (verse)	Holt (NY) 1962	B
	Holt (UK) 1962	B
16 **The Poetry of Robert Frost**	Holt 1969	B
	Cape 1971	B

In addition to 5, a further **Selected Poems** was published in England by Cape in 1936, with several introductory essays, including one by W.H. Auden. (**D**).
Very many of the above were issued simultaneously with a limited, signed edition, but the prices here refer to the ordinary trade editions.

Gibbons, Stella Born in London, 1902.

Although one has heard very little from her lately, Stella Gibbons is still alive and, as far as I know, well. She has published upwards of thirty books, but it is her first published novel for which she will always be remembered. Very, very scarce in first edition.

Cold Comfort Farm	Longman 1932	H
(novel)	Longman (US) 1933	E

Ginsberg, Allen Born in New Jersey, 1926.

Despite the resurgence of the Beats among the young, none of them is truly *collected* in this country, as they are in America. This is largely due to the old reason of availability, for during the sixties there were many more bookshops in London specializing in imported books (particularly American) than there are now. Ginsberg remains popular, though – the most popular of the Beats, probably – and there follows a selection of highlights.

1 **Howl and Other Poems**	City Lights 1956	G
Ginsberg's first book.		
2 **Kaddish and Other Poems**	City Lights 1961	D

3 **Penguin Modern Poets 5**   Penguin 1963   **A**
This book, shared with Gregory Corso
and Lawrence Ferlinghetti, established
the Beat Poets in this country.

Golding, William   Born in Cornwall, 1911.

Other than a knighthood, or the OM, it is difficult to imagine an accolade
that has not been heaped on to Mr Golding. He has now won the Booker
Prize and been awarded the Nobel Prize and seen *Lord of the Flies* placed high
on every single list yet compiled (and there have been many) of the best
novels of our time, Anthony Burgess including *The Spire* as well in his *99
Novels*.
   Golding certainly deserves it. Young collectors, though, might be
dismayed by it all, for although Golding has been collected for over twenty
years, it is only comparatively recently that prices have taken off, and one
would be very fortunate indeed these days to find a first of *Lord of the Flies* for
less than several hundred pounds, unless it was a wreck, and as for his 1934
Poems – it's worth its weight in rubies.

1 **Poems**   Macmillan 1934   **T**
Very, very scarce: one of these books   Macmillan (NY) 1935   **R**
that is worth what a collector is willing
to pay!

2 **Lord of the Flies** (novel)   Faber 1954   **Q**
Not only Golding's highlight, but one   Coward McCann 1955   **K**
of the key novels of recent years. It is a
small volume, with a d/w bearing fine
artwork and the magnificent Faber
Albertus type, as do most of his works.
It is very scarce. E.M. Forster singled it
out for special attention on publication,
and the second and third impressions
came swiftly. By now, the editions are
beyond count, and it has long been a
'set book' in schools. Very satisfying,
then, to have the 1st and, although it is
rising fast, any price is a good price, as
a collection of modern fiction would
never be complete without it.

3 **The Inheritors** (novel)   Faber 1955   **J**
Similar in format to 2. Quite scarce.   Harcourt Brace 1962   **C**

4 **Pincher Martin** (novel)   Faber 1956   **I**

5 **The Two Deaths of Christopher**   Harcourt Brace 1957   **F**
Martin (same as 4)

6 **The Brass Butterfly**   Faber 1958   **H**
(play)   NAL 1962   **C**

7 **Free Fall** (novel)	Faber 1959	**F**
	Harcourt Brace 1960	**C**
8 **The Spire** (novel)	Faber 1964	**E**
	Harcourt Brace 1965	**C**
9 **The Hot Gates** (occasional pieces)	Faber 1965	**E**
	Harcourt Brace 1965	**C**
10 **The Pyramid** (novel)	Faber 1967	**D**
	Harcourt Brace 1967	**C**
11 **The Scorpion God** (stories)	Faber 1971	**C**
One of the stories – *Envoy Extraordinary* –	Harcourt Brace 1972	**B**

One of the stories – *Envoy Extraordinary* – was first published in **Sometime, Never – Three Tales of Imagination** Eyre & Spottiswoode 1956; Ballantine 1956. (**I**)

12 **Darkness Visible** (novel)	Faber 1979	**C**
	Farrar Straus 1979	**B**
13 **Rites of Passage** (novel)	Faber 1980	**C**
	Farrar Straus 1980	**B**
14 **A Moving Target** (essays)	Faber 1982	**B**
	Farrar Straus 1982	**B**
15 **The Paper Men** (novel)	Faber 1984	**B**
	Farrar Straus 1984	**B**

Film:
Lord of the Flies British Lion 1963

There have been many books on the writings of Golding, and the following are recommended:
Bernard S. Oldsey and Stanley Weintraub **The Art of William Golding** Harcourt Brace 1965   Mark Kinkead-Weekes and Ian Gregor **William Golding: A Critical Study** Faber 1967   Leighton Hodson **Golding** Oliver & Boyd 1969

Grahame, Kenneth   Born in Edinburgh, 1859. Died 1932.

Grahame published few works, and three of the most notable – including the absolute highlight – are listed below.

1 **The Golden Age** (juvenile)	Lane 1895	**D**
	Stone & Kimball 1895	**D**
2 **Dream Days** (juvenile)	Lane 1898	**E**
	Lane (US) 1898	**D**
3 **The Wind in the Willows** (juvenile)	Methuen 1908	**H**
	Scribner 1908	**G**

The Wind in the Willows is the real highlight here, but as all the great illustrators have at one stage rendered their interpretations, these later editions often exceed the prices of the 1sts. For example, Lane published an edition of 1 in 1900 illustrated by Maxfield Parrish – very much in vogue at the moment. This would probably be Grade I now.

Films (cartoons):
The Reluctant Dragon (story) Disney 1941   **The Adventures of Ichabod and Mr Toad** Disney 1949 (based in part on *The Wind in the Willows*)

Grass, Günter   Born in Danzig, 1927.

I don't often list works that have first been published in a language other than English, but even in translation the author's first book is an important addition to a collection of modern fiction, and a desirable item.

The Tin Drum (novel)	Random House 1963	**E**
This was, of course, originally published	Secker & Warburg	**E**
in Germany as *Die Blechtrommel* in 1959.	1963	
The English language editions, however,		
are by no means common.		

Graves, Robert   Born in London, 1895.

Graves has been on this earth for close on ninety years, and has produced over one hundred and thirty books, less than half of them poetry. There must be collectors anxious to obtain every single item (there always are) but in my experience I find it is more usual for collectors to restrict themselves to just the areas of greatest interest to them – say, just the novels and maybe a *Collected Poems*, or so. Amongst the vast *œuvre*, there are a couple of highlights – very fine and very famous books (indeed, the first of these is *essential*) and these I find are usually the most wanted items. For the serious collector, however, I recommend: Fred H. Higginson *A Bibliography of the Works of Robert Graves* Vane 1966

1 **Good-bye to All That: An**	Cape 1929	**J–G**
Autobiography		(see below)
This is Graves' best-known work, though	Cape & Smith 1930	**G**
there is an important issue point which		
greatly affects the value. In the first issue		
(**J**), there is a long poem by Siegfried		
Sassoon, beginning on page 341. This is		
replaced in the second issue (**G**) by		
asterisks. The title pages are identical.		
Both, however, are very scarce in the		
d/w, which is a black-and-white		
montage of artwork and photographs.		

2 **I, Claudius** (novel)	Barker 1934	**F**
	Smith & Haas 1934	**D**
3 **Claudius the God** (novel)	Barker 1934	**D**
Sequel to 2.	Smith & Haas 1935	**C**

Although the prose works are the best
known, the poetry is very desirable –
particularly the very early books. Many
are called simply **Poems**, followed by
the relevant dates. The first was **Over
the Brazier** Poetry Bookshop 1916; the
seemingly definitive **Collected Poems
1975** was published by Cassell.

Green, Henry   Born in England, 1905. Died 1973.
Pseudonym for Henry Vincent Yorke.

Very sought after by collectors, and very elusive – almost impossible in dust-wrapper. Dust-wrappers are particularly important here, actually, as because all the books came from The Hogarth Press, the artists employed were of the calibre you might expect: Vanessa Bell, Lynton Lamb, John Piper, etc.

1 **Blindness** (novel)	Dutton 1926	**H**
	Dent 1926	**G**
2 **Living** (novel)	Dutton 1929	**G**
	Dent 1929	**F**
3 **Party Goff** (novel)	Hogarth Press 1939	**G**
	Longman (Toronto) 1939	**C**
4 **Pack My Bag** (autobiog.)	Hogarth Press 1940	**F**
	Macmillan (Toronto) 1940	**D**
5 **Caught** (novel)	Hogarth Press 1943	**E**
	Macmillan (Toronto) 1943	**D**
6 **Loving** (novel)	Hogarth Press 1945	**D**
	Macmillan (Toronto) 1945	**C**
7 **Back** (novel)	Hogarth Press 1946	**D**
	Oxford (Toronto) 1946	**C**
8 **Concluding** (novel)	Hogarth Press 1948	**D**
	Viking 1950	**C**
9 **Nothing** (novel)	Hogarth Press 1950	**C**
	Viking 1950	**B**
10 **Doting** (novel)	Hogarth Press 1952	**C**
	Viking 1952	**B**

Greene, Graham   Born in Hertfordshire, 1904.

Certainly one of the most collected authors in Britain today. I am convinced that new people must start collecting him every day, for even the usual recent titles go on selling within days of their being put out. It is easy to understand. Everyone enjoys reading Greene, everyone recognizes his status and importance, and one can fairly rapidly gather half his *œuvre* without declaring oneself a bankrupt. As for the other half . . .

1 **Babbling April: Poems**   Blackwell (Oxford)   **O**
  Of legendary scarcity, despite the fact   1925
  that it appears at sales not irregularly.
2 **The Man Within** (novel)   Heinemann 1929   **M**
  Very scarce, particularly in d/w.   Doubleday 1929   **J**
3 **The Name of Action** (novel)   Heinemann 1930   **M**
  Same situation as 2.   Doubleday 1931   **J**
4 **Rumour at Nightfall** (novel)   Heinemann 1931   **K**
  Again, very scarce.   Doubleday 1932   **H**
5 **Stamboul Train** (novel)   Heinemann 1932   **E**
  Classed by Greene as 'An
  entertainment', this was published in
  America as *Orient Express* by Doubleday
  in 1933, anticipating Agatha Christie's
  Murder . . . by just one year. This is the
  easiest of the early Greenes, though
  difficult in d/w and correspondingly
  more expensive than the grade given.
6 **It's a Battlefield** (novel)   Heinemann 1934   **G**
  Again, scarce and more expensive in   Doubleday 1934   **G**
  d/w.
7 **England Made Me** (novel)   Heinemann 1935   **H**
  Scarce.   Doubleday 1935   **H**
8 **The Basement Room** (stories)   Cresset Press 1935   **I**
  Very scarce.
9 **A Gun for Sale** (novel)   Heinemann 1936   **F**
  This Gun for Hire   Doubleday 1936   **F**
  An entertainment.
10 **Journey Without Maps** (travel)   Heinemann 1936   **I**
  Quite scarce.   Doubleday 1936   **G**
11 **Brighton Rock** (novel)   Heinemann 1938   **I**
  Greene's highlight. Not only scarce in   Viking 1938   **F**
  d/w, this, but legendary. I know several
  ardent Greene collectors who despair of
  ever seeing it, let alone acquiring it. If
  one came up in d/w, the price could be
  R. In America only it was classed as
  'An entertainment'.

12	**The Confidential Agent** (novel)	Heinemann 1939	G
	Scarce.	Viking 1939	E
13	**Twenty-Four Stories**	Cresset Press 1939	E
	With James Laver and Sylvia Townsend Warner. An unusual item.		
14	**The Lawless Roads** (travel)	Longman 1939	N
	Another Mexico	Viking 1939	N
15	**The Power and the Glory** (novel)	Heinemann 1940	P
	The Labyrinthine Ways	Viking 1940	N
16	**British Dramatists** (non-fiction)	Collins 1942	C
	One of the Britain in Pictures series. Not published separately in America, but included in *The Romance of English Literature* Hastings House 1944 (**B**).		
17	**The Ministry of Fear** (novel)	Heinemann 1943	E
	Not too difficult.	Viking 1943	D
18	**The Little Train** (juvenile)	Eyre & Spottiswoode 1946	L
	Published anonymously while Greene was a director at E. & S. Scarce.	Lothrop 1958	E
19	**Nineteen Stories**	Heinemann 1947	D
	Heinemann published a supplemented edition as **Twenty-One Stories** in 1954 (**C**).	Viking 1949	C
20	**The Heart of the Matter** (novel)	Heinemann 1948	C
	One of the easy Greenes, but beware the Book Society edition – these are very common (**A**).	Viking 1948	C
21	**Why Do I Write?: An Exchange of Views Between Elizabeth Bowen, Graham Greene, and V.S. Pritchett**	Marshall 1948	D
	Quite scarce.		
22	**The Little Fire Engine** (juvenile)	Parrish 1950	H
	Scarce.		
	The Little Red Fire Engine	Lothrop 1952	E
23	**The Third Man** (novel)	Viking Press 1950	E
	An entertainment. Quite scarce.		
24	**The Third Man** and **The Fallen Idol** (novels)	Heinemann 1950	D
	Quite difficult.		
25	**The End of the Affair** (novel)	Heinemann 1951	C
	Quite easy.	Viking 1951	C
26	**The Lost Childhood** (essays)	Eyre & Spottiswoode 1951	D
		Viking 1952	C
27	**The Little Horse Bus** (juvenile)	Parrish 1952	H
	Scarce.	Lothrop 1954	E
28	**The Little Steam Roller** (juvenile)	Parrish 1953	H
	Scarce.	Lothrop 1955	E

29 **The Living Room** (play)	Heinemann 1953	D
His first play, and not common.	Viking 1954	C
30 **Loser Takes All** (novel)	Heinemann 1955	C
	Viking Press 1957	C
31 **The Quiet American** (novel)	Heinemann 1955	C
	Viking 1956	C
32 **The Potting Shed** (play)	Viking 1957	D
	Heinemann 1958	C
33 **Our Man in Havana**	Heinemann 1958	C
(novel)	Viking 1958	C
An entertainment.		
34 **The Complaisant Lover**	Heinemann 1959	C
(play)	Viking 1961	C
35 **In Search of a Character: Two**	Bodley Head 1961	C
African Journals	Viking 1961	C
One of the journals, *Convoy to West Africa*, was first published in Geoffrey Grigson (ed.) *The Mint* Routledge 1946		
36 **A Burnt-Out Case** (novel)	Heinemann 1961	C
	Viking Press 1961	C
37 **A Sense of Reality** (stories)	Bodley Head 1963	C
	Viking 1963	C
38 **Carving a Statue** (play)	Bodley Head 1964	C
39 **The Comedians** (novel)	Bodley Head 1966	B
	Viking 1966	B
40 **May We Borrow Your Husband?**	Bodley Head 1967	B
(stories)	Viking 1967	B
There is also a signed, limited British edition (**F**).		
41 **The Third Man: A Film**	Lorrimer 1969	C
(screenplay)		
With Carol Reed.		
42 **Collected Essays**	Bodley Head 1969	C
	Viking 1969	C
43 **Travels with My Aunt**	Bodley Head 169	B
(novel)	Viking 1970	B
44 **A Sort of Life** (autobiog.)	Bodley Head 1971	B
	Simon & Schuster 1971	B
45 **The Pleasure Dome: The Collected**	Secker & Warburg 1972	C
Film Criticism 1935–40		
	Simon & Schuster 1972	C
46 **The Collected Stories**	Bodley Head/ Heinemann 1972	C
	Viking 1973	C
47 **The Honorary Consul** (novel)	Bodley Head 1973	B
	Viking 1973	B

48	**The Portable Graham Greene**	Viking 1973	**B**
49	**Lord Rochester's Monkey** (biog.)	Bodley Head 1974	**B**
		Viking 1974	**B**
50	**Shades of Greene** (stories)	Bodley Head/ Heinemann 1975	**A**
51	**The Return of A.J. Raffles** (play) 250 copies of the first edition were specially bound in boards and signed by the author. Only numbers 81–250 were for sale, at £25 (F)	Bodley Head 1975 Simon & Schuster 1978	**B** **B**
52	**The Human Factor** (novel)	Bodley Head 1978 Simon & Schuster 1978	**B** **B**
53	**Dr Fischer of Geneva or The Bomb Party** (novel)	Bodley Head 1980 Simon & Schuster 1980	**A** **A**
54	**Ways of Escape** (autobiog.)	Bodley Head 1980 Simon & Schuster 1981	**B** **B**
55	**The Great Jowett** (play) Published *only* as a limited, signed edition of 500.	Bodley Head 1981	**G**
56	**Monsignor Quixote** (novel) A typical Greene perversity. *Why* was it first published in Canada?	Lester & Orpen Dennys (Canada) 1982 Bodley Head 1982 Simon & Schuster 1982	**E** **A** **A**
57	**J'Accuse: The Darker Side of Nice** (non-fiction) Greene's rather brave exposé of corruption in Nice, published in wrappers with both an English and a French text.	Bodley Head 1982 Simon & Schuster 1982	**A** **A**
58	**Marie-Françoise Allain The Other Man: Conversations with Graham Greene**	Bodley Head 1983 Simon & Schuster 1983	**A** **A**
59	**For Whom the Bell Chimes** and **Yes and No** (plays) Again issued solely as a limited, signed edition, the limitation this time having risen to 775 copies.	Bodley Head 1983	**F**

Greene has edited the following:

The Old School: Essays by Divers Hands	Cape 1934	**F**
Greene also has an essay in this. Scarce.	Smith 1934	**F**
The Spy's Bedside Book With Hugh Greene.	Hart-Davis 1957	**E**

An Impossible Woman: The	Bodley Head 1975	**B**
Memories of Dottoressa Moor of	Viking Press 1976	**B**
Capri		

Films:
Orient Express (*Stamboul Train*) 20th Century Fox 1934 **This Gun for Sale** (*A Gun for Sale*) Paramount 1942 **Ministry of Fear** Paramount 1944 **Confidential Agent** Warner Bros 1945 **The Man Within** 20th Century Fox 1947 **The Fugitive** (*The Power and the Glory*) RKO 1947 **The Fallen Idol** 20th Century Fox 1948 **Brighton Rock** Associated British 1948 **The Third Man** General 1950 **The Heart of the Matter** British Lion 1953 **The End of the Affair** Columbia 1954 **Loser Takes All** British Lion 1956 **Short Cut to Hell** (*A Gun for Sale*) Paramount 1957 **Across the Bridge** (story) Rank 1957 **The Quiet American** United Artists 1957 **Our Man in Havana** Columbia 1959 **The Power and the Glory** Paramount 1962 **The Comedians** MGM 1967 **England Made Me** Hemdale 1972 **Travels with My Aunt** MGM 1972 **The Human Factor** Rank 1980 **The Honorary Consul** 20th Century Fox 1983

Greene wrote the screenplays for **Brighton Rock, The Fallen Idol, The Third Man, Our Man in Havana** and **The Comedians**, though they have not been published.

Greenwood, Walter   Born in Lancashire, 1903. Died 1974.

Author of several books, though notable for one in particular – destined for revival, one would think, in these dark days of rife unemployment. Love is, after all, free. It was declared so in the sixties, and will remain so until the Government subjects it to VAT.

Love on the Dole	Cape 1933	**D–E**
It is scarce.	Doubleday 1934	**D–E**

Film:
Love on the Dole United Artists 1941

Grossmith, George and Weedon
George, 1847–1912. Weedon, 1854–1919.

They wrote only one book, and I *know* it's not a twentieth century work, but it's going in anyway – for its influence on modern journalism, if you like; but really because it's so funny, and it has never been bettered.

The Diary of a Nobody	Arrowsmith 1892	**H**
Originally a series of contributions to		

Punch, and then enlarged and developed
for this book. Illustrated by Weedon,
and published in Arrowsmith's Three-
and-sixpenny series.

There is now a biography:
Tony Joseph **George Grossmith** published by the author, and printed
by none other than J.W. Arrowsmith of Bristol (1982).

Gunn, Thom   Born in Kent, 1929.

Still a very popular poet, but now tending to publish more and more in
America in the form of limited (often *extremely* limited) issues from private
presses. He lives in California now, but he used to live in Hampstead and
drops back from time to time.

1 **Poetry from Cambridge 1951–1952**	Fortune Press 1952	H
An anthology introduced by Gunn, and containing four of his poems.		
2 **The Fantasy Poets No. 16**	Fantasy Press 1953	G
There were about 300 copies of this pamphlet.		
3 **Fighting Terms** (verse)	Fantasy Press 1954	G
Again, around 300 copies. The first	Hawk's Well Press	D
state contains a printing error on page	1958	
38, where the last letter of the word 'thought' is omitted.		
4 **The Sense of Movement** (verse)	Faber 1957	D
	University of	B
	Chicago Press 1959	
5 **My Sad Captains** (verse)	Faber 1961	D
	University of	C
	Chicago Press 1961	
6 **Selected Poems** (verse)	Faber 1962	B
With Ted Hughes.		
7 **A Geography** (verse)	Stone Wall Press	D
Limitation of 220 copies, but	(Iowa) 1966	
apparently only 216 were printed.		
8 **Positives** (verse)	Faber 1966	D
Large format, illustrated with	University of	C
photographs by Ander Gunn, Thom's	Chicago Press 1967	
brother.		
9 **Touch** (verse)	Faber 1967	C
	University of	B
	Chicago Press 1968	

10 **The Garden of the Gods** (verse)   Pym-Randall 1968   **D**
A limitation of 200 numbered, 26
lettered. A first impression was
destroyed (save 10 copies) as
production was deemed to be
inadequate.

11 **The Explorers** (verse)   Gilbertson 1969   **H**
Only 6 copies of this were published (at
£60 each), and bound to order. Later
issues do not add very many to the
total: 'deluxe issue' (10 copies), 'special
issue' (20 copies) and 'ordinary issue'
(64 copies).

12 **The Fair in the Woods** (verse)   Sycamore Press 1969   **C**
Single-sheet folded broadside. 500
printed.

13 **Poems 1950–1966: A Selection**   Faber 1969   **B**

14 **Sunlight** (verse)   Albondocani Press   **D**
Only 150 numbered copies for sale.   1969

15 **Moly** (verse)   Faber 1971   **C**
    Farrar Straus 1973   **B**

16 **Last Days at Teddington** (verse)   John Roberts Press   **C**
Single-sheet broadside. 1000 copies.   1971

17 **Poem After Chaucer**   Albondocani Press   **E**
Christmas greeting from the publisher.   1971
320 printed, none for sale.

18 **The Spell** (verse)   Steane 1973   **C**
Single-sheet broadside (500 copies)
published at 20p.

19 **Songbook** (verse)   Albondocani Press   **C**
230 copies, 200 for sale.   1973

20 **To the Air** (verse)   Godine 1974   **B**

21 **Mandrakes** (verse)   Rainbow Press 1974   **G**
150 copies, numbered and signed.

22 **Jack Straw's Castle** (verse)   Hallman 1975   **D**
300 paperbound copies for sale. 100
hardbound (signed) copies were on sale
the following year.

23 **The Missed Beat** (verse)   Janus Press 1976   **E**
50 copies. An English edition of 'about
70 copies' was published in the same
year by the Gruffyground Press (**D**).

24 **Jack Straw's Castle and Other**   Faber 1976   **B**
Poems   Farrar Straus 1976   **B**
Of the English edition, 750 hardback
and 4000 paper.

25 **A Crab** (verse)   The Pirates 1978   **D**
A pirated, freely distributed poem. 30
copies.

26 **Games of Chance** (verse)	Abattoir 1979	C
27 **Selected Poems 1950–1975**	Faber 1979	B
	Farrar Straus 1979	B
28 **The Passages of Joy** (verse)	Faber 1982	B
	Farrar Straus 1982	B

Gunn has edited the following:

Five American Poets	Faber 1963	C
With Ted Hughes.		
Selected Poems of Fulke Greville	Faber 1968	C
	University of Chicago Press 1968	B
Ben Jonson	Penguin 1974	A

An excellent bibliography now exists: Jack W.C. Hagstrom and George Bixby **Thom Gunn: A Bibliography 1940–1978** Rota 1979. This contains an introductory biographical essay by Thom Gunn.

Hall, Radclyffe Born in Bournemouth, 1886. Died 1943.

I include this one work (she wrote quite a few) more as a landmark in twentieth-century publishing than anything. Declared obscene at the time (it is a lesbian confession, rather stilted, occasionally touching) and ordered to be destroyed – quite as if the pulping of such books would quell the spirit from which they sprang. As with all prohibition, the article in question came to be disproportionately attractive and was eagerly sought out as a source of vicarious pleasure. It achieved the reputation of being a dirty book (which it isn't) before the backlash pronounced it a great work (which it isn't). A period piece, then, and quite difficult to acquire, if inexpensive.

| **The Well of Loneliness** (novel) | Cape 1928 | B |
| | Covici 1928 | B |

The American edition might well be a lot easier, as the book was cleared of charges in the States. Grade C if in the scarce d/w.

Hammett, Dashiell Born in Maryland, 1894. Died 1961.

There has been such a rise in interest in detective fiction – particularly the 'tough guy' school of Hammett and Chandler – that it is worth while giving a complete listing.

1 **Red Harvest** (novel)	Knopf 1929	P
	Cassell 1929	M
2 **The Dain Curse** (novel)	Knopf 1929	N
	Cassell 1929	K

3 **The Maltese Falcon** (novel)	Knopf 1930	P
The highlight, this.	Cassell 1930	M
4 **The Glass Key** (novel)	Knopf 1931	L
	Cassell 1931	J
5 **The Thin Man** (novel	Knopf 1934	N
	Barker 1934	K
6 **$106,000 Blood Money** (novel)	Spivak (NY) 1943	H

This was republished the same year by World as *Blood Money*, and reissued in 1948 by Spivak as *The Big Knock-over*.

7 **The Adventures of Sam Spade** (stories)	Spivak 1944	E

Ed. Ellery Queen. This was reissued in 1949 as *They Can Only Hang You Once*.

8 **The Continental Op** (stories)	Spivak 1945	C
Ed. Ellery Queen.		
9 **The Return of the Continental Op** (stories)	Spivak 1945	C
Ed. Ellery Queen.		
10 **Hammett Homicides** (stories)	Spivak 1946	C
Ed. Ellery Queen.		
11 **Dead Yellow Women** (stories)	Spivak 1947	C
Ed. Ellery Queen.		
12 **Nightmare Town** (stories)	Spivak 1948	C
Ed. Ellery Queen.		
13 **The Creeping Siamese** (stories)	Spivak 1950	C
Ed. Ellery Queen.		
14 **Woman in the Dark** (stories)	Spivak 1951	C
Ed. Ellery Queen.		
15 **A Man Named Thin and Other Stories**	Ferman (NY) 1952	C
Ed. Ellery Queen.		
16 **The Big Knockover: Selected Stories and Short Novels**	Random House 1966	C
Ed. Lillian Hellman.		
17 **The Hammett Story Omnibus** (same as 16)	Cassell 1966	C

Films:
The Maltese Falcon Warner Bros 1931 (remade by First National in 1937 as *Satan Met a Lady*, and under its original title by Warner Bros in 1941)   **The Thin Man** MGM 1934   **The Glass Key** Paramount 1935 (remade by Paramount in 1942)   **The Black Bird** Columbia/Warner 1975 (based upon *The Maltese Falcon*)

Bibliography:
Richard Layman **Dashiell Hammett: A Descriptive Bibliography** University of Pittsburgh Press 1979

Hammett

Biography:
Diane Johnson **The Life of Dashiell Hammett** Chatto & Windus 1984

Hartley, L.P. Born in Cambridgeshire, 1895. Died 1972.

Never a 'popular' success with readers or collectors, Hartley is still very much followed by a select band who are very determined to complete their collections. It is not easy – all the books that come up tend to be post-1950.

1	**Night Fears and Other Stories**	Putnam (UK) 1924	I
2	**Simonetta Perkins** (novel)	Putnam 1925	I
		Putnam (US) 1925	I
3	**The Killing Bottle** (stories)	Putnam 1932	E
4	**The Shrimp and the Anemone** (novel)	Putnam 1944	E
5	**The West Window** (same as 4)	Doubleday (NY) 1945	D
6	**The Sixth Heaven** (novel)	Putnam 1946	D
		Doubleday 1947	C
7	**Eustace and Hilda** (novel) 4, 6 and 7 form a trilogy.	Putnam 1947	C⁻
8	**The Travelling Grave** (stories)	Arkham House (US) 1948	C
		Barrie 1951	C
9	**The Boat** (novel)	Putnam 1950	C
		Doubleday 1950	C
10	**My Fellow Devils** (novel)	Barrie 1951	D
11	**The Go-Between** (novel)	Hamilton 1953	C
		Knopf 1954	C
12	**A White Wand and Other Stories**	Hamilton 1954	C
13	**A Perfect Woman** (novel)	Hamilton 1955	B
		Knopf 1956	B
14	**The Hireling** (novel)	Hamilton 1957	B
		Rinehart 1958	B
15	**Facial Justice** (novel)	Hamilton 1960	B
		Doubleday 1961	B
16	**Two for the River** (stories)	Hamilton 1961	B
17	**The Brickfield** (novel)	Hamilton 1964	B
18	**The Betrayal** (novel)	Hamilton 1966	B
19	**Poor Clare** (novel)	Hamilton 1968	B
20	**The Collected Stories**	Hamilton 1968	B
		Horizon Press 1969	B
21	**The Love-Adept** (novel)	Hamilton 1969	B
22	**My Sister's Keeper** (novel)	Hamilton 1970	B
23	**The Harness Room** (novel)	Hamilton 1971	B
24	**Mrs Carteret Receives** (stories)	Hamilton 1971	B
25	**The Will and the Way** (novel)	Hamilton 1973	B

Films:
The Go-Between MGM/EMI 1971   **The Hireling** Columbia/Warner
Bros 1973

Heaney, Seamus   Born in County Derry, 1939.

Rising in fame and popularity all the time, his early slim volumes come up
but rarely, now. Heaney has, in a way, consolidated his position as one of the
country's leading poets by collaborating with Ted Hughes on *The Rattle-Bag*,
a really excellent anthology of verse for all ages which, I think, will become a
standard that will be around for a very long time to come.

1	**Eleven Poems**	Festival (Belfast) 1965	N
2	**Death of a Naturalist** (verse)	Faber 1966	H
		OUP (US) 1966	D
3	**A Lough Neagh Sequence**	Phoenix Pamphlet Poets Press 1969	F
4	**Door into the Dark** (verse)	Faber 1969	G
		OUP (US) 1969	C
5	**Night Drive: Poems** Limited to 100 copies, signed, 25 of which contain a poem in the author's hand (**K**).	Gilbertson (Crediton) 1970	I
6	**Boy Driving His Father to Confession** Limited to 150 numbered copies, 50 signed. (**I**).	Sceptre Press 1970	H
7	**Wintering Out** (verse)	Faber 1972	D
		OUP (US) 1973	C
8	**The Fire i' the Flint: Reflections on the Poetry of Gerard Manley Hopkins** (lecture)	OUP (US) 1975	C
9	**North** (verse)	Faber 1975	C
		OUP (US) 1976	B
10	**Bog Poems**	Rainbow Press 1975	E
11	**Stations** (verse)	Ulsterman (Belfast) 1975	D
12	**Robert Lowell: A Memorial Lecture and an Eulogy**	Privately printed 1978	E
13	**Field Work** (verse)	Faber 1979	B
		Farrar Straus 1979	B
14	**Selected Poems 1965–1975**	Faber 1980	B
15	**Preoccupations: Selected Prose 1968–1978**	Faber 1980	B
		Farrar Straus 1980	B
16	**The Rattle-bag** (anthology) Edited with Ted Hughes.	Faber 1982	B

Heaney

Heaney has edited **New Poems
1970–1971** (with Alan Brownjohn and
Jon Stallworthy) Hutchinson 1971 (**A**)
and **Soundings 72** Blackstaff Press
(Belfast) 1972 (**A**).

Heller, Joseph   Born in Brooklyn, 1923.

As may be seen from the following list, Heller has published very little in
twenty-odd years, and it's all fairly available, and fairly cheap – all, that is,
except one: *Catch-22*. Which tends to be the only one people want: *Catch-22*.

1	**Catch-22** (novel)	Simon & Schuster 1961	G
		Cape 1962	E
2	**We Bombed in New Haven** (play)	Knopf 1968	C
		Cape 1969	B
3	**Catch-22** (play)	French (NY) 1971	B
4	**Clevinger's Trial** (play)	French (NY) 1973	B
5	**Something Happened** (novel)	Knopf 1974	C
		Cape 1974	B
6	**Good as Gold** (novel)	Simon & Schuster 1979	B
		Cape 1979	B

Film:
Catch-22 Paramount 1969

Hemingway, Ernest   Born in Illinois, 1899. Died 1961.

England has always had a rather love-hate relationship with Hemingway –
collectors have, anyway. His importance is recognized – some even find him
readable – but there is a sort of a feeling that one would not care to make him
too prominent a feature of one's collection; we maybe feel that all that macho
and all that gore are not quite *nice*. Americans, of course, have no such
mealy-mouthed doubts – they deify him. It is true, of course, that
Hemingway is not easy to collect in this country, and nor are the early items
by any means cheap. *The Old Man and the Sea* (an atypical work) seems the
favourite in this country, and it is not too hard to find. If, however, a *serious*
collection of Hemingway is contemplated, one ought to be forewarned that
American first editions are very pricey – and the prices asked in America!
Well, you'd have to be American to pay them.

1	**Three Stories and Ten Poems**	Privately printed (Paris 1923)	O–P upwards
2	**In Our Time** (stories)	Boni & Liveright 1924	K

		Cape 1924	I
3	**The Torrents of Spring** (novel)	Scribner 1926	K
4	**The Sun Also Rises** (novel)	Scribner 1926	J
5	**Fiesta** (same as 4)	Cape 1927	H
6	**Men Without Women** (stories)	Scribner 1927	F
		Cape 1927	C
7	**A Farewell to Arms** (novel)	Scribner 1929	E
		Cape 1929	B
8	**Death in the Afternoon** (non-fiction)	Scribner 1932	H
		Cape 1932	G
9	**Winner Take Nothing** (stories)	Scribner 1933	E
		Cape 1934	C
10	**Green Hills of Africa** (non-fiction)	Scribner 1935	H
		Cape 1936	E
11	**To Have and Have Not** (novel)	Scribner 1937	F
		Cape 1937	C
12	**The Fifth Column and the first Forty-Nine Stories** (play and stories)	Scribner 1938	F
		Cape 1941	C
13	**For Whom the Bell Tolls** (novel)	Scribner 1940	E
		Cape 1941	B
14	**Across the River and into the Trees** (novel)	Cape 1950	C
		Scribner 1950	B
15	**The Old Man and the Sea** (novel)	Scribner 1952	C
		Cape 1952	B
16	**A Moveable Feast** (non-fiction)	Scribner 1964	D
		Cape 1964	C
17	**Islands in the Stream** (novel)	Scribner 1970	B
		Collins 1970	B

In 1947 Cape published **The Essential Hemingway,** which contains extracts from his works.

Films:
A Farewell to Arms Paramount 1932; 20th Century Fox 1957   **For Whom the Bell Tolls** Paramount 1943   **To Have and Have Not** Warner Bros 1944 (as *The Breaking Point*) Warner Bros 1950 (as *The Gun Runners*) United Artists 1958   **The Killers** (story) Universal 1946; Rank 1964   **The Macomber Affair** (story) Universal 1947   **Under My Skin** 20th Century Fox 1950 (*My Old Man* – story)   **The Snows of Kilimanjaro** (story) 20th Century Fox 1952   **The Sun Also Rises** 20th Century Fox 1957   **The Old Man and the Sea** Warner Bros 1958   **Hemingway's Adventures of a Young Man** 20th Century Fox 1962   **Islands in the Stream** Paramount 1977

Highsmith, Patricia   Born in Fort Worth, Texas, 1921.

'The Queen of Psychological Crime' she has been dubbed, and it is not hard to see why. The books are not only gripping, but eerie – to say nothing of extremely well written, and faultlessly plotted. It is no wonder that Hitchcock was drawn to her first novel *Strangers on a Train*. Images haunt, as usual – the reflection of the merry-go-round in the murder victim's fallen spectacles, accompanied by the sounds of her strangulation – but it was a phrase that caught me: let's swap crimes.

1	**Strangers on a Train** (novel)	Harper 1950	H
		Cresset Press 1951	G
2	**The Price of Salt** (novel)	Coward McCann (NY)	H
	Pseud. Claire Morgan.	1952	
3	**The Blunderer** (novel)	Coward McCann 1954	F
		Cresset Press 1956	E
4	**The Talented Mr Ripley**	Coward McCann 1955	F
	(novel)	Cresset Press 1957	E
5	**Deep Water** (novel)	Harper 1957	E
		Heinemann 1958	D
6	**A Game for the Living** (novel)	Harper 1958	E
		Heinemann 1959	D
7	**Miranda the Panda is on the**	Coward McCann 1958	D
	Verandah (juvenile)		
	With Doris Sanders.		
8	**This Sweet Sickness** (novel)	Harper 1960	D
		Heinemann 1961	C
9	**The Cry of the Owl** (novel)	Harper 1962	D
		Heinemann 1963	C
10	**The Two Faces of January** (novel)	Doubleday 1964	C
		Heinemann 1964	B
11	**The Glass Cell** (novel)	Doubleday 1964	C
		Heinemann 1965	B
12	**The Story-Teller** (novel)	Doubleday 1965	C
13	**A Suspension of Mercy**	Heinemann 1965	B
	(same as 12)		
14	**Plotting and Writing Suspense**	Writer (Boston) 1966	C
	Fiction		
15	**Those Who Walk Away** (novel)	Doubleday 1967	C
		Heinemann 1967	B
16	**The Tremor of Forgery**	Doubleday 1969	C
	(novel)	Heinemann 1969	B
17	**Ripley Under Ground** (novel)	Doubleday 1970	C
		Heinemann 1971	B
18	**The Snail-Watchers** (stories)	Doubleday 1970	C
19	**Eleven** (same as 18)	Heinemann 1970	B
20	**A Dog's Ransom** (novel)	Knopf 1972	B
		Heinemann 1972	B

21 **Ripley's Game** (novel)	Knopf 1974	B
	Heinemann 1974	B
22 **The Animal Lover's Book of Beastly Murder** (stories)	Heinemann 1975	C
23 **Edith's Diary** (novel)	Heinemann 1977	B
24 **Little Tales of Misogyny** (stories) First published in German, Zürich 1974 (**D**).	Heinemann 1977	B
25 **Slowly, Slowly in the Wind** (stories)	Heinemann 1979	B
26 **The Boy Who Followed Ripley** (novel)	Heinemann 1980	B
	Lippincott 1980	B
27 **The Black House** (novel)	Heinemann 1981	B
28 **The People Who Knock on the Door** (novel)	Heinemann 1983	B

Films:
Strangers on a Train Warner Bros 1951 **Purple Noon** Hillcrest 1961 (*The Talented Mr Ripley*) **The American Friend** Cinegate 1978 (based on *Ripley's Game*) **This Sweet Sickness** Artificial Eye 1979

Hill, Susan   Born in Yorkshire, 1942.

Susan Hill apparently became disenchanted by the business of writing novels about ten years ago, announced her retirement from the profession (rare among writers) and settled down to the work of reviewing others. But she's back now. Artists just *can't* retire; it's not as if they were human, or anything.

1 **The Enclosure** (novel)	Hutchinson 1961	F
2 **Do Me a Favour** (novel)	Hutchinson 1963	D
3 **Gentlemen and Ladies** (novel)	Hamilton 1968	D
	Walker 1969	C
4 **A Change for the Better** (novel)	Hamilton 1969	C
5 **I'm the King of the Castle** (novel)	Hamilton 1970	C
	Saturday Review Press 1970	B
6 **Strange Meeting** (novel)	Hamilton 1971	B
	Saturday Review Press 1972	B
7 **The Albatross and Other Stories**	Hamilton 1971	B
8 **The Bird of Night** (novel)	Hamilton 1972	B
	Saturday Review Press 1972	B
9 **The Custodian** (story)	Covent Garden Press 1972	C
10 **A Bit of Singing and Dancing** (stories)	Hamilton 1973	B

11 **In the Springtime of the Year** (novel)	Hamilton 1974 Saturday Review Press 1974	B B
12 **The Cold Country and Other Plays for Radio**	BBC 1975	B
13 **The Magic Apple-tree** (prose)	Hamilton 1982 Holt Rinehart 1983	B B
14 **The Woman in Black** (novel)	Hamilton 1983	B
15 **Ghost Stories**	Hamilton 1983	B

Household, Geoffrey Born in Bristol, 1900. Pseudonym for Edward West.

Was the taking of the pseudonym his bid to become a household name? Unlikely, for he was thirty-nine when his most celebrated novel was published (*Rogue Male*) and eighty-two when he brought us the sequel.

1 **The Terror of Villadonga** (juvenile)	Hutchinson 1936	H
2 **The Spanish Cave** (same as 1, revised)	Little Brown 1936	G
3 **The Third Hour** (novel)	Chatto & Windus 1937 Little Brown 1938	G F
4 **The Salvation of Pisco Gabar** (stories)	Chatto & Windus 1938 Little Brown 1940	E D
5 **Rogue Male** (novel)	Chatto & Windus 1939 Little Brown 1939	G F
6 **Arabesque** (novel)	Chatto & Windus 1948 Little Brown 1948	E D
7 **The High Place** (novel)	Joseph 1950 Little Brown 1950	D C
8 **A Rough Shoot** (novel)	Joseph 1951 Little Brown 1951	D C
9 **A Time to Kill** (novel)	Little Brown 1951 Joseph 1952	D C
10 **Tales of Adventurers** (stories)	Joseph 1952 Little Brown 1952	D C
11 **Fellow Passenger** (novel)	Joseph 1955 Little Brown 1955	C C
12 **The Exploits of Xenophon** (juvenile) **Xenophon's Adventure**	Random House 1955 Bodley Head 1961	C C
13 **The Brides of Solomon** (stories)	Joseph 1958 Little Brown 1958	C B
14 **Watcher in the Shadows** (novel)	Joseph 1960 Little Brown 1960	B B
15 **Thing to Love** (novel)	Joseph 1963 Little Brown 1963	B B

16 **Olura** (novel)	Joseph 1965	B
	Little Brown 1965	B
17 **Sabres on the Sand** (stories)	Joseph 1966	B
	Little Brown 1966	B
18 **Prisoner of the Indies** (juvenile)	Bodley Head 1967	B
	Little Brown 1967	B
19 **The Courtesy of Death** (novel)	Joseph 1967	B
	Little Brown 1967	B
20 **Dance of the Dwarfs** (novel)	Joseph 1968	B
	Little Brown 1968	B
21 **Doom's Caravan** (novel)	Joseph 1971	B
	Little Brown 1971	B
22 **The Three Sentinels** (novel)	Joseph 1972	B
	Little Brown 1972	B
23 **The Lives and Times of Bernardo Brown** (novel)	Joseph 1973	B
	Little Brown 1974	B
24 **Red Anger** (novel)	Joseph 1975	B
	Little Brown 1976	B
25 **Escape Into Daylight** (juvenile)	Bodley Head 1976	B
26 **Hostage: London** (novel)	Joseph 1977	B
	Little Brown 1977	B
27 **The Last Two Weeks of George Rivac** (novel)	Joseph 1978	B
	Little Brown 1978	B
28 **The Europe That Was** (stories)	David & Charles 1979	B
	St Martin's 1979	B
29 **The Sending** (novel)	Joseph 1980	B
	Little Brown 1980	B
30 **Summon the Bright Water** (novel)	Joseph 1981	B
	Little Brown 1981	B
31 **Capricorn and Cancer** (stories)	Joseph 1981	B
32 **Rogue Justice** (novel)	Joseph 1982	B
	Little Brown 1983	B

Films:
Manhunt (*Rogue Male*) 20th Century Fox 1941 **Brandy for the Parson** (story) MGM 1952 **Rough Shoot** United Artists 1953

Howard, Elizabeth Jane   Born in London, 1923.

Fairly recently, Elizabeth Jane Howard published her first novel for seven years, the main reason being that she has given much of her time to adapting her work for television, anthologizing, and being one of the three judges of the 'twelve best novels of our time' – an unenviable task for a working novelist, one would have thought – unless one can do it with all the singular confidence and brio of Anthony Burgess, and round it up to 99 while one is about it.

1 **The Beautiful Visit** (novel)	Cape 1950	D
	Random House 1950	C

2 **We Are for the Dark: Six Ghost Stories** With Robert Aickman.	Cape 1951	**C**
3 **The Long View** (novel)	Cape 1956	**C**
	Reynal 1956	**B**
4 **The Sea Change** (novel)	Cape 1959	**B**
	Harper 1960	**A**
5 **After Julius** (novel)	Cape 1965	**C**
	Viking 1965	**B**
6 **Something in Disguise** (novel)	Cape 1969	**B**
	Viking 1970	**A**
7 **Odd Girl Out** (novel)	Cape 1972	**B**
	Viking 1972	**A**
8 **Mr Wrong** (stories)	Cape 1975	**B**
	Viking 1975	**A**
9 **The Lover's Companion** (verse) An anthology of other people's poetry, selected and introduced by E.J.H., to coincide with Valentine's Day.	David & Charles 1978	**A**
10 **Getting it Right** (novel)	Hamilton 1982	**A**
	Viking 1982	**A**

Hughes, Richard   Born in Surrey, 1900. Died 1976.

It is rather sad that Richard Hughes embarked so late in life upon his *Human Predicament* – the umbrella title for what was to have been an epic sequence of novels, the exact number unspecified. Not that sixty-one is a terribly great age to publish the first volume – but he was seventy-three when he published the second, which was to be the last. It is, however, his very early works which are rare and command the high prices, while a representative work would be *A High Wind in Jamaica* – still the highlight, and still reasonably priced.

Hughes published a fair amount of private press material which does not appear here. A list may be found in *The New Cambridge Bibliography of English Literature* vol. 4, and the Golden Cockerel Press items may be found in their own checklist of publications.

1 **The Sister's Tragedy** (play)	Blackwell 1922	**G**
2 **The Sister's Tragedy and Other Plays** Incl. *The Man Born to be Hanged, A Comedy of Good and Evil* and *Danger*.	Heinemann 1924	**E**
A Rabbit and a Leg: Collected Plays	Knopf 1924	**D**
3 **Confessio Juvenis: Collected Poems**	Chatto & Windus 1925	**E**
4 **A Moment of Time** (stories)	Chatto & Windus 1926	**E**

5 **A High Wind in Jamaica** (novel) Also limited ed. of 150 copies (F).	Chatto & Windus 1929	C
6 **The Innocent Voyage** (same as 5)	Harper (NY) 1929	C
7 **Richard Hughes: An Omnibus** (stories, plays and poems)	Harper 1931	C
8 **The Spider's Palace** (juvenile stories)	Chatto & Windus 1931 Harper 1932	G F
9 **In Hazard** (novel)	Chatto & Windus 1938 Harper 1938	C C
10 **Don't Blame Me and Other Stories** (juvenile)	Chatto & Windus 1940 Harper 1940	D C
11 **The Fox in the Attic** (novel)	Chatto & Windus 1961 Harper 1961	B B
12 **Gertrude's Child** (juvenile)	Harlin Quist (NY) 1966 Allen 1967	C B
13 **The Wooden Shepherdess** (novel)	Chatto & Windus 1973 Harper 1973	B B
14 **The Wonder-Dog: The Collected** **Stories** (juvenile)	Chatto & Windus 1977	B
15 **In the Lap of Atlas: Stories of** **Morocco** Ed. Richard Poole.	Chatto & Windus 1979 Merrimack 1980	B B

Film:
A High Wind in Jamaica 20th Century Fox 1964

Hughes, Ted Born in Yorkshire, 1930.

The reputation of Ted Hughes as one of our foremost poets is perfectly sound, despite the fact that more and more admirers are being prevented from enjoying his latest offerings by Hughes' penchant for publishing very small print runs with private presses, often at very high prices indeed. Certainly a 'Collected Poems' seems overdue, though one hopes that when it comes it does not merely reproduce all that work freely available from Faber for years. You need to be very dedicated to collect *everything* by Hughes, to say nothing of an early bird, lucky, and rich. The ensuing checklist is, I hope, exhaustive, though a bibliography now exists – up to 1980 – details of which I append after the listing.

1 **The Hawk in the Rain** (verse)	Faber 1957 Harper 1957	J H
2 **Pike** (poem) A single-sheet broadside in an edition of 150.	Gehenna Press 1959	F
3 **Lupercal** (verse)	Faber 1960 Harper 1960	H F

Hughes, T.

4 **Meet My Folks!** (juvenile)   Faber 1961   **E**
                                          Bobbs-Merrill 1973   **B**
5 **Selected Poems**   Faber 1962   **B**
  With Thom Gunn.
6 **How the Whale Became**   Faber 1963   **D**
  (juvenile)   Atheneum 1964   **C**
7 **The Earth-Owl and Other Moon-**   Faber 1963   **D**
  People (juvenile)
8 **Nessie the Mannerless Monster**   Faber 1964   **D**
  (juvenile)   Bobbs-Merrill 1974   **C**
  The American edition omits the word
  'mannerless' from the title.
9 **The Burning of the Brothel** (verse)   Turret Books 1966   **E**
  300 copies, 75 numbered and signed
  (**H**).
10 **Recklings** (verse)   Turret Books 1966   **G**
  150 copies, numbered and signed.
11 **Scapegoats and Rabies** (verse)   Poet & Printer 1967   **C**
  400(ish) copies.
12 **Wodwo** (miscellany)   Faber 1967   **C**
                                          Harper 1967   **B**
13 **Animal Poems**   Gilbertson 1967
  100 copies, as follows:
  1–6: poems hand-written by T.H. next
  to text (**N**)
  7–16: with 3 manuscript poems (**K**)
  17–36: with 1 manuscript poem (**I**).
  37–100: signed (**E**).
14 **Poetry in the Making** (prose)   Faber 1967   **D**
  The American edition was entitled   Doubleday 1970   **D**
  Poetry Is.
15 **Gravestones** (verse)   Bartholemew 1967   **I**
  A set of six broadsides; linocuts by
  Gavin Robbins. 40 sets printed.
16 **Seneca's Oedipus** (play)   Faber 1969   **C**
                                          Doubleday 1972   **C**
17 **The Iron Man** (juvenile)   Faber 1968   **D**
18 **The Iron Giant**   Harper 1968   **C**
  The American edition of 17.
19 **Five Autumn Songs for Children's**   Gilbertson 1968
  Voices (verse)
  500 copies, as follows (for sale):
  3–11: a verse in manuscript & a
  watercolour (**I**).
  12–37: a verse in manuscript (**H**)
  38–188: signed (**D**)
  189–500: numbered (**B**).

20 **I Said Goodbye to Earth** (poem)   Turret Books 1969   **E**
Broadside. 75 copies, signed.
21 **A Crow Hymn** (poem)   Sceptre Press 1970
21 signed (**G**), 64 unsigned (**C**) for sale.
22 **The Martyrdom of Bishop Farrar**   Gilbertson 1970   **F**
100 copies, signed.
23 **The Coming of the Kings and**   Viking 1974   **A**
Other Plays   Faber 1970   **C**
The Tiger's Bones and Other Plays
for Children.
24 **A Few Crows** (verse)   Rougemont Press 1970   **E**
150 copies, 75 signed (**H**).
25 **Crow** (verse)   Faber 1970   **C**
        Harper 1971   **B**
26 **Fighting for Jerusalem** (poem)   Northumberland Arts   **D**
Broadside, number of copies unknown.   1970
27 **Crow Wakes** (verse)   Poet & Printer 1971   **D**
100 for sale.
28 **Poems**   Rainbow Press 1971   **I**
With Ruth Fainlight and Alan Sillitoe.
300 copies, numbered and signed by
the three poets.
29 **Shakespeare's Poem**   Lexham Press 1971   **E**
150 copies, 75 (signed) for sale.
30 **Eat Crow** (verse)   Rainbow Press 1971   **I**
150 copies, signed and numbered.
31 **Selected Poems 1957–1967**   Faber 1972   **B**
        Harper 1973   **B**
32 **Orpheus** (play)   Dramatic Publishing   **C**
1023 copies.   Company (US) 1973
33 **Prometheus on His Crag** (verse)   Rainbow Press 1973   **I**
160 copies signed by T.H. and Leonard
Baskin.
34 **Spring Summer Autumn Winter**   Rainbow Press 1974   **J**
(verse)
140 copies, numbered and signed.
35 **Season Songs**   Doubleday 1975   **B**
First trade editions of 34.   Faber 1976   **B**
36 **Cave Birds** (verse)   Scolar Press 1975
Ten sheets in a box, illustrated by
Leonard Baskin. 125 copies printed, at
£125 each (**K**). *Sensible* editions were
published by Faber in 1978 (**B**) and the
Viking Press in 1979 (**B**).
37 **Earth-Moon** (verse)   Rainbow Press 1976   **H**
226 signed and numbered copies, 200
for sale.

Hughes, T.

38 **Eclipse** (verse) 250 copies, 50 signed (**E**).	Sceptre Press 1976	**C**
39 **Moon-Whales and Other Poems** Previously published verse, but new to America.	Viking 1976	**B**
40 **Gaudete** (verse)	Faber 1977 Harper 1977	**B** **B**
41 **Chiasmadon** (verse) 175 signed copies, 120 for sale.	Janus Press (US) 1977	**G**
42 **Sunstruck** (verse) 300 copies, as follows: 100 signed (50 for sale) (**E**). 200 numbered (**B**).	Sceptre Press 1977	
43 **A Solstice** (verse) 350 copies, as follows. 100 signed (50 for sale) (**E**). 250 numbered (**B**).	Sceptre Press 1978	
44 **Orts** (verse) 200 copies, numbered and signed.	Rainbow Press 1978	**H**
45 **Moortown Elegies** (verse) 175 copies, as follows: 6 author's copies. 26 lettered A–Z (£175)(**L**). 143 numbered (£140) (**K**).	Rainbow Press 1978	
46 **The Threshold** (poem) 12 leaves, illustrated by Ralph Steadman. Signed by R.S. and T.H. 100 copies at £105 each.	Steam Press 1979	**J**
47 **Adam and the Sacred Nine** (verse) 200 copies, numbered and signed.	Rainbow Press 1979	**G**
48 **Remains of Elmet** (verse) With photographs by Fay Godwin. 180 copies, as follows: 1–70: bound, signed by T.H. and F.G. (£140) (**K**). 71–180: ordinary binding, signed by T.H. (£48) (**F**). Attainable editions were published by Faber and Harper & Row later in the year (**B**).	Rainbow Press 1979	
49 **Night Arrival of Sea-Trout, The Iron Wolf, Puma** (verse) Three broadsides. 30 sets printed at £15 each. The Press is owned by Hughes's son Nicholas.	Morrigu Press 1979	**C**
50 **Brooktrout** (poem) Broadside. 60 copies printed.	Morrigu Press 1979	**C**

51	**Four Tales Told by an Idiot** 450 numbered copies, 100 signed (**C**).	Sceptre Press 1979	**B**
52	**Pan** (poem) Broadside. 60 copies printed.	Morrigu Press 1979	**C**
53	**Woodpecker** (poem) Broadside. 60 copies printed.	Morrigu Press 1979	**C**
54	**Moortown** (verse)	Faber 1979	**C**
		Harper 1980	**C**
55	**Henry Williamson** (tribute) 200 copies, 125 for sale.	Rainbow Press 1979	**E**
56	**Wolverine** (poem) Broadside. 75 copies.	Morrigu Press 1979	**C**
57	**Eagle** (poem) Broadside. 75 copies.	Morrigu Press 1980	**C**
58	**Mosquito** (poem) Broadside. 60 copies.	Morrigu Press 1980	**C**
59	**Catadrome** (poem) Broadside. 75 copies.	Morrigu Press 1980	**C**
60	**Caddis** (poem) Broadside. 75 copies.	Morrigu Press 1980	**C**
61	**Visitation** (poem) Broadside. 75 copies.	Morrigu Press 1980	**C**
62	**Under the North Star** (verse)	Faber 1981	**B**
		Viking 1981	**B**
63	**The Rattle-bag** An anthology of everyone, edited by T.H. and Seamus Heaney.	Faber 1982	**B**
64	**Selected Poems 1957–1981** The Harper edition was entitled **New Selected Poems.**	Faber 1982	**B**
		Harper 1982	**B**
65	**River** (verse) With photographs by Peter Keen, which the American edition omits.	Faber 1983	**B**
		Harper 1984	**B**
66	**Weasels at Work** (poem) Booklet. 75 copies.	Morrigu Press 1983	**C**
67	**Fly Inspects** (poem) Booklet. 75 copies.	Morrigu Press 1983	**C**
68	**Mice are Funny Little Creatures** Booklet. 75 copies.	Morrigu Press 1983	**C**
69	**What is the Truth?** (juvenile)	Faber 1984	**B**
		Harper 1984	**B**

Huxley, Aldous   Born in Surrey, 1894. Died 1963.

In *Collecting Modern First Editions* (1977) I recorded only Huxley's highlight, *Brave New World*. Even then, this was a little cavalier and dismissive, but by now interest has certainly grown to the extent where a complete listing is called for.

1	**The Burning Wheel** (verse)	Blackwell 1916	L
2	**Jonah** (verse)	Holywell 1917	L
	Approximately 50 signed copies.		
3	**The Defeat of Youth and Other Poems**	Blackwell 1918	K
	250 copies only.		
4	**Leda** (verse)	Chatto & Windus 1920	H
	In addition to the trade edition, Chatto	Doran 1920	G
	put out 160 numbered and signed		
	editions (**J**). The Doran edition		
	contained only the title poem, and was		
	illustrated by Eric Gill.		
5	**Limbo** (6 stories and a play)	Chatto & Windus 1920	F
		Doran 1920	E
6	**Crome Yellow** (novel)	Chatto & Windus 1921	H
		Doran 1922	G
7	**Mortal Coils** (stories)	Chatto & Windus 1922	F
	Includes Huxley's most celebrated story	Doran 1922	E
	'The Gioconda Smile'.		
8	**Antic Hay** (novel)	Chatto & Windus 1923	F
		Doran 1923	E
9	**On the Margin** (essays)	Chatto & Windus 1923	D
		Doran 1923	C
10	**Little Mexican and Other Stories**	Chatto & Windus 1924	E
		Doran 1924	D
11	**Along the Road** (essays)	Chatto & Windus 1925	D
	As well as the trade edition, Doran	Doran 1925	C
	issued 250 signed numbered copies (**I**).		
12	**Selected Poems**	Blackwell 1925	D
		Appleton 1925	D
13	**Those Barren Leaves** (novel)	Chatto & Windus 1925	D
	Doran edition: as with 11.	Doran 1925	D
14	**Essays New and Old**	Chatto & Windus 1926	H
	The Chatto edition comprised 650	Doran 1927	D
	signed, numbered copies.		
15	**Jesting Pilate** (travel)	Chatto & Windus 1926	D
		Doran 1926	D
16	**Two or Three Graces and Other Stories**	Chatto & Windus 1926	D
		Doran 1926	D

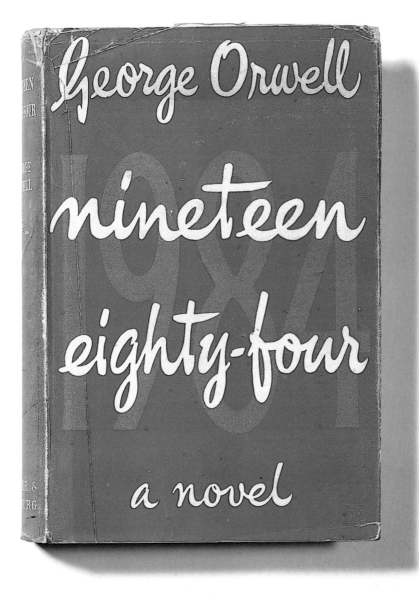

The book of the year, in the less common maroon dust-wrapper

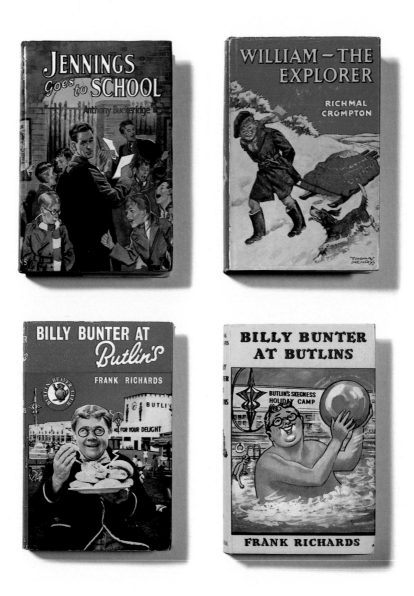

The three most famous fictional schoolboys. The *Jennings* is the first in the series, while the two *Bunters* are explained by the fact that one version was issued free as a Christmas gift by the Butlin's holiday camps, while the other is the standard edition

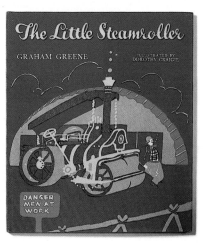

Graham Greene's first juvenile (published anonymously) and a couple of sequels

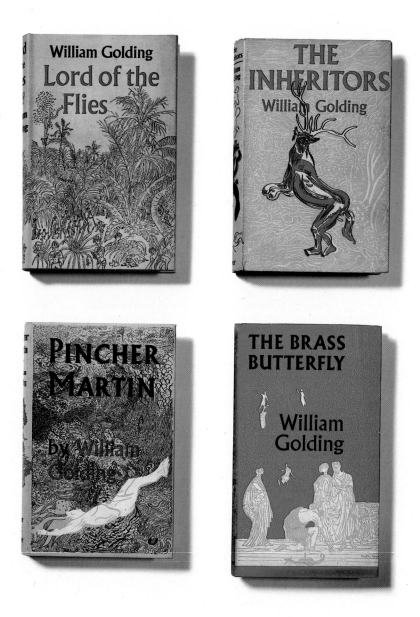

Golding's first and most famous novel, together with the two that followed it, and his very scarce play

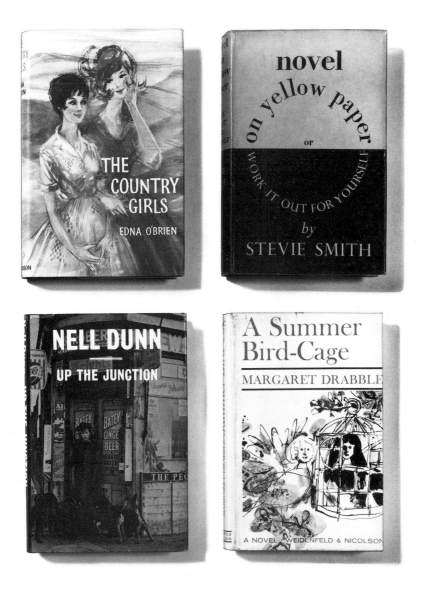

Four very different first novels by women writers

LUPERCAL
LUPERCAL
LUPERCAL
LUPERCAL
LUPERCAL
LUPERCAL
LUPERCAL
LUPERCAL

TED·HUGHES·

Crossing
the
Water
SYLVIA
PLATH

The Sense
of
Movement

THOM
GUNN

Death
of a
Naturalist

by
Seamus
Heaney

Representative works from four of Faber's leading poets

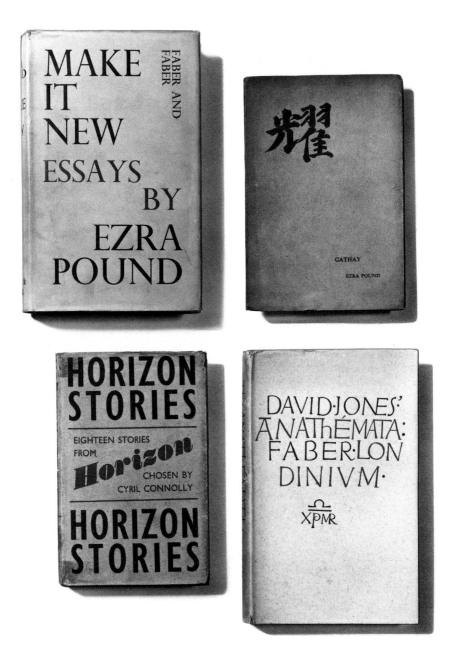

Middle-period Pound next to a very early translation by him from the Chinese, a selection of stories culled from Connolly's *Horizon*, and David Jones's highlight, in a dust-wrapper designed by the author

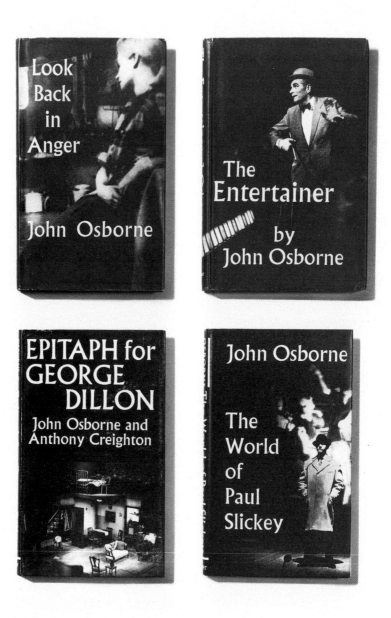

The first four plays from the leading 'angry young man' of the fifties

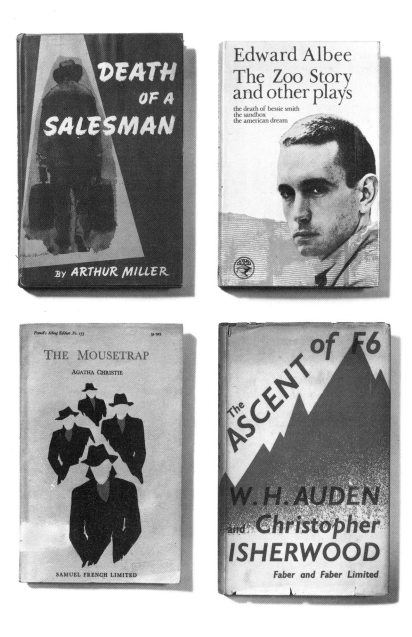

Poetry, prose and poser in the theatre

The first (pseudonymous) edition of *A Grief Observed* together with the later issue.
The first edition of *Animal Farm* and the curious first illustrated edition

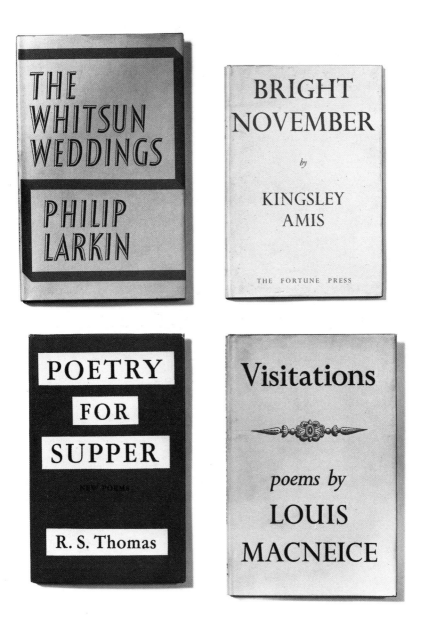

Four highly regarded slim volumes from four highly collected poets

Isherwood's most sought-after early works

The key novel by Virginia Woolf, with artwork by Vanessa Bell

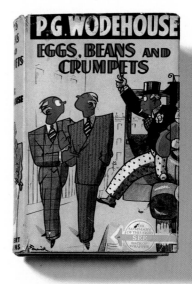
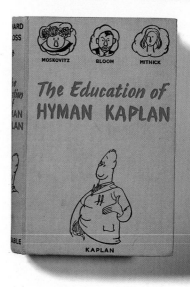

Four very funny books, two by The Master

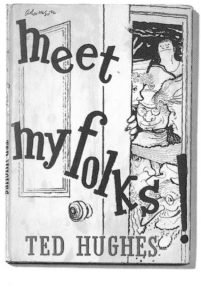
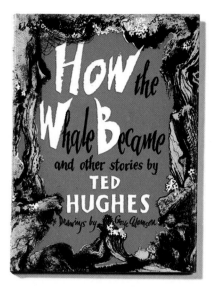

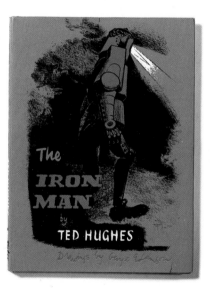

Ted Hughes's four early juveniles

The Alexandria Quartet, in the four separate first editions

17	**Proper Studies** (essays)	Chatto & Windus 1927	C
		Doubleday Doran 1928	C
18	**Point Counter Point** (novel)	Chatto & Windus 1928	E
		Doubleday Doran 1928	D
19	**Arabia Infelix** (verse) Comprising 692 signed, numbered copies in all.	Fountain Press (NY) 1929	H
20	**Do What You Will** (essays)	Chatto & Windus 1929	H
		Chatto & Windus 1929	C
		Doubleday Doran 1929	C
21	**Holy Face and Other Essays** Drawings by Albert Rutherston. 300 numbered copies.	The Fleuron Press 1929	G
22	**Apennine** (verse) 91 signed, numbered copies.	Slide Mountain Press (US) 1930	H
23	**Brief Candles** (stories)	Chatto & Windus 1930	D
		Doubleday Doran 1930	D
24	**Vulgarity in Literature** (essay) Published as 260 signed, numbered copies (**G**), and also as No. 1 in Chatto's 'Dolphin Books' series (**C**).	Chatto & Windus 1930	
25	**The Cicadas and Other Poems** Chatto published 160 signed, numbered copies simultaneously (**H**).	Chatto & Windus 1931 Doubleday Doran 1931	D D
26	**Music at Night and Other Essays** By now the simultaneous publication of signed, numbered editions was established, and for this book – between Britain and America – no less than 1684 such numbered copies were published (**G**).	Chatto & Windus 1931 Doubleday Doran 1931	D D
27	**The World of Light** (play) Chatto also published 160 signed, numbered copies (**G**).	Chatto & Windus 1931 Doubleday Doran 1931	C C
28	**Brave New World** (novel) Of this classic, both Chatto and Doubleday issued a signed numbered edition, of 324 and 250, respectively (**L**).	Chatto & Windus 1932 Doubleday Doran 1932	I G
29	**Rotunda** (essays) A selection of previously published work.	Chatto & Windus 1932	C
30	**T.H. Huxley as a Man of Letters** 28 pages. The Huxley Memorial Lecture.	Macmillan 1932	C
31	**Texts and Pretexts** (essays)	Chatto & Windus 1932	C
		Harper 1933	C
32	**Retrospect: An Omnibus of Aldous Huxley's Books**	Doubleday Doran 1933	C

33 **Beyond the Mexique Bay** (essays)   Chatto & Windus 1934   C
In addition to the trade edition, Chatto   Harper 1934   C
issued 210 signed, numbered copies (**G**).

34 **Eyeless in Gaza** (novel)   Chatto & Windus 1936   C
Chatto also issued 200 signed,   Harper 1936   C
numbered copies (**H**).

35 **The Olive Tree and Other Essays**   Chatto & Windus 1936   C
Harper 1937   C

36 **What Are You Going to do About**   Chatto & Windus 1936   C
It? The Case for Constructive   Harper 1937   B
Peace
35-page pamphlet.

37 **Ends and Means** (essays)   Chatto & Windus 1937   B
Chatto also issued 160 signed,   Harper 1937   B
numbered copies (**G**).

38 **Stories, Essays and Poems**   Dent 1937   B
An anthology of previously published
material, in the Everyman's Library.

39 **After Many a Summer**   Chatto & Windus 1939   B
(novel)   Harper 1939   B

40 **Grey Eminence** (non-fiction)   Chatto & Windus 1941   B
Harper 1941   B

41 **The Art of Seeing** (non-fiction)   Chatto & Windus 1942   B
Harper 1942   B

42 **Time Must Have a Stop** (novel)   Chatto & Windus 1944   B
Harper 1944   B

43 **The Perennial Philosophy**   Chatto & Windus 1945   B
Harper 1945   B

44 **Science, Liberty and Peace**   Chatto & Windus 1946   B
(non-fiction)   Harper 1946   B

45 **Verses and a Comedy**   Chatto & Windus 1946   B
46 **Ape and Essence** (novel)   Chatto & Windus 1949   B
Harper 1948   B

47 **The Gioconda Smile** (play)   Chatto & Windus 1948   C
Dramatized version of the story in 7.   Harper 1948   B

48 **The Prisons** (essay)   Trianon Press 1949
The English (Trianon) edition   Zeitlin & Ver Brugge
comprised 1000 unsigned copies (**B**)   1949
and 212 signed and numbered (**E**), and
the American just 212 signed and
numbered (**E**).

49 **Themes and Variations** (essays)   Chatto & Windus 1950   B
Harper 1950   B

50 **The Devils of Loudun**   Chatto & Windus 1952   C
(non-fiction)   Harper 1952   C

51 **The Doors of Perception**   Chatto & Windus 1954   B
A seminal work, revived in the sixties at   Harper 1954   B
the height of the drug culture.

52	**The Genius and the Goddess** (novel)	Chatto & Windus 1955	B
		Harper 1955	B
53	**Adonis and the Alphabet** (essays)	Chatto & Windus 1956	B
54	**Tomorrow and Tomorrow and Tomorrow** (essays)	Harper 1956	B
	Same as 53.		
55	**Heaven and Hell** (non-fiction)	Chatto & Windus 1956	B
		Harper 1956	B
56	**Collected Short Stories**	Chatto & Windus 1957	B
		Harper 1957	B
57	**Brave New World Revisited** (novel)	Chatto & Windus 1958	B
	The sequel to 28.	Harper 1958	B
58	**Collected Essays**	Harper 1959	B
59	**Island**	Chatto & Windus 1961	B
		Harper 1961	B

Films:
A Woman's Vengeance (based upon *The Gioconda Smile*) Universal 1947 **Prelude to Fame** (based upon the story *Young Archimedes*) General Film 1950 **The Devils** (based upon *The Devils of Loudun*) Warner Bros 1971

Bibliography:
Claire John Eschelbach & Joyce Lee Shober **Aldous Huxley: A Bibliography 1916–1959** University of California Press 1961

Biography:
The essential and definitive biography: Sybille Bedford **Aldous Huxley** Vol. 1: **1894–1939** Chatto/Collins 1973; Vol. 2: **1939–63** Chatto/Collins 1974

Isherwood, Christopher   Born in Cheshire, 1904.

It seems extraordinary to me that *Sally Bowles* is nearly fifty years old – it always comes up so fresh, and feeling very modern, despite the passé and much parodied 'decadence' that it depicts. But then, Isherwood is eighty. Sad too that in the twenty years since the hauntingly stark *A Single Man*, he has published only one other novel, his other books having been given over to autobiography and gurus.

As will be seen from the values below, however, it is really only pre-war (and particularly Berlin) Isherwood that is of great interest to collectors. The post-1950 stuff – though not rare – is, I think, undervalued.

1	**All the Conspirators** (novel)	Cape 1928	I
		New Directions 1958	C
2	**The Memorial** (novel)	Hogarth Press 1932	G
		New Directions 1946	C

Isherwood

25 **My Guru and His Disciple** (non-fiction)	Farrar Straus 1980	B
	Eyre Methuen 1980	B
26 **October** (prose)	Twelvetrees Press (US) 1980	M
The American limited edition was printed on hand-made paper, leather bound, and $400 on publication. The Methuen edition was paperback, limited to 1000 copies, and priced at £12.50.	Methuen 1982	C
27 **People One Ought to Know** (verse)	Doubleday 1982	B
Nonsense verse, illustrated by Sylvain Mangeot.	Macmillan 1982	B

Isherwood's interest in Vedanta is shown by the two books he wrote – **An Approach to Vedanta** and **Essentials of Vedanta** Vedanta Press (USA) 1963 and 1969, as well as the two books he edited: **Vedanta and the Western World** Rodd 1946; Allen & Unwin 1948, **Vedanta for Modern Man** Harper 1951; Allen & Unwin 1952

Films:
I Am a Camera Monogram 1955 (based on the *Berlin Stories*)   **Cabaret** Cinerama 1972 (based on *I Am a Camera*)   **Frankenstein: The True Story** Universal 1973

James, P.D.   Born in Oxford, 1920.

The name recalls the great M.R. James, but P.D. conceals none other than Phyllis Dorothy, and the lady is fast on her way to becoming the Queen of Crime, in the tradition of Dorothy L. Sayers – or maybe Michael Innes or Edmund Crispin. Anyway, she is very literary and very good, and collectors are taking a lot of notice. She was written surprisingly few books, as will be seen below, but none is easy to come by.

1 **Cover Her Face** (novel)	Faber 1962	J
	Scribner 1966	C
2 **A Mind to Murder** (novel)	Faber 1963	I
	Scribner 1967	C
3 **Unnatural Causes** (novel)	Faber 1967	F
	Scribner 1967	D
4 **Shroud for a Nightingale** (novel)	Faber 1971	E
	Scribner 1971	D
5 **An Unsuitable Job for a Woman** (novel)	Faber 1972	D
	Scribner 1972	C
6 **The Black Tower** (novel)	Faber 1975	C
	Scribner 1975	C
7 **Death of an Expert Witness** (novel)	Faber 1977	B
	Scribner 1977	B

8 **Innocent Blood** (novel)	Faber 1980	**B**
	Scribner 1980	**B**
9 **P.D. James Omnibus**	Faber 1982	**B**
Includes 3, 4 and 5.		
10 **The Skull Beneath the Skin** (novel)	Faber 1982	**B**
	Scribner 1982	**B**

Film:
An Unsuitable Job for a Woman Boyd 1981

Jellicoe, Ann   Born in Yorkshire, 1927.

Well, yes, still notable for the following – but nothing since has come close to *The Knack*. Can she have lost it?

1 **The Sport of My Mad Mother** (play)	Faber 1958	**B**
This was published in *The Observer Plays* along with other plays, including N.F. Simpson's *A Resounding Tinkle*. The Preface is by Kenneth Tynan.		
2 **The Knack** (play)	Encore 1962	**C**
	French (NY) 1962	**C**

Two Plays: The Knack and The Sport of My Mad Mother was published in America by Dell in 1964.

Film:
The Knack United Artists 1965

Jerome, Jerome K.   Born in Walsall, 1859. Died 1927.

Yes, I *know* not strictly within the brief of the modern first edition (although he did publish over twenty books during the twentieth century) – but I'm biased. Since publishing my biography of Jerome in 1982, the amount of correspondence I have received convinces me that interest is very strong – and indeed much more of Jerome's *œuvre* is now back in print than was a few years ago. A revival was well overdue.

1 **On the Stage – And Off** (pieces)	Field & Tuer 1885	**G**
This tiny book (about four inches by three) was soon followed by an illustrated edition, Leadenhall Press, illus. by Kenneth M. Skeaping (**D**).		
2 **Barbara** (play)	Lacy 1886	**C**

3	**The Idle Thoughts of an Idle Fellow** (essays)	Field & Tuer 1886	**D**

The earliest editions make no mention of 'edition' on cover.

4	**Sunset** (play)	Fitzgerald (NY) n.d.(1888)	**B**
5	**Fennel** (play)	French n.d. (1888)	**B**
6	**Woodbarrow Farm** (play)	French n.d. (1888)	**B**
7	**Stage-Land** (satire)	Chatto & Windus 1889	**D**
8	**Three Men in a Boat** (novel)	Arrowsmith 1889	**H**

The famous novel, bound in Thames-green cloth, the front bearing a silhouette and black lettering, while the spine is lettered in gold. Subsequent issues may easily be mistaken for the very first edition, as superficially all are similar. The basic distinction remains that the publisher's address at the foot of the title page should read 'Quay Street' and *not* '11 Quay Street'. The heading over the advertisements on the front fixed endpaper, however, should read 'J.W. Arrowsmith, Bristol' and *not* '11 Quay Street, Bristol'. Questions have been raised as to the relevance of inverted ornamental capitals opening chapters, but the above two points remain the only really reliable guides. The book is illustrated by A. Fredrics, and the title page bears the date of publication.

9	**Told After Supper** (essays)	Leadenhall Press 1891	**D**
10	**The Diary of a Pilgrimage** (novel)	Arrowsmith 1891	**C**

Earliest editions also contain six essays, and make no mention of edition on cover.

11	**Novel Notes** (articles)	Leadenhall Press 1893	**C**
12	**John Ingerfield** (stories)	McClure 1894	**D**
13	**My First Book** (essays, with other writers)	Chatto & Windus 1894	**D**

Blue cloth. The 1897 red-bound edition is often mistaken for the 1st.

14	**The Prude's Progress** (play)	French 1895	**B**
15	**Sketches in Lavender, Blue and Green** (stories)	Longman 1897	**D**
16	**The Second Thoughts of an Idle Fellow**	Hurst & Blackett 1898	**D**
17	**Three Men on the Bummel** (novel)	Arrowsmith 1900	**D**

18	**The Observations of Henry** (stories)	Arrowsmith 1901	D
19	**Miss Hobbs** (play)	French 1902	B
20	**Paul Kelver** (novel)	Hutchinson 1902	C
21	**Tea-Table Talk** (essays)	Hutchinson 1903	C
22	**Tommy and Co.** (novel)	Hutchinson 1904	C
23	**American Wives and Others** (essays)	Stokes 1904	C
	A miscellany published only in USA.		
24	**Idle Ideas in 1905** (essays)	Hurst & Blackett 1905	C
25	**The Passing of the Third Floor Back** (essays, stories)	Hurst & Blackett 1907	C
26	**The Angel and the Author** (essays)	Hurst & Blackett 1908	C
27	**They and I** (novel)	Hutchinson 1909	C
28	**Fanny and the Servant Problem** (play)	Lacy 1909	B
29	**The Passing of the Third Floor Back** (play)	Hurst & Blackett 1910	C
30	**The Master of Mrs Chilvers** (play)	T. Fisher Unwin 1911	B
31	**Robina in Search of a Husband** (play)	Lacy 1914	B
32	**Malvina of Brittany** (stories)	Cassell 1916	C
33	**All Roads Lead to Calvary** (novel)	Hutchinson 1919	C
34	**Anthony John** (novel)	Cassell 1923	C
35	**A Miscellany of Sense and Nonsense**	Arrowsmith 1923	C
36	**The Celebrity** (play)	Hodder & Stoughton 1926	B
37	**My Life and Times** (autobiog.)	Hodder & Stoughton 1926	D
38	**The Soul of Nicholas Synders** (play)	Hodder & Stoughton 1927	B

The list above is of English 1st editions, though it should be noted that in America 17 was published as **Three Men on Wheels**, 32 as **The Street of the Blank Wall**, 28 as **Lady Bantock** and 36 as **Cook**.

In addition to the above, the following works should be noted:
Playwriting: A Handbook for Would-Be Dramatic Authors This booklet, published by the Stage Office in 1888 by 'A Dramatist' is almost certainly by J.K.J., as has been reasonably established in Arnott & Robinson, **English Theatrical Literature, 1559–1900**. **K** Arrowsmith 1892. The story 'K' was published by a writer cloaked beneath the pseudonym 'McK'. Jerome never owned to having written the piece, but a letter written to Arrowsmith and auctioned by Sotheby's in 1968 revealed that McK was none other than Jerome. It appears that the story was to have been entitled *Weeds*, and it is not at all certain that any copies went on sale. **Humours of Cycling** Bowden 1897. Jerome contributes

an essay entitled 'Women on Wheels'. The volume was reissued in 1905
by Chatto & Windus. **Songs From the Heart of England: An
Anthology of Walsall Poetry** T. Fisher Unwin 1920. Jerome
contributed a short foreword to this, compiled by Alfred Moss.
Jerome also edited two magazines, *The Idler* and *Today*. *The Idler* was
founded in 1892 by Robert Barr, who offered Jerome the joint editorship.
They edited it until 1898, although the magazine ran until 1911. *The Idler*
was issued in bound volumes. (**B** each). *Today* was a weekly founded by
Jerome himself in 1893. He edited it until 1898 and the magazine ran
until 1905, when it merged with *London Opinion*. Bound volumes of *Today*
were also published, but these are much more scarce than *The Idler*
(**C** each).

Films:
The Passing of the Third Floor Back Gaumont British 1936   **Three
Men in a Boat** British Lion 1956

Biography (including bibliography):
Joseph Connolly **Jerome K. Jerome: A Critical Biography** Orbis
1982

Jhabvala, Ruth Prawer   Born in Cologne, 1927. British.

Although she has been publishing for thirty years, Jhabvala is a comparatively recent discovery for collectors, and therefore it should still be possible
to gather the bulk of her *œuvre* without too much trouble or expense –
although her first two or three books are scarce, and the recent film *Heat and
Dust* (coinciding as it did with Britain's great Indian revival) has attracted
great attention to its author, so if a collection is contemplated at all either
now is the time, or else you are just too late.

1	**To Whom She Will** (novel)	Allen & Unwin 1955	**E**
2	**Amrita** (same as 1)	Norton (US) 1956	**C**
3	**The Nature of Passion** (novel)	Allen & Unwin 1956	**D**
		Norton 1957	**C**
4	**Esmond in India** (novel)	Allen & Unwin 1957	**D**
		Norton 1958	**C**
5	**The Householder** (novel)	Murray 1960	**C**
		Norton 1960	**C**
6	**Get Ready for Battle** (novel)	Murray 1962	**C**
		Norton 1963	**C**
7	**Like Birds, Like Fishes**	Murray 1963	**C**
	and Other Stories	Norton 1964	**C**
8	**A Backward Place** (novel)	Murray 1965	**C**
		Norton 1965	**C**
9	**A Stronger Climate: 9 stories**	Murray 1968	**B**
		Norton 1969	**B**

10 **An Experience of India** (stories)	Murray 1971		B
	Norton 1972		B
11 **A New Dominion** (novel)	Murray 1973		B
12 **Travelers** (same as 11)	Harper & Row 1973		B
13 **Heat and Dust** (novel)	Murray 1975		C
	Harper 1976		B
14 **How I Became a Holy Mother** (stories)	Harper 1976		B
	Harper 1976		B
15 **In Search of Love and Beauty** (novel)	Murray 1983		B
	Morrow 1983		B

Film:
Heat and Dust Merchant Ivory 1983

Johns, W.E.   Born in Hertford, 1893. Died 1968.

As well as fifteen miscellaneous books of fact and fiction for adults, Johns wrote no less than one hundred and forty adventures concerning our old chums Gimlet, Steeley, Worrals and (this one you will have heard of) – Biggles. Far too many to list here, then, but they include such wonders as *Biggles Sees It Through* OUP 1941, *Biggles Defies The Swastika* OUP 1941, *Biggles in Borneo* OUP 1943, *Biggles Works It Out* Hodder 1951 and – as will have become apparent – *No Rest for Biggles* Hodder 1956.

Johns' first book, however, was:

1 **The Camels are Coming** (novel) and the first Biggles followed two years later:	J. Hamilton 1932		F
2 **Biggles of the Camel Squadron** (novel)	J. Hamilton 1934		E

Jones, David   Born in Kent, 1895. Died 1974.

I had *heard* of *In Parenthesis* and *The Anathemata* – this mainly because of Auden's enthusiasm for it – but I hadn't read them. My first awareness of David Jones was as an artist, when I was devastated by the beauty of an ordination certificate he had done for Peter Levi. The lettering is as easy to feel as the poetry can be difficult to understand, so chock full of learning and allusion is it – recalling, in this respect, Auden and Pound. Jones's main work is worth the struggle. The later stuff – and the posthumous pieces – might always remain a conundrum understood fully only by its creator.

1 **In Parenthesis**	Faber 1937		I
Although the Amer. ed. is 24 years after the English, it contains an Intro. by T.S. Eliot, reprinted in the first English paperback edition, Faber 1963	Chilmark 1961		E

2 **The Anathemata**	Faber 1952	**H**
	Chilmark 1963	**C**
3 **Epoch and Artist**	Faber 1959	**F**
	Chilmark 1964	**C**
4 **The Tribune's Visitation**	Fulcrum Press 1969	**C**
5 **The Sleeping Lord**	Faber 1974	**C**
6 **The Kensington Mass**	Agenda Editions 1975	**B**
7 **Letters to Vernon Watkins**	University of Wales Press 1976	**B**
8 **The Dying Gaul and Other Writings**	Faber 1978	**B**
9 **Introducing David Jones: A Selection of His Writings** Ed. John Matthias	Faber 1980	**B**
10 **Dai Greatcoat: A Self-Portrait in His Letters** Ed. René Hague.	Faber 1980	**C**
11 **The Painted Inscriptions of David Jones** by Nicolette Gray	Gordon Fraser 1980	**D**
12 **The Roman Quarry and Other Sequences**	Agenda 1981	**B**
	Sheap Meadow (US) 1982	**B**

D/ws are extremely important with David Jones, as those of 2, 3, 4 and 5 bear his exquisite typography. There have been two *Agenda* special numbers devoted to David Jones, Vol. 5 Nos 1–3 1967, and Vol. 11 No. 4–Vol. 12 No. 1 1973/74; and one slight book on his art, Penguin Modern Painters 1949; it is one of the most scarce of the series, and Grade **C**. One book of literary criticism has appeared: David Blamires **David Jones, Artist and Writer** Manchester University Press 1971, Grade **D** In 1975, *The Tablet* published Peter Levi **In Memory of David Jones**. The d/w and frontis. of Peter Levi **Fresh Water, Sea Water** Black Raven Press 1966 reproduces Jones's superb design for Levi's ordination certificate.

Joyce, James   Born in Ireland, 1882. Died 1941.

Joyce is scarce. There is really no such thing as a common or easy Joyce first edition; even the three volumes of his letters issued in the sixties have gone to ground. To collect Joyce seriously, then, you need to have a lot of luck in coming across the items, and a whole lot more money with which to pay for them. And Joyce's signature too, incidentally – whether upon a limited edition, or a trade edition, or a letter – is very valuable and rare. For example, the Faber 1st of *Finnegans Wake* might fetch £200 for a decent copy, but an inscribed copy could be four or five times that.

Joyce

1 **Chamber Music** (poems)   Elkin Mathews 1907   **U**
The American first was   Cornhill Co. 1918   **L**
unauthorized. The authorized
edition was published later in the
same year by Huebsch (**L**).

2 **Dubliners** (stories)   Grant Richards 1914   **L**
    Huebsch 1916   **I**

3 **A Portrait of the Artist as a Young**   Huebsch 1916   **K**
Man   Egoist Ltd 1917   **I**
The 1st English was American sheets.
In the following year The Egoist Ltd
published a 2nd edition, printed in
England.

4 **Exiles** (play)   Grant Richards 1918   **I**
This play was reissued in 1951 by the   Huebsch 1918   **I**
Viking Press 'with hitherto unpublished
notes by the author' (**D**). It was
published in this form in England by
Cape in 1952 (**D**).

5 **Ulysses** (novel)   Shakespeare Press   **Q**
Limited to 1000 copies, 100 signed (**V**).   (Paris) 1922
Published in France.

6 **Ulysses**   Egoist Press 1922   **M**
This was the 1st English edition,
though printed in France. Limited to
2000 numbered copies.

7 **Ulysses**   Shakespeare Press   **L**
This was the 1st American edition,   (Paris) 1929
though unauthorized. The 1st
authorized American edition was
published in 1934 by Random House,
though set up from the Shakespeare
edition. The first printing of the
Random House ed., due to copyright,
was only 100 copies (**N**), and the
second printing 10,300 (**I**).

8 **Ulysses**   Bodley Head 1936   **J**
This was the 1st English edition
actually printed in England. 100 were
signed (**R**).

9 **Pomes Penyeach**   Shakespeare & Co   **L**
100 were signed (**Q**). The 1st American   (Paris) 1927
edition was published by Sylvia Beach
in 1931 (**I**). The 1st English edition –
but printed in France – was by the
Obelisk Press in 1932 (**H**), and the 1st
English edition printed in England was
by Faber in 1933 (**F**).

10 **Anna Livia Plurabelle** (fragment) Crosby Gaige (NY)   I
 The American ed. was limited to 850   1928
 signed copies, but the Faber ed. was in Faber 1930   C
 the Criterion Miscellany series, and
 unlimited.

11 **Tales Told of Shem and Shaun**   Black Sun Press   M
 Limited to 650 copies, 100 signed (**O**). (Paris) 1929

12 **Two Tales of Shem and Shaun**   Faber 1932   E
 Extract from 11; 1st English.

13. **Haveth Childers Everywhere**   Fountain Press 1930   I
 (fragment)
 Printed in France, but published in
 America. Limited to 685 copies, 100
 signed (**O**). The 1st English edition was
 published by Faber in the following
 year, in an unlimited edition (**D**).

14 **Collected Poems**   Black Sun Press 1936   H
 Limited to 800 copies, 50 signed (**M**).
 A trade edition followed in 1937 from
 Viking (**E**).

15 **Finnegans Wake**   Faber 1939   L
                Viking 1939   J

16 **Stephen Hero** (draft)   Cape 1944   H
                New Directions 1944 G

17 **The Essential James Joyce**   Cape 1948   B
 (extracts)

18 **The Letters** Vol. I   Faber 1957   D
19 **The Critical Writings**   Faber 1959   C
20 **The Cat and the Devil** (juvenile) Faber 1965   C
21 **The Letters** Vol. II   Faber 1966   D
22 **The Letters** Vol. III   Faber 1966   D
23 **Giacomo Joyce**   Viking 1968   D
                Faber 1968   D

Films:
Ulysses British Lion 1966   **Passages from Finnegans Wake**
Expanding Cinema 1965   **Portrait of the Artist as a Young Man**
Ulysses 1977

Bibliography:
John J. Slocum & Herbert Cahoon
A Bibliography of James Joyce Yale University Press 1953

There have been a vast number of books on Joyce, but below appears a
selection of the best:
T.S. Eliot **Introducing James Joyce** Faber 1942   Harry Levin **James
Joyce: A Critical Introduction** Faber 1944   Richard Ellmann **James
Joyce** OUP 1959; new edition OUP 1983.   Anthony Burgess **Here**

Joyce

Comes Everybody Faber 1965   John Gross **Joyce** Fontana 1971   A good deal of information is also given in Stanislaus Joyce **My Brother's Keeper** Faber 1958. This was edited by Richard Ellmann, and has a Preface by T.S. Eliot.

Kästner, Erich   Born in Germany, 1899. Died 1974.

Although a translation, a children's classic, and one that seems to be remembered by all with great fondness. Kästner wrote other books, and the character Emil appears again, but none captures the great appeal of the following:

Emil and the Detectives (juvenile)	Cape 1930	**C–D**
This was first published in Germany in 1929 as *Emil und die Detektive*. The 1st English edition is scarce.	Doubleday 1930	**C**

Film:
Emil and the Detectives United Artists 1931; Disney 1965.

Kazantzakis, Nikos   Born in Greece, 1885. Died 1957.

The author of quite a few novels, but still remembered for the one – and damnably hard to find it is, too.

Zorba the Greek (novel)	Lehmann 1952	**D**
The novel was originally published in Greek in 1946. The Lehmann edition spells his name Kazantzaki. It is scarce.	Simon & Schuster 1953	**C**

Film:
Zorba the Greek 20th Century Fox 1964.

Keneally, Thomas   Born in Sydney, 1935.

Keneally is very much an Australian author, and much of his output concerns Australia, as is usual – indeed *mandatory* – with all Commonwealth (or ex-Commonwealth) authors. How strange, then, that the book that firmly established his name upon the literary map (*Schindler's Ark*) concerned the Jews, for it is an equally strictly adhered to principle in literature that only Jews write about Jews.

The main controversy surrounding *Schindler's Ark* when it won the Booker Prize was whether the book could indeed be classed as fiction at all, so documentary were its contents, but apparently it *is* a novel, because Hodder & Stoughton say so. It was the first book that Keneally had done for Hodder, and they were justly proud of their new acquisition. It should not be too difficult to assemble a collection of Keneally – indeed, until recently, collectors expressed little interest. Prices for the time being, then, should be low.

The first seven of Keneally's books were published in Britain and Australia simultaneously.

1 **The Place at Whitton** (novel)	Cassell 1964	G
	Walker 1965	D
2 **The Fear** (novel)	Cassell 1965	F
3 **Bring Larks and Heros** (novel)	Cassell 1967	E
	Viking 1968	D
4 **Three Cheers for the Paraclete** (novel)	Angus & Robertson 1968	B
	Viking 1969	B
5 **The Survivor** (novel)	Angus & Robertson 1969	B
6 **A Dutiful Daughter** (novel)	Angus & Robertson 1971	B
	Viking 1971	B
7 **The Chant of Jimmie Blacksmith** (novel)	Angus & Robertson 1972	C
	Viking 1972	C
8 **Blood Red, Sister Rose** (novel)	Collins 1974	B
	Viking 1974	B
9 **Moses the Lawgiver** (novelization)	Harper 1975	B
	Collins 1976	B
10 **Gossip from the Forest** (novel)	Collins 1975	B
	Harcourt Brace 1976	B
11 **Season in Purgatory** (novel)	Collins 1976	B
	Harcourt Brace 1977	B
12 **A Victim of the Aurora** (novel)	Collins 1977	B
	Harcourt Brace 1978	B
13 **Ned Kelly and the City of Bees** (juvenile)	Cape 1978	B
	Godine 1981	B
14 **Passenger** (novel)	Collins 1979	B
	Harcourt Brace 1979	B
15 **The Confederates** (novel)	Collins 1979	B
	Harcourt Brace 1980	B
16 **The Cut-Rate Kingdom**	Wild Cat Press (Australia; periodical) 1980	B
	1st book form Penguin (Australia) 1984	B
	Allen Lane (UK) 1984	B
17 **Schindler's Ark** (novel)	Hodder & Stoughton 1982	C
18 **Schlinder's List** (same as 16)	Simon & Schuster 1982	C

19 **Outback** (non-fiction)	Hodder & Stoughton 1983	B

Films:
The Chant of Jimmie Blacksmith Fox 1979   **Schindler's Ark**
Universal 1984/5

Kerouac, Jack   Born in Massachussets, 1922. Died 1969.

Kerouac has a following, and is hard to gather. The novels are, I think, infinitely more desirable than the verse, and the highlight is *On the Road*.

1 **The Town and the City** (novel)	Harcourt Brace 1950	H
(Author's name appears as *John*	Eyre & Spottiswoode	F
Kerouac)	1951	
2 **On the Road** (novel)	Viking 1957	H
	Deutsch 1958	F
3 **The Subterraneans** (novel)	Grove Press 1958	G
	Deutsch 1960	F
4 **The Dharma Bums** (novel)	Viking 1958	G
	Deutsch 1959	F
5 **Mexico City Blues** (verse)	Grove Press 1959	E
6 **Hymn – God Pray For Me** (verse)	Privately printed 1959	G
7 **Doctor Sax: Faust Part Three**	Grove Press 1959	D
(novel)	Evergreen 1961	C
8 **Maggie Cassidy** (novel)	Avon 1959	C
	Panther 1960	B
9 **Excerpts from 'Visions of Cody'**	New Directions 1959	C
(novel)		
10 **Tristessa** (novel)	Avon 1960	B
11 **Rimbaud** (verse)	City Lights 1960	C
12 **Book of Dreams** (verse)	City Lights 1960	C
13 **The Scripture of the Golden**	Totem-Corinth (US)	C
Eternity (verse)	1960	
14 **Lonesome Traveler** (prose)	McGraw Hill 1960	C
Drawings by Larry Rivers.	Deutsch 1962	B
15 **Big Sur** (novel)	Farrar Straus 1962	C
	Deutsch 1963	B
16 **Poem**	Privately printed 1962	E
17 **Visions of Gerard** (novel)	Farrar Straus 1963	C
The Deutsch edition includes 10.	Deutsch 1964	B
18 **Desolation Angels** (novel)	Coward McCann 1965	C
	Deutsch 1966	B
19 **Satori in Paris** (novel)	Grove Press 1966	C
	Deutsch 1967	B
20 **Hugo Weber** (verse)	Portents (US) 1967	B
21 **Someday You'll be Lying** (verse)	Privately printed 1968	E

22 **Vanity of Duluoz:**	Coward McCann 1968	C
An Adventurous Education 1935–46	Deutsch 1969	B
(novel)		
23 **A Last Haiku** (verse)	Privately printed 1969	E
24 **Pic** (novel)	Grove Press 1971	B
The Deutsch edition includes 3.	Deutsch 1973	B
25 **Scattered Poems**	City Lights 1971	D
26 **Trip, Trap** (verse)	Grey Fox Press 1973	D
27 **Heaven and Other Poems**	Grey Fox Press 1977	D
28 **Baby Driver: A Story about Myself**	St Martin's 1981	B
Ed. Jan Kerouac.	Deutsch 1982	B

Bibliography:
Ann Charters **A Bibliography of Works by Jack Kerouac (Jean Louis de Kerouac) 1939–1967** Phoenix Bookshop 1967; revised edition 1975.

Kesey, Ken   Born in Colorado, 1935.

Still the author of only two novels, one of which remains very well known (largely because of the film) and is hard to find in either American or English editions. I have heard of an American in America paying $1000 for the American 1st of *Cuckoo*, and he must have been, a bit, to pay that sort of money.

1 **One Flew over the Cuckoo's Nest**	Viking 1962	I
(novel)	Methuen 1963	F
2 **Sometimes a Great Notion** (novel)	Viking 1964	D
	Methuen 1966	C

Film:
One Flew over the Cuckoo's Nest United Artists 1975.

Koestler, Arthur   Born in Hungary, 1905. Died 1983.

Although *Darkness at Noon* has always been a scarce and sought after first edition, it is true that Koestler has in recent years languished in the shade, as far as collectors are concerned. His death in 1983, however – as is so often the way – stimulated a new wave of interest, this fuelled by the bizarre death itself (he and his wife both committed suicide, calmly and with premeditation) and also the unique (if disappointingly dull) document which they left behind them – *Stranger on the Square*. What is most unusual from the collector's point of view (one might even say unique) is that Koestler's first book remains one of the easiest of all to find – this because it was printed in abnormally large quantities for distribution by The Left Book Club.

Koestler

1 **Spanish Testament** (autobiog.)   Gollancz 1937   B
This is the orange-wrapped Left Book
Club edition. An abridged edition was
published in America by Macmillan in
1942 as **Dialogue with Death**.

2 **The Gladiators** (novel)   Cape 1939   C
                                         Macmillan (US) 1939   B

3 **Darkness at Noon** (novel)   Cape 1940   F
                                         Macmillan 1941   D

4 **Scum of the Earth** (autobiog.)   Cape 1941   C
                                         Macmillan 1941   B

5 **Arrival and Departure** (novel)   Cape 1943   B
                                         Macmillan 1943   B

6 **The Yogi and the Commissar**   Cape 1945   B
(essays)   Macmillan 1945   B

7 **Thieves in the Night** (novel)   Macmillan (UK) 1946   B
                                         Macmillan (US) 1946   B

8 **Insight and Outlook** (essay)   Macmillan (UK) 1949   B
                                         Macmillan (US) 1949   B

9 **Promise and Fulfilment** (non-   Macmillan (UK) 1949   B
fiction)   Macmillan (US) 1949   B

10 **The Age of Longing** (novel)   Collins 1951   B
                                         Macmillan 1951   B

11 **Arrow in the Blue** (autobiog.)   Collins/Hamilton 1952 C
                                         Macmillan 1952   B

12 **The Invisible Writing** (autobiog.) Collins/Hamilton 1954 C
                                         Macmillan 1954   B

13 **The Trail of the Dinosaur** (essays) Collins 1955   B
                                         Macmillan 1955   B

14 **Reflections on Hanging** (essay)   Gollancz 1957   B
                                         Macmillan 1957   B

15 **The Sleepwalkers** (non-fiction)   Hutchinson 1959   B
                                         Macmillan 1959   B

16 **The Lotus and the Robot** (essays) Hutchinson 1960   B
                                         Macmillan 1961   B

17 **Hanged by the Neck** (essay)   Penguin 1961   A
18 **The Act of Creation** (non-fiction) Hutchinson 1964   B
                                         Macmillan 1964   B

19 **The Ghost in the Machine** (non-   Hutchinson 1967   B
fiction)   Macmillan 1968   B

20 **Drinkers of Infinity: Essays**   Hutchinson 1968   B
1955–1967   Macmillan 1969   B

21 **The Case of the Midwife Toad**   Hutchinson 1971   B
(non-fiction)   Random House 1972   B

22 **The Call-Girls** (novel)   Hutchinson 1972   B
                                         Random House 1973   B

23 **The Roots of Coincidence** (non-   Hutchinson 1972   B
fiction)   Random House 1972   B

24 **The Lion and the Ostrich** (essay)	OUP 1973	B
25 **The Challenge of Chance** (non-fiction)	Hutchinson 1973	B
	Random House 1975	B
With Alister Hardy and Robert Harvie.		B
26 **The Heel of Achilles: Essays 1968–1973**	Hutchinson 1974	B
	Random House 1975	B
27 **The Thirteenth Tribe** (non-fiction)	Hutchinson 1976	B
	Random House 1976	B
28 **Janus: A Summing Up** (essays)	Hutchinson 1978	B
	Random House 1978	B
29 **Bricks to Babel** (essays)	Hutchinson 1980	C
	Random House 1981	C
30 **Stranger on the Square**	Hutchinson 1984	B
This is the third, unfinished, volume of autobiography, following 11 and 12. It is billed as having been written by Arthur and Cynthia Koestler.	Random House 1984	B

Larkin, Philip   Born in Warwickshire, 1922.

Probably the most *revered* living poet, being avidly read and acknowledged by his peers as a master of his craft. A great deal of this respect emanates from the fact that he publishes so very little. This convinces us (and we are never disappointed) that each new volume, when it comes, will be *worth* it. It is very telling that in the seven years since I composed a checklist of his works for *Collecting Modern First Editions*, Larkin has published only one more work – and that a collection of previously published reviews and articles. *And* it won the W.H. Smith literary award.

1 **The North Ship** (verse)	Fortune Press 1945	P
Black cloth, the maroon d/w describing it as being one of the Fortune Poets series. There was an unauthorized edition published in 1965 (though stating 'first published 1945' on the verso of the title page) in maroon cloth. About 500 were printed, but the edition was recalled when Larkin became aware of its existence. Faber published an edition in 1966, with a new introduction and an extra poem (**C**).		
2 **Jill** (novel)	Fortune Press 1946	N
A revised edition was published in 1964 by Faber, and in America by the St Martin's Press (**E**).		
3 **A Girl in Winter** (novel)	Faber 1947	M
	St Martin's 1957	E

4	**XX Poems** Only 100 printed, all for the author – none for sale.	Privately printed 1951	Q
5	**The Fantasy Poets No. 21** About 300 copies.	Fantasy Press 1954	M
6	**The Less Deceived** (verse)	Marvell Press 1955 St Martin's 1960	M I
7	**The Whitsun Weddings** (verse)	Faber 1964 Random House 1964	E D
8	**All What Jazz: A Record Diary** **1961–68**	Faber 1970 St Martin's 1970	C C
9	**The Explosion** This was a single-sheet poem, in a signed limited edition of 1000 available at five guineas, only on subscription.	Poem-of-the-Month Club 1970	H
10	**The Oxford Book of Twentieth-** **Century English Verse** This very important book was edited by Larkin.	OUP 1973	C
11	**High Windows** (verse)	Faber 1974 Farrar Straus 1974	C C
12	**Required Writing** (prose) Larkin also wrote the Preface for **The** **Arts Council Collection of Modern** **Literary Manuscripts 1963–72** Turret Books 1974, a fascinating and valuable book in itself (**B**).	Faber 1983 Farrar Straus 1983	B B

Also of note:
    Larkin at Sixty   Faber 1982
    A tribute, with contributions by
    Kingsley Amis, John Betjeman, and
    Seamus Heaney, among others.

Bibliography:
B.C. Blomfield **Philip Larkin: A Bibliography 1933–76** Faber 1979

Lawrence, D.H.   Born in Nottinghamshire, 1885. Died 1930.

Still very much collected, and at last living down the reputation bestowed upon him by the idiots as having been the man who wrote that dirty book, for to a whole new generation The Trial of Lady Chatterley is ancient history. I do wish they would stop filming Lawrence, though. It is a personal view, of course, but I have never seen any film version of a Lawrence novel or story that has not been in some way *embarrassing* – something the books are not. Certainly, the films do nothing to enhance the author's reputation.

As will be seen from the following valuations, a great deal of the *œuvre* remains scarce and expensive. This position will persist.

Below is all his main work, though I have omitted a few privately printed items, special editions, etc. In some cases, however – notably *Lady Chatterley's Lover* – there are several relevant editions, and these have been included.

1	**The White Peacock** (novel)	Duffield (NY) 1911	N
		Heinemann 1911	M
2	**The Trespasser** (novel)	Duckworth 1912	L
		Kennerley 1912	K
3	**Love Poems and Others**	Duckworth 1913	K
		Kennerley 1913	J
4	**Sons and Lovers** (novel)	Duckworth 1913	K
		Kennerley 1913	J
5	**The Widowing of Mrs Holroyd** (play)	Kennerley 1914	I
		Duckworth 1914	H
6	**The Prussian Officer** (stories)	Duckworth 1914	H
		Huebsch 1916	G
7	**The Rainbow** (novel)	Methuen 1915	J
		Huebsch 1916	H
8	**Twilight in Italy** (travel)	Duckworth 1916	I
		Huebsch 1916	I
9	**Amores** (verse)	Duckworth 1916	H
		Huebsch 1916	F
10	**New Poems**	Secker 1918	G
		Huebsch 1920	E
11	**The Last Girl** (novel)	Secker 1920	H
		Seltzer 1921	G
12	**Women in Love** (novel) This was the 1st trade edition, preceded by 50 numbered and signed (**N**).	Secker 1921	H
13	**Sea and Sardinia** (travel)	Seltzer 1921	I
		Secker 1923	H
14	**Aaron's Rod** (novel)	Seltzer 1922	K
		Secker 1922	I
15	**Fantastia of the Unconscious** (non-fiction)	Seltzer 1922	H
		Secker 1923	H
16	**England, My England** (essays)	Seltzer 1922	H
		Secker 1924	H
17	**The Ladybird** (novelettes) Incl. **The Fox** and **The Captain's Doll**.	Secker 1923	G
18	**The Captain's Doll** (as in 17)	Seltzer 1923	F
19	**Kangaroo** (novel)	Secker 1923	G
		Seltzer 1923	G
20	**Birds, Beasts and Flowers** (verse)	Seltzer 1923	I
		Secker 1923	H
21	**The Boy in the Bush** (novel)	Secker 1924	K
		Seltzer 1924	I

Lawrence, D. H.

22	**The Plumed Serpent** (novel)	Secker 1926	I
		Knopf 1926	H
23	**David** (play)	Secker 1926	G
		Knopf 1926	F
24	**Mornings in Mexico** (travel)	Secker 1927	I
		Knopf 1927	H
25	**The Woman Who Rode Away** (stories)	Secker 1928	G
		Knopf 1928	F
26	**Lady Chatterley's Lover** (novel) Printed and published in Florence	Privately printed 1928	O
27	**Lady Chatterley's Lover** These are the first English and American *expurgated* editions.	Secker 1932	K
		Knopf 1932	I
28	**Lady Chatterley's Lover** These are the first American and English *unexpurgated* editions, the Penguin following the infamous trial. The Heinemann edition is really a hardback version of the Penguin.	Grove Press 1959	B
		Penguin 1960	B
		Heinemann 1961	B
29	**Collected Poems** (2 vols)	Secker 1928	D
30	**Pornography and Obscenity** (essay)	Faber 1929	C
31	**Pansies** (verse)	Secker 1929	E
32	**Nettles** (verse)	Faber 1930	E
33	**The Virgin and the Gypsy** (novel) These were preceded by a limited edition published by Orioli in Florence (**L**).	Secker 1930	H
		Knopf 1930	G
34	**The Man Who Died** (novelette) This had been published as **The Escaped Cock** in Paris in 1929.	Secker 1931	E
35	**The Letters** Ed. Aldous Huxley.	Heinemann 1932	D
36	**The Lovely Lady** (stories)	Secker 1933	E
		Viking 1933	E
37	**Last Poems**	Secker 1933	D
38	**The Plays**	Secker 1933	D
39	**The Tales**	Secker 1934	D
40	**A Collier's Friday Night** (play)	Secker 1934	D
41	**Pornography and So On** (essay)	Faber 1936	C
42	**Poems** (2 vols)	Heinemann 1939	D
43	**The Complete Poems** (3 vols)	Heinemann 1957	D
44	**The Complete Poems** (2 vols)	Heinemann 1964	C
45	**The Complete Plays**	Heinemann 1965	C
46	**The Letters of D. H. Lawrence** Volume I. 1901–13	CUP 1979	C
47	**The Letters of D. H. Lawrence** Volume II. 1913–16	CUP 1981	C

Films:
The Rocking Horse Winner (story) Two Cities 1949 **Lady Chatterley's Lover** Columbia 1956 **Sons and Lovers** 20th Century Fox 1960 **The Fox** Warner Bros 1968 **Women in Love** United Artists 1969 **The Virgin and the Gypsy** London Screenplays 1971 **Lady Chatterley's Lover** Columbia–EMI–Fox 1981 **The Trespasser** Colin Gregg 1981.

Bibliography:
Warren Roberts **A Bibliography of D. H. Lawrence** CUP 1982.

Biography:
Harry T. Moore **The Priest of Love** Heinemann 1974.

Lawrence, T.E.   Born in Caernarvonshire, 1888. Died 1935.

Peter O'Toole wandered into the shop one Christmas Eve in quest of a first edition (a *real* first edition – see below) of *Seven Pillars of Wisdom*. It was sad to have to disappoint him, for that would have been a very satisfying placing of a book. He ended up buying the *Annotated Sherlock Holmes*, which seemed bizarre at the time, and no less so now.

The real rarities by Lawrence remain so (somewhere in editions of single figures and may be seen only in such places as the British Museum or the Bodleian) but first trade editions of his best known works remain quite freely available and are still good value.

Variously known as J.H. Ross, T.E. Shaw and T.E. Lawrence, he is very difficult and expensive to collect seriously, though trade editions of his major works may be acquired quite easily, and usually at surprisingly low prices.

The New Cambridge Bibliography of English Literature vol. 4 lists all of Lawrence's works, and gives a few bibliographies, but these all seem to have been limited editions, or duplicated in small numbers.

Below are the major works.

1	**Revolt in the Desert** There were also simultaneous limited editions – of 315 and 250 copies, respectively, in England and America.	Cape 1927 Doran 1927	D D
2	**Seven Pillars of Wisdom** This, it must be noted, is the first *trade* edition. The 1st edition was privately printed in Oxford in 1922 in an edition of 8 copies. It was printed again in 1925, privately, in a revised edition of 100 copies, and once more, in 1926 – text completely revised, with a new prefatory note – privately printed in England and America in editions of 202 and 22 copies, respectively.	Cape 1936 Doubleday 1936	D D

Lawrence, T. E.

3	**The Letters of T. E. Lawrence** Edited by David Garnett, who also edited **The Essential T. E. Lawrence**, Cape 1951 (**B**).	Cape 1938 Doubleday 1939	C C
4	**The Mint** Once more, this is the first *trade* edition. It was first published in New York in 1936 in an edition of 50.	Cape 1955 Doubleday 1955	C C

There is a vast number of books on Lawrence, though no definitive biography has yet emerged. One outstanding title is: Robert Graves *Lawrence and the Arabs* Cape 1927. Published by Doubleday in America in 1928 as *Lawrence and the Arabian Adventure*.

Film:
Lawrence of Arabia British Lion 1962 (*Seven Pillars of Wisdom*).

Leacock, Stephen   Born in Hampshire 1869. Died 1944.

Although the author of many serious works – *Elements of Political Science* (1906), to give an example – he is remembered for his humorous stuff. There are a great number of these, and collectors have recently shown fair interest in them. The early titles, such as the two examples quoted below, might reach Grade C, but generally speaking, Grade A–B is the norm.

1	**Literary Lapses**	Dodd 1910 Lane 1910	B–C B–C
2	**Moonbeams from the Larger Lunacy**	Lane (US) 1915 Lane (UK) 1915	B–C B–C

Le Carré, John   Born in Dorset, 1931. Pseudonym for David Cornwell.

Always well known, and always collected, since publication of the Smiley trilogy, le Carré has become one of the most famous – and certainly one of the highest-earning – authors in the world. Still best loved for Smiley, he nonetheless had a huge success in 1983 with *The Little Drummer Girl*, despite some criticism of the politics involved. Indeed, some eight months after publication it was *still* among the top ten selling novels every *week*.

1	**Call for the Dead** (novel)	Gollancz 1960 Walker 1962	N I
2	**A Murder of Quality** (novel)	Gollancz 1962 Walker 1963	L H
3	**The Spy Who Came in from the Cold** (novel)	Gollancz 1963 Coward McCann 1963	H F

4 **The Looking-Glass War** (novel)	Heinemann 1965	**D**
	Coward McCann 1965	**C**
5 **A Small Town in Germany** (novel)	Heinemann 1968	**D**
	Coward McCann 1968	**C**
6 **The Naive and Sentimental Lover** (novel)	Hodder & Stoughton 1971	**C**
	Knopf 1971	**C**
7 **Tinker, Tailor, Soldier, Spy** (novel)	Hodder & Stoughton 1974	**C**
	Knopf 1974	**C**
8 **The Honourable Schoolboy** (novel)	Hodder & Stoughton 1977	**B**
	Knopf 1977	**B**
9 **Smiley's People** (novel) 7, 8 and 9 form the Smiley trilogy. See also 10.	Hodder & Stoughton 1980	**B**
	Knopf 1980	**B**
10 **The Quest for Karla** This is an omnibus, containing 7, 8 and 9.	Hodder & Stoughton 1982	**B**
	Knopf 1982	**B**
11 **The Little Drummer Girl** (novel)	Hodder & Stoughton 1983	**B**
	Knopf 1983	**B**

Films:
The Spy Who Came In from the Cold Paramount 1963 **The Deadly Affair** British Lion 1966 (*Call for the Dead*) **The Looking-Glass War** Columbia 1969

Lee, Laurie   Born in Gloucestershire, 1914.

It is unusual that an autobiographical work written by a man who up till then had published nothing but verse should become so very, very famous. *Cider With Rosie* has long been a set text at schools, and continues to sell strongly in hardback and Penguin every year. Sales are just about to be given another massive boost as Century publish their lavishly illustrated version, in a distinctive green and white spotted binding, following in style 1983's *Lark Rise to Candleford* by Flora Thompson. It is a great tribute to Lee that his book should be chosen to follow on this success, when one considers all the other past classics that might have been selected. But sometimes it is hard to believe that *Cider With Rosie* is a contemporary book, for it has from the first possessed this air of timelessness which, I suppose, singles out the classic. In the fifteen years since *As I Walked Out One Midsummer Morning* Lee has published only prose pieces; it would be nice to see another full-length work from him.

1 **The Sun My Monument** (verse)	Hogarth Press 1944	**E**
	Doubleday 1947	**C**

2 **Land at War** (non-fiction) Anonymous.	HMSO 1945	**D**
3 **We Made a Film in Cyprus** With Ralph Keene.	Longman 1947	**C**
4 **The Bloom of Candles** (verse)	Lehmann 1947	**C**
5 **Peasant's Priest** (play)	Goulden (Canterbury) 1947	**C**
6 **The Voyage of Magellan** (play)	Lehmann 1948	**C**
7 **My Many-Coated Man** (verse)	Deutsch 1955	**C**
	Coward McCann 1957	**B**
8 **A Rose for Winter** (travel)	Hogarth Press 1955	**C**
	Morrow 1956	**B**
9 **Cider with Rosie** (autobiog.)	Hogarth Press 1959	**C**
10 **The Edge of Day** (same as 9)	Morrow 1960	**C**
11 **Poems**	Studio Vista 1960	**B**
12 **Man Must Move** (juvenile)	Rathbone 1960	**C**
13 **The Wonderful World of Transportation** (same as 12)	Doubleday 1961	**B**
14 **As I Walked Out One Midsummer Morning** (autobiog)	Deutsch 1969	**B**
	Atheneum 1969	**B**
15 **I Can't Stay Long** (pieces)	Deutsch 1975	**A**
	Atheneum 1975	**A**
16 **Innocence in the Mirror** (prose)	Morrow 1978	**B**
17 **Selected Poems**	Deutsch 1983	**B**
18 **Two Women** (photographic essay)	Deutsch 1983	**B**

Lehmann, John   Born in Buckinghamshire, 1907.

Important mainly for his fine work in publishing and editing. Once partner in the Hogarth Press, he founded John Lehmann Ltd, which published quite a few of the books mentioned in this volume. He then founded *New Writing*, *Daylight*, *Penguin New Writing* and *The London Magazine*. Between them, these publications printed the work of just about everybody, many single issues having become collectors' items, although sets are pursued as well. Particularly collected lately is the *Penguin New Writing* (40 vols, 1936–50), a nice run being Grade H.

   Also of note is his three-volume autobiography:

1 **The Whispering Gallery**	Longman 1955
	Harcourt Brace 1955
2 **I Am My Brother**	Longman 1960
	Reynal 1960
3 **The Ample Proposition** The three together would be Grade **D**.	Eyre & Spottiswoode 1966

Lehmann, Rosamond   Born in Buckinghamshire, 1901.

A tremendous upsurge of interest has taken place with Rosamond Lehmann – due in part to the reprinting of many of her earlier titles by the estimable Virago Press – and certainly now if a bookseller is asked for 'Lehmann' it is Rosamond, and not her younger brother John, whom is being referred to.

1	**Dusty Answer** (novel)	Chatto & Windus 1927	I
		Holt 1927	H
2	**A Note in Music** (novel)	Chatto & Windus 1930	H
		Holt 1930	G
3	**Letter to a Sister** (essay)	Hogarth Press 1931	G
		Harcourt Brace 1932	F
4	**Invitation to the Waltz** (novel)	Chatto & Windus 1932	H
		Holt 1932	G
5	**The Weather in the Streets** (novel)	Collins 1936	H
		Reynal Hitchcock 1936	G
6	**No More Music** (play)	Collins 1939	D
		Reynal Hitchcock 1945	C
7	**The Ballad and the Source** (novel)	Collins 1944	C
		Reynal Hitchcock 1945	C
8	**The Gipsy's Baby and Other Stories**	Collins 1946	D
		Reynal Hitchcock 1947	C
9	**The Echoing Grove** (novel)	Collins 1953	B
		Harcourt Brace 1953	B
10	**A Man Seen Afar** (prose) With W. Tudor Pole.	Spearman 1965	C
11	**The Swan in the Evening: Fragments of an Inner Life**	Collins 1967	C
		Harcourt Brace 1967	C
12	**Letters from Our Daughters** 2 vols. With Cynthia Hill Sandys.	College of Psychic Studies 1972	C
13	**The Sea-Grape Tree** (novel)	Collins 1976	B
		Harcourt Brace 1977	B

Lennon, John   Born in Liverpool, 1940. Died 1980.

From the collector's point of view, although the collecting boom in *Beatles* material was well under way before the murder of John Lennon, his death has not had the expected result of a huge rise in the value of his two books (possibly they were already over-valued) and, it must be admitted, neither is very difficult to acquire. I re-read them recently, and I think they hold up very well. Of course, Cape wouldn't have published these little ditties and doodles in 1964 and 1965 if the 24-year old author hadn't happened to be one of the most famous people then on earth, but they are very funny, and they do display a dexterity with, and a love for, words.

Lennon

Unless one is a fanatical Beatles collector (in which case all the flimsy, tasteless tin and plastic trash that one's parents said one was mad to spend three-and-eleven on in the sixties, one will now buy all over again at fifty quid a throw) only two extraneous items stand out as relevant – both of which were contemporary – and they are listed below.

1	**In His Own Write**	Cape 1964	C
		Simon & Schuster 1964	C
2	**A Spaniard in the Works**	Cape 1965	C
		Simon & Schuster 1965	C

Also of note:

Brian Epstein **A Cellarful of Noise**	Souvenir Press 1964	C
Hunter Davies **The Beatles**	Heinemann 1968	D

Lessing, Doris   Born in Persia (Iran), 1919. British.

Still highly collectable, but getting more difficult every year. The recent stuff too seems to vanish fairly quickly – I suspect because the print runs are lower than one might expect for an author of such renown, as the sequence in which Lessing is presently engaged (five volumes, to date) is very involved, not at all 'popular', and very much aimed at the Lessing connoisseur. It is not a sequence one can casually pick up in the middle, certainly, and it remains to see whether it will become the monument that Lessing clearly intends. At the moment, though, *The Golden Notebook* is still the highlight.

1	**The Grass is Singing** (novel)	Joseph 1950	I
		Crowell 1950	G
2	**This was the Old Chief's Country** (stories)	Joseph 1951	H
		Crowell 1952	F
3	**Martha Quest** (novel)	Joseph 1952	F
4	**Five: Short Novels**	Joseph 1953	H
5	**Retreat to Innocence** (novel)	Joseph 1953	F
6	**A Proper Marriage** (novel)	Joseph 1954	F
	The American ed. includes 3.	Simon & Schuster 1964	B
7	**Going Home** (non-fiction)	Joseph 1957	D
		Ballantine 1968	C
8	**The Habit of Loving** (stories)	MacGibbon & Kee 1957	D
		Crowell 1958	C
9	**A Ripple from the Storm** (novel)	Joseph 1958	D
10	**Fourteen Poems**	Scorpion Press 1959	D
11	**In Pursuit of the English: A Documentary**	Joseph 1960	D
12	**Portrait of the English** (same as 11)	Simon & Schuster 1961	C

13	**Play with a Tiger** (play)	Joseph 1962	E
14	**The Golden Notebook** (novel)	Joseph 1962	G
		Simon & Schuster 1962	F
15	**A Man and Two Women: Stories**	MacGibbon & Kee 1963	C
		Simon & Schuster 1963	C
16	**African Stories**	Joseph 1964	C
		Simon & Schuster 1965	C
17	**Landlocked** (novel) The Amer. ed. includes 9.	MacGibbon & Kee 1965	C
		Simon & Schuster 1966	C
18	**Particularly Cats** (non-fiction)	Joseph 1967	C
		Simon & Schuster 1967	C
19	**Nine African Stories**	Longman 1968	C
20	**The Four-Gated City** (novel) This completes the **Children of Violence** sequence, the other volumes being 3, 6, 9 and 17.	MacGibbon & Kee 1969	C
		Knopf 1969	B
21	**Briefing for a Descent into Hell** (novel)	Cape 1971	B
		Knopf 1971	B
22	**The Story of a Non-Marrying Man** (stories)	Cape 1972	B
23	**The Temptation of Jack Orkney** (same as 22)	Knopf 1972	B
24	**The Summer Before the Dark** (novel)	Cape 1973	B
		Knopf 1973	B
25	**A Small Personal Voice** (pieces)	Knopf 1974	B
26	**The Memoirs of a Survivor** (novel)	Octagon Press 1974	B
		Knopf 1975	B
27	**A Small Personal Voice: Essays, Reviews and Interviews**	Knopf 1974	B
28	**Collected Stories** 2 volumes. All the stories appear in the one-volume **Stories**, published by Knopf in the same year (**C**).	Cape 1978	C
29	**Shikasta** (novel)	Cape 1979	B
		Knopf 1979	B
30	**The Marriages between Zones Three Four and Five** (novel)	Cape 1980	B
		Knopf 1980	B
31	**The Sirian Experiments** (novel)	Cape 1981	B
		Knopf 1981	B
32	**The Making of the Representative for Planet 8** (novel)	Cape 1982	B
		Knopf 1982	B

33 **The Sentimental Agents in the**   Cape 1983   **B**
      Volyen Empire (novel)   Knopf 1983   **B**

Lewis, C.S.   Born in Belfast, 1898. Died 1963.

My old English master at school had been under Lewis at Oxford, and he confirmed my impression that here was indeed a remarkable man. A convert to Catholicism, much of his writing was given over to religion, but with none of the dullness that this might imply – *The Screwtape Letters* and *Surprised By Joy* (his autobiographical account of his religious conversion) being minor classics. In all other fields of writing he established classics, too – literary criticism, science fiction, philosophy and children's books. Certainly, if all the children of my acquaintance are anything to go by, *The Lion, The Witch and the Wardrobe* will be around for ever.

In passing, I should like to heartily recommend *Experiment in Criticism* to any student of literature. It is short enough to digest completely, and it really helps one to *understand*, instead of merely confusing the reader or condescending, as do so many works purporting to be its equal.

Lewis published a large number of books, many of them theological, and many of very specific literary criticism. A checklist may be found in *The New Cambridge Bibliography of English Literature* vol. 4, but below are his absolute highlights, of which there are quite a few.

1 **The Allegory of Love** (non-fiction)	OUP 1936	**G**
	OUP (US) 1936	**F**
2 **Out of the Silent Planet** (novel)	Bodley Head, Lane 1938	**H**
	Macmillan (US) 1943	**C**
3 **The Screwtape Letters** (religious)	Bles 1942	**E**
	Saunders 1942	**C**
4 **Perelandra** (novel)	Bodley Head, Lane 1943	**F**
	Macmillan 1944	**D**
5 **That Hideous Strength** (novel)	Bodley Head, Lane 1945	**F**
2, 4 and 5 form his SF trilogy.	Macmillan 1946	**D**
6 **The Lion, the Witch, and the**	Bles, 1950	**I**
Wardrobe (juvenile)	Macmillan 1950	**H**
7 **Prince Caspian** (juvenile)	Bles 1951	**H**
	Macmillan 1951	**G**
8 **The Voyage of the Dawn**	Bles 1952	**F**
Treader (juvenile)	Macmillan 1952	**E**
9 **The Silver Chair** (juvenile)	Bles 1953	**E**
	Macmillan 1953	**D**
10 **The Horse and His Boy** (juvenile)	Bles 1954	**E**
	Macmillan 1954	**D**

11	**The Magician's Nephew** (juvenile)	Bodley Head 1955	E
		Macmillan 1955	D
12	**Surprised by Joy** (autobiog.)	Bles 1955	B
		Harcourt Brace 1956	B
13	**The Last Battle** (juvenile)	Bodley Head 1956	D
	6, 7, 8, 9, 10, 11 and 13 form the	Macmillan 1956	C
	Chronicles of Narnia.		
14	**The Four Loves** (philosophy)	Bles 1960	C
		Harcourt Brace 1960	B
15	**Studies in Words** (essay)	CUP 1960	C
		Macmillan 1960	B
16	**Experiment in Criticism**	CUP 1961	C
		Macmillan 1961	B
17	**A Grief Observed** (essay)	Faber 1961	F
	Pseud. N.W. Clerk.	Seabury 1963	F

Lewis, Wyndham   Born in 1882. Died 1957.

It is not clear where Wyndham Lewis was born. According to him, it was on board a ship bound for Canada, during a thunderstorm. This is thought to be a less than reliable piece of autobiography, as Lewis was forever inventing for himself more and more glamorous 'pasts' so that art dealers would find the genesis of his paintings more 'interesting'. He always saw himself as a painter first, and in the early days, affected the garb: long hair, cape, wide-brimmed hat. With such trappings *and* so wild and romantic a history, people could not *fail* to accept him as a serious artist, he reasoned. Fortunately, his art – his painting and his writing was more than equal to his extravagant claims, and Lewis has become a landmark figure of the century.

He published nearly fifty books, many of them from private presses, and in limited editions. An immensely detailed bibliography now exists, and is appended below. I record here the various editions of his highlight.

The Apes of God (novel)   The Arthur Press
                                     1930

This was published in a signed limited edition of 750 copies at the then very high price of three guineas. This is the absolute first edition (**I**). A trade edition was published in 1931 by Nash & Grayson, in a print run of 1900 copies (**E**). The first American edition was published in 1932 by McBride (**D**).

In 1955 a 'twenty-fifth anniversary' edition was published by Arco, in a signed, limited edition of 1000 copies, selling for exactly the same price as the first edition – 3 guineas (**D**).

Bibliography:
Bradford Morrow and Bernard LaFourcade **Wyndham Lewis: A Bibliography** Black Sparrow 1978.

Loos

Loos, Anita   Born in California, 1893.

The author is still living well on the reputation of her most famous book and its sequel. As she says in the book, 'fate keeps on happening'.

1	**Gentlemen Prefer Blondes**	Boni & Liveright 1925	E
	Scarce. The sequel seems an attempt to redress the balance. (Note that preference comes more expensive than marriage.)	Brentano's 1926	B
2	**But Gentlemen Marry Brunettes**	Boni & Liveright 1928	C
		Brentano's 1928	C

Films:
Gentlemen Prefer Blondes 20th Century Fox 1953
Gentlemen Marry Brunettes United Artists 1955.

Lovecraft, H.P.   Born in Providence, 1890. Died 1937.

Lovecraft is an unusual literary figure, for although now verging upon being a cult, collectors (particularly of SF) standing on each other's backs to get at the few 1sts around, this popularity occurred considerably after his death. Amis said in *New Maps Of Hell*: 'Lovecraft's intrinsic importance is small', and although the reference books and bibliographies seem to agree with him – information is extremely hard to come by – it is evident that collectors do not.

Many of Lovecraft's books are being reissued in whole and in part by the paperback companies, and some title changes seem to have taken place, to add to the confusion. It is possible, therefore, that the list below is not as complete as I should have wished.

1	**Shadow over Innsmouth** (novel)	Visionary Puolications 1936	I
2	**Notes and Commonplace Book Employed by the Author**	Futile Press 1938	I
3	**The Outsider and Others** (stories)	Arkham House 1939	I
4	**Beyond the Wall of Sleep** (novel)	Arkham House 1943	H
5	**Best Supernatural Stories**	World Publishers 1945	G
		Gollancz 1952	G
6	**Marginalia**	Arkham House 1945	H
7	**The Lurker at the Threshold**	Arkham House 1948	G
	With A.W. Derleth.	Museum Press 1948	F
8	**Something About Cats** (stories)	Arkham House 1949	F
9	**The Haunter of the Dark** (stories)	Gollancz 1951	E

10 **The Case of Charles Dexter Ward** (novel)	Gollancz 1952	E
11 **Dream Quest of Unknown Kadath**	Dawn Press 1955	E
12 **Survivor, and Others** (stories) With A.W. Derleth.	Arkham House 1957	E
13 **Cry Horror** (stories)	Corgi 1959	C
14 **The Shuttered Room** (stories)	Arkham House 1959	C
15 **Dreams and Fancies** (stories)	Arkham House 1962	C
16 **Collected Poems**	Arkham House 1963	C
17 **The Dunwich Horror and Other Stories**	Arkham House 1963	C
18 **The Mountains of Madness** (stories)	Gollancz 1966	C
19 **Dagon** (novel)	Gollancz 1967	B
20 **Shadow out of Time** (stories)	Gollancz 1968	B

Films:
The Haunted Palace American International 1963 (*The Case of Charles Dexter Ward*) **Monster of Terror** (**Die Monster Die**) American International 1965 (*Color Out of Space* – story) **Dunwich Horror** American International 1969

Bibliography:
Mark Owings **The Revised Lovecraft Bibliography** Mirage Press 1973.

Biography:
L. Sprague de Camp **Lovecraft** NEL 1976.

Lowell, Robert   Born in Boston, 1914. Died 1977.

That Lovell is still avidly collected was amply demonstrated to me just last autumn. I occasionally (*very* occasionally) decide to thin out my collection of modern firsts, and when I do, it generally means disposing of an author's output, unless there is a discernible highlight. I put my Lowell collection into the modern first edition section in the shop (the Faber editions, in d/w, from *Life Studies* onwards) and they all sold within three days.

1 **The Land of Unlikeness** (verse)	Cummington Press (US) 1944	I
2 **Lord Weary's Castle** (verse)	Harcourt Brace 1946	G
3 **Poems 1938–1949**	Faber 1950	F
4 **The Mills of the Kavanaughs**	Harcourt Brace 1951	F
5 **Life Studies** (verse)	Faber 1959	C
	Farrar Straus 1959	C
6 **Imitations** (verse)	Farrar Straus 1961	C
	Faber 1962	C
7 **Phaedra and Figaro** (plays trans.)	Farrar Straus 1961	D
8 **Phaedra** (as in 7)	Faber 1963	C

Lowell

9 **For the Union Dead** (verse)	Farrar Straus 1964	D
	Faber 1965	C
10 **The Old Glory** (play)	Farrar Straus 1964	C
An expanded version was published by		
Faber in 1966, and by Farrar Straus in		
1968 (**B**).		
11 **Selected Poems**	Faber 1965	B
12 **Near the Ocean** (verse)	Farrar Straus 1967	B
	Faber 1967	B
13 **The Voyage** (Baudelaire trans.)	Farrar Straus 1968	B
	Faber 1968	B
14 **Notebook 1967–1968**	Farrar Straus 1969	D
An augmented edition, called simply		
Notebook, was published in 1970 by		
Faber and Farrar Straus (**C**).		
15 **Prometheus Bound** (adapt.)	Farrar Straus 1969	C
	Faber 1970	B
16 **For Lizzie and Harriet** (verse)	Faber 1973	B
	Farrar Straus 1973	B
17 **History** (verse)	Faber 1973	B
	Farrar Straus 1973	B
18 **The Dolphin** (verse)	Faber 1973	B
	Farrar Straus 1973	B
19 **Poems: A Selection**	Faber 1974	B
20 **Day by Day** (verse)	Farrar Straus 1978	B
	Faber 1978	B
21 **The Oresteia of Aeschylus** (trans.)	Farrar Straus 1979	B
	Faber 1979	D

Bibliography:
Ian Hamilton **Robert Lowell** Faber 1983.

Lowry, Malcolm   Born in Cheshire, 1909. Died 1957.

A complex, and a rather sad character, who is now assuming the status of a cult figure among younger readers and collectors. He was born of a wealthy family, but sought to be a loner, a tramp, a bum. Several times, he drank himself nearly to death, and was at all times said to be in an alcoholic stupor of varying degree. The pain and the horror of this he anchored well in his highlight *Under The Volcano*. He needed this success (not financially, but psychologically) for his first novel fourteen years earlier had sold only half of its modest print run of 1500, the remaining 750 of which were pulped.

1 **Ultramarine** (novel)	Cape 1933	L
A revised edition of this novel was		
published in 1962 by Lippincott in the		
USA and in 1963 by Cape in the UK (**D**).		

2 **Under the Volcano** (novel)	Reynal & Hitchcock 1947	G
	Cape 1947	F
3 **Hear Us O Lord from Heaven**	Lippincott 1961	E
Thy Dwelling Place (stories)	Cape 1962	D
4 **Selected Poems of Malcolm Lowry**	City Lights 1962	C
5 **Selected Letters of Malcolm Lowry**	Lippincott 1965	C
	Cape 1967	C
6 **Lunar Caustic** (novel)	Grossman 1968	D
	Cape 1968	C
7 **Dark as the Grave Wherein My**	NAL 1968	C
Friend is Laid (stories)	Cape 1969	C
8 **October Ferry to Gabriola** (novel)	World 1970	C
	Cape 1971	C
9 **Notes on a Screenplay for F. Scott**	Bruccoli 1976	B
Fitzgerald's Tender is the Night		

Biography:
Douglas Day **Malcolm Lowry: A Biography** OUP 1973.

Lurie, Alison   Born in Chicago, 1926.

A very elegant writer, just coming to the attention of collectors. Although American, she seems a very *English* writer, the novels contriving to be very tightly crafted comedies of manners – not an avenue much explored by American writers. Although her name is known, prices might well be low, as many book catalogues do not yet rate her as collectable. Conversely, her books are far from easy to come by.

1 **Love and Friendship** (novel)	Heinemann 1962	F
	Macmillan (US) 1962	E
2 **The Nowhere City** (novel)	Heinemann 1965	E
	Coward McCann 1966	D
3 **Imaginary Friends** (novel)	Heinemann 1967	D
	Coward McCann 1967	C
4 **Real People** (novel)	Random House 1969	C
	Heinemann 1970	C
5 **The War Between the Tates** (novel)	Random House 1974	B
	Heinemann 1974	B
6 **Only Children** (novel)	Random House 1979	B
	Heinemann 1979	B
7 **The Heavenly Zoo** (juvenile)	Eel Pie 1979	B
	Farrar Straus 1980	B
8 **Clever Gretchen and Other**	Harper 1980	B
Forgotten Folk Tales (juvenile)	Heinemann 1980	B
9 **The Language of Clothes** (non-fiction)	Random House 1981	B
	Heinemann 1982	B

Macdonald, Ross   Born in California, 1915.
Pseudonym for Kenneth Millar.

In line with the current vogue for detective fiction, Ross Macdonald is of very big interest now, but the early titles are hard to get, particularly with those all-important dust wrappers (with detective novels, it always seems more important than ever, I think because the books look so deliciously lurid *with* them, and so much like any other book without).

Macdonald (or Millar, to give him his real name) wrote under several names. As well as Ross Macdonald we have Kenneth Millar, John Ross Macdonald and John Macdonald. It's the last of these that could cause confusion, as there is *another* writer of detective fiction called John Macdonald – the author of nearly sixty books and the creator of Travis McGee. This is *not* the author under discussion, who was the creator of Lew Archer, as will be seen below.

As Kenneth Millar:
The following feature the character Chet Gordon.

1	**The Dark Tunnel** (novel)	Dodd Mead 1944	H
2	**I Die Slowly** (English edition of 1)	Lion 1955	C
3	**Trouble Follows Me** (novel)	Dodd Mead 1946	G
4	**Night Train** (English edition of 3)	Lion 1955	C
5	**Blue City** (novel)	Knopf 1947	E
		Cassell 1949	C
6	**The Three Roads** (novel)	Knopf 1948	E
		Cassell 1950	C

As John Ross Macdonald:
7	**The Drowning Pool** (novel)*	Knopf 1950	H
		Cassell 1952	F
8	**The Way Some People Die** (novel)*	Knopf 1951	G
		Cassell 1953	F
9	**The Ivory Grin** (novel)*	Knopf 1952	F
		Cassell 1953	E
10	**Meet Me at the Morgue** (novel)	Knopf 1953	E
11	**Experience with Evil** (English edition of 10)	Cassell 1954	E
12	**Find a Victim** (novel)*	Knopf 1954	E
		Cassell 1955	D
13	**The Name is Archer** (stories)*	Bantam 1955	D

As John Macdonald:
14	**The Moving Target** (novel)	Knopf 1949	F
		Cassell 1951	E

The above, and all those below marked *, feature the character Lew Archer.

As Ross Macdonald:

15 **The Barbarous Coast** (novel)*	Knopf 1956	H
	Cassell 1957	G
16 **The Doomsters** (novel)*	Knopf 1958	E
	Cassell 1958	D
17 **The Galton Case** (novel)*	Knopf 1959	D
	Cassell 1960	C
18 **The Fergusson Affair** (novel)	Knopf 1960	D
	Collins 1961	C
19 **The Wycherley Woman** (novel)	Knopf 1961	D
	Collins 1962	C
20 **The Zebra-Striped Hearse** (novel)*	Knopf 1962	D
	Collins 1963	C
21 **The Chill** (novel)*	Knopf 1964	D
	Collins 1964	C
22 **The Far Side of the Dollar** (novel*)	Knopf 1965	D
	Collins 1965	C
23 **Black Money** (novel)*	Knopf 1966	C
	Collins 1966	C
24 **The Instant Enemy** (novel)*	Knopf 1968	C
	Collins 1968	C
25 **The Goodbye Look** (novel)*	Knopf 1969	C
	Collins 1969	C
26 **The Underground Man** (novel*)	Knopf 1971	C
	Collins 1971	C
27 **Sleeping Beauty** (novel)*	Knopf 1973	C
	Collins 1973	C
28 **The Blue Hammer** (novel)*	Knopf 1976	B
	Collins 1976	B

Film:
The Moving Target Warner Bros. 1967.

Bibliography:
Matthew J. Broccoli **Kenneth Millar/Ross Macdonald: A Checklist**
Gale US 1971.

McEwan, Ian   Born in Aldershot, 1948.

When I published *Collecting Modern First Editions* McEwan had brought out *one* book – but that was of short stories, and no one took any notice of short stories. But they did, actually – and his follow-up was short stories too; that must be some sort of record. Anyway, all these years on, McEwan has still published only half-a-dozen short works, and yet there he is, right up at the top of the young British novelists (or joint first with Martin Amis – I don't know; they can fight it out between them). Such is success in Britain. McEwan is seen to be intensely *literary* – an image much underlined by his publicity pictures in which he seems to be forever peering out dolefully from the bowels of a slum through a cracked window pane and old LCC glasses. Still, his writing is very fine, and very poetic – if you can stand the (often scatalogical) imagery.

1 **First Loves, Last Rites** (stories)	Cape 1975	D
	Random House 1975	C
2 **In Between the Sheets** (stories)	Cape 1978	C
	Simon & Schuster 1978	C
3 **The Cement Garden** (novel)	Cape 1978	B
	Simon & Schuster 1978	B
4 **The Imitation Game: Three Plays for Television** (includes **Solid Geometry** and **Jack Flea's Birthday Celebration**)	Cape 1981	B
5 **The Comfort of Strangers** (novel)	Cape 1981	B
	Simon & Schuster 1981	B
6 **Or Shall We Die?** (oratorio)	Cape 1983	B

The words to an oratorio by Michael Berkeley.

MacInnes, Colin   Born in London, 1914. Died 1976.

One of Burne-Jones's grandchildren was the novelist Angela Thirkell. Thirkell's son was Colin MacInnes. MacInnes, in the late fifties and sixties, became a chronicler and a champion of the teenage rebellion, pop music, the plight of blacks in Britain, and the drug scene. In life, MacInnes was seen to be a rebel, a drunk, and a homosexual, who died prematurely. It is little wonder, then, that he has now risen to the level of a cult, and he has an eager following.

1 **To The Victors The Spoils** (novel)	MacGibbon & Kee 1950	D
2 **June in Her Spring** (novel)	MacGibbon & Kee 1952	D
3 **City of Spades** (novel)	MacGibbon & Kee 1957	C
	Macmillan (US) 1958	C
4 **Absolute Beginners** (novel)	MacGibbon & Kee 1959	D
	Macmillan 1960	C
5 **Mr Love and Justice** (novel)	MacGibbon & Kee 1960	B
	Dutton 1961	B

6 **England, Half English** (essays)	MacGibbon & Kee 1961	C
	Random House 1962	C
7 **London: City of Any Dream** (non-fiction)	Thames & Hudson 1962	C
8 **Australia and New Zealand** (non-fiction) In collaboration with the editors of **Life**.	Time (US) 1964	C
9 **All Day Saturday** (novel)	MacGibbon & Kee 1966	C
10 **Sweet Saturday Night** (prose)	MacGibbon & Kee 1967	B
11 **Visions of London** An omnibus containing 3, 4 and 5.	MacGibbon & Kee 1969	B
12 **The London Novels** (same as 11)	Farrar Straus 1969	B
13 **Westward to Laughter** (novel)	MacGibbon & Kee 1969	B
	Farrar Straus 1970	B
14 **Three Years to Play** (novel)	MacGibbon & Kee 1970	B
	Farrar Straus 1970	B
15 **Loving Them Both: A Study of Bisexuality and Bisexuals** (non-fiction)	Brian & O'Keefe 1973	B
16 **Out of the Garden** (novel)	Hart-Davis MacGibbon 1974	B
17 **'No Novel Reader'** (non-fiction)	Brian & O'Keefe 1975	B
18 **Posthumous Essays**	Brian & O'Keefe 1977	B
19 **Out of the Way: Later Essays**	Brian & O'Keefe 1980	B

Biography:
Tony Gould **Inside Outsider: The Life and Times of Colin MacInnes** Chatto & Windus 1983.

MacNeice, Louis   Born in Belfast, 1907. Died 1963.

One of the great poets of the century – below Auden and Eliot, but above most others. Very collectable – and the larger part of his *œuvre* fairly available. It is, as usual, the early items that are difficult.

1 **Blind Fireworks** (verse)	Gollancz 1929	K
2 **Roundabout Way** (novel) Pseud. Louis Malone.	Putnam 1932	K

MacNiece

3	**Poems**	Faber 1935	**G**
		Random House 1937	**F**
4	**The Agamemnon of Aeschylus** (trans.)	Faber 1936	**C**
		Harcourt Brace 1937	**C**
5	**Out of the Picture** (play)	Faber 1937	**C**
		Harcourt Brace 1938	**C**
6	**Letters from Iceland** (non-fiction) With W.H. Auden.	Faber 1937	**E**
		Harcourt Brace 1937	**E**
7	**I Crossed the Minch** (travel)	Longman 1938	**I**
8	**Zoo** (non-fiction)	Joseph 1938	**H**
9	**Modern Poetry: A Personal Essay**	OUP 1938	**D**
10	**The Earth Compels** (verse)	Faber 1938	**D**
11	**Autumn Journal** (verse)	Faber 1939	**C**
		Random House 1939	**C**
12	**The Last Ditch** (verse)	Cuala Press (Dublin) 1940	**G**
13	**Selected Poems**	Faber 1940	**B**
14	**Poems 1925–1940**	Random House 1940	**C**
15	**Plant and Phantom** (verse)	Faber 1941	**D**
16	**The Poetry of W. B. Yeats** (criticism)	OUP 1941	**E**
17	**Meet the U.S. Army** (essay)	Board of Education 1943	**H**
18	**Springboard: Poems 1941–44**	Faber 1944	**C**
		Random House 1945	**C**
19	**Christopher Columbus** (play)	Faber 1944	**D**
20	**The Dark Tower** (plays)	Faber 1947	**C**
21	**Holes in the Sky: Poems 1944–47**	Faber 1948	**C**
		Random House 1949	**C**
22	**Collected Poems 1925–48**	Faber 1949	**C**
		OUP (US) 1949	**C**
23	**Goethe's Faust Parts I & II** (trans.)	Faber 1952	**C**
		OUP 1952	**C**
24	**Ten Burnt Offerings** (verse)	Faber 1952	**D**
		OUP 1953	**C**
25	**Autumn Sequel** (verse)	Faber 1954	**B**
26	**The Other Wing** (Ariel Poem)	Faber 1954	**B**
27	**The Penny That Rolled Away** (juvenile) This was published in England, no doubt for sound economic reasons, as **The Sixpence That Rolled Away** by Faber in 1956. **E**	Putnam 1954	**E**
28	**Visitations** (verse)	Faber 1957	**B**
		OUP 1958	**B**
29	**Eighty-Five Poems**	Faber 1959	**B**
		OUP 1959	**B**
30	**Solstices** (verse)	Faber 1961	**B**
		OUP 1961	**B**

31 **The Burning Perch** (verse)	Faber 1963	B
	OUP 1963	B
32 **Selected Poems**	Faber 1964	C
Ed. and Intro. by W.H. Auden.		
33 **The Mad Islands** and	Faber 1964	C
The Administrator (plays)		
34 **Astrology** (non-fiction)	Aldus 1964	C
	Doubleday 1964	C
35 **The Strings are False** (autobiog.)	Faber 1965	C
	OUP 1966	C
36 **Varieties of Parable** (lecture)	CUP 1965	C
37 **Collected Poems**	Faber 1966	C
	OUP 1967	C
38 **One for the Grave** (play)	Faber 1968	B
39 **Persons from Porlock and Other**	BBC 1969	B
Plays		
Intro. by W.H. Auden.		

Bibliography:
Christopher Armitage and Neil Clark **A Bibliography of the Works of Louis MacNeice** Kaye & Ward 1973.

Mailer, Norman   Born in New Jersey, 1923.

Mailer is larger than life. He has always been *celebrated* as a personality as much as a writer. His non-fiction, always provocative (*Marilyn, Cannibals and Christians*) took an even more bizarre turn with *The Executioner's Song* – a massive book chronicling the life and last days of Gary Gilmore, a murderer who had requested relief from 'Death Row' in the form of the electric chair. And then Mailer came up with *Ancient Evenings* – a huge novel, and the final entry in Anthony Burgess's *99 Novels*. It concerns Ancient Egypt, and yet it is baroque. It is majestic, funny, powerful, rude, irresistible (but skippable) and it presents the land of the Cleopatras as just as weird as present-day America. Below appears his fictional work, in addition to which Mailer has published about two dozen books.

1 **The Naked and the Dead** (novel)	Rinehart 1948	H
	Wingate 1949	E
2 **Barbary Shore** (novel)	Rinehart 1951	D
	Cape 1952	C
3 **The Deer Park** (novel)	Putnam 1955	D
	Wingate 1957	B
4 **Advertisements for Myself**	Putnam 1959	C
(miscellany)	Deutsch 1961	B
5 **Deaths for the Ladies and**	Putnam 1962	C
Other Disasters (verse)	Deutsch 1962	C

Mailer

6	**An American Dream** (novel)	Dial Press 1965	C
		Deutsch 1965	B
7	**The Deer Park** (play)	Dial Press 1967	C
		Weidenfeld 1970	B
8	**Why are We in Vietnam?** (novel)	Putnam 1967	C
		Weidenfeld	B
9	**Ancient Evenings** (novel)	Little Brown 1983	B
		Macmillan 1983	B

Films:

The Naked and the Dead Warner Bros 1958 **See You in Hell, Darling** Warner Bros 1966 (*An American Dream*) **Marilyn: The Untold Story** Rank 1980.

Bibliography:
Laura Adams **Norman Mailer: A Comprehensive Bibliography** Scarecrow Press (New Jersey) 1974.

Manning, Olivia Born in Portsmouth, 1915. Died 1980.

Always a respected writer, but only quite recently of interest to collectors. It was apparently marriage to a British official in the Balkans that alerted her interest, and gave rise to her most celebrated works, now gathered together under the umbrella title 'The Balkan Trilogy' (although now there is a 'Levant Trilogy' as well).

1	**The Wind Changes** (novel)	Cape 1937	H
		Knopf 1938	F
2	**The Remarkable Expedition: The Story of Stanley's Rescue of Emin Pasha from Equatorial Africa** (non-fiction)	Heinemann 1947	F
3	**The Reluctant Rescue** (same as 2)	Doubleday 1947	D
4	**Growing Up: A Collection of Short Stories**	Heinemann 1948	C
		Doubleday 1948	C
5	**Artist Among the Missing** (novel)	Heinemann 1949	C
6	**The Dreaming Shore** (travel)	Evans 1950	C
7	**School for Love** (novel)	Heinemann 1951	C
8	**A Different Face** (novel)	Heinemann 1953	C
		Abelard 1957	B
9	**Doves of Venus** (novel)	Heinemann 1955	C
		Abelard 1958	B
10	**My Husband Cartright** (novel)	Heinemann 1956	C
11	**The Great Fortune** (novel)	Heinemann 1960	D
		Doubleday 1961	C

12 **The Spoilt City** (novel)	Heinemann 1962	C
	Doubleday 1963	B
13 **Friends and Heroes** (novel)	Heinemann 1965	C
11, 12 and 13 form **The Balkan**	Doubleday 1966	B
Trilogy.		
14 **A Romantic Hero and**	Heinemann 1967	B
Other Stories		
15 **Extraordinary Cats** (non-fiction)	Joseph 1967	C
16 **The Playroom** (novel)	Heinemann 1969	B
17 **The Camperlea Girls**	Coward McCann 1969	B
(same as 16)		
18 **The Rain Forest** (novel)	Heinemann 1974	B
19 **The Danger Tree** (novel)	Weidenfeld 1977	B
	Atheneum 1977	B
20 **The Battle Lost and Won** (novel)	Weidenfeld 1978	B
	Atheneum 1979	B
21 **The Sum of Things** (novel)	Weidenfeld 1980	B
19, 20 and 21 form **The Levant**	Atheneum 1981	B
Trilogy.		

Marcus, Frank   Born in Germany, 1928. British.

Not at all what you would call a 'collected' author. Indeed, most people have never heard of him; but he does remain the author of one of the most powerful plays of the sixties, which was in turn made into one of the most powerful and memorable films.

The Killing of Sister George	Hamilton 1965	C
	Random House 1966	B

Film:
The Killing of Sister George Cinerama 1968.

Marsh, Ngaio   Born in Christchurch, New Zealand, 1899.

Eighty-five years old now, still writing, and probably the best known woman of crime fiction after Agatha Christie and Dorothy L. Sayers. I have met many collectors who are very enthusiastic about her work, but never one who was *wholly* confident about pronouncing her Christian name.

1 **A Man Lay Dead** (novel)	Bles 1934	H
	Sheridan 1942	G
2 **Enter a Murderer** (novel)	Bles 1935	G
	Sheridan 1942	F
3 **Death in Ecstasy** (novel)	Bles 1936	G
	Sheridan 1941	F

4	**The Nursing Home Murder** (novel) With H. Jellett.	Bles 1936 Sheridan 1941	G F
5	**Vintage Murder** (novel)	Bles 1937 Sheridan 1940	G F
6	**Artists in Crime** (novel)	Bles 1938 Furman 1938	E D
7	**Death in a White Tie** (novel)	Bles 1938 Furman 1938	E D
8	**Overture to Death** (novel)	Collins 1939 Little Brown 1939	D C
9	**Death at the Bar** (novel)	Collins 1940 Little Brown 1940	C C
10	**Death of a Peer** (novel)	Little Brown 1940	C
11	**Surfeit of Lampreys** (same as 10)	Collins 1941	C
12	**Death and the Dancing Footman** (novel)	Collins 1941 Little Brown 1941	C C
13	**Colour Scheme** (novel)	Collins 1943 Little Brown 1943	C C
14	**Died in the Wool** (novel)	Collins 1945 Little Brown 1945	C C
15	**Final Curtain** (novel)	Collins 1947 Little Brown 1947	B B
16	**Swing Brother Swing** (novel)	Collins 1949	B
17	**Wreath for Riviera** (same as 16)	Little Brown 1949	B
18	**Opening Night** (novel)	Collins 1951	B
19	**Night at the Vulcan** (same as 18)	Little Brown 1951	B
20	**Spinsters in Jeopardy** (novel)	Little Brown 1953 Collins 1954	C C
21	**Scales of Justice** (novel)	Collins 1955 Little Brown 1955	B B
22	**Death of a Fool** (novel)	Little Brown 1956	B
23	**Off with His Head** (same as 22)	Collins 1957	B
24	**Singing in the Shrouds** (novel)	Little Brown 1958 Collins 1959	B B
25	**False Scent** (novel)	Little Brown 1959 Collins 1960	B B
26	**Hand in Glove** (novel)	Little Brown 1962 Collins 1962	B B
27	**Dead Water** (novel)	Little Brown 1963 Collins 1964	B B
28	**Killer Dolphin** (novel)	Little Brown 1966	B
29	**Death at the Dolphin** (same as 28)	Collins 1967	B
30	**Clutch of Constables** (novel)	Collins 1968 Little Brown 1969	C B
31	**When in Rome** (novel)	Collins 1970 Little Brown 1970	B A

32 **Tied up in Tinsel** (novel)	Collins 1972	B
	Little Brown 1972	A
33 **Black as He's Painted** (novel)	Collins 1974	B
	Little Brown 1974	A
34 **Last Ditch** (novel)	Collins 1977	B
	Little Brown 1977	A
35 **Grave Mistake** (novel)	Collins 1978	A
	Little Brown 1978	A
36 **Photo-Finish** (novel)	Collins 1980	A
	Little Brown 1980	A
37 **Light Thickens** (novel)	Collins 1982	A
	Little Brown 1982	A

Miller, Arthur   Born in New York, 1915.

Today, more famous for having married Marilyn Monroe than for having written plays. Some years ago, one could have asserted with confidence that his plays would long outlast his sometime-wife's film appearances, but such is the way of the world that this now seems doubtful; shaky, even. But his work is safe – even the title *Death of a Salesman* being famous.

Of his works (about two dozen) the following are stage classics:

1 **All My Sons** (play)	Reynal & Hitchcock 1947	F
2 **Death of a Salesman** (play)	Viking 1949	F
	Cresset 1949	E
3 **The Crucible** (play)	Viking 1953	D
	Cresset 1956	C
4 **A View from the Bridge** and **A Memory of Two Mondays**	Viking 1955	D
5 **A View from the Bridge** (revised)	Cresset 1956	B
6 **Collected Plays** Incl. 1, 2, 3 and 4.	Viking 1957	C
	Cresset 1958	C
7 **Incident at Vichy** (play)	Viking 1965	C
	Secker 1966	B

Films:
All My Sons Universal 1948   **Death of a Salesman** Columbia 1951   **The Witches of Salem** Films de France 1957 (*The Crucible*)   **A View from the Bridge** Transcontinental 1961
The Misfits (story) United Artists 1961   The screenplay of **The Misfits** was published by Dell in 1961 and Secker & Warburg in 1961.

Bibliography:
Tetsumaro Hayashi **Arthur Miller: A Checklist of his Published Works** Kent, Ohio 1967.

Miller, Henry   Born in New York, 1891. Died 1980.

His staying power has been quite remarkable. I detect, however, that although Miller is still avidly *read* (his reputation will always ensure this) there is less interest from collectors than there used to be, say, ten years ago. His classic, though, remains scarce and expensive (in its original form) and still a sought-after book in its subsequent 'firsts', as is its sequel, and these are appended below.

1	**Tropic of Cancer** (novel)	Obelisk Press (Paris)	R
	As will be seen, there is a world of	1934	
	difference between the Paris edition and	Grove Press 1961	F
	the later American and English editions,	Calder 1963	C
	and therefore this is reflected in the		
	prices.		
2	**Tropic of Capricorn** (novel)	Obelisk Press 1939	P
	The same situation applies as in 1.	Grove Press 1961	E
		Calder 1964	B

It ought to be noted that in addition to the above highlights, Miller has published upwards of seventy books.

Film:
Tropic of Cancer Paramount 1969.

Bibliography:
Maxine Renken **A Bibliography of Henry Miller 1945–1961** Swallow 1962.

Milne, A.A.   Born in London, 1882. Died 1956.

I suppose that lovers of Winnie the Pooh et al. find it difficult to believe that Milne wrote anything else, but in fact he published about sixty books (many of them plays). Only those below pertain to Pooh and all his friends. The other works range from the tolerable to the frankly unreadable.

1	**When We were Very Young** (verse)	Methuen 1924	J
		Dutton 1924	H
2	**Winnie the Pooh** (stories)	Methuen 1926	I
		Dutton 1926	G
3	**Now We are Six** (verse)	Methuen 1927	H
		Dutton 1927	E
4	**The House at Pooh Corner** (stories)	Methuen 1928	H
		Dutton 1928	E

5 **Toad of Toad Hall** (play)	Methuen 1929	**E**
This is an adaptation of Kenneth	Scribner 1929	**C**
Grahame's *The Wind in the Willows*.		

Films (cartoons):
Winnie the Pooh and the Honey Tree Disney 1965 **Winnie the Pooh and the Blustery Day** Disney 1968 **Winnie the Pooh and Tigger Too** Disney 1974.

Mitchell, Margaret   Born in Atlanta, 1900. Died 1949.

For the one and only time, I do not have to say 'author of loads of old rubbish, but notable for just one'. No. Margaret Mitchell was that rare bird who today would have been hard put to resist a publisher's ministrations. But after the success of the film, when she was asked for a sequel, all she said was: 'I know good work and I know good writing, and I didn't think mine good.' The first edition is scarce, and such is the change of mood among collectors since I wrote *Collecting Modern First Editions* that I entirely withdraw what I said in that book – 'It is very uncommon in a 1st, but would probably never rise above Grade C (then, up to £10) such is its image.' No – it is so popular, kitsch, even, that I can see it fetching £100 today. In America, it could fetch anything between two hundred and a billion dollars; it's a part of their heritage.

Gone With the Wind	Macmillan (US) 1936	**K** up
	Macmillan (UK) 1936	**I** down

Film:
Gone With the Wind MGM 1939.

Mitford, Nancy   Born in London, 1904. Died 1973.

Best known for having coined the term 'U' and 'non-U'; but apart from that she remains a respected writer, who managed superb economy and wit and she reminds me of Waugh. Author of a few historical works, she is most notable for the following.

1 **The Pursuit of Love** (novel)	Hamilton 1945	**C**
	Random House 1946	**B**
2 **Love in a Cold Climate** (novel)	Hamilton 1949	**B**
	Random House 1949	**B**
3 **The Blessing** (novel)	Hamilton 1951	**B**
	Random House 1951	**A**
4 **Don't Tell Alfred** (novel)	Hamilton 1960	**B**
	Harper 1960	**A**

Also notable is the following volume
which she edited, responsible for the
whole U and non-U 'controversy' of the
fifties:

Noblesse Oblige	Harper 1956	C
	Hamilton 1957	B

Film:
Count Your Blessings MGM 1959 (*The Blessing*).

Biography:
Harold Acton **Nancy Mitford** Hamilton 1975; Harper 1976.

Monsarrat, Nicholas   Born in Liverpool, 1910. Died 1979.

Not really a collected author, but still notable for his most famous novel and
the film it inspired.

The Cruel Sea	Cassell 1951	C
The American edition actually	Knopf 1951	B
preceded, by about three weeks.		
The Book Society edition – issued		
simultaneously – is very common, and		
very cheap.		

Films:
The Cruel Sea General Films 1952.   Two more films have been made
from Monsarrat's books.

Mortimer, John   Born in Hampstead, London 1923.

It is difficult to get it firmly fixed in one's mind that Mortimer is *not*
Rumpole, and that Leo McKern is really an actor who *plays* Rumpole – who,
of course, does not exist. But like all really great fictional characters, he is
more real than anyone one can think of. When he says 'my old darling',
though (he says 'my old darling' a lot) I always think it sounds more actor
than barrister, but Mortimer is a QC, so he should know. The Pomeroy's
claret is bang on, though, as is Mrs Rumpole (who calls him 'Rumpole') and
whom he refers to as 'she who must be obeyed' – the "'er indoors' of the
professional classes.

Mortimer has had an unusual publishing history, as will be seen below.
Hugely prolific and hardworking (he is an active QC, a journalist, a tireless
adaptor for TV – as exemplified by his brilliant *Brideshead Revisited* – and an
interviewer, as well as a playwright and novelist) until Rumpole he was best
known for his stage work, the bulk of his published *œuvre*. His *A Voyage Round*

My Father was autobiographical (memorably televised with Laurence Olivier and Alan Bates) and his actual autobiography, *Clinging to the Wreckage*, was a bestseller. I imagine, though, that it is Rumpole for whom he will be remembered. Rumpole is here to stay.

1	**Charade** (novel)	Lane 1947	C
2	**Rumming Park** (novel)	Lane 1948	C
3	**Answer Yes or No** (novel)	Lane 1950	C
4	**The Silver Hook** (American edition of 3)	Morrow 1950	C
5	**Like Men Betrayed** (novel)	Collins 1953	C
		Lippincott 1954	C
6	**The Narrowing Stream** (novel)	Collins 1954	C
7	**Three Winters** (novel)	Collins 1956	C
8	**No Moaning at the Bar** (humour) Published under the pseudonym Geoffrey Lincoln.	Bles 1957	C
9	**With Love and Lizards** (travel) Written with Penelope Mortimer.	Joseph 1957	C
10	**Three Plays** Includes **The Dock Brief, What Shall We Tell Caroline?** and **I Spy**.	Elek 1958 Grove Press 1962	D C
11	**The Wrong Side of the Park** (play)	Heinemann 1960	B
12	**Lunch Hour** (play)	French 1960	A
13	**Lunch Hour** and **Other Plays** Includes **Collect Your Hand Baggage, David and Broccoli,** and **Call Me a Liar**.	Methuen 1960	B
14	**Two Stars For Comfort** (play)	Methuen 1962	B
15	**A Flea in Her Ear** (play) An adaptation of Feydeau.	French (UK) 1967 French (US) 1967	A A
16	**The Judge** (play)	Methuen 1967	A
17	**A Choice of Kings** (play) Published in **Playbill Three**, edited by Alan Durband.	Hutchinson 1969	A
18	**Cat Among the Pigeons** (play) An adaptation of Feydeau.	French 1970	A
19	**Five Plays** Includes **The Dock Brief, What Shall We Tell Caroline?, I Spy, Lunch Hour,** and **Collect Your Hand Baggage**.	Methuen 1970	B
20	**Come As You Are: Four Short Plays** Includes **Mill Hill, Bermondsey, Gloucester Road,** and **Marble Arch**.	Methuen 1971	B
21	**The Captain of Kopenick** (play) An adaptation of Carl Zuckmayer.	Methuen 1971	A

Mortimer

22 **A Voyage Round My Father** (play)	Methuen 1971	C
23 **Knightsbridge** (play)	French 1973	A
24 **Collaborations** (play)	Methuen 1973	A
25 **The Lady from Maxim's** (play)	Heinemann 1977	A
An adaptation of Feydeau.		
26 **Will Shakespeare:**	Hodder 1977	A
The Untold Story (novel)	Delacorte 1978	A
27 **The Fear of Heaven** (play)	French 1978	A
28 **Heaven and Hell** (plays)	French 1978	A
Contains 27 and **The Prince of**		
Darkness.		
29 **Rumpole of the Bailey** (novel)	Penguin 1978	B
30 **The Trials of Rumpole** (novel)	Penguin 1979	B
29 and 30 were paperback originals.		
The two were published together in		
hardback by Allen Lane in 1980.		
31 **Rumpole's Return** (novel)	Penguin 1981	B
32 **Regina v Rumpole** (novel)	Lane 1981	B
33 **Clinging to the Wreckage**	Weidenfeld 1982	B
(autobiography)	Ticknor & Fields 1982	B
34 **In Character** (interviews)	Lane 1983	B

Film:
The Dock Brief MGM 1962.

Muldoon, Paul   Born in Northern Ireland, 1951.

One of the 'Ulster' poets, the best known of whom is Seamus Heaney.
Muldoon is greatly respected, and is a man to watch from the collecting
point of view, I believe. He started publishing very young, and already has
seven slim volumes to his credit. It must be very rare indeed for Faber – still
probably the most prestigious publisher of poetry – to bring out a book of
verse by a twenty-two-year-old. This accolade is a fair testimony to the
quality of much of his work.

1 **Knowing My Place** (verse)	Ulsterman (Belfast) 1971	E
2 **New Weather** (verse)	Faber 1973	D
3 **Spirit of Dawn** (verse)	Ulsterman 1975	C
4 **Mules** (verse)	Faber 1977	B
5 **Names and Addresses** (verse)	Ulsterman 1978	B
6 **Why Brownlee Left** (verse)	Faber 1980	A
7 **Quoof** (verse)	Faber 1983	A

Murdoch, Iris   Born in Dublin, 1919.

Iris Murdoch – in my opinion, the very best living novelist – is far more avidly collected than she was a few years ago. My only puzzlement is as to why, a few years ago, interest was not so strong. Then as now, of course, *Under the Net* was a scarce and sought after book, but five years ago everything later than 1960 might have been gathered at a couple of pounds each. This is no longer possible, but Murdoch is still very undervalued – I urge you to fill your gaps *now*, for it cannot be long before everyone wakes up to the truth that fine 1sts in dust-wrapper are not as common as dealers and collectors alike seem to imagine they are. Contract the Iris-virus.

1	**Sartre: Romantic Rationalist** (non-fiction)	Bowes & Bowes 1953	G
		Yale University Press 1953	E
2	**Under the Net** (novel)	Chatto & Windus 1954	I
		Viking 1954	F
3	**The Flight from the Enchanter** (novel)	Chatto & Windus 1956	H
		Viking 1956	E
4	**The Sandcastle** (novel)	Chatto & Windus 1957	G
		Viking 1957	E
5	**The Bell** (novel)	Chatto & Windus 1958	E
		Viking 1958	D
6	**A Severed Head** (novel)	Chatto & Windus 1961	C
		Viking 1961	B
7	**An Unofficial Rose** (novel)	Chatto & Windus 1962	B
		Viking 1962	A
8	**The Unicorn** (novel)	Chatto & Windus 1963	C
		Viking 1963	B
9	**The Italian Girl** (novel)	Chatto & Windus 1964	C
		Viking 1964	B
10	**A Severed Head** (play) With J.B. Priestley.	Chatto & Windus 1964	D
11	**The Red and the Green** (novel)	Chatto & Windus 1965	B
		Viking 1965	A
12	**The Time of the Angels** (novel)	Chatto & Windus 1966	C
		Viking 1966	B
13	**The Sovereignty of Good** (lecture)	CUP 1967	D
14	**The Nice and the Good** (novel)	Chatto & Windus 1968	C
		Viking 1968	B
15	**Bruno's Dream** (novel)	Chatto & Windus 1969	C
		Viking 1969	B
16	**The Italian Girl** (play) With James Saunders.	French 1969	C
17	**A Fairly Honourable Defeat** (novel)	Chatto & Windus 1970	C
		Viking 1970	B

Murdoch

18 **The Sovereignty of Good** (essays) Cont. 13, together with other unpublished essays.	Routledge 1971	C
19 **An Accidental Man** (novel)	Chatto & Windus 1971 Viking 1972	B A
20 **The Black Prince** (novel)	Chatto & Windus 1973 Viking 1973	C B
21 **The Three Arrows** and **The Servants and the Snow: Two Plays**	Chatto & Windus 1973 Viking 1974	C B
22 **The Sacred and Profane Love Machine** (novel)	Chatto & Windus 1974 Viking 1974	B A
23 **A Word Child** (novel)	Chatto & Windus 1975 Viking 1975	B A
24 **Henry and Cato** (novel)	Chatto & Windus 1976 Viking 1976	B A
25 **The Fire and the Sun: Why Plato Banished the Artists** (philosophy)	OUP 1977	B
26 **The Sea, the Sea** (novel)	Chatto & Windus 1978 Viking 1978	C B
27 **A Year of Birds** (verse) A lovely slim volume, and Murdoch's only published poetry. It is limited to 350 copies, each numbered and signed by Iris Murdoch and by Reynolds Stone, who illustrated it (see 29).	Compton Press 1978	G
28 **Nuns and Soldiers** (novel)	Chatto & Windus 1980 Viking 1981	B B
29 **Reynolds Stone** A four-page address given in St James's Church, Piccadilly, in memory of Stone. Limited to 750 copies, but none is numbered and there is no mention of whether all or some were signed. My own copy bears a signature.	Warren Editions 1981	D
30 **The Philosopher's Pupil** (novel)	Chatto & Windus 1983 Viking 1983	B B
A story entitled 'Something Special' appears in **Winter's Tales** 3	Macmillan 1957	C

Film:
A Severed Head Columbia 1969.

Bibliography:
Thomas A. Tominaga and Wilma Schneidermeyer **Iris Murdoch and Muriel Spark: A Bibliography** Scarecrow Press (US) 1976.

Nabokov, Vladimir Born in St Petersburg
(now Leningrad), 1899. Died 1977.

Now that the notorious image of *Lolita* has faded, Nabokov is much better known for the power of such novels as *Pale Fire* and *Ada*, and for his recently published lectures on literature.

Nabokov is a difficult author to collect; not least because most collections must probably be compromises, for many of his works were first published in Russian in different countries, sometimes long before the first English editions, although in most cases the translations into English were by Nabokov himself. In the checklist below, I have taken the chronology of the English editions, though stating whether Russian-language publication preceded.

1	**Camera Obscura** (novel) A revised edition was published in America by Bobbs Merrill in 1938 as **Laughter in the Dark** (**J**), and by Weidenfeld in 1961 (**E**). First publication, in Russian, was in Paris and Berlin 1933.	Long (London) 1937	**O**
2	**Despair** (novel) A revised edition was published in 1966 in America by Putnam (**C**) and in England by Weidenfeld (**C**). First publication was in Berlin 1936.	Long (London) 1937	**L**
3	**The Real Life of Sebastian Knight** (novel)	New Directions 1941	**I**
		Editions Poetry 1945	**H**
4	**Nikolai Gogol** (non-fiction)	New Directions 1944	**G**
		Editions Poetry 1947	**G**
5	**Bend Sinister** (novel)	Holt 1947	**G**
		Weidenfeld 1960	**E**
6	**Nine Stories**	New Directions 1947	**F**
7	**Conclusive Evidence: A Memoir** Published in England by Gollancz in 1952 as **Speak, Memory: A Memoir** (**F**). A revised edition **Speak, Memory: An Autobiography Revisited** was published in America by Putnam in 1966 (**C**), and in England by Weidenfeld in 1967 (**C**).	Harper 1951	**H**
8	**Lolita** (novel) The Paris edition is in two volumes.	Olympia Press (Paris) 1955	**H**
		Putnam 1958	**D**
		Weidenfeld 1959	**C**

Nabokov

9	**Pnin** (novel)	Doubleday 1957	D
		Heinemann 1957	C
10	**Nabokov's Dozen** (stories)	Doubleday 1958	C
		Heinemann 1959	C
11	**Invitation to a Beheading** (novel)	Putnam 1959	E
	First publication, in Russian, was in Paris 1938.	Weidenfeld 1960	D
12	**Poems**	Doubleday 1959	C
		Weidenfeld 1961	C
13	**Pale Fire** (novel)	Putnam 1962	D
		Weidenfeld 1962	C
14	**The Gift** (novel)	Putnam 1963	C
	First published, in Russian, in New York 1952.	Weidenfeld 1963	C
15	**The Defense** (novel)	Putnam 1964	C
	English title **The Defence**. First published, in Russian, in Berlin 1930.	Weidenfeld 1964	C
16	**Nabokov's Quartet** (stories)	Phaedra 1966	C
		Weidenfeld 1967	C
17	**King, Queen, Knave** (novel)	McGraw-Hill 1968	C
		Weidenfeld 1968	C
18	**Nabokov's Congeries** (anthology)	Viking Press 1968	C
19	**Ada** (novel)	McGraw-Hill 1969	C
		Weidenfeld 1969	C
20	**Mary** (novel)	McGraw-Hill 1970	C
	This was, in fact, his first novel, and was originally published in Russian in Berlin 1926.	Weidenfeld 1971	C
21	**Glory** (novel)	McGraw-Hill 1971	C
	First publication, in Russian, was in Paris 1932	Weidenfeld 1972	C
22	**Poems and Problems**	McGraw-Hill 1971	C
		Weidenfeld 1972	C
23	**Transparent Things** (novel)	McGraw-Hill 1973	C
		Weidenfeld 1973	C
24	**A Russian Beauty and Other Stories**	McGraw-Hill 1973	B
		Weidenfeld 1973	B
25	**Strong Opinions** (essays)	McGraw-Hill 1973	B
		Weidenfeld 1974	B
26	**Look at the Harlequins!** (novel)	McGraw-Hill 1974	C
		Weidenfeld 1975	B
27	**Lolita: A Screenplay**	McGraw-Hill 1974	C
28	**Tyrants Destroyed and Other Stories**	McGraw-Hill 1975	B
		Weidenfeld 1975	B
29	**Details of a Sunset and Other Stories**	McGraw-Hill 1976	B
		Weidenfeld 1976	B

30 **The Nabokov/Wilson Letters 1940–1971** Correspondence between Nabokov and Edmund Wilson.	Farrar Straus 1978 Weidenfeld 1979	C C
31 **Lectures on Literature**	Harcourt Brace 1980 Weidenfeld 1980	C C
32 **Lectures on Russian Literature**	Harcourt Brace 1981 Weidenfeld 1982	C C
33 **Lectures on Don Quixote**	Harcourt Brace 1983 Weidenfeld 1983	C C

Films:
Lolita MGM 1962   **Laughter in the Dark** United Artists 1969
Despair Gala 1978.
Some works – notably the very early verse – did not appear under their original titles in English, but details of these and of his translations of other works, etc., may be found in
Andrew Field **Nabokov: A Bibliography** McGraw-Hill 1974.

Naipaul, V.S.   Born in Trinidad, 1932. British.

A highly regarded author, the most desirable highlights of whom are still *The Mystic Masseur* (his first book) and *A House for Mr Biswas*. Lately, he has been leaning towards non-fiction, and this is of considerably less interest to the collector.

1 **The Mystic Masseur** (novel)	Deutsch 1957 Vanguard Press 1959	J G
2 **The Suffrage of Elvira** (novel)	Deutsch 1958	I
3 **Miguel Street** (novel)	Deutsch 1959 Vanguard Press 1960	I F
4 **A House for Mr Biswas** (novel)	Deutsch 1961 McGraw-Hill 1962	H F
5 **The Middle Passage** (non-fiction)	Deutsch 1962 Macmillan (US) 1963	F E
6 **Mr Stone and the Knights Companion** (novel)	Deutsch 1963 Macmillan 1964	E D
7 **An Area of Darkness** (travel)	Deutsch 1964 Macmillan 1965	D C
8 **The Mimic Men** (novel)	Deutsch 1967 Macmillan 1967	F E
9 **A Flag on the Island** (stories)	Deutsch 1967 Macmillan 1968	D C

Naipaul

10 **The Loss of El Dorado** (history)	Deutsch 1969	C
	Knopf 1970	C
11 **In a Free State** (novel)	Deutsch 1971	C
	Knopf 1971	C
12 **The Overcrowded Barracoon** (articles)	Deutsch 1972	C
	Knopf 1972	C
13 **Guerrillas** (novel)	Deutsch 1975	C
	Knopf 1975	B
14 **India: A Wounded Civilisation** (non-fiction)	Deutsch 1977	B
	Knopf 1977	B
15 **A Bend in the River** (novel)	Deutsch 1979	B
	Knopf 1979	B
16 **The Return of Eva Peron** (essays)	Deutsch 1980	B
	Knopf 1980	B
17 **Among the Believers: An Islamic Journey** (travel)	Deutsch 1981	B
	Knopf 1981	B
18 **Finding the Centre: Two Narratives**	Deutsch 1984	B
	Knopf 1984	B

Nash, Ogden   Born in New York, 1902. Died 1971.

What can one say about Nash? One of the great romantic poets of our time – indeed, of any time. He makes Byron seem crass, Shelley inept, and Keats downright insensitive. It is with tears of joy that I bring you the following:

'Many people have asked me what was the most beautiful sight I
  saw during the recent summer,
And I think the most beautiful sight was the day the water
  wouldn't stop running and in came the plumber.'

The master of these unique rhymes has published quite a few volumes, though no one in particular stands out as a highlight. Each seems as delightful as the next, however, and so I print a representative selection.

1 **Hard Lines**	Simon & Schuster 1931	G
	Duckworth 1931	F
2 **The Primrose Path**	Simon & Schuster 1935	E
	Bodley Head 1935	D
3 **The Bad Parent's Garden of Verse**	Simon & Schuster 1936	D
4 **The Face is Familiar**	Little Brown 1940	D
	Dent 1942	C
5 **Verses from 1929 on**	Little Brown 1961	B
This was published in England as **Collected Verses** by Dent during the same year. **B**		

Naughton, Bill   Born in County Mayo, Ireland, 1910.

Still best known for one key, seminal sixties novel which was in turn made into a key, seminal sixties film notable for Michael Caine and a nasal little ditty by Cilla Black which didn't actually feature in the film at all. Not a lot of people know that.

Alfie	MacGibbon & Kee 1966	C
	Ballantine 1966	C

Films:
Alfie Paramount 1965.

O'Brien, Edna   Born in County Clare, Ireland, 1932.

Although her touch is as soft and sure as ever, Edna O'Brien continues to be underrated by the collectors. People seem to seek *The Country Girls* because it is her first book, and to largely ignore the rest. This is (she will enjoy the adjective) scandalous. A unique writer – the power and the gentleness balanced as evenly as the black and the white in a well-kept Guinness – she should be valued more highly. This said, she really *must* get back to writing novels – it's what she is made for.

1	**The Country Girls** (novel)	Hutchinson 1960	E
		Knopf 1960	C
2	**The Lonely Girl** (novel)	Cape 1962	D
		Random House 1962	B
3	**Girls in Their Married Bliss** (novel) 1, 2 and 3 form a trilogy.	Cape 1964	C
		Houghton Mifflin 1968	B
4	**August is a Wicked Month** (novel)	Cape 1965	B
		Simon & Schuster 1965	B
5	**Casualties of Peace** (novel)	Cape 1966	B
		Simon & Schuster 1967	B
6	**The Love Object** (stories)	Cape 1968	B
		Knopf 1969	B
7	**A Pagan Place** (novel)	Weidenfeld 1970	B
		Knopf 1970	A
8	**Zee & Co** (screenplay)	Weidenfeld 1971	A
9	**Night** (novel)	Weidenfeld 1972	A
		Knopf 1973	A
10	**A Pagan Place** (play)	Faber 1973	B

O'Brien, E.

11 **A Scandalous Woman** (stories)	Weidenfeld 1974	A
	Harcourt Brace 1974	A
12 **Mother Ireland** (autobiog.)	Weidenfeld 1976	B
	Harcourt Brace 1976	B
13 **Johnnie, I Hardly Knew You** (novel)	Weidenfeld 1977	A
The American edition was entitled	Doubleday 1978	A
simply **I Hardly Knew You**.		
14 **Arabian Days** (travel)	Horizon Press (NY) 1977	B
	Quartet 1977	B
15 **The Collected Edna O'Brien**	Collins 1978	B
Contains 1, 2, 3, 4, 5, 6, 7, 11, together with a new introduction.		
16 **Mrs Reinhardt and Other Stories**	Weidenfeld 1978	A
17 **A Rose in the Heart**	Doubleday 1979	A
(American edition of 16)		
18 **Some Irish Loving** (anthology)	Weidenfeld 1979	A
A selection of Irish writing, edited and	Harper 1979	A
introduced by E. O'B.		
19 **Virginia** (play)	Hogarth Press 1981	B
	Harcourt Brace 1981	B
20 **The Dazzle** (juvenile)	Hodder & Stoughton 1981	B
21 **James and Nora** (essay)	Lord John Press (US) 1981	E
Concerning the marriage of Joyce, in a signed edition published at $35.		
22 **Returning** (stories)	Weidenfeld 1982	B
23 **A Christmas Treat** (juvenile)	Hodder & Stoughton 1982	A

Films:
The Girl with Green Eyes United Artists 1964 (*The Lonely Girl*)
Zee & Co Columbia 1971.

O'Brien, Flann   Pseudonym of Brian O'Nolan, also known as Myles na Gopaleen.
Born in Tyrone, Ireland, 1912. Died 1966.

I am not going to even begin to try to explain what sort of a book the following is, but I will say that it is unique, brilliant, funny and very scarce. It remains the highlight.

At-Swim-Two-Birds	Longman 1939	I
	Pantheon 1951	H

O'Casey, Sean   Born in Dublin, 1880. Died 1964.

As is so often the way, O'Casey is most popular with the Irish, because he is Irish. In order to forestall the barrage, I should like to make clear that *of course* O'Casey is highly thought of in Britain (indeed, internationally) but only for the recognized highlights – unless one is a *student* of O'Casey, in which case the most arcane fragments appear to be compulsively attractive. It is interesting, then – to say nothing of economical – to note that his two highlights were published within the same volume:

> **Two Plays: Juno and the Paycock;**   Macmillan 1925   **G**
> **The Shadow of a Gunman**
> This is quite scarce.
> A checklist of O'Casey's work may be
> found in *The New Cambridge
> Bibliography of English Literature*
> vol. 4, but the only bibliographies,
> strangely enough, appear in German
> and Russian.

Films:
Juno and the Paycock British International 1930. Two other films have been made from O'Casey's work.

Orton, Joe   Born in Leicester, 1933. Died 1967.

Very well known and popular even *before* his rather horrible murder by his live-in friend. Orton was possessed of a very dry, black, cynical humour, and his dialogue was as sharp as a razor. He published only a small body of work, the following two remaining the highlights.

1	**Entertaining Mr Sloane** (play)	Hamilton 1964	**D**
		Grove Press 1965	**C**
2	**Loot** (play)	Methuen 1967	**C**
		Grove Press 1968	**B**

Films:
Entertaining Mr Sloane Warner Bros 1969   **Loot** British Lion 1971.

Biography:
John Lahr **Prick Up Your Ears** Lane 1976; Knopf 1976.

Orwell, George   Born in Bengal, 1903. Died 1950. Pseudonym for Eric Blair

Demand for the first edition of *Nineteen Eighty-Four* has been predictably high in that year, with prices to match. However, lest we forget, Orwell *did* write other books, and most of them – as will be seen from the ensuing price guide – are far more scarce than *Nineteen Eighty-Four*. Orwell remains very, very popular, and extremely difficult and expensive to collect. The hope of finding the early titles, fine in dust-wrapper, are virtually nil – and if you did find them you'd have to sell the house to pay for them, and where do you and your books (and your family too, now I come to think of it) go then?

1 **Down and Out in Paris and London** (non-fiction)	Gollancz 1933	**Q**
	Harper 1933	**M**
2 **Burmese Days** (novel)	Harper 1934	**O**
	Gollancz 1935	**L**
3 **A Clergyman's Daughter** (novel)	Gollancz 1935	**N**
	Harper 1936	**I**
4 **Keep the Aspidistra Flying** (novel)	Gollancz 1936	**M**
	Harcourt Brace 1956	**G**
5 **The Road to Wigan Pier** (non-fiction) The 1st was published in orange wrpps under The Left Book Club imprint (**I**). A hard-covered trade edition followed.	Gollancz 1937	**D**
	Harcourt Brace 1958	**D**
6 **Homage to Catalonia** (non-fiction)	Secker 1938	**K**
	Harcourt Brace 1952	**D**
7 **Coming Up for Air** (novel)	Gollancz 1939	**K**
	Harcourt Brace 1950	**D**
8 **Inside the Whale** (essays)	Gollancz 1940	**D**
9 **The Lion and the Unicorn** (non-fiction) This was published as Searchlight Books No. 1. Orwell was the editor, with T.R. Fyvel, of ten Searchlight Books, published between 1941 and 1943. Although this was the only one he wrote, he contributed Forewords to two more: T.C. Worsley **The End of the Old School Tie** and J. Cary **The Case for African Freedom**.	Secker 1941	**D**
10 **Animal Farm** (novel)	Secker 1945	**H**
	Harcourt Brace 1946	**F**
11 **James Burnham and the Managerial Revolution**	Socialist Book Centre 1946	**F**
12 **Critical Essays**	Secker 1946	**E**
13 **Dickens, Dali and Others** (same as 12)	Reynal (NY) 1946	**E**

14 **The English People** (essay)   Collins 1947   **D**
This was No. 100 in the Britain in
Pictures series.

15 **Nineteen Eighty-Four**   Secker 1949   **I**
Much play is made of the d/w. There   Harcourt Brace 1949   **H**
are two states – maroon (often faded to
pink) and green. No one can say with
absolute certainty which preceded, but
it is true that the maroon is far scarcer,
and therefore, I suppose, the more
desirable. It could cost twice as much (**L**).
    It is also worth acquiring the
Cambridge revised edition, out this
year, if only for the copyright date
reading '1984'. The reissued Secker
edition also bore this date, actually, but
this was quite unjustified as it was an
unrevised text.

16 **Shooting an Elephant** (essays)   Secker 1950   **E**
                                        Harcourt Brace 1950   **D**
17 **Such, Such Were the Joys** (essays)   Harcourt Brace 1953   **E**
18 **England, Your England** (essays)   Secker 1953   **D**
Substantially the same as 17.

19 **Animal Farm: Illustrated Edition**   Secker 1954   **D**
20 **Selected Essays**   Penguin 1957   **C**
21 **Selected Writings**   Heinemann 1958   **C**
22 **Collected Essays**   Secker 1961   **C**
Inc. 12, 16 and 18.

23 **The Collected Essays, Journalism**   Secker 1968   **G**
   and Letters (4 vols)   Harcourt-Brace 1968   **G**

Films:
Animal Farm Associated British 1954   **1984** Associated British 1956.

Bibliography:
Z.G. Zeke and W. White **George Orwell: A Selected Bibliography**
Boston 1962.

Biography:
Bernard Crick **George Orwell: A Life** Secker 1980; revised edition 1982.

Osborne, John   Born in London, 1929.

Much less prolific, these days, his plays tending to be for television rather
than stage, and consequently shorter. The recent first volume of his
autobiography made up for the silence, though. His first prose work, and one
of the best things he has ever done. Osborne's cynical amusement and rather

Osborne

stylish assumed lethargy have always been compelling spectator sports, and it is nice to see that the anger in the original *Angry Young Man* has not been lost – merely reduced (in the culinary sense) to a seething intolerance, rising occasionally to a rather healthy hatred.

1	**Look Back in Anger** (play)	Faber 1957	**D**
		Criterion 1957	**C**
2	**The Entertainer** (play)	Faber 1957	**D**
		Criterion 1958	**C**
3	**Epitaph for George Dillon** (play)	Faber 1958	**C**
	With Anthony Creighton.	Criterion 1958	**B**
4	**The World of Paul Slickey** (play)	Faber 1959	**D**
		Criterion 1961	**C**
5	**A Subject of Scandal and Concern** (play)	Faber 1961	**C**
6	**Luther** (play)	Faber 1961	**C**
		Dramatic Publishing Co. 1961	**B**
7	**Plays for England**	Faber 1963	**C**
	Inc. **The Blood of the Bambergs** and **Under Plain Cover**.	Criterion 1964	**B**
8	**Tom Jones: A Film Script**	Faber 1964	**C**
		Grove Press 1964	**B**
9	**Inadmissible Evidence** (play)	Faber 1965	**C**
		Grove Press 1965	**B**
10	**A Bond Honoured** (play)	Faber 1966	**B**
11	**A Patriot for Me** (play)	Faber 1966	**B**
		Random House 1970	**B**
12	**Time Present** and **Hotel in Amsterdam** (plays)	Faber 1968	**B**
13	**The Right Prospectus** (play)	Faber 1970	**B**
14	**Very Like a Whale** (play)	Faber 1971	**B**
15	**West of Suez** (play)	Faber 1971	**B**
16	**Hedda Gabler** (play: adapt. from Ibsen)	Faber 1972	**A**
17	**The Gift of Friendship** (play)	Faber 1972	**A**
18	**A Sense of Detachment** (play)	Faber 1973	**A**
19	**A Place Calling Itself Rome** (play)	Faber 1973	**A**
20	**The Picture of Dorian Gray** (play)	Faber 1973	**A**
21	**The End of Me Old Cigar** (play)	Faber 1975	**A**
22	**Watch It Come Down** (play)	Faber 1975	**A**
23	**You're Not Watching Me, Mummy** and **Try A Little Tenderness** (plays)	Faber 1978	**A**
24	**A Better Class of Person** (autobiog.)	Faber 1981	**B**
		Dutton 1981	**B**

Films:
Look Back in Anger Associated British 1959   **The Entertainer** British Lion 1960   **Inadmissible Evidence** Paramount 1968   The film **Tom**

Jones (8) was made in 1962 by United Artists. **Luther** Seven Keys 1973   **The Entertainer** Seven Keys 1975

Two works about Osborne are recommended: John Russell Taylor **Anger and After** Methuen 1962   Simon Trussler **The Plays of John Osborne** Gollancz 1969.

Owen, Wilfred   Born in Shropshire, 1893. Died 1918.

Still the favourite of the war poets, young girls in particular, I have noticed, responding to the sensitivity in his work, as well as the tragic romance of his early death. Although selections of his work have always been readily available, it seems sad that the definitive collected edition had to be published at £55, scholarly two-volume work though it is, when the collected works of almost any other poet one would care to name is available at an infinitely more accessible figure. Maybe soon there will be a compact one-volume edition, minus the annotations.

1 **Poems**	Chatto & Windus	I
Intro. by Siegfried Sassoon.	1920	
2 **The Poems of Wilfred Owen**	Chatto & Windus 1931	F
	Viking 1931	E
3 **The Čollected Poems of Wilfred Owen**	Chatto & Windus 1963	D
Intro. by C. Day Lewis, memoir by Edmund Blunden.	New Directions 1964	C
4 **Collected Letters**	OUP 1967	C
5 **The Complete Poems and Fragments**	Chatto & Windus 1983	G
2 volumes, edited by Jon Stalworthy.		

Biography:
Jon Stalworthy **Wilfred Owen** OUP/Chatto 1974.

Parkinson, C. Northcote   Born in Durham, 1909.

Parkinson's Law expounds the theory that work will expand to fill the time available. This appears to be a truism, today, but only since Parkinson set it down. This is why the following highlight is collectable, while Parkinson's other (more whimsical, less vital) offerings are not.

Parkinson's Law	Houghton Mifflin	C
Quite uncommon.	1957	
	Murray 1958	C

Pasternak, Boris   Born in Moscow, 1890. Died 1960.

Not the force he was (he is distinctly unfashionable, these days) but still notable for the one famous novel, made into a highly successful film with a haunting theme tune – or an annoying theme tune, depending upon your outlook. Pasternak is a Russian noun which translated means Parsnip.

Dr Zhivago	Collins/Harvill 1958	**C**
First publication was in Italy in 1957.	Pantheon 1958	**C**

Film:
Doctor Zhivago MGM 1965.

Peake, Mervyn   Born in China, 1911. Died 1968.

Although there is still very strong collectors' interest in the likes of Peake and Tolkien (people who like one tend to like the other) there is not any more the *passion* that was evident ten years ago. The **Gormenghast** trilogy remains a very important and very desirable set, while I find there is little demand for the posthumous fragments. Always an important factor with Peake is the presence of the dust-wrapper, as it was often designed by him – just as the books often carry illustrations by him (all of which, it seems facile to mention, must be present). So I shouldn't say that interest is on the way down, but rather that it has, as it were, peaked.

1	**Captain Slaughterboard Drops Anchor** (juvenile)	Country Life 1939 Macmillan (US) 1967	**N** **C**
2	**Shapes and Sounds** (verse)	Chatto & Windus 1941	**K**
3	**Rhymes Without Reason** (verse)	Eyre & Spottiswoode 1944	**I**
4	**The Craft of the Lead Pencil** (non-fiction)	Wingate 1946	**I**
5	**Titus Groan** (novel)	Eyre & Spottiswoode 1946 Reynal & Hitchcock 1946	**I** **H**
6	**Letters from a Lost Uncle from Polar Regions** (stories)	Eyre & Spottiswoode 1948	**G**
7	**The Drawings of Mervyn Peake**	Grey Walls Press 1949	**F**
8	**The Glassblowers** (verse)	Eyre & Spottiswoode 1950	**E**

Everything you ever wanted to know about Life, but were afraid to ask

Murdoch's second and third novels, and two big novels from J. B. Priestley, with whom she collaborated on her dramatized version of *A Severed Head*

First novels by three of the younger bloods, and Rushdie's prizewinning second
book

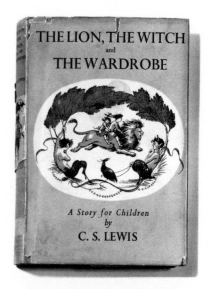

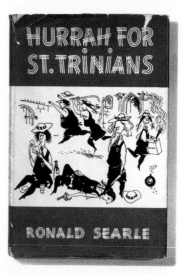

A quartet of childrens' (?) classics

An early Spark, Keith Waterhouse's first novel, Storey's scarce second novel, and Wyndham's homicidal plant

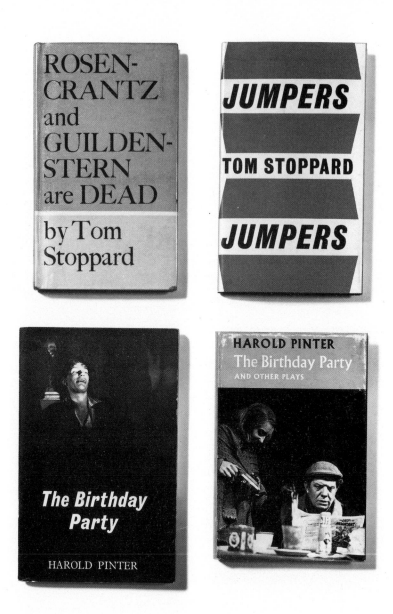

Stoppard's first play, together with probably his most representative work, and Pinter's first play in the Encore edition (1959) and the Methuen edition (1960)

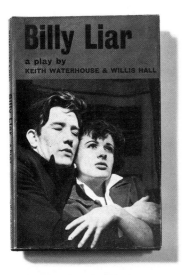

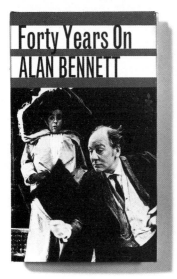

Changing fashions in drama over the last three decades

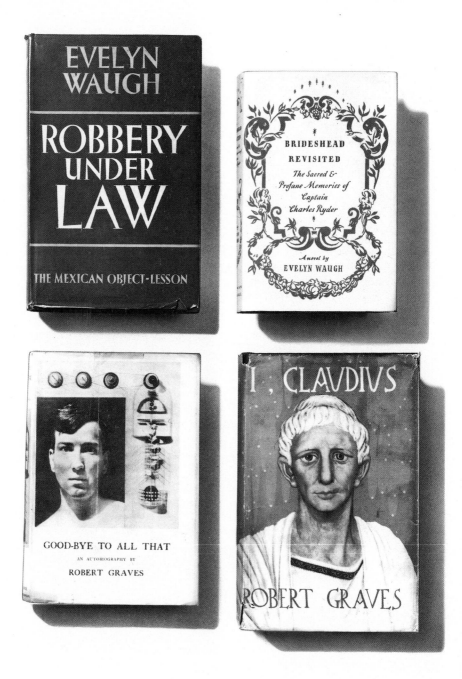

A very scarce Waugh, with his celebrated novel, and the two best-known titles by
Robert Graves

9 **Gormenghast** (novel)	Eyre & Spottiswoode 1950	G
	Weybright & Talley 1967	C
10 **Mr Pye** (story)	Heinemann 1953	D
11 **Titus Alone** (novel) This, with 5 and 9, completes the trilogy. A revised ed. of **Titus Alone** was published by Eyre & Spottiswoode in 1970.	Eyre & Spottiswoode 1959 Weybright & Talley 1967	D C
12 **The Rhyme of the Flying Bomb** (verse)	Dent 1962	C
13 **Poems and Drawings** Limited to 150 copies.	Keepsake Press 1965	G
14 **A Reverie of Bone** (verse) Limited to 300 copies.	Rota 1967	H
15 **Selected Poems**	Faber 1972	B
16 **A Book of Nonsense**	Owen 1972	B
	Dufour 1975	B
17 **The Drawings of Mervyn Peake**	Davis-Poynter 1974	C
18 **Mervyn Peake: Writings and Drawings**	Academy 1974 St Martin's 1974	C C
19 **Twelve Poems**	Bran's Head 1975	E
20 **Peake's Progress: Selected Writings and Drawings** Ed. Maeve Gilmore.	Lane 1979 Overlook Press 1981	B B

Biography:
John Watney **Mervyn Peake** Joseph 1976.

Perelman, S.J.   Born in Brooklyn, 1904. Died 1979.

Perelman has written about thirty books – novels, stories, plays, screenplays, miscellaneous insanities – all in his own inimitable style. There are no highlights as such, though below appears a selection which deserves to be preserved, if only for the titles – or, should I say, not least for the titles.

1 **Keep It Crisp**	Random House 1946	C
	Heinemann 1947	B
2 **Acres and Pains**	Reynal & Hitchcock 1947	C
	Heinemann 1948	B
3 **Westward Ha! or, Around the World in 80 Clichés**	Simon & Schuster 1947	C
	Reinhardt & Evans 1949	B

Perelman

4	**The Swiss Family Perelman**	Simon & Schuster 1950	C
		Reinhardt & Evans 1951	B
5	**A Child's Garden of Curses**	Heinemann 1951	B
6	**The Rising Gorge**	Simon & Schuster 1961	B
		Heinemann 1962	B
7	**The Last Laugh**	Simon & Schuster 1981	B
	This – posthumously published – was, appropriately, his last book.	Methuen 1981	B

Pinter, Harold   Born in London, 1930.

Pinter seems to be as strong a force just lately as he was in the sixties, when it was all truly exciting and new. He has adapted, and all his more recent publications are notable. From the collector's point of view, of course, the early stuff remains the most rare and sought after, because it was then that his reputation was made (this makes such works as *The Birthday Party* and *The Caretaker* eminently desirable) and the concept of collecting playscripts in those days was unheard of – indeed, they were published only in order to be used by theatrical companies, not to be gathered up by the collector of modern first editions. Assemble a collection while it is still possible – treasure every word, and every pause.

1	**The Birthday Party** (play)	Encore Publishing 1959	H
2	**The Birthday Party and Other Plays** Incl. **The Dumb Waiter** and **The Room**.	Methuen 1960	D
3	**The Caretaker** Methuen published an edition later the same year.	Encore Publishing 1960	F
			C
4	**A Slight Ache and Other Plays** Incl. **A Night Out, The Dwarfs** and 5 revue sketches.	Methuen 1961	C
5	**The Birthday Party** and **The Room** (same as 2)	Grove Press 1961	C
6	**The Collection** (play)	French 1962	B
7	**The Caretaker** and **The Room** (plays)	Grove Press 1962	B
8	**Three Plays** Incl. **A Slight Ache, The Collection, The Dwarfs**.	Grove Press 1962	B
9	**The Lover** (play)	Dramatists Play Service (NY) 1965	C

10 **The Dwarfs** and **Eight Revue Sketches**	Dramatists Play Service 1965	C
11 **The Homecoming** (play)	Methuen 1965	C
	Grove Press 1966	B
12 **The Collection** and **The Lover** (plays) Incl. **The Examination**, a prose piece.	Methuen 1966	B
13 **Tea Party** (play)	Grove Press 1966	B
14 **Tea Party and Other Plays** Incl. **The Basement** and **Night School**.	Methuen 1967	B
		B
15 **Early Plays** Incl. **A Night Out, Night School**, revue sketches.	Grove Press 1968	B
16 **Poems** A revised edition was published in 1971, with extra poems (**B**).	Enitharmon Press 1968	C
17 **Mac** (memoir)	Pendragon Press 1968	D
18 **Landscape** and **Silence** (plays) Incl. **Night**.	Methuen 1969	B
	Grove Press 1970	B
19 **Five Screenplays** Cont. **The Caretaker, The Servant, The Pumpkin Eater, Accident, The Quiller Memorandum**.	Methuen 1971	C
20 **Old Times** (play)	Eyre Methuen 1971	B
	Grove Press 1971	B
21 **Monologue**	Covent Garden Press 1973	B
22 **No Man's Land** (play)	Eyre Methuen 1975	B
	Grove Press 1975	B
23 **The Proust Screenplay**	Grove Press 1977	B
	Eyre Methuen 1978	B
24 **Poems and Prose 1949–1977**	Grove Press 1978	B
	Eyre Methuen 1978	B
25 **Betrayal** (play)	Eyre Methuen 1978	B
	Grove Press 1979	B
26 **I Know The Place** (verse)	Greville Press 1979	C
27 **The Hothouse** (play)	Eyre Methuen 1980	B
	Grove Press 1980	B
28 **The Screenplay of The French Lieutenant's Woman**	Cape 1981	B
	Little Brown 1981	B
29 **The French Lieutenant's Woman and Other Screenplays** Includes **The Last Tycoon** and **Langrishe, Go Down**.	Methuen 1982	A
30 **Other Places** (play)	Methuen 1982	A
	Grove Press 1983	A

Pinter

Films:
The Caretaker British Lion 1963   **The Birthday Party** Cinerama
1968   **The Homecoming** Seven Keys 1973   **Betrayal** Horizon 1983.

In addition to those in 19, Pinter also wrote the screenplay for **The Go-Between** (MGM/EMI 1971), though this has not been published.

Plath, Sylvia   Born in Boston, 1932. Died 1963.

Phenomally popular during the sixties and seventies, Plath is now felt to have been perhaps over-valued from a collector's point of view, for while it is true that there are genuine rarities (notably *The Bell Jar*) such as *Ariel* have never been scarce, and I think were fetching more ten years ago than they would today. That said, it cannot be denied that she has a great following, and certainly the slim volumes (provided they are sensibly priced) never stay on the shelves for long.

1	**A Winter Ship** (verse) Published anonymously	Tragara Press (Edinburgh) 1960	O
2	**The Colossus** and **Other Poems** Reissued by Heinemann as **The Colossus** in 1967.	Heinemann 1960 Knopf 1962	M H
3	**The Bell Jar** (novel) Reissued in the Contemporary Fiction series (**E**) and then by Faber – as by Sylvia Plath – in 1966 (**D**), and Harper in the US in 1971 (**C**). The original edition was under the pseudonym Victoria Lucas.	Heinemann 1963	M
4	**Ariel** (verse)	Faber 1965 Harper 1966	F E
5	**Uncollected Poems** Limited to 150 copies.	Turret Books 1965	F
6	**Three Women** (play) Limited to 150 copies.	Turret Books 1968	F
7	**The Art of Sylvia Plath** A symposium, ed. Charles Newman, containing much new material.	Faber 1970 Indiana University 1970	D C
8	**Wreath for a Bridal** (verse) Limited to 150 copies.	Sceptre Press 1970	F
9	**Million Dollar Month** (verse) Limited to 150 copies.	Sceptre Press 1971	F
10	**Fiesta Melons: Poems** Limited to 150 copies.	Rougemont Press 1971	H
11	**Child** (verse) Limited to 325 copies.	Rougement Press 1971	E

12 **Crystal Gazer** (verse)	Rainbow Press 1971	**F**
Limited to 480 copies, 80 specially bound (**H**).		
13 **Lyonesse** (verse)	Rainbow Press 1971	
Limited to 400 copies, as follows:		
10 vellum **K**		
90 full calf **H**		
300 quarter leather **E**.		
14 **Crossing the Water** (verse)	Faber 1971	**C**
	Harper 1971	**B**
15 **Winter Trees** (verse)	Faber 1971	**C**
	Harper 1972	**B**
16 **Pursuit** (verse)	Rainbow Press 1973	**H**
Limited to 100 copies.		
17 **Letters Home** (letters)	Harper 1975	**C**
	Faber 1976	**C**
18 **The Bed Book** (juvenile)	Faber 1976	**A**
	Harper 1976	**A**
19 **Johnny Panic and the Bible of Dreams and Other Writings** (miscellany)	Faber 1977	**C**
20 **Johnny Panic and the Bible of Dreams: Short Stories, Prose and Diary Excerpts**	Harper 1979	**D**
21 **Collected Poems**	Faber 1981	**C**
Ed. Ted Hughes.	Harper 1981	**C**
22 **Dialogue Over A Ouija Board** (verse)	Rainbow Press 1981	**I**
Limited to 140 copies.		

Potter, Stephen   Born in London, 1900. Died 1969.

Lifemanship – that's the key. The art of always being on top, always being the centre of attention, always winning – without appearing to *try*, and without actually breaking the rules. This was exemplified by Potter himself, while a guest of Roy Plomley on BBC Radio's *Desert Island Discs*:

R.P.:   Mr Potter, as I've known you for so many years, do you think that on this programme I might call you Stephen?

S.P.:   Well – why not, Plomley?

Potter wrote other books, but it is the quartet below with which we are concerned.

1 **The Theory and Practice of Gamesmanship or The Art of Winning Games Without Actually Cheating**	Hart-Davis 1947	**B**

2 **Lifemanship, Including Further Researches in Gamesmanship**	Hart-Davis 1950	**B**
3 **One-Upmanship, Being Some Account of the Activities and Teaching of the Lifemanship Correspondence College of One-Upness and Gameslifemastery**	Hart-Davis 1952	**B**
4 **Supermanship: How To Try To Continue To Stay Top Without Actually Falling to Pieces**	Hart-Davis 1958	**B**

This gorgeous title is how it appears on the dust-wrapper. The title page says . . . **Without Actually Falling Apart**, but you get the idea.

Film:
School For Scoundrels Warner Bros 1960 (based upon 1, 2 and 3).

Pound, Ezra   Born in Idaho, 1885. Died 1972.

Pound has been accused of being unreadable. This because a great deal of his verse (*The Cantos*, mainly) is so chock-full of allusion, obscurity and foreign words and phrases as to render it impossible unless one is a hyper-educated linguist armed with a battery of classical dictionaries. Such criticism is harsh, and rather silly. Pound is not *easy* (of course not – never was) but most of *The Cantos* is worth the struggle. Young people, I have noticed, seem not at all deterred by Pound (possibly because they are taught that anything good *has* to be hard work) and I discern a very definite upturn in collectors' interest – although, of course, Pound has never really fallen from favour, except within pockets of resistance who have never been able to get down his known Fascist sympathies. Not at all easy to collect – most are rare and expensive, as will be seen – but his place in literature as well as in the world of book collecting (not always synonymous) is as solid as a rock. There is a fine bibliography, which I append to the following checklist of Pound's best known works.

1 **A Lume Spento** (verse)	Antonini (Venice) 1908	**T–V**
2 **Personae** (verse)	Mathews 1909	**N**
3 **Exultations** (verse)	Mathews 1909	**M**
4 **The Spirit of Romance** (prose)	Dent 1910	**L**
	Dutton 1910	**K**
5 **Canzoni** (verse)	Mathews 1911	**K**

For item 1: This, Pound's first book, was an edition of only 100 copies. Now extremely rare and near priceless, it was reissued in 1965 by New Directions in the USA (**C**), and by Faber in England (**C**).

6 **Ripostes** (verse)	Swift 1912	K
	Small Maynard 1913	I
7 **Cathay** (translations)	Mathews 1915	H
8 **Gaudier-Brzeska** (memoir)	Bodley Head 1916	I
	Lane 1916	H
9 **Lustra** (verse)	Elkin Matthews 1916	K
10 **Quia Pauper Amavi** (verse)	The Egoist 1919	I
11 **Umbra** (verse)	Elkin Matthews 1920	I
12 **Poems 1918–21**	Boni & Liveright 1921	H
13 **Selected Poems**	Faber & Gwyer 1928	G
Intro. by T.S. Eliot.		
14 **A Draft of XXX Cantos**	Hours Press (Paris)	J
The Paris ed. was limited to 210 copies,	1930	
10 signed (**M**).	Farrar & Rinehart	F
	1933	
	Faber 1933	F
15 **How to Read** (prose)	Harmsworth 1931	H
16 **ABC of Economics** (prose)	Faber 1933	G
	New Directions 1940	F
17 **ABC of Reading** (prose)	Routledge 1934	H
	Yale 1934	G
18 **Make It New** (essays)	Faber 1934	F
	Yale University	E
	Press 1935	
19 **Eleven New Cantos: XXXI–XLI**	Farrar & Rinehart	E
	1934	
20 **Draft of Cantos XXXI–XLI**	Faber 1935	D
(same as 19)		
21 **Homage to Sextus Propertius**	Faber 1934	G
(verse)		
22 **Polite Essays**	Faber 1937	E
	New Directions 1940	E
23 **The Fifth Decad of Cantos**	Faber 1937	F
	Farrar & Rinehart 1937	F
24 **Guide to Kulchur** (prose)	Faber 1938	D
	New Directions 1938	D
25 **Cantos LII–LXXI**	Faber 1940	D
	New Directions 1940	D
26 **The Pisan Cantos**	New Directions 1948	D
	Faber 1949	D
27 **The Cantos**	New Directions 1948	D
Seventy Cantos	Faber 1950	D
28 **The Cantos of Ezra Pound**	Faber 1954	D
This is as above, but including 19. New		
Collected Editions of the *Cantos* were		
published by Faber in 1964 and 1976.		
29 **Patria Mia** (prose)	Seymour 1950	D
	Owen 1962	D

30 **The Letters of Ezra Pound**	Harcourt Brace 1950	D
	Faber 1951	D
31 **The Translations of Ezra Pound**	Faber 1953	D
	New Directions 1953	D
32 **Literary Essays of Ezra Pound**	Faber 1954	D
Intro. by T.S. Eliot.	New Directions 1954	D
33 **Section Rock-Drill** (cantos)	Pesce d'Oro (Milan)	G
The Milan edition consisted of 506	1955	
copies.	New Directions 1956	C
	Faber 1957	C
34 **Thrones** (cantos)	Pesce d'Oro (Milan)	G
The Milan edition consisted of 300	1959	
copies.	New Directions 1959	C
	Faber 1960	C
35 **Pound/Joyce** (letters)	New Directions 1967	C
	Faber 1968	C
36 **Drafts and Fragments of Cantos**	New Directions 1969	C
CX–CXVII	Faber 1970	C
37 **Selected Prose 1909–65**	Faber 1973	C
	New Directions 1975	C
38 **Collected Early Poems**	Faber 1977	C

Bibliography:
Donald Gallup **A Bibliography of Ezra Pound** Hart-Davis 1969

Biography:
Noel Stock **The Life of Ezra Pound** Pantheon 1970 Routledge 1970

Powell, Anthony   Born in London, 1905.

As predicted, the prices for the *Music of Time* sequence have risen sharply. Still not too late to gather most of them, though, but one would probably have to pay for a dust-wrappered first of *A Question of Upbringing* the value of the other eleven put together.

1 **Afternoon Men** (novel)	Duckworth 1931	Q
	Holt 1932	O
2 **Venusberg** (novel)	Duckworth 1932	P
	Holliday 1952	D
3 **From a View to a Death** (novel)	Duckworth 1933	P
This was published as *Mr Zouch:*		
Superman by the Vanguard Press in 1934		
(**K**), though the Little Brown reissue of		
1964 mercifully returns to the original		
title (**D**).		
4 **Caledonia: A Fragment**	Privately printed 1934	Q
Limited to 100 copies.		

5 **Agents and Patients** (novel)	Duckworth 1936	**N**
	Holliday 1952	**E**
6 **What's Become of Waring** (novel)	Cassell 1939	**N**
	Little Brown 1963	**D**
7 **John Aubrey and His Friends** (non-fiction)	Heinemann 1948	**H**
	Scribner 1949	**F**

The following comprise **A Dance to the Music of Time**:

8 **A Question of Upbringing** (novel)	Heinemann 1951	**L**
	Scribner 1951	**I**
9 **A Buyer's Market** (novel)	Heinemann 1952	**H**
	Scribner 1953	**F**
10 **The Acceptance World** (novel)	Heinemann 1955	**F**
	Farrar Straus 1956	**D**
11 **At Lady Molly's** (novel)	Heinemann 1957	**E**
	Little Brown 1958	**D**
12 **Casanova's Chinese Restaurant** (novel)	Heinemann 1960	**E**
	Little Brown 1960	**D**
13 **The Kindly Ones** (novel)	Heinemann 1962	**E**
	Little Brown 1962	**D**
14 **The Valley of Bones** (novel)	Heinemann 1964	**E**
	Little Brown 1964	**D**
15 **The Soldier's Art** (novel)	Heinemann 1966	**E**
	Little Brown 1966	**D**
16 **The Military Philosophers** (novel)	Heinemann 1968	**D**
	Little Brown 1969	**C**
17 **Books Do Furnish a Room** (novel)	Heinemann 1971	**C**
	Little Brown 1971	**B**
18 **Temporary Kings** (novel)	Heinemann 1973	**C**
	Little Brown 1973	**B**
19 **Hearing Secret Harmonies** (novel)	Heinemann 1975	**B**
	Little Brown 1975	**B**

Powell has also published:

20 **The Garden God** and **The Rest I'll Whistle** (plays)	Heinemann 1971	**B**
	Little Brown 1972	**B**
21 **Infants of the Spring** (autobiography)	Heinemann 1976	**B**
	Holt Rinehart 1976	**B**
22 **Messengers of Day** (autobiography)	Heinemann 1978	**B**
	Holt Rinehart 1978	**B**
23 **Faces in My Time** (autobiography)	Heinemann 1980	**B**
	Holt Rinehart 1981	**B**
24 **The Strangers All Are Gone** (autobiography)	Heinemann 1982	**B**
	Holt Rinehart 1983	**B**

21–24 comprise *To Keep the Ball Rolling*.

25 **O, How the Wheel Becomes It!** (novel)	Heinemann 1983	**B**
	Holt Rinehart 1983	**B**

Powell has edited and introduced the
following:

26	**The Barnard Letters 1778–1884**	Duckworth 1928	H
27	**Novels of High Society from the Victorian Age**	Pilot 1947	C
28	**Brief Lives and Other Selected Writings of John Aubrey**	Cresset 1949 Scribner 1949	C C
29	E.W. Hornung **Raffles** Introduced by A.P.	Eyre & Spottiswoode 1950	C
30	**The Complete Ronald Firbank**	Duckworth 1961	C
31	Jocelyn Brooke **The Orchid Trilogy** Introduced by A.P.	Secker 1981	B

The following work should also be noted:
Hilary Spurling **Handbook to Anthony Powell's Dance to the Music of Time** Heinemann 1977; Little Brown 1978

The Powys Brothers

As with the Sitwells, there are quite a few collectors who collect all three, which is illogical but neat. Very often too, I find, Powys collectors do not collect anybody else – understandable in a way, for they published a lot of books, most of which are pretty elusive and pricey. Rather limited as a collection, though, I should have thought. Still. I record here only the highlights of each of them (J.C. Powys is still by far the most popular) and I append bibliographies where applicable.

Powys, J.C.   Born in Derbyshire, 1872. Died 1963.

1	**Wolf Solent** (novel) The Amer. ed. is in two volumes, the English in one.	Simon & Schuster 1929 Cape 1929	K I
2	**The Meaning of Culture** (prose)	Norton 1929 Cape 1930	F E
3	**In Defense of Sensuality** (philosophy)	Simon & Schuster 1930 Gollancz 1930	E D
4	**A Glastonbury Romance** (novel)	Simon & Schuster 1932 Bodley Head 1933	F E
5	**A Philosophy of Solitude**	Simon & Schuster 1933 Cape 1933	D D
6	**Weymouth Sands** (novel) **Jobber Skald**	Simon & Schuster 1934 Bodley Head 1935	G D

Bibliography:
L.E. Siberell **A Bibliography to the First Editions of J.C. Powys**
Folcroft (Cincinnati) 1934. Intro. by Powys.

Powys, Llewelyn   Born in Dorchester, 1884. Died 1939.

1 **Apples Be Ripe** (novel)	Harcourt Brace 1930	**E**
	Longman 1930	**E**
2 **Dorset Essays**	Bodley Head 1935	**D**
	Simon & Schuster 1938	**C**
3 **Love and Death** (novel)	Bodley Head 1939	**C**
	Simon & Schuster 1941	**C**

Bibliography:
Kenneth Hopkins **Llewelyn Powys: A Selection** Macdonald 1952.
(Contains a checklist.)

Powys, T.F.   Born in Dorset, 1875. Died 1953.

1 **Mr Weston's Good Wine** (novel)	Viking 1928	**F**
The American edition was preceded by	Chatto & Windus 1928	**E**
a limited ed. (660 copies) (H)		
2 **The White Paternoster** (stories)	Chatto & Windus 1930	**D**
	Viking 1931	**C**

Bibliography:
A.P. Riley **A Bibliography of T.F. Powys** Hastings 1967

Biography:
Kenneth Hopkins **The Powys Brothers** Dickinson (Phoenix) 1967

Priestley, J.B.   Born in Yorkshire, 1894. Died 1984.

The grand old Yorkshireman died just short of his ninetieth birthday, and has been paid the tribute of a biography by fellow Yorkshireman, John Braine. Still very much a British institution, but less and less collected, I find. He had published over one hundred and fifty books, but it is the two novels listed below that remain his highlights. They were published in his heyday, when Priestley was, in his mid-thirties, one of the most sought-after authors by collectors of first editions. In the thirties, each of these books would have fetched about fifteen or twenty *pounds* each – indeed, more than they would today, relatively. Be warned – always follow your taste, never fashion; this way, if your collection fails to appreciate in value – or, worse, declines – so what? You still have the books you love.

1 **The Good Companions**	Heinemann 1929	**F**
(novel)	Harper 1929	**D**

2 **Angel Pavement** (novel)	Heinemann 1930	E
	Harper 1930	C

Film:
The Good Companions 20th Century Fox 1933; Associated British 1957

Puzo, Mario   Born in New York, 1920.

Author of upwards of half a dozen novels, and many screenplays, but notable for the big one.

The Godfather (novel)	Putnam 1969	C
	Heinemann 1969	C

Films:
The Godfather Paramount 1971   **The Godfather Part II** Cinema International 1974

Pym, Barbara   Born in Shropshire, 1913. Died 1980.

Barbara Pym's is a strange story. She published her first novel in 1950, and five more within the decade. Only one of them was taken by America, and sales declined with each new book. Although the reviews she received were always respectful, it seemed as if the book-buying public were simply no longer interested in her view of the world. In the early sixties, she had a novel turned down. The publishers no longer wished to be involved with an uncommercial enterprise. Barbara Pym stopped writing. All her books were out of print. There the matter would no doubt have rested, but in 1977, a clutch of eminent literati was asked by the *TLS* to put forward the names of underrated writers of the century, and two very big names – Lord David Cecil and Philip Larkin – put their full weight behind Barbara Pym. The reaction of most people at the time – whether or not they now care to admit it – was 'Who?' But Cape remembered who, and they reissued her out-of-print novels, selling the American rights while they were about it. More to the point, Macmillan offered her a three-book contract, and Barbara Pym was in print again, writing again, and now collected – all after a gap of sixteen years. Barbara Pym wrote the novels, they were published, and she died.

I really don't know if this is a happy story, or a sad one.

1 **Some Tame Gazelle** (novel)	Cape 1950	H
2 **Excellent Women** (novel)	Cape 1952	G
	Dutton 1978	B
3 **Jane and Prudence** (novel)	Cape 1953	G
	Dutton 1981	A
4 **Less Than Angels** (novel)	Cape 1955	F
	Vanguard 1957	C
5 **A Glass of Blessings** (novel)	Cape 1959	E
	Dutton 1980	A

6 **No Fond Return of Love** (novel)	Cape 1961	D
	Dutton 1982	A
7 **Quartet in Autumn** (novel)	Macmillan 1977	C
	Dutton 1978	B
8 **The Sweet Dove Died** (novel)	Macmillan 1978	C
	Dutton 1979	B
9 **A Few Green Leaves** (novel)	Macmillan 1980	B
	Dutton 1980	B
10 **An Unsuitable Attachment** (novel)	Macmillan 1982	B
	Dutton 1982	B
11 **A Very Private Eye** (journals)	Macmillan 1984	B
	Dutton 1984	B

Pynchon, Thomas   Born in New York, 1937.

Pynchon has published only three novels and a couple of collections of stories in twenty years, but all of his books are avidly read (particularly the novels) and are now collected – for Pynchon has become something of a cult, and hence the prices at present might be artificially high. I think that there is no shortage of people willing to pay them, however, for I hear quite a few people these days saying that they adore Pynchon's novels, and would love to get hold of them in firsts.

1 **V** (novel)	Lippincott 1963	H
	Cape 1963	G
2 **The Crying of Lot 49** (novel)	Lippincott 1966	F
	Cape 1967	E
3 **Gravity's Rainbow** (novel)	Viking 1973	D
	Cape 1973	C
4 **Mortality and Mercy in Vienna** (stories)	Aloes Editions 1976	C
5 **Low-Lands** (stories)	Aloes Editions 1978	C
6 **The Secret Integration** (story)	Aloes Editions 1981	C

Ransome, Arthur   Born in Leeds, 1884. Died 1967.

It is Ransome's centenary this year (1984), and a biography was published in celebration (see below). It even nudged into the best sellers, proving that Ransome is remembered with great fondness in this country – and rightly, for *Swallows and Amazons* really is a deathless work. I quote it here as his highlight, though it was the first of a very long line of childrens' books.

| **Swallows and Amazons** | Cape 1930 | G |
| | Lippincott 1931 | E |

Film:
Swallows and Amazons EMI 1973

Ransome

Biography:
Hugh Brogan **Arthur Ransome: A Life** Cape 1984

Raven, Simon Born in London, 1927.

A known author, but possibly rather underrated by collectors. His books do
not come up that often (I know of several people trying to complete their
Alms for Oblivion sequence) but when they do, prices are always surprisingly
low.

1	**The Feathers of Death** (novel)	Blond 1959	**D**
		Simon & Schuster 1960	**B**
2	**Brother Cain** (novel)	Blond 1959	**C**
		Simon & Schuster 1960	**B**
3	**Doctors Wear Scarlet** (novel)	Blond 1960	**C**
		Simon & Schuster 1961	**B**
4	**The English Gentleman** (essay)	Blond 1961	**B**
	The Decline of the English Gentleman	Simon & Schuster 1962	**B**
5	**Close of Play** (novel)	Blond 1962	**C**
6	**Boys Will Be Boys and Other Essays**	Blond 1963	**B**

The following ten novels form the *Alms
for Oblivion* sequence:

7	**The Rich Pay Late**	Blond 1964	**C**
		Putnam 1965	**B**
8	**Friends in Low Places**	Blond 1965	**C**
		Putnam 1966	**B**
9	**The Sabre Squadron**	Blond 1966	**C**
		Harper 1967	**B**
10	**Fielding Gray**	Blond 1967	**B**
11	**The Judas Boy**	Blond 1968	**B**
12	**Places Where They Sing**	Blond 1970	**B**
13	**Sound the Retreat**	Blond 1971	**B**
14	**Come Like Shadows**	Blond & Briggs 1972	**B**
15	**Bring Forth the Body**	Blond & Briggs 1974	**B**
16	**The Survivors**	Blond & Briggs 1976	**B**

This completes the sequence.

17	**The Fortunes of Fingel** (stories)	Blond & Briggs 1976	**A**
18	**The Roses of Picardie** (novel)	Blond & Briggs 1980	**A**
19	**An Inch of Fortune** (novel)	Blond & Briggs 1980	**A**

This was the first novel he wrote.

Blond also published, in 1966, **Royal Foundation and Other Plays**. Raven has written many television and radio plays, though unpublished.

Film:
Incense for the Damned Gaumont 1970 (*Doctors Wear Scarlet*)

Read, Herbert   Born in Yorkshire, 1893. Died 1968.

Most people are surprised by the number of books published by Read – over 100. Most collectable are his art philosophy books, the highlights of which (see below) have remained in print since publication. As most of his books were done by Faber, the bold graphics of the case design as well as that of the dust-wrappers, well becomes the contents – or, at least, it did during Read's lifetime; the present editions look just like any other books. In the case of Herbert Read, then, there is very much an aesthetic consideration to collecting the original editions, in addition to all the other reasons for amassing first editions, whatever they may be.

Below are some highlights.

1	**Collected Poems 1913–25**	Faber & Gwyer 1926	C
2	**English Prose Style** (criticism)	Bell 1928	C
		Holt 1928	B
3	**The Meaning of Art**	Faber 1931	C
4	**Art Now**	Faber 1933	D
	A particularly fine piece of book production, with its bold blue and white graphics on black cloth, handsome sans-serif type, and Jean Cocteau frontis.	Harcourt Brace 1937	C
5	**Art and Industry**	Faber 1934	D
6	**The Green Child** (novel)	Heinemann 1935	C
		New Directions 1948	B
7	**Surrealism** (ed. by H.R.)	Faber 1936	D
8	**Art and Society**	Heinemann 1937	D
		Macmillan 1937	C
9	**Education Through Art**	Faber 1943	C
		Pantheon n.d.	C
10	**Collected Poems**	Faber 1946	B
	A revised edition was published by the Horizon Press in 1966 (**B**)		
11	**The Contrary Experience**	Faber 1963	B
	(autobiog.)	Horizon Press 1963	B

Biography:
George Woodcock **Herbert Read: The Stream and the Source** Faber 1972. This work includes a checklist.

Rhys, Jean   Born in Dominica, West Indies, 1894. Died 1979. British.

A small output, but a very big reputation. None of her books is common, but of course the early titles are far scarcer than the later clutch, for as will be seen from the following checklist, there was a twenty-seven year gap somewhere in the middle.

1	**The Left Bank and Other Stories**	Cape 1927	J
		Harper 1927	I
2	**Postures** (novel)	Chatto & Windus 1928	I
3	**Quartet**	Simon & Schuster 1929	G
	Same as 2		
4	**After Leaving Mr Mackenzie** (novel)	Cape 1931	H
		Knopf 1931	F
5	**Voyage in the Dark** (novel)	Constable 1934	F
		Morrow 1935	E
6	**Good Morning, Midnight** (novel)	Constable 1939	E
7	**Wide Sargasso Sea** (novel)	Deutsch 1966	C
		Norton 1966	C
8	**Tigers Are Better Looking** (stories)	Deutsch 1968	C
		Harper 1974	B
9	**Sleep It Off Lady** (stories)	Deutsch 1976	B
		Harper 1976	B
10	**Letters 1931–1966**	Deutsch 1984	B
		Viking 1984	B

Richards, Frank   Born in Middlesex, 1876. Died 1961. Pseudonym of Charles Hamilton.

Reputed to be the most prolific author *ever*, disputes arising only over the number of million words that he produced. For decades, he singlehandedly wrote every issue of *The Gem* and *The Magnet*, under many pseudonyms – Martin Clifford, Owen Conquest, Hilda Richards and, of course, Frank Richards. Always very moral and upstanding, his books stress the importance of being a clean living gentleman. In the Bunter books, he was particularly down on smoking, drinking and gambling, attributing these habits only to his nasty characters; alas, Richards was very prone to all of these vices himself, but they didn't stop him living 85 years, and bringing delight to millions of boys. And he still does, he still does. When the public libraries withdrew the Bunter books from the shelves for the reason that they discriminated against the overweight child (or fat, as we say) they were missing the point. Bunter was not disliked at Greyfriars because he was *fat*, but because he was a coward, a liar, a cheat, a tuck-thief, a sneak, an egomaniac, a snob and a toady – as well as being ignorant and quite the most insufferably idle child that ever lived. Had he been as skinny as a rake, his demeanour would hardly have endeared him to the Famous Five, would it?

Recently – and I can hardly bring myself to write this – a trio of Bowdlerized versions has appeared, no doubt tailored to the requirements of the libraries. You do not need me to tell you to give these leprous articles the very wide berth they deserve.

But the originals are great – go for them. The collectfulness is terrific!

The following were published by Skilton:

1	**Billy Bunter of Greyfriars School**	1947	F
2	**Billy Bunter's Banknote**	1948	D
3	**Billy Bunter's Barring-Out**	1948	D
4	**Billy Bunter's Christmas Party**	1949	D
5	**Billy Bunter in Brazil**	1949	D
6	**Billy Bunter's Benefit**	1950	C
7	**Billy Bunter among the Cannibals**	1950	C
8	**Billy Bunter's Postal Order**	1951	C
9	**Billy Bunter Butts In**	1951	C
10	**Billy Bunter and the Blue Mauritius**	1952	C

The following were published by Cassell:

11	**Billy Bunter's Beanfeast**	1952	B
12	**Billy Bunter's Brain-Wave**	1953	B
13	**Billy Bunter's First Case**	1953	B
14	**Billy Bunter the Bold**	1954	B
15	**Bunter Does His Best**	1954	B
16	**Billy Bunter's Double**	1955	B
17	**Backing Up Billy Bunter**	1955	B
18	**Lord Billy Bunter**	1956	B
19	**The Banishing of Billy Bunter**	1956	B
20	**Billy Bunter's Bolt**	1957	B
21	**Billy Bunter Afloat**	1957	B
22	**Billy Bunter's Bargain**	1958	B
23	**Billy Bunter the Hiker**	1958	B
24	**Bunter Out of Bounds**	1959	B
25	**Bunter Comes for Christmas**	1959	B
26	**Bunter the Bad Lad**	1960	B
27	**Bunter Keeps It Dark**	1960	B
28	**Billy Bunter's Treasure-Hunt**	1961	B
29	**Billy Bunter at Butlin's**	1961	B
30	**Bunter the Ventriloquist**	1961	B
31	**Bunter the Caravanner**	1962	B
32	**Billy Bunter's Bodyguard**	1962	B
33	**Big Chief Bunter**	1963	B
34	**Lust Like Bunter**	1963	B
35	**Bunter the Stowaway**	1964	B
36	**Thanks to Bunter**	1964	B
37	**Bunter the Sportsman**	1965	B

38 **Bunter's Last Fling**	1965	**B**

Richards also published:

39 **Bessie Bunter of Cliff House School**	Skilton 1949	**C**

Pseud. Hilda Richards.
The only Bessie Bunter novel published.

40 **The Autobiography of Frank Richards**	Skilton 1952	**C**

Biography:
W.O. Lofts & D.J. Adley **The World of Frank Richards** Howard Baker 1975

Rosenberg, Isaac   Born in Bristol, 1890. Died 1918.

Another casualty of the Great War – much less known than Brooke and Owen, but very popular again of late, largely through the publication of his collected works five years ago.

1 **Night and Day** (verse)	Privately printed 1915	**O**
2 **Moses: A Play**	Privately printed 1916	**N**
3 **Youth** (verse)	Privately printed 1918	**N**
4 **Poems**	Heinemann 1922	**H**
5 **The Collected Works of Isaac Rosenberg**	Chatto & Windus 1937	**F**
6 **Collected Poems**	Chatto & Windus 1949	**E**
	Schocken 1949	**D**
7 **The Collected Works of Isaac Rosenberg: Poetry, Prose, Letters, Paintings and Drawings**	Chatto & Windus 1979	**C**
	OUP (US) 1979	**C**

Rosten, Leo   Born in Poland, 1908.

Rosten is a genius. Anyone who could create Hyman Kaplan – or H*Y*M*A*N K*A*P*L*A*N, to give him his full name – would have to be. The book is very, very, very funny, and so is its sequel. Written largely in phonetics, you might think the style would weary, the joke stale: not a bit of it. Rosten *understands* words – he loves them. His books on Yiddish (or, Yinglish, as he says) are also well worth looking into, but Kaplan is unmissable.

1 **The Education of Hyman Kaplan** (novel)	Harcourt Brace 1938	**F**
	Constable 1938	**E**

Pseud. Leonard Q. Ross.

2 **The Return of Hyman Kaplan** (novel)	Harper 1959	**D**
	Gollancz 1959	**C**

Roth, Philip   Born in New Jersey, 1933.

I think that *Portnoy's Complaint* was so read and so famous at the time was because we were all thrilled by another taboo being broken – they were falling like ninepins in the sixties – and in hard covers, yet. It's just as well that the book is funny, though, because the 'hero' (oh, God – can we really call him a hero?) was so *awful*, and his Jewish mother was so *awful*, and we had only just got over *The Graduate*.

Roth is popular in this country, but very much more so – and very much more collected – in America, where they can actually identify with people like this.

1	**Goodbye Columbus** and **Five Short Stories**	Houghton Mifflin 1959	G
		Deutsch 1959	F
2	**Letting Go** (novel)	Random House 1962	F
		Deutsch 1962	E
3	**When She Was Good** (novel)	Random House 1967	D
		Cape 1967	C
4	**Portnoy's Complaint** (novel)	Random House 1969	F
		Cape 1970	C
5	**Our Gang** (novel)	Random House 1971	C
		Cape 1971	B
6	**The Breast** (novel)	Holt Rinehart 1972	C
		Cape 1973	B
7	**The Great American Novel** (novel)	Holt Rinehart 1973	C
		Cape 1973	B
8	**My Life as a Man** (novel)	Holt Rinehart 1974	C
		Cape 1974	B
9	**Reading Myself and Others** (prose)	Farrar Straus 1975	C
		Cape 1975	B
10	**The Professor of Desire** (novel)	Farrar Straus 1977	B
		Cape 1978	A
11	**The Ghost Writer** (novel)	Farrar Straus 1979	B
		Cape 1979	A
12	**A Philip Roth Reader** (anthology)	Farrar Straus 1980	B
		Cape 1981	B
13	**Zuckerman Unbound** (novel)	Farrar Straus 1981	B
		Cape 1981	A
14	**The Anatomy Lesson** (novel)	Farrar Straus 1983	B
		Cape 1984	A

Films:
Goodbye Columbus Paramount 1969   **Portnoy's Complaint** Columbia/Warner Bros 1972

Bibliography:
Bernard F. Rodgers **Philip Roth: A Bibliography** Scarecrow Press 1974

Rushdie, Salman   Born in Bombay, 1947.

Four years ago, Rushdie was completely unheard of. Today, he is one of the most famous writers in Britain. So fast and meteoric has been his success that I believe that this is the first reference book in which he appears; the first, no doubt, of many. As everybody knows, Rushdie won the Booker Prize with his second novel, and the book became an enormous bestseller in hard and paperback, and suddenly the Booker was glamorized, and Rushdie became a star. He nearly won again with his next book too. Shame. Whether the books hold their very high current value will have to be seen.

1	**Grimus** (novel)	Gollancz 1975	F
		Overlook Press 1979	E
2	**Midnight's Children** (novel)	Cape 1981	H
		Knopf 1981	F
3	**Shame** (novel)	Cape 1983	B
		Knopf 1983	B

Russell, Bertrand   Born in Wales, 1872. Died 1970.

Bertrand Russell is a singular phenomenon in the collecting world, in that although a philosopher and a mathematician, he is collected because he is *literary*. Not that he concerned himself primarily with literature (although his essays as well as his rare forays into the short story are damnably good) but simply because he wrote so utterly lucidly, this quality exemplified, I think, in his three-volume autobiography – a work that could be enjoyed by any right-thinking character. His *History of Western Philosophy* is probably his most popular work today, although here once again we have a book that people talk of 'tackling' or even 'ploughing through'. This is ridiculous. It is a fat book, yes – but as readable as anything on the subject could be. Russell published over 120 books in his long lifetime, and made contributions to 50 more. The more popular titles appear below, though a checklist of his works may be found in *The New Cambridge Bibliography of English Literature* vol. 4.

1	**Sceptical Essays**	Allen & Unwin 1928	C
		Norton 1928	C
2	**Marriage and Morals** (philosophy)	Allen & Unwin 1929	C
		Liveright 1929	C
3	**The Conquest of Happiness** (philosophy)	Allen & Unwin 1930	C
		Liveright 1930	C
4	**In Praise of Idleness** (philosophy)	Allen & Unwin 1935	C
		Norton 1935	C
5	**History of Western Philosophy**	Allen & Unwin 1945	C
		Simon & Schuster 1946	C

6 **Satan in the Suburbs**	Bodley Head 1953	C
(stories)	Simon & Schuster 1953	C
7 **Nightmares of Eminent Persons** (stories)	Bodley Head 1954	C
	Simon & Schuster 1955	C
8 **Portraits from Memory**	Allen & Unwin 1956	C
(memoirs)	Simon & Schuster 1956	C
9 **Fact and Fiction** (miscellany)	Allen & Unwin 1961	C
	Simon & Schuster 1962	C
10 **Autobiography** (3 vols)	Allen & Unwin 1967–9	D
	Little Brown 1967–9	D

In 1983, Allen & Unwin published the first volume of Russell's **Collected Papers**. They do not say precisely how many volumes there will be, but they do talk of the series extending unto and beyond the year 2000. Well, volume I was £48, so clearly – to have any hope of assembling this lot – one has to be young and rich, in which case one is probably doing other things.

Sagan, Françoise   Born in France, 1935. Pseudonym of Françoise Quoirez.

Not a collected author at all, really, but her one key work remains important.

Bonjour Tristesse (novel)	Murray 1955	B
This was previously published in France in 1954 (**D**).	Smithers 1955	B

Films:
Bonjour Tristesse Columbia 1957
In addition to the above, three other Sagan novels have been filmed.

Salinger, J.D.   Born in New York, 1919.

The Catcher in the Rye, make no mistake, is a very fine book: everyone talks about it as being in the great American tradition of *Huckleberry Finn*. Published in 1951, it was followed by three volumes of stories published in the next ten years or so, and then – *nothing*. Very big news would be made by a new Salinger, but after twenty years' silence, it looks unlikely.

1 **Catcher in the Rye**	Little Brown 1951	K
(novel)	Hamilton 1951	I
Later *The Catcher in the Rye*.		

2 **Nine Stories**	Little Brown 1953	G
3 **For Esmé – With Love and Squalour**	Hamilton 1953	E
and Other Stories (same as 2)		
4 **Franny & Zooey** (stories)	Little Brown 1961	C
	Heinemann 1962	B
5 **Raise High the Roof Beam and**	Little Brown 1963	B
Seymour: An Introduction	Heinemann 1963	A

Sandford, Jeremy   Born in England, 1934.

Silly, in one way, to include Sandford in a select band of collected authors, but the works he produced – 'faction', it is now called – were important at the time, and memorable. The two works below were presented as semi-scripted '*cinéma vérité*' TV plays. The paperbacks recorded here are 'novelized' versions of the scripts.

1 **Cathy Come Home**	Pan 1967	C
2 **Edna, The Inebriate Woman**	Pan 1971	B

Sapper   Born in England, 1888. Died 1937. Pseudonym of Herman Cyril McNeile.

His first few books met with indifference, and then came Bulldog Drummond. The character was an almost immediate success, and was featured in a long series of novels – but beware, for the series was continued even after McNeile's death by one Gerard T. Fairlie, retaining the Sapper pseudonym.
    Examples of *true* Sapper–Drummond are as follows:

1 **Bulldog Drummond**	Hodder 1920	L
2 **The Return of Bulldog Drummond**	Hodder 1932	D
Bulldog Drummond Returns	Doubleday 1932	C

Films:
Five Bulldog Drummond novels were filmed.

Sassoon, Siegfried   Born in London, 1886. Died 1967.

There is a steady interest in Sassoon – he attracts little new interest, I think, but the diehard collectors are loyal. The publication of his Diaries recently has brought him back to the fore, though, so maybe the younger set will 'discover' him, as the young are prone to do.
    Sassoon is particularly difficult to collect seriously, as his first fourteen works were either privately printed, or else published by a small press, as were many subsequent books by him. These cannot be listed here, but a bibliography exists, listing them all in some detail:

Below are all the commercially published Sassoon titles.

1 **The Old Huntsman** (verse)	Heinemann 1917	I
	Dutton 1917	H
2 **Counter-Attack** (verse)	Heinemann 1918	G
	Dutton 1918	F
3 **The War Poems of Siegfried Sassoon**	Heinemann 1919	G
4 **Selected Poems**	Heinemann 1925	D
5 **Satirical Poems**	Heinemann 1926	G
	Viking 1926	F
6 **Nativity** (Ariel Poem)	Faber 1927	E
7 **The Heart's Journey** (verse)	Heinemann 1928	H
This was preceded by a limited edition in 1927 (**M**).	Harper 1929	G
8 **To My Mother** (Ariel Poem)	Faber 1928	C
9 **Memoirs of a Fox-Hunting Man** (novel)	Faber 1928	G
	Coward McCann 1929	F
This was published anonymously, and 1928 and 1929 also saw a limited edition (**I**) and an illustrated edition (**H**) of the work.		
10 **Memoirs of an Infantry Officer** (novel)	Faber 1930	D
	Coward McCann 1930	D
The initial British print of this title was 20,000, compared with 1500 for 9.		
11 **In Sicily** (Ariel Poem)	Faber 1930	C
12 **Poems by Pinchbeck Lyre**	Duckworth 1931	F
13 **To the Red Rose** (Ariel Poem)	Faber 1931	C
14 **Prehistoric Burials** (poem)	Knopf 1932	C
No. 1 of the Borzoi Chap Books.		
15 **The Road to Ruin** (verse)	Faber 1933	D
16 **Vigils** (verse)	Heinemann 1935	D
	Viking 1936	D
These trade editions were preceded by a limited edition (**K**), a large-paper edition (**I**), and also a vellum edition (**H**).		
17 **Sherston's Progress** (novel)	Faber 1936	C
This, with 9 and 10, forms a trilogy.		
18 **The Complete Memoirs of George Sherston**	Faber 1937	C
	Doubleday 1937	C
Contains 9, 10 and 17.		
19 **The Old Century** (prose)	Faber 1938	C
The t/p bears a Gwen Raverat engraving.	Viking 1939	C
20 **Rhymed Ruminations** (verse)	Faber 1940	C
A private press edition of 75 copies appeared in 1939 (**H**).	Viking 1941	B

Sassoon

21 **Poems Newly Selected**	Faber 1940	B
22 **The Flower Show Match** (extracts)	Faber 1941	C
23 **The Weald of Youth** (Prose)	Faber 1942	C
The d/w and t/p bear an engraving by Reynolds Stone.	Viking 1942	B
24 **Siegfried's Journey** (prose)	Faber 1945	C
As above, this too has a Reynolds Stone engraving.	Viking 1946	B
25 **Collected Poems**	Faber 1947	C
	Viking 1949	C
26 **Meredith** (prose)	Constable 1948	B
	Viking 1948	B
27 **Sequences** (verse)	Faber 1956	B
	Viking 1957	B
28 **Collected Poems 1908–1956**	Faber 1961	B
29 **Diaries 1920–1922**	Faber 1981	B
30 **Diaries 1915–1918**	Faber 1983	B

Bibliography:
Geoffrey Keynes **A Bibliography of Siegfried Sassoon** Hart-Davis 1962

Sayers, Dorothy L.   Born in Oxford, 1893. Died 1957.

Always one of the most popular and collected detective fiction writers of all, and not easy to come by. In later life, Sayers tended towards the religious and the philosophical, but below I list the really good stuff which stretches from 1923 until 1940 – the period during which she still indulged in Wimsey.

1 **Whose Body?** (novel)	Unwin 1923	L
	Boni & Liveright 1923	J
2 **Clouds of Witness** (novel)	Unwin 1926	J
	Dial Press 1927	H
3 **Unnatural Death** (novel)	Benn 1927	J
The Dawson Pedigree	Dial Press 1928	I
4 **Lord Peter Views the Body** (stories)	Gollancz 1928	J
	Brewer 1929	H
5 **The Unpleasantness at the Bellona Club** (novel)	Benn 1928	J
	Brewer 1928	I
6 **Strong Poison** (novel)	Gollancz 1930	I
	Harcourt 1930	H
7 **The Documents in the Case** (novel)	Benn 1930	G
With Robert Eustace.	Brewer 1930	G
8 **The Five Red Herrings** (novel)	Gollancz 1931	H
Suspicious Characters	Harcourt 1931	H
9 **Have His Carcase** (novel)	Gollancz 1932	H
	Harcourt 1932	G

10 **Hangman's Holiday** (stories)	Gollancz 1933	**H**
	Harcourt 1933	**G**
11 **Murder Must Advertise** (novel)	Gollancz 1933	**H**
	Harcourt 1933	**G**
12 **The Nine Tailors** (novel)	Gollancz 1934	**H**
	Harcourt 1934	**G**
13 **Gaudy Night** (novel)	Gollancz 1935	**G**
	Harcourt 1936	**F**
14 **Busman's Honeymoon** (novel)	Gollancz 1937	**G**
	Harcourt 1937	**F**
15 **In the Teeth of the Evidence** (stories)	Gollancz 1940	**F**
	Harcourt 1940	**E**

A checklist of Sayers work may be found in: **The New Cambridge Bibliography of English Literature** vol. 4

Film:
Busman's Holiday MGM 1940 (*Busman's Honeymoon*)

Biography:
Janet Hitchman **Such a Strange Lady** NEL 1975

Scott, Paul Born in India, 1920. Died 1978. British.

A highly successful literary agent, turned highly successful writer, whose colossal standing and fame was largely posthumous. *The Raj Quartet*, of course, is his highlight, but it was the sequel *Staying On* that won him the Booker Prize and triggered a major reappraisal of his work, for before this moment it is true to say that Scott was barely collected at all. *The Raj Quartet* (together with its sequel) now features on most 'best of . . .' lists, and the recent television adaptation hurled both the reissued hardback omnibus and the separate paperback editions to the top of their relative bestseller lists. Television does indeed sell books, but Scott's reputation was secure before all the razzmatazz.

1 **I Gerontius** (novel)	Favil Press 1941	**K**
2 **Pillars of Salt** (play) Contained in *Four Jewish Plays*, edited by H.F. Rubinstein.	Gollancz 1948	**F**
3 **Johnny Sahib** (novel)	Eyre & Spottiswoode 1952	**G**
4 **The Alien Sky** (novel)	Eyre & Spottiswoode 1953	**G**
5 **Six Days in Marapore** American edition of 4.	Doubleday 1953	**F**
6 **A Male Child** (novel)	Eyre & Spottiswoode 1956	**F**
	Dutton 1957	**E**

Scott

7 **The Mark of the Warrior** (novel)	Eyre & Spottiswoode 1958	E
	Morrow 1958	D
8 **The Chinese Love Pavilion** (novel)	Eyre & Spottiswoode 1960	D
9 **The Love Pavilion** American edition of 8.	Morrow 1960	C
10 **The Birds of Paradise** (novel)	Eyre & Spottiswoode 1962	C
	Morrow 1962	B
11 **The Bender: Pictures From an Exhibition of Middle Class Portraits** (novel) The American edition omits the subtitle.	Secker 1963 Morrow 1963	C B
12 **The Corrida at San Feliu** (novel)	Secker 1964	C
	Morrow 1964	B
13 **The Jewel in the Crown** (novel)	Heinemann 1966	F
	Morrow 1966	E
14 **The Day of the Scorpion** (novel)	Heinemann 1968	D
	Morrow 1968	D
15 **The Towers of Silence** (novel)	Heinemann 1971	C
	Morrow 1972	C
16 **A Division of the Spoils** (novel) 13, 14, 15 and 16 comprise *The Raj Quartet*.	Heinemann 1975 Morrow 1976	C C
17 **The Raj Quartet** (omnibus) Contains 13, 14, 15 and 16.	Heinemann 1976 Morrow 1976	C C
18 **Staying On** (novel)	Heinemann 1977	D
	Morrow 1977	D
19 **After the Funeral** (story)	Whittington Press 1979	E

Searle, Ronald   Born in Cambridge, 1920.

Although very much more collected as an artist than as an author (his originals fetch a fortune) Searle's books are very sought after – and so are his dust-wrapper designs, no matter who wrote the book, or what it is about. None the less, it is for St Trinian's that he will be for ever remembered and also – hardly to a lesser extent, Nigel Molesworth & Co. Now, credit must be given here to Geoffrey Willans who wrote such wondrous effusions as 'it is peason, he is my grate frend which means we touough each other up continually', to say nothing of all the stuff about fotherington-tomas, who keep dollies at home, sa hullo cloud hullo sky, hav a face like a squished tomato and couldn't hurt a flea. The Searle cartoons, of course, are more than mere illustrations accompanying the text – they make Molesworth *LIVE!* (Hem-hem.)

1	**Hurrah for St Trinian's**	Macdonald (UK) 1948	C
		Macdonald (US) 1948	C
2	**The Terror of St Trinian's**	Parrish 1952	C

This was written by 'Timothy Shy' (D.B. Wyndham Lewis), who wrote the introduction to 1.

The Molesworth quartet:

3	**Down with Skool!**	Parrish 1953	B

The title note deserves quoting: 'Contanes Full Lowdown on Skools, Swots, Snekes, Cads, Prigs Bulies Headmasters Criket Foopball, Dirty Roters Funks, Parents, Masters Wizard Wheezes, Weeds Aple Pie Beds and Various other Chizzes – in fact THE LOT.'

4	**How to be Topp**	Parrish 1954	B
5	**Whizz for Atomms**	Parrish 1956	B
6	**Back in the Jug Agane**	Parrish 1959	B

Shaffer, Peter   Born in Liverpool, 1926.

Author of nearly twenty books, mostly plays, and included in *Collecting Modern First Editions* for just one, which was then fast becoming a classic. To this may now be added one more.

1	**Equus** (play)	Deutsch 1973	D
		Atheneum 1974	C
2	**Amadeus** (play)	Deutsch 1980	C
		Harper 1981	B

Film:
Equus United Artists 1977

Sharpe, Tom   Born in London, 1928.

Can be wildly funny, Tom Sharpe, and can sometimes be merely wild. His earlier books are best, I think – up to *Wilt*. It all gets rather too over the top after that, to my mind. But Sharpe is extremely popular, and very much-loved as a humourist; he has even been compared with P.G. Wodehouse, which is rather over the top in itself.

1	**Riotous Assembly** (novel)	Secker 1971	C
2	**Indecent Exposure** (novel)	Secker 1973	B
3	**Porterhouse Blue** (novel)	Secker 1974	B

Sharpe

4 **Blott on the Landscape** (novel)	Secker 1975	B
5 **Wilt** (novel)	Secker 1976	B
6 **The Great Pursuit** (novel)	Secker 1977	A
	Harper 1978	A
7 **The Throwback** (novel)	Secker 1978	A
8 **The Wilt Alternative** (novel)	Secker 1979	A
9 **Ancestral Vices** (novel)	Secker 1980	A
	St Martin's 1980	A
10 **Vintage Stuff** (novel)	Secker 1983	A

10 **Vintage Stuff** (novel)
At the time of writing, this title –
together with 5 and 7 – has been
contracted to Random House, in
America.

Sillitoe, Alan   Born in Nottingham, 1928.

Arthur Seaton takes his place among the deathless heroes (?) of fifties fiction
– alongside such as Jimmy Porter, Vic Brown, and Joe Lampton.

The characters and strength of such novels aside, isn't it extraordinary
that the very *titles* in each case were so well chosen as to have entered the
language as phrases, and are endlessly adapted for use in other contexts?
*Room at the Top, Look Back in Anger, A Kind of Loving, A Taste of Honey, The L-
Shaped Room* – as well as Sillitoe's two, *Saturday Night and Sunday Morning* and
The Loneliness of the Long Distance Runner. Story's *Live Now, Pay Later* was
another one, but that came a few years later.

1 **Without Beer or Bread** (verse)	Outpost Publications 1957	H
2 **Saturday Night and Sunday Morning** (novel)	Allen 1958	H
	Knopf 1958	G
3 **The Loneliness of the Long Distance Runner** (stories)	Allen 1959	F
	Knopf 1959	E
4 **The General** (novel)	Allen 1960	C
	Knopf 1960	B
5 **The Rats and Other Poems**	Allen 1960	C
6 **Key to the Door** (novel)	Macmillan 1961	B
	Knopf 1961	A
7 **The Ragman's Daughter** (stories)	Allen 1963	B
	Knopf 1963	A
8 **A Falling out of Love and Other Poems**	Allen 1964	B
9 **The Road to Volgograd** (travel)	Allen 1964	B
	Knopf 1964	B
10 **The Death of William Posters** (novel)	Macmillan 1965	C
	Knopf 1965	B
11 **A Tree on Fire** (novel)	Macmillan 1967	B
	Knopf 1967	A

12 **The City Adventures of**   Macmillan 1967   **B**
   Marmalade Jim (juvenile)
13 **Guzman Go Home** (stories)   Macmillan 1968   **B**
                                           Doubleday 1968   **B**
14 **Love in the Environs of Voronezh**   Macmillan 1968   **A**
   (verse)   Doubleday 1968   **A**
15 **All Citizens Are Soldiers** (play)   Macmillan 1969   **B**
   Adaptation with Ruth Fainlight.   Dufour 1969   **B**
16 **A Start in Life** (novel)   Allen 1970   **A**
                                           Scribner 1971   **A**
17 **Travels in Nihilon** (novel)   Allen 1971   **A**
                                           Scribner 1972   **A**
18 **Raw Material** (novel)   Allen 1972   **A**
                                           Scribner 1973   **A**
19 **Men, Women, and Children**   Allen 1973   **A**
   (stories)   Doubleday 1974   **A**
20 **Flame of Life** (novel)   Allen 1974   **A**
21 **Storm: New Poems**   Allen 1974   **A**
22 **Mountains and Caverns**   Allen 1975   **A**
   (prose)
23 **The Widower's Son** (novel)   Allen 1976   **A**
                                           Harper 1977   **A**
24 **Big John and the Stars** (juvenile)   Robson 1977   **A**
25 **The Incredible Fencing Fleas**   Robson 1978   **A**
   (juvenile)
26 **Three Plays**   Allen 1978   **B**
27 **Snow on the North Side of Lucifer**   Allen 1979   **A**
   (verse)
28 **The Storyteller** (novel)   Allen 1979   **A**
                                           Simon & Schuster 1980 **A**
29 **Marmalade Jim at the Farm**   Robson 1980   **A**
   (juvenile)
30 **The Second Chance and Other**   Cape 1981   **A**
   Stories   Simon & Schuster 1981 **A**
31 **Her Victory** (novel)   Granada 1982   **A**
                                           Watts 1982   **A**
32 **The Saxon Shore Way** (non-fiction)   Hutchinson 1983   **A**
33 **The Lost Flying Boat** (novel)   Granada 1983   **A**
34 **Sun Before Departure: Poems**   Granada 1984   **A**
   1974–1984

Films:
Saturday Night and Sunday Morning British Lion 1960   **The
Loneliness of the Long Distance Runner** British Lion
1962   **Counterpoint** Universal 1968 (*The General*)   **The Ragman's**

Daughter 20th Century Fox 1972   Sillitoe wrote the screenplays for all but **Counterpoint**.

Simenon, Georges   Born in Liège, Belgium, in 1903.

Creator, of course, of Maigret. Prior to his recent divulgences, it was Simenon's output of books of which one was in awe. But now we learn that he has been couched in intimacy with *thousands* of different women (not all at once, you understand). He also wrote hundreds of novels – you just wouldn't think there were the hours in the day. Simenon is eighty now, and still consumes large quantities of Cognac and pipe tobacco. I think these health people are fools and killjoys and have been lying to us for years. The very first Maigret appears below, although Simenon's first novel was published in 1920.

> **The Crime of Inspector Maigret**   Covici 1932   **J**
> The first appearance in England was
> **Introducing Inspector Maigret**, from
> Hurst & Blackett in 1933 (**H**).

In addition to the very popular television series, eight Simenon novels have been filmed.

Simon, Neil   Born in New York, 1937.

Most famous for *The Odd Couple*; very prolific, the highest paid playwright and screen writer in America, and that's saying something. But he probably deserves it.

1 **Adventures of Marco Polo: A Musical Fantasy** With William Friedberg.	French (US) 1959	**C**
2 **Heidi** (play) Adaptation from Johanna Spyri's novel, written with William Friedberg.	French (US) 1959	**C**
3 **Come Blow Your Horn** (play)	French (US) 1961 French (UK) 1961	**C** **B**
4 **Barefoot in the Park** (play)	Random House 1964 French (UK) 1967	**C** **B**
5 **The Odd Couple** (play)	Random House 1966	**C**
6 **Sweet Charity** (play)	Random House 1966	**C**

7 **The Star-Spangled Girl** (play)	Random House 1967	B
8 **Plaza Suite** (play)	Random House 1969	B
9 **Promises, Promises** (play)	Random House 1969	B
10 **Last of the Red Hot Lovers** (play)	Random House 1970	B
11 **The Gingerbread Lady** (play)	Random House 1971	B
12 **The Prisoner of Second Avenue** (play)	Random House 1972	B
	French (UK) 1972	A
13 **The Good Doctor** (play)	Random House 1974	A
	French (UK) 1975	A
14 **God's Favorite** (play)	Random House 1975	A
15 **California Suite** (play)	Random House 1977	B
16 **Chapter Two** (play)	Random House 1979	A
	French 1979	A
17 **They're Playing Our Song** (play)	Random House 1980	A
18 **I Ought to be in Pictures** (play)	Random House 1981	A
19 **Fools** (play)	Random House 1982	A

Films:
Come Blow Your Horn Paramount 1963   **Barefoot in the Park**
Paramount 1966   **The Odd Couple** Paramount 1968   **Sweet Charity**
Universal 1969   **The Last of the Red Hot Lovers** Paramount
1972   **Plaza Suite** Paramount 1972   **Prisoner of Second Avenue**
Columbia/Warner Bros 1975   **The Sunshine Boys** MGM
1975   **California Suite** Columbia 1979   **Chapter Two**
Columbia/EMI/Warner 1980   **Only When I Laugh** Columbia 1981
(*The Gingerbread Lady*)

The Sitwells

Although there remains considerable interest in the Sitwells, I find that the
more common items hang around the shelves for ages – everyone either has
them, or doesn't want them. There are collectors who collect nothing but the
Sitwells, but in a general collection of literature it seems to me that while they
must certainly be represented, the Collected Poems, autobiographies, and
one or two selected highlights of each might suffice. It is Edith, of course, who
really lives on as a poet, but because my shop is heavily biased in favour of
art, I find more demand for Sacheverell than for the others – his
architectural travel books, mainly – but this may not be typical of the trend
in bookshops generally. Before this (highly selective) listing, then, I shall give
details of the bibliography, essential reading for anyone with more than a
passing interest: Richard Fifoot *A Bibliography of Edith, Osbert and Sacheverell
Sitwell* Hart-Davis 1971.

Sitwell, Edith   Born in Scarborough, 1887. Died 1964.

1 **Poetry and Criticism** (prose)	Hogarth Press 1925	E
	Holt 1926	D
2 **Rustic Elegies** (verse)	Duckworth 1927	D
	Knopf 1927	C
3 **Collected Poems**	Duckworth 1930	C
This was preceded by a signed, limited edition published by Duckworth and in America by Houghton Mifflin (**G**).		
4 **The English Eccentrics** (prose)	Faber 1933	E
	Houghton Mifflin 1933	D
5 **A Poet's Notebook** (prose)	Macmillan 1943	B
6 **Taken Care Of** (autobiog.)	Hutchinson 1965	B
	Atheneum 1965	B

Sitwell, Osbert   Born in London, 1892. Died 1969.

1 **Collected Satires and Poems**	Duckworth 1931	D
2 **Left Hand, Right Hand!**	Little Brown 1944	B
(autobiog.)	Macmillan 1945	B
3 **The Scarlet Tree** (autobiog.)	Little Brown 1946	B
	Macmillan 1946	B
4 **Great Morning** (autobiog.)	Little Brown 1947	B
	Macmillan 1948	B
5 **Laughter in the Next Room**	Little Brown 1948	B
(autobiog.)	Macmillan 1949	B
6 **Noble Essences** (autobiog.)	Macmillan 1950	C
	Little Brown 1950	B

Sitwell, Sacheverell   Born in Scarborough, 1897.

1 **Southern Baroque Art**	Grant Richards 1924	D
	Knopf 1924	C
2 **Collected Poems**	Duckworth 1936	C
3 **Conversation Pieces** (art)	Batsford 1936	C
	Scribner 1937	C
4 **Edinburgh** (prose)	Faber 1938	C
	Houghton Mifflin 1939	B
5 **British Architects and Craftsmen**	Batsford 1945	C
	Scribner 1946	B
6 **Journey to the Ends of Time**	Cassell 1959	B
Vol. 1 (autobiog.)	Random House 1959	A
Vol. 1 only published.		

Smith, Stevie   Born in Hull, 1902. Died 1971.

Stevie Smith is such a *refreshing* poet – good *and* fun. I like her a lot, and most people seem to. Not easy to collect, though, but I know one chap who has a first edition of everything except *Novel on Yellow Paper*, which was her first book.

1 **Novel on Yellow Paper** (novel)	Cape 1936	**K**
	Morrow 1937	**I**
2 **A Good Time was Had by All** (verse)	Cape 1937	**I**
3 **Over the Frontier** (novel)	Cape 1939	**G**
4 **Tender Only to One** (verse)	Cape 1938	**F**
5 **Mother, What is Man?** (verse)	Cape 1942	**D**
6 **The Holiday** (novel)	Chapman & Hall 1949	**F**
	Smithers 1950	**E**
7 **Harold's Leap** (verse)	Chapman & Hall 1950	**D**
8 **Not Waving but Drowning** (verse)	Deutsch 1957	**D**
9 **Cats in Colour** (photo essay)	Batsford 1959	**C**
10 **Selected Poems**	Longman 1962	**B**
	New Directions 1964	**B**
11 **The Frog Prince and Other Poems**	Longman 1966	**B**
12 **Two in One**	Longman 1971	**B**
Cont. 10 and 11.		
13 **Scorpion and Other Poems**	Longman 1971	**B**
14 **Collected Poems**	Lane 1975	**B**
	OUP (US) 1976	**B**
15 **Me Again: Uncollected Writings**	Virago 1981	**B**
	Farrar Straus 1982	**B**
16 **Stevie Smith: A Selection** Edited by Hermione Lee.	Faber 1983	**A**

Snow, C.P.   Born in Leicester, 1905. Died 1980.

In addition to the celebrated *Strangers and Brothers* sequence, listed below, Snow published about twenty other works, half a dozen of them plays written in collaboration with his wife, Pamela Hansford Johnson. Interest had flagged after *Last Things*, but Lord Snow's death – as is so often rather ghoulishly the way – realerted people to his work, and now I find that the younger generation of collectors is taking notice, which I should not have foreseen.

1 **Strangers and Brothers**	Faber 1940	**G**
	Scribner 1960	**B**
2 **The Light and the Dark**	Faber 1947	**D**
	Macmillan (US) 1948	**C**

3 **Time of Hope**	Faber 1949	D
	Macmillan (US) 1950	C
4 **The Masters**	Macmillan (UK) 1951	C
	Macmillan (US) 1951	B
5 **The New Men**	Macmillan (UK) 1954	C
	Scribner 1954	B
6 **Homecomings**	Macmillan (UK) 1956	C
The Scribner edition omitted the 's' in the title.	Scribner 1956	B
7 **The Conscience of the Rich**	Macmillan (UK) 1958	C
	Scribner 1958	B
8 **The Affair**	Macmillan (UK) 1960	B
	Scribner 1960	B
9 **Corridors of Power**	Macmillan (UK) 1964	B
	Scribner 1964	B
10 **The Sleep of Reason**	Macmillan (UK) 1968	B
	Scribner 1969	B
11 **Last Things**	Macmillan (UK) 1970	B
	Scribner 1970	B

Solzhenitsyn, Alexander   Born in Rostov, Russia, 1918.

When I started collecting Solzhenitsyn, he was *it*. His work was not merely published, it was *smuggled out*. When one of his 'messages' to the West was published in pamphlet form, it reprinted four, five times within weeks. And then, to my mind the USSR did a very clever thing: they deported him. Solzhenitsyn was then accessible, rich (vast royalties had been piling up all over the world) and no longer had access to the *feel* of his motherland. The mystique dissolved, and although Solzhenitsyn was – is still – read and reviewed, we no longer hang upon every syllable. Politics aside, Solzhenitsyn remains a very fine writer – even in translation – but the sequence of his published *œuvre* remains confusing and bitty. Where, for instance, is the promised sequel to *August 1914*, published twelve years ago?

Collecting Solzhenitsyn is a task fraught with problems and uncertainties unless one decides precisely what the aim is. To acquire the *absolute* 1st editions in each case would be very difficult, unless one had contacts in several countries. Assuming that the English-language editions are of most interest, I list here the English and American details only. Most collectors in England would settle for the complete English 1st editions, and those in the USA, I imagine, would be satisfied with their American counterparts.

1 **One Day in the Life of Ivan Denisovich** Trans. Max Hayward and Ronald Hingley.	Praeger 1963	E
2 **One Day in the Life of Ivan Denisovich** Trans. Ralph Parker. 1 and 2 appeared simultaneously.	Dutton 1963 Gollancz 1963	D D

258

3 **We Never Make Mistakes: Two Short Novels** Trans. Paul W. Blackstock.	University of South Carolina 1963	**D**
4 **The First Circle** Trans. Thomas P. Whitney.	Harper & Row 1968	**C**
5 **The First Circle** Trans. Michael Guybon.	Collins 1968	**C**
6 **Cancer Ward** Trans. Nicholas Bethell and David Burg. The English ed. is in two vols, the American in one.	Bodley Head 1968–9 Farrar Straus 1969	**D** **C**
7 **The Cancer Ward** Trans. Rebecca Frank.	Dial Press (NY) 1968	**C**
8 **The Love-Girl and the Innocent** (play) Trans. Nicholas Bethell and David Burg.	Bodley Head 1969 Farrar Straus 1970	**B** **A**
9 **Stories and Prose Poems** Trans. Michael Glenny.	Bodley Head 1971 Farrar Straus 1971	**B** **A**
10 **August 1914** Trans. Michael Glenny.	Bodley Head 1972 Farrar Straus 1972	**B** **B**
11 **'One Word of Truth . . .'** (Nobel Lecture)	Bodley Head 1972 Farrar Straus 1973	**A** **A**
12 **Candle in the Wind** (play) Trans. Keith Armes.	University of Minnesota 1973 Bodley Head/OUP 1973	**A** **A**
13 **The Gulag Archipelago** Trans. Thomas P. Whitney.	Harper 1974 Collins 1974	**B** **B**
14 **Letter to Soviet Leaders** Trans. Hilary Sternberg.	Index on Censorship 1974 Harper 1974	**A** **A**
15 **The Gulag Archipelago (2)** Trans. as 13.	Harper 1975 Collins 1975	**B** **B**
16 **From under the Rubble** With others. Trans. and ed. by Michael Scammell.	Little Brown 1975 Collins 1975	**A** **A**
17 **Lenin in Zurich** Trans. H.T. Willetts.	Farrar Straus 1976 Bodley Head 1976	**A** **A**
18 **Warning to the Western World**	Bodley Head/BBC 1976	**A**
19 **Speeches to the Americans** American edition of 18	Farrar Straus 1976	**A**
20 **The Gulag Archipelago (3)** Trans. H.T. Willetts.	Harper 1976 Collins 1978	**B** **B**
21 **Prussian Nights** (poem) Trans. Robert Conquest.	Collins/Harvill 1977	**A**

Solzhenitsyn

22	**Alexander Solzhenitsyn Speaks to the West**	Bodley Head 1979	**A**
23	**A World Split Apart** American edition of 22.	Harper 1979	**A**
24	**The Mortal Danger**	Bodley Head 1980 Harper 1980	**A** **A**
25	**The Oak and the Calf**	Harper 1980 Bodley Head 1980	**B** **B**
26	**Victory Celebrations** (play)	Bodley Head 1983	**A**
27	**Prisoners** (play)	Bodley Head 1983	**A**

Film:
One Day in the Life of Ivan Denisovich Cinerama 1971

Spark, Muriel   Born in Edinburgh, 1918.

The twinkling wit of Muriel Spark is always a joy to behold, and never more so, in my opinion, than in *The Prime of Miss Jean Brodie, The Girls of Slender Means* and the rather underrated novella *The Abbess of Crewe*. This was seen to be an allegorical work pertaining to Watergate (which is either rubbish or not rubbish, it hardly matters) and made into an awful film which they re-christened *Nasty Habits*, which is about as subtle as a bus.

1	**Tribute to Wordsworth** (non-fiction) Ed. with Derek Stanford.	Wingate 1950	**D**
2	**Child of Light: A Reassessment of Mary Shelley**	Tower Bridge 1951	**D**
3	**The Fanfarlo and Other Verse** The 1st issue is red-lettered on buff wrpps.	Hand & Flower Press 1952	**E**
4	**A Selection of Poems by Emily Bronte** (ed. M.S.)	Grey Walls Press 1952	**C**
5	**Emily Bronte: Her Life and Work** With Derek Stanford.	Owen 1953	**D**
6	**John Masefield** (non-fiction)	Nevill 1953	**D**
7	**My Best Mary: The Letters of Mary Shelley** Ed. with Derek Stanford.	Wingate 1953 Folcroft Editions 1972	**D** **B**
8	**The Bronte Letters** (ed. M.S.)	Nevill 1954	**D**
9	**Letters of J.H. Newman** Ed. with Derek Stanford.	Owen 1957	**C**
10	**The Comforters** (novel)	Macmillan 1957 Lippincott 1957	**D** **C**
11	**Robinson** (novel)	Macmillan 1958 Lippincott 1958	**D** **C**

12 **The Go-Away Bird and Other Stories**	Macmillan 1958 Lippincott 1960	D C
13 **Memento Mori** (novel)	Macmillan 1959 Lippincott 1959	D C
14 **The Ballad of Peckham Rye** (novel)	Macmillan 1960 Lippincott 1960	D C
15 **The Bachelors** (novel)	Macmillan 1960 Lippincott 1961	D C
16 **Voices at Play** (stories and plays)	Macmillan 1961	C
17 **The Prime of Miss Jean Brodie** (novel)	Macmillan 1961 Lippincott 1962	D C
18 **Doctors of Philosophy** (play)	Macmillan 1963	C
19 **The Girls of Slender Means** (novel)	Macmillan 1963 Knopf 1963	D C
20 **The Mandelbaum Gate** (novel)	Macmillan 1965 Knopf 1965	A A
21 **Collected Stories I**	Macmillan 1967 Knopf 1968	C C
22 **Collected Poems I**	Macmillan 1967	C
23 **The Public Image** (novel)	Macmillan 1968 Knopf 1968	A A
24 **The Very Fine Clock** (juvenile)	Knopf 1968 Macmillan 1969	C C
25 **The Driver's Seat** (novel)	Macmillan 1970 Knopf 1970	A A
26 **Not to Disturb** (novel)	Macmillan 1971 Viking Press 1972	A A
27 **The Hothouse by the East River** (novel)	Macmillan 1972 Viking 1972	A A
28 **The Abbess of Crewe** (novel)	Macmillan 1974 Viking 1974	B B
29 **The Takeover** (novel)	Macmillan 1976 Viking 1976	A A
30 **Territorial Rights** (novel)	Macmillan 1979 Coward McCann 1979	A A
31 **Loitering With Intent** (novel)	Bodley Head 1981 Coward McCann 1981	A A

Film:
The Prime of Miss Jean Brodie 20th Century Fox 1969 **Nasty Habits** Scotia-Barber 1977 (*The Abbess of Crewe*)

Bibliography:
Thomas A. Tominaga and Wilma Schneidermeyer **Iris Murdoch and Muriel Spark: A Bibliography** Scarecrow Press (US) 1976

Spender, Stephen   Born in London, 1909.

There has been a decline in collectors' interest in Spender, but certainly a market remains for the verse and the stories, if not for the prose works and the essays. In addition to his fictional work and poetry listed below, however, I append three non-fictional works which are of importance. Spender at 75 seems to be going from strength to strength. Newly back from a tour of China with David Hockney (the book *A China Diary* was the result) he has just been knighted for his services to literature. Whether or not this honour will prompt a re-evaluation (it sometimes does) remains to be seen.

1 **20 Poems**	Blackwell 1930	I
2 **Poems**	Faber 1933	G
	Random House 1934	F
3 **Vienna** (verse)	Faber 1934	E
	Random House 1935	D
4 **The Burning Cactus** (stories)	Faber 1936	G
	Random House 1936	E
5 **Trial of a Judge** (play)	Faber 1938	C
	Random House 1938	C
6 **The Still Centre** (verse)	Faber 1939	D
7 **Danton's Death** (play)	Faber 1939	C
Adapt. with Goronwy Rees.		
8 **Selected Poems**	Faber 1940	C
9 **The Backward Son** (novel)	Hogarth Press 1940	G
10 **Ruins and Visions** (verse)	Faber 1942	D
	Random House 1942	C
11 **Poems of Dedication**	Faber 1946	C
	Random House 1947	B
12 **The Edge of Being** (verse)	Faber 1949	C
	Random House 1949	B
13 **Sirmione Peninsula**	Faber 1954	A
(Ariel Poem)		
14 **Collected Poems**	Faber 1955	C
	Random House 1955	C
15 **Engaged in Writing and The Fool**	Hamilton 1958	C
and the Princess (stories)	Farrar Straus 1958	C
16 **Mary Stuart** (play)	Faber 1959	C
Adapt. from Schiller.		
17 **Selected Poems**	Random House 1964	B
	Faber 1965	B
18 **The Generous Days** (verse)	Faber 1971	B
	Random House 1971	B
Three prose works of importance:		
19 **World Within World**	Hamilton 1951	B
(autobiography)	Harcourt Brace 1951	B

20	**W.H. Auden: A Tribute**	Weidenfeld 1975	C
		Macmillan 1975	C
21	**Eliot**	Fontana 1975	A
	In the 'Fontana Modern Masters' series.		

Steinbeck, John   Born in California, 1902. Died 1968.

According to the letters I received after the publication of *Collecting Modern First Editions*, Steinbeck was my greatest omission. My point was that I didn't believe collectors in *Britain* to be *that* interested. I still don't. But I agree that Steinbeck is of the *calibre* to be included, so here he is.

1	**Cup of Gold** (novel)	McBride 1929	L
		Heinemann 1937	G
2	**The Pastures of Heaven** (novel)	Brewer 1932	J
		Allan 1933	H
3	**To a God Unknown** (novel)	Ballou 1933	I
		Heinemann 1935	G
4	**Tortilla Flat** (novel)	Covici Friede 1935	I
		Heinemann 1935	G
5	**In Dubious Battle** (novel)	Covici Friede 1936	H
		Heinemann 1936	G
6	**Of Mice and Men** (novel)	Covici Friede 1937	H
		Heinemann 1937	G
7	**Of Mice and Men** (play)	Covici Friede 1937	D
8	**The Red Pony** (novel)	Covici Friede 1937	F
	Enlarged edition published by Viking in 1945 (**C**).		
9	**The Long Valley** (novel)	Viking 1938	J
		Heinemann 1939	G
10	**The Grapes of Wrath** (novel)	Viking 1939	I
		Heinemann 1939	G
11	**Sea of Cortez: A Leisurely Journal of Travel and Research**	Viking 1941	G
	This was republished as **The Log from the Sea of Cortez** by Viking and Heinemann (1951 and 1958, respectively) together with a new essay by J.S. on Edward F. Ricketts, the co-writer of the book (**D,C**).		
12	**The Moon is Down** (novel)	Viking 1942	D
		Heinemann 1942	B
13	**Bombs Away: The Story of a Bomber Team** (non-fiction)	Viking 1942	F
14	**Cannery Row** (novel)	Viking 1945	D
		Heinemann 1945	C

15 **The Wayward Bus** (novel)	Viking 1947	D
	Heinemann 1947	C
16 **The Pearl** (novel)	Viking 1947	D
	Heinemann 1948	C
17 **A Russian Journal**	Viking 1948	C
(non-fiction)	Heinemann 1949	C
18 **Burning Bright** (novel)	Viking 1950	C
	Heinemann 1951	B
19 **Viva Zapata!** (screenplay)	Edizioni Filmcritica	C
New edition published by Viking in	(Italy) 1952	
1975.		
20 **East of Eden** (novel)	Viking 1952	E
	Heinemann 1952	C
21 **Sweet Thursday** (novel)	Viking 1954	C
	Heinemann 1954	B
22 **The Short Reign of Pippin IV: A**	Viking 1957	B
Fabrication (fiction)	Heinemann 1957	A
23 **Once There Was a War** (non-fiction)	Viking 1958	C
	Heinemann 1959	B
24 **The Winter of Our Discontent**	Viking 1961	C
(novel)	Heinemann 1961	B
25 **Travels With Charley in Search of**	Viking 1962	C
America (non-fiction)	Heinemann 1962	B
26 **Speech Accepting the Nobel Prize**	Viking 1962	C
for Literature		
27 **America and Americans**	Viking 1966	C
(non-fiction)	Heinemann 1966	B
28 **The Acts of King Arthur and His**	Farrar Straus 1976	B
Noble Knights	Heinemann 1977	A

Films:
Of Mice and Men United Artists 1939   **The Grapes of Wrath** Fox
1940   **The Forgotten Village** MGM 1941   **Tortilla Flat** MGM
1942   **The Moon is Down** Fox 1943   **The Pearl** RKO 1948   **The
Red Pony** British Lion 1949   **East of Eden** Warner Bros. 1954 **The
Pearl** RKO 1954 **The Wayward Bus** Fox 1957   **The Red Pony**
British Lion 1976   **Cannery Row** MGM 1981

Stevens, Wallace   Born in Pennsylvania, 1879. Died 1955.

That Stevens trained as a lawyer and became vice-president of an insurance
company is, perhaps, not in itself amazing – Eliot, as we all know, was a
banker. What strikes me as *absolutely* amazing, however, is that throughout
his career as a poet – during which he was repeatedly hailed as one of
America's greatest – he steadfastly held on to his position on the board of the

insurance company! He said – no doubt to the bewildered fury of poets everywhere – that poetry was 'a leisure pursuit'. This remained, as it were, his policy. A checklist of his major work appears below.

1	**Harmonium** (verse) A revised ed. was published by Knopf in 1931.	Knopf 1923	N
2	**Ideas of Order** (verse) This was preceded by a limited, signed ed. from Alcestis in 1935 (**L**).	Knopf 1936	J
3	**The Man with the Blue Guitar and Other Poems**	Knopf 1937	J
4	**Parts of a World** (verse)	Ryerson Press 1942	H
5	**Transport to Summer** (verse)	Knopf 1947	G
6	**The Auroras of Autumn** (verse)	Knopf 1950	F
7	**The Necessary Angel** (essays)	Knopf 1951	F
		Faber 1960	D
8	**Selected Poems**	Faber 1953	E
		Vintage 1959	C
9	**Collected Poems**	Knopf 1954	E
		Faber 1955	D
10	**Opus Posthumous** (verse)	Knopf 1957	E
		Faber 1959	D
11	**The Letters**	Knopf 1966	D
		Faber 1967	C
12	**The Palm at the End of the Mind: Selected Poems and a Play**	Knopf 1971	C

Bibliography:
J.M. Edelstein **Wallace Stevens: A Descriptive Bibliography**
University of Pittsburgh Press 1973

Stewart, J.I.M.   Born in Edinburgh, 1906.

Stewart is better known by his pseudonym, Michael Innes. He has written over seventy books now, but I list here just the first five Innes, and the first five Stewarts.

Michael Innes:

1	**Death at the President's Lodging** **Seven Suspects**	Gollancz 1936 Dodd Mead 1937	I H
2	**Hamlet, Revenge!**	Gollancz 1937 Dodd Mead 1937	H G
3	**Lament for a Maker**	Gollancz 1938 Dodd Mead 1938	H G
4	**Stop Press** **The Spider Strikes**	Gollancz 1939 Dodd Mead 1939	H G

5 **The Secret Vanguard**	Gollancz 1940	**F**
	Dodd Mead 1941	**D**

J.I.M. Stewart:

1 **Mark Lambert's Supper**	Gollancz 1954	**G**
2 **The Guardians**	Gollancz 1955	**F**
	Norton 1957	**D**
3 **The Use of Riches**	Gollancz 1957	**D**
	Norton 1957	**C**
4 **The Man Who Wrote Detective Stories and Other Stories**	Gollancz 1959	**D**
	Norton 1959	**C**
5 **The Man Who Won the Pools**	Gollancz 1961	**C**
	Norton 1961	**C**

Stoppard, Tom   Born in Czechoslovakia, 1937. British.

An astounding playwright – his work gets better and better, stronger and funnier, more and more clever, but never clever-clever. He will always be collected.

1 **Lord Malquist and Mr Moon** (novel)	Blond 1966	**G**
	Knopf 1968	**E**
2 **Rosencrantz and Guildenstern are Dead** (play)	Faber 1967	**F**
	Grove Press 1967	**E**
3 **The Real Inspector Hound** (play)	Faber 1968	**E**
	Grove Press 1969	**C**
4 **Enter a Free Man** (play)	Faber 1968	**D**
This play has an interesting history, for it was originally televised in 1963 as *A Walk on the Water*, and then a revised version was televised the following year as *The Preservation of George Riley*.	Grove Press 1972	**B**
5 **Albert's Bridge and If You're Glad I'll Be Frank: Two Plays for Radio**	Faber 1969	**C**
6 **After Magritte** (play)	Faber 1971	**C**
	Grove Press 1972	**B**
7 **Jumpers** (play)	Faber 1972	**C**
	Grove Press 1972	**C**
8 **Artist Descending a Staircase and Where Are They Now?: Two Plays for Radio**	Faber 1973	**C**
9 **Travesties** (play)	Faber 1975	**C**
	Grove Press 1975	**C**
10 **Dirty Linen and New-Found-Land** (plays)	Ambiance/Almost Free Playscript 1976	**C**

An edition was published by Faber a month later (**B**).	Grove Press 1976	**B**
11 **The Fifteen Minute Hamlet** (play)	French 1976	**B**
12 **Every Good Boy Deserves Favour and Professional Foul** (plays)	Faber 1978 Grove Press 1978	**B** **B**
13 **Night and Day** (play)	Faber 1978	**B**
A revised edition was published by Faber in 1979 (**B**).	Grove Press 1979	**B**
14 **Undiscovered Country**	Faber 1980	**B**
A version of Arthur Schnitzler's play.		
15 **Dogg's Hamlet, Cahoot's Macbeth** (play)	Faber 1980	**B**
16 **On the Razzle** (play)	Faber 1981	**B**
17 **The Real Thing** (play)	Faber 1982	**B**
18 **The Dog It was That Died and Other Plays**	Faber 1983	**B**
Includes *The Dissolution of Dominic Boot*, *'M' is for Moon Among Other Things*, *Teeth*, *Another Moon Called Earth*, *Neutral Ground* and *A Separate Peace*.		

Storey, David   Born in Yorkshire, 1933.

Storey's career is unusual in that it is precisely divided into success as a novelist, and success as a playwright: he is equally well known in each sphere. His Yorkshire background emerges very strongly in his first novel *This Sporting Life* (and later in his play *The Changing Room*) but disillusion with the North caused him to come to London. He draws on this in *Flight Into Camden*, his second novel (and almost as scarce as his first). Camden, it might be explained, in 1961 would have meant Camden *Town*. It is only quite recently that Camden has come to mean a London borough.

1 **This Sporting Life** (novel)	Longmans 1960	**G**
	Macmillan 1960	**E**
2 **Flight into Camden** (novel)	Longmans 1961	**G**
	Macmillan 1961	**E**
3 **Radcliffe** (novel)	Longmans 1963	**C**
	Coward McCann 1964	**B**
4 **The Restoration of Arnold Middleton** (play)	Cape 1967	**B**
5 **In Celebration** (play)	Cape 1969	**B**
	Grove Press 1975	**B**
6 **The Contractor** (play)	Cape 1970	**B**
	Random House 1971	**A**
7 **Home** (play)	Cape 1970	**B**
	Random House 1971	**A**
8 **The Changing Room** (play)	Cape 1972	**B**
	Random House 1972	**A**

9 **Pasmore** (novel)	Longman 1972	B
	Dutton 1974	B
10 **Edward** (humour)	Lane 1973	B
11 **A Temporary Life** (novel)	Lane 1973	B
	Dutton 1974	A
12 **The Farm** (play)	Cape 1973	B
13 **Cromwell** (play)	Cape 1973	B
14 **Life Class** (play)	Cape 1975	B
15 **Saville** (novel)	Cape 1976	B
	Harper 1977	A
16 **Mother's Day** (play)	Cape 1977	B
17 **Early Days** (play)	Penguin 1980	A
18 **Sisters** (play)	Penguin 1980	A
19 **A Prodigal Child** (novel)	Cape 1982	B
	Dutton 1983	B
20 **Present Times** (novel)	Cape 1984	B

Film:
This Sporting Life Rank 1962   **In Celebration** Seven Keys 1976

Story, Jack Trevor   Born in Hertfordshire, 1917.

A very prolific author, but one would be hard put to name any of his books but one, the title of which has entered the language. Because it captures so well the mood of the time – and because it was so memorably filmed (with Ian Hendry as the tally boy) – it is an important work for collectors of modern fiction. Story is now the 'writer in residence' in Milton Keynes. He likes it there, he says.

Live Now, Pay Later (novel)	Secker 1963	C
Unusually for the time, this was	Penguin 1963	B
published simultaneously in hard and		
paperback. Both editions are hard to		
come by.		

Films:
Live Now, Pay Later Regal 1962
In addition to this, two other Story novels have been filmed.

Strachey, Lytton   Born in London, 1880. Died 1932.

Interest in the Bloomsbury Group has declined since the heyday of the seventies, but although books on the subject continue to be published, only the ones *really* vital to the thing are taken seriously and, apart from standard biographies, none is of any interest to the collector unless written *by* the person in question, and not *about* him or her. Strachey seems to have been spared being dug and re-dug, but then Holroyd did the job so thoroughly in the sixties that it would be folly to try. Nor do any posthumous writings seem to have emerged recently, and so Strachey's checklist remains the same, as does collectors' interest – it never boomed, but it never went away.

1	**Landmarks in French Literature** This is a very small, fragile item in the Home University Library series, but there are many variant issues, chronicled in Percy Muir *Points*.	Williams & Norgate 1912 Holt 1912	F D
2	**Eminent Victorians**	Chatto & Windus 1918 Putnam 1918	F D
3	**Queen Victoria**	Chatto & Windus 1921 Harcourt 1921	D C
4	**Books and Characters**	Chatto & Windus 1922 Harcourt 1922	C C
5	**Pope: The Leslie Stephen Lecture**	CUP 1925	C
6	**Elizabeth and Essex**	Chatto & Windus 1928 Harcourt 1928	C C
7	**Portraits in Miniature**	Chatto & Windus 1931 Harcourt 1931	C C
8	**Characters and Commentaries**	Chatto & Windus 1933 Harcourt 1933	C C
9	**Spectatorial Essays**	Chatto & Windus 1964 Harcourt 1965	C C
10	**Ermyntrude and Esmerelda** This is illustrated by Erté, and has an Intro. by Michael Holroyd.	Blond 1969 Stein & Day 1969	C B

A volume of letters between Virginia Woolf and Lytton Strachey was published by the Hogarth Press in 1956, though of course the great work on Strachey is: Michael Holroyd *Lytton Strachey* (2 vols) Heinemann 1967, 1968.

Styron, William   Born in Virginia, 1925.

Sophie's Choice was Styron's fifth novel in thirty years, and something of a *cause célèbre* even before it was published. There were rumblings about 'the new Styron' in America as soon as page proofs were released, and the feeling that here was something 'big' soon spread to this country. It was a fat American novel, to be sure, but it was not to be a blockbuster *à la* Harold Robbins, nor 'big' in the sense that, say, James Michener's novels are big. It was a very literary novel, with too thin a thread, one would have thought, to sustain it. But the power and the intrigue persisted unto the end. It is the much-honoured film that now consolidates the success. Anyway, Styron does now appear to be collectable – and if his past record is anything to go by, it looks as if there will be no new novel until about 1990.

1	**Lie Down in Darkness**	Bobbs-Merrill 1951	H
	(novel)	Hamilton 1952	F
2	**The Long March** (novel)	Random House 1956	F
		Hamilton 1962	B
3	**Set The House on Fire** (novel)	Random House 1960	E
		Hamilton 1961	C
4	**The Confessions of Nat Turner**	Random House 1967	C
	(novel)	Cape 1968	C
5	**Sophie's Choice** (novel)	Random House 1979	D
		Cape 1979	C
6	**This Quiet Dust** (essays)	Random House 1982	B
		Cape 1983	B

Films:
The Confessions of Nat Turner Fox 1969   **Sophie's Choice** ITC 1983

Swift, Graham   Born in London, 1949.

Swift published his first book only four years ago, and so it might appear somewhat premature to include him in rather select listing of collected authors; but his reputation was strong even before his sizeable success with *Waterland*, which was short listed for the Booker Prize. It is certainly a unique novel, and from it I get the right 'feel' – it feels that Graham Swift will be very sought after, very soon.

1	**The Sweet-Shop Owner** (novel)	Lane 1980	C
2	**Shuttlecock** (novel)	Lane 1981	C
3	**Learning to Swim** (stories)	London Magazine Editions 1982	B
4	**Waterland** (novel)	Heinemann 1983	B
		Poseidon 1984	B

Symons, Julian   Born in London, 1912.

An undisputed master of his genre, Symons is not as collected as one might expect. He *is* collected, but he is rarely eagerly pursued. About half his work is non-fiction – essays, criticism, histories, and two very early volumes of verse. It is, of course his crime fiction that is of the most interest, and that is what is listed below.

1 **The Immaterial Murder Case**	Gollancz 1945	E
	Macmillan 1957	D
2 **A Man Called Jones**	Gollancz 1947	D
3 **Bland Beginning**	Gollancz 1949	D
	Harper 1949	C
4 **The 31st of February**	Gollancz 1950	D
	Harper 1950	C
5 **The Broken Penny**	Gollancz 1952	C
	Harper 1953	C
6 **The Narrowing Circle**	Gollancz 1954	C
	Harper 1954	C
7 **The Paper Chase**	Collins 1956	C
This was published as *Bogue's Fortune* in America by Harper in 1957 (C).		
8 **The Colour of Murder**	Collins 1957	C
	Harper 1957	B
9 **The Gigantic Shadow**	Collins 1958	C
This was published in America by Harper in the same year, with the title *Pipe Dream* (C).		
10 **The Progress of a Crime**	Collins 1960	B
	Harper 1960	B
11 **Murder, Murder** (stories)	Fontana 1961	B
12 **The Killing of Francie Lake**	Collins 1962	C
This was published during the same year by Harper in America with the title *The Plain Man* (C).		
13 **The End of Solomon Grundy**	Collins 1964	B
	Harper 1964	B
14 **The Belting Inheritance**	Collins 1965	B
	Harper 1965	B
15 **Francis Quarles Investigates** (stories)	Panther 1965	B
16 **The Julian Symons Omnibus**	Collins 1966	B
Cont. 4, 10 and 13.		
17 **The Man Who Killed Himself**	Collins 1967	B
	Harper 1967	A
18 **The Man Whose Dreams Came True**	Collins 1969	B
	Harper 1969	A
19 **The Man Who Lost His Wife**	Collins 1971	B
	Harper 1971	A
20 **The Players and the Game**	Collins 1972	A
	Harper 1972	A
21 **The Plot Against Roger Rider**	Collins 1973	B
	Harper 1973	A
22 **A Three Pipe Problem**	Collins 1975	B
	Harper 1975	A

23 **The Blackheath Poisonings**	Collins 1978	A
	Harper 1979	A
24 **Sweet Adelaide**	Collins 1980	A
	Harper 1980	A
25 **The Detling Murders**	Macmillan 1982	A
26 **The Detling Secret**	Viking 1983	A
American edition of 25.		
27 **The Tigers of Subtopia and Other**	Macmillan 1982	A
Stories	Viking 1983	A
28 **The Name of Annabel Lee**	Macmillan 1983	A
	Viking 1983	A

Film:
The Narrowing Circle Eros 1955

Taylor, Elizabeth   Born Reading, 1912. Died 1976.

'Not one of the most collected authors,' I wrote in *Collecting Modern First Editions*, 'though the quality of her work has lately received more notice.' I still stand by that. I then went on to record the fact that Elizabeth Taylor had published fifteen books, and I listed three of the best, as I shall do again. One of them – *Angel* – was in the list of the 'Thirteen Best Novels of Our Time', but I still have not witnessed a stampede towards the author.

1 **At Mrs Lippincote's** (novel)	Davies 1945	F
	Knopf 1946	D
2 **Angel** (novel)	Davies 1957	D
	Viking 1957	C
3 **Mrs Palfrey at the Claremont**	Chatto & Windus 1971	C
(novel)	Viking 1971	C

Tennant, Emma   Born in London, 1937.

The popularity of Emma Tennant has grown largely by word of mouth, for she appears in almost no reference works, and her books are published very quietly and without fuss (which, for an author, is an appallingly anti-climactic way to be published). She has been very big news with detective and crime collectors for years, it is true, but now the more general collector of modern firsts is beginning to take notice, and would be pleased to have at least a representation of her work on his or her shelves.

1 **The Colour of Rain**	Weidenfeld 1964	F
(novel)		
Pseud. Catherine Aydy.		
2 **The Time of the Crack** (novel)	Cape 1973	C

3 **The Last of the Country House Murders** (novel)	Cape 1974	C
	Nelson (US) 1974	B
4 **Hotel de Dream** (novel)	Gollancz 1976	B
5 **The Bad Sister** (novel)	Gollancz 1978	B
	Coward McCann 1978	B
6 **Wild Nights** (novel)	Cape 1979	B
	Harcourt Brace 1980	B
7 **The Boggart** (juvenile)	Granada 1980	B
8 **Alice Fell** (novel)	Cape 1980	B
9 **The Search for Treasure Island** (juvenile)	Puffin 1981	A
10 **Queen of Stones** (novel)	Cape 1982	B
11 **Woman Beware Woman** (novel)	Cape 1983	B

Thomas, D.M.   Born in Cornwall, 1935.

Thomas was known to a very élite few as a poet, long before the publication of his celebrated novel *The White Hotel*. He was not collected then, and I am not *completely* convinced that he is now, but sufficient numbers of people seemed concerned that the subsequent novel – *Ararat* – should still be in first edition before they bought it to make it appear likely that a stirring has begun. Or was it only because *The White Hotel* was – after a long time 'sleeping' – reprinted six times in six months, and they did not wish to be caught out again? As it is, they needn't have worried, for *Ararat* is still freely available and, at time of writing, *Swallow* is as yet unpublished. But *The White Hotel* remains famous for being famous, and seems to have been enjoyed greatly and vilified by similarly vast numbers of people. In addition to the works listed below, Thomas has also published a few translations from the Russian: Akhamatova, Pushkin and Yevtushenko.

1 **Penguin Modern Poets 11** With D.M. Black and Peter Redgrove.	Penguin 1968	C
2 **Two Voices** (verse)	Cape Golliard 1968	E
3 **Logan Stone** (verse)	Cape Golliard 1971	D
4 **The Shaft** (verse)	Arc 1973	D
5 **Lilith-Prints** (verse) Illustrated by Martin Dutton. Limited to 400 copies.	Second Aeon (Cardiff) 1974	C
6 **Love and Other Deaths** (verse)	Elek 1975	C
7 **The Devil and the Floral Dance** (juvenile)	Robson 1978	C
8 **In the Fair Field** (verse) Limited to 120 signed copies.	Five Seasons Press (Hereford) 1978	E
9 **The Honeymoon Voyage** (verse)	Secker 1978	C

Thomas, D. M.

10 **The Flute Player** (novel)	Dutton 1979	C
	Gollancz 1979	C
11 **Protest** (poem) Limited to 500 copies.	Privately printed 1980	C
12 **Birthstone** (novel) A revised edition of this novel was published in paperback by King Penguin in 1982, and in hardback by Gollancz in 1983.	Viking 1980 Gollancz 1980	D C
13 **Dreaming in Bronze** (verse)	Secker 1981	C
14 **The White Hotel** (novel)	Viking 1981	H
	Gollancz 1981	E
15 **Ararat** (novel)	Viking 1983	B
	Gollancz 1983	B
16 **Selected Poems**	Viking 1983	B
	Secker 1983	B
17 **Swallow** (novel)	Viking 1984	B
	Gollancz 1984	B

Thomas, Dylan   Born in Swansea, 1914. Died 1953.

Dylan Thomas remains one of the really great writers of the century, and this is reflected in the scarceness and high prices of most of his work. This situation will not alter: he will always be collected – isn't it?

1 **18 Poems** Black cloth, lettered in gold, with grey d/w. The second issue is distinguishable in many ways, two being the rounded spine, as opposed to the flat spine of the first issue, and the advert on the verso for slim volumes by George Barker, Dylan Thomas and David Gascoyne, not present in first issue. The spine lettering tends to discoloration on the second issue, due to inferior gold. The 1st issue is Grade S and over now, though the 2nd issue is Grade P in fine condition. A 2nd edition was published by the Fortune Press in, it is thought, 1942, the first issue of this having red boards, and a yellow d/w. Subsequent issues retain the yellow d/w, but have various coloured boards (**F**).	Sunday Referee & The Parton Bookshop 1934	**S** **upwards**
2 **Twenty-Five Poems** Grey boards, grey d/w.	Dent 1936	I

274

3 **The Map of Love**   Dent 1939   **I**
(verse and prose)
Mauve cloth, grey and purple d/w.
Three subsequent issues exist, the first
identifiable by its smooth-grained cloth,
and gold lettering.

4 **The World I Breathe**   New Directions 1939   **F**
This American anthology was bound in
brown, with cream d/w. It contains
selections from 1, 2 and 3, though two
stories appear for the first time.

5 **Portrait of the Artist as a Young**   Dent 1940   **H**
   Dog   New Directions 1940   **G**
English ed. is green cloth with scarlet
d/w, American ed. is red cloth with
cream d/w.

6 **New Poems**   New Directions 1943   **E**
Mauve boards in mauve d/w.

7 **Deaths and Entrances**   Dent 1946   **E**
$5\frac{1}{2}$ in. × $4\frac{1}{2}$ in. only. Orange cloth,
vermilion d/w.

8 **Selected Writings**   New Directions 1946   **E**
Pinkish cloth in pinkish d/w.

9 **Twenty-six Poems**   Dent/New   **L**
This consisted of 150 signed copies, the   Directions 1950
first ten on Japanese vellum (**M**), the
remainder on handmade paper, divided
between Dent and New Directions, all
printed in Italy.

10 **In Country Sleep**   New Directions 1952   **D**
100 signed copies (**L**), and 5000
ordinary copies.

11 **Collected Poems**   Dent 1952   **E**
Published simultaneously with the   New Directions 1953   **D**
English ed. was a signed, limited issue
of 65 copies, 60 for sale (**N**).

12 **The Doctor and the Devils**   Dent 1953   **C**
The American ed. was printed off from New Directions 1953   **C**
the English 2nd impression.

13 **Under Milk Wood**   Dent 1954   **G**
                                       New Directions 1954   **E**

14 **Quite Early One Morning**   Dent 1954   **C**
                                       New Directions 1954   **C**

15 **Conversation About Christmas**   New Directions 1954   **D**
2000 printed for distribution by the
publisher.

16	**Adventures in the Skin Trade and Other Stories**	New Directions 1955	**D**
	The title story was published alone by Putnam in 1955, with a Foreword by Vernon Watkins (**D**)		
17	**A Prospect of the Sea**	Dent 1955	**C**
18	**Letters to Vernon Watkins**	Faber/Dent 1957	**B**
		New Directions 1957	**B**
19	**The Beach of Falesa**	Stein & Day 1963	**B**
		Cape 1964	**B**
20	**Twenty Years A-Growing**	Dent 1964	**C**
21	**Rebecca's Daughters**	Triton 1965	**B**
		Little Brown 1965	**B**
22	**Me and My Bike**	McGraw-Hill 1965	**B**
		Triton 1965	**B**
23	**Selected Letters of Dylan Thomas**	Dent 1966	**C**
		New Directions 1967	**C**
24	**The Notebooks of Dylan Thomas Poet in the Making**	New Directions 1967	**C**
		Dent 1968	**C**
25	**Early Prose Writings**	Dent 1971	**B**
		New Directions 1972	**B**
26	**The Death of the King's Canary**	Hutchinson 1976	**A**
	With John Davenport.		

Film:
Under Milk Wood Rank 1971

Bibliography:
Ralph Maud **Dylan Thomas in Print: A Bibliographical History** Dent 1970; University of Pittsburgh Press 1970

Biography:
Constantine FitzGibbon **The Life of Dylan Thomas** Dent 1965; Little Brown 1965

Thomas, R.S. Born in Cardiff, 1913.

Probably the best known Welsh poet after Dylan – and possibly David Jones. His reputation remains high, his early works remain scarce, and his *œuvre* as a whole remains highly collectable. Only seventeen books – and the very devil to gather up the lot. In addition to the checklist following, Thomas has edited five volumes of verse.

1	**The Stones of the Field** (verse)	Druid Press 1946	**N**
2	**An Acre of Land** (verse)	Montgomery Printing Co. 1952	**L**

3 **The Minister** (verse)	Montgomery Printing Co. 1953	K
4 **Song at the Year's Turning** (verse)	Hart-Davis 1955	F
5 **Poetry for Supper** (verse)	Hart-Davis 1958	D
	Dufour 1961	B
6 **Judgement Day** (verse)	Poetry Book Society 1960	D
7 **Tares** (verse)	Hart-Davis 1961	D
	Dufour 1961	C
8 **The Bread of Truth** (verse)	Hart-Davis 1963	D
	Dufour 1963	C
9 **Pieta** (verse)	Hart-Davis 1966	D
10 **Not That He Brought Flowers** (verse)	Hart-Davis 1968	C
11 **The Mountains** (verse)	Chilmark Press (NY) 1968	D
12 **H'm: Poems**	Macmillan 1972	C
	St Martin's 1972	B
13 **Selected Poems: 1946–1968**	Hart-Davis 1973	B
	St Martin's 1974	B
14 **Laboratories of the Spirit** (verse)	Macmillan 1975	B
	St Martin's 1976	A
15 **Frequencies** (verse)	Macmillan 1978	A
16 **Between Here and Now** (verse)	Macmillan 1981	A
17 **Later Poems**	Macmillan 1983	A

Thurber, James   Born in Ohio, 1894. Died 1961.

The cynical, world-wise, off-beat American humorist, *par excellence*. Quite apart from his writing, his cruelly economical cartoons would have assured him of a place in the history of humour. His dogs are not nearly as funny (or as grotesque) as his women. All these women are shaped like a cardboard box, bear expressions of unyielding malevolence (unless they are drunk) and their hair resembles a charred and sparse floor mop. It was to escape such harridans that Walter Mitty entered his dream world, and who can blame him. The wonderful Danny Kaye film, it might be noted here, was spun out of the original short story of only nine pages.

1 **Is Sex Necessary? Or: Why You Feel the Way You Do** With E.B. White.	Harper 1929	H
	Heinemann 1930	E
2 **The Owl in the Attic and Other Perplexities**	Harper (US) 1931	F
	Harper (UK) 1931	F
3 **The Seal in the Bedroom and Other Predicaments**	Harper (US) 1932	F
	Harper (UK) 1932	F
4 **My Life and Hard Times**	Harper (US) 1933	E
	Harper (UK) 1933	E

5	The Middle-Aged Man on the Flying Trapeze	Harper 1935	E
		Heinemann 1935	D
6	Let Your Mind Alone! and Other More or Less Inspirational Pieces	Harper 1937	D
		Hamilton 1937	C
7	Cream of Thurber (anthology)	Hamilton 1939	C
8	The Last Flower: A Parable in Pictures	Harper 1939	D
		Hamilton 1939	C
9	Fables of Our Time and Famous Poems Illustrated	Harper 1940	D
		Hamilton 1940	C
10	The Male Animal (play)	Random House 1940	C
	With Elliott Nugent.	Hamilton 1950	B
11	My World – and Welcome to It	Harcourt Brace 1942	E
	This contains the story *The Secret Life of Walter Mitty*.	Hamilton 1942	D
12	Many Moons (juvenile)	Harcourt Brace 1943	E
		Hamilton 1945	D
13	Men, Women and Dogs	Harcourt Brace 1943	D
		Hamilton 1945	C
14	The Great Quillow (juvenile)	Harcourt Brace 1944	E
15	The White Deer (juvenile)	Harcourt Brace 1945	C
		Hamilton 1945	C
16	The Thurber Carnival (anthology)	Harper 1945	C
		Hamilton 1945	C
17	The Beast in Me and Other Animals	Harcourt Brace 1948	C
		Hamilton 1949	C
18	The 13 Clocks (juvenile)	Simon & Schuster 1950	D
		Hamilton 1951	C
19	The Thurber Album	Simon & Schuster 1952	C
		Hamilton 1952	C
20	Thurber Country	Simon & Schuster 1953	C
		Hamilton 1953	C
21	The Wonderful O (juvenile)	Simon & Schuster 1955	D
		Hamilton 1955	C
22	Thurber's Dogs	Simon & Schuster 1955	C
		Hamilton 1955	C
23	A Thurber Garland (anthology)	Hamilton 1955	B
24	Further Fables of Our Time	Simon & Schuster 1956	C
		Hamilton 1956	B
25	Alarms and Diversions	Harper 1957	B
		Hamilton 1957	B

26 **The Years with Ross**	Little Brown 1959	**B**
(non-fiction)	Hamilton 1959	**B**
27 **Lanterns and Lances**	Harper 1961	**B**
	Hamilton 1961	**B**
28 **A Thurber Carnival** (play)	French (US) 1962	**B**
29 **Credos and Curios**	Harper 1962	**B**
	Hamilton 1962	**B**
30 **Vintage Thurber**	Hamilton 1963	**C**
(anthology, 2 vols)		
31 **Thurber and Company**	Harper 1967	**B**
	Hamilton 1967	**B**

Films:
Rise and Shine 20th Century fox 1941 (*My Life and Hard Times*) **The Secret Life of Walter Mitty** RKO 1949. This last film is adapted from a short story, possibly his most famous work.

Bibliography:
Edwin T. Bowden **James Thurber: A Bibliography** Ohio State University Press 1968

Tolkien, J.R.R.   Born in Birmingham, England, 1892. Died 1973.

Tolkien has published a dozen books since his death in 1973. It is quite extraordinary how some writers leave such a mass of writing behind them, while others publish everything they write, as they write it, hence leaving nothing whatever for posthumous publication. Tolkien is not the most prolific dead author, of course (Virginia Woolf has published *twenty-six* books since her death in 1941) but certainly he does seem to have stored away an awful lot. Witness, indeed, the title of his latest, at time of writing: *The Book of Lost Tales Part I*. Anyway, it all affords great scope for the collector – bearing in mind that it is always up to the collector how far he wishes to go. Few, of course, would turn down firsts of the *Lord of the Rings* trilogy, or of *The Hobbit* (provided he was possessed of the necessary wealth) but what of this, published in 1982: a leather-bound edition of *The Silmarillion* (first published five years earlier) at £75, or at £100 signed by Tolkien's son, Christopher?

1 **A Middle English Vocabulary**	OUP 1922	**K**
	OUP (US) 1922	**I**
2 **Sir Gawain and the Green Knight**	OUP 1925	**I**
Ed. with E.V. Gordon.	OUP (US) 1925	**I**
3 **Songs for the Philologists** (verse)	Privately printed 1936	**O**
4 **Beowulf: The Monsters and the**	OUP 1936	**H**
Critics (lecture)	Folcroft Editions 1972	**B**

279

Tolkein

5	**The Hobbit** (novel)	Allen & Unwin 1937	**T**
		Houghton Mifflin 1938	**R**
6	**Farmer Giles of Ham** (novel)	Allen & Unwin 1949	**F**
		Houghton Mifflin 1950	**D**
7	**The Fellowship of the Ring** (novel)	Allen & Unwin 1954	**N**
		Houghton Mifflin 1954	**L**
8	**The Two Towers** (novel)	Allen & Unwin 1954	**M**
		Houghton Mifflin 1955	**K**
9	**The Return of the King** (novel)	Allen & Unwin 1955	**M**
		Houghton Mifflin 1956	**K**

7, 8 and 9 form the trilogy *The Lord of the Rings*. Revised editions of these three volumes were published by the same publishers, in 1966 and 1967 respectively.

10	**The Adventures of Tom Bombadil** (verse)	Allen & Unwin 1962	**E**
		Houghton Mifflin 1963	**D**
11	**Tree and Leaf** (essay)	Allen & Unwin 1964	**D**
		Houghton Mifflin 1965	**C**
12	**The Tolkien Reader**	Ballantine (NY) 1966	**B**
13	**Smith of Wootton Major** (novelette)	Allen & Unwin 1967	**D**
		Houghton Mifflin 1967	**C**
14	**The Road Goes Ever On** (verse)	Houghton Mifflin 1967	**C**
	Music by Donald Swann.	Allen & Unwin 1968	**C**
15	**Bilbo's Last Song** (poster poem)	Houghton Mifflin 1974	**B**
		Allen & Unwin 1974	**B**
16	**Sir Gawain and the Green Knight, Pearl, and Sir Orfeo** (trans.)	Allen & Unwin 1975	**B**
		Houghton Mifflin 1975	**B**
17	**The Homecoming of Beorhtnoth** (poem)	Allen & Unwin 1975	**B**

Published together with reprints of 11 and 13.

18	**The Father Christmas Letters**	Allen & Unwin 1976	**B**
		Houghton Mifflin 1976	**B**
19	**The Silmarillion** (novel)	Allen & Unwin 1977	**C**
		Houghton Mifflin 1977	**B**
20	**Pictures by J.R.R. Tolkien**	Allen & Unwin 1979	**B**
	The Pictures of J.R.R.Tolkien	Houghton Mifflin 1979	**B**
21	**Poems and Stories**	Allen & Unwin 1980	**B**
		Houghton Mifflin 1980	**B**
22	**Unfinished Tales**	Allen & Unwin 1980	**B**
		Houghton Mifflin 1980	**B**
23	**Letters**	Allen & Unwin 1981	**B**
		Houghton Mifflin 1981	**B**
24	**Mr Bliss** (juvenile)	Allen & Unwin 1982	**B**
		Houghton Mifflin 1983	**B**
25	**Finn and Hengest: The Fragment**	Allen & Unwin 1983	**B**

and the Episode	Houghton Mifflin 1983	B
26 **The Monsters and the Critics**	Allen & Unwin 1983	B
	Houghton Mifflin 1983	B
27 **The Book of Lost Tales Part I**	Allen & Unwin 1983	B
	Houghton Mifflin 1984	B

Film:
Lord of the Rings United Artists 1980

Biography:
Humphrey Carpenter **J.R.R. Tolkien** Allen & Unwin 1977; Houghton Mifflin 1977

Travers, P.L.   Born in Queensland, 1906.

Famous for Mary Poppins, a character who featured in a series of books for children, the first of which is listed below. The film raised Poppins from well known to universally known, though Travers's own name was largely forgotten in the process.

Mary Poppins	Howe 1934	F
A difficult book to find.	Reynal 1934	F

Film:
Mary Poppins Disney 1964

Trevor, William   Born in Cork, 1928.

A craftsman *and* an artist. The fusion is sublime, for Trevor rarely falls short of the perfection for which he is striving. He has been publishing every single year for the past twenty, and although his novels are always extremely well reviewed (often by his peers), collectors' interest has emerged only recently. Although not too common, it ought to be possible to assemble the latter half of Trevor's *œuvre* without too much difficulty or expense, for some booksellers, I think, would even now not rate him as collectable. Until they read this. Be quick!

1 **A Standard of Behaviour** (novel)	Hutchinson 1958	G
2 **The Old Boys** (novel)	Bodley Head 1964	D
	Viking 1964	C
3 **The Boarding House** (novel)	Bodley Head 1965	C
	Viking 1965	B
4 **The Love Department** (novel)	Bodley Head 1966	C
	Viking 1967	B
5 **The Day We Got Drunk on Cake** (novel)	Bodley Head 1967	C
	Viking 1968	B

6	**The Girl** (play)	French 1968		**B**
7	**Mrs Eckdorf in O'Neill's Hotel**	Bodley Head 1969		**C**
	(novel)	Viking 1970		**B**
8	**The Old Boys** (play)	Poynter 1971		**B**
9	**Miss Gomez and the Brethren**	Bodley Head 1971		**C**
	(novel)			
10	**A Night With Mrs Da Tonka** (play)	French 1972		**B**
11	**The Ballroom of Romance**	Bodley Head 1972		**B**
	(novel)	Viking 1972		**A**
12	**Going Home** (play)	French 1972		**B**
13	**Elizabeth Alone** (novel)	Bodley Head 1973		**C**
		Viking 1974		**B**
14	**Marriages** (play)	French 1973		**B**
15	**Angels at the Ritz and Other Stories**	Bodley Head 1975		**C**
		Viking 1976		**B**
16	**The Children of Dynmouth** (novel)	Bodley Head 1976		**C**
		Viking 1977		**B**
17	**Old School Ties** (story)	Lemon Tree Press 1976		**D**
18	**Lovers of Their Time and Other Stories**	Bodley Head 1978		**B**
		Viking 1978		**A**
19	**Other People's Worlds** (novel)	Bodley Head 1980		**B**
		Viking 1981		**A**
20	**Beyond the Pale** (stories)	Bodley Head 1981		**B**
		Viking 1982		**A**
21	**Fools of Fortune** (novel)	Bodley Head 1983		**B**
		Viking 1983		**A**
22	**A Writer's Ireland**	Viking 1984		**B**
	(non-fiction)	Thames & Hudson 1984		**B**

In addition to the above, Trevor has written about twenty plays for television, none of which has been published.

Updike, John Born in Pennsylvania, 1932.

An extremely popular and prolific author, with ever-increasing numbers of fans for his *Bech* books, and even more for the *Rabbit* series. In the late sixties *Couples* was just about the most fashionable novel to be seen with. There are, as well, Updike fanatics who recently were pleased to buy in pretty healthy numbers his collected essays and reviews at £21 a throw; when you get into this bracket for a newly published unillustrated book, you really have to *like* an author. Collecting Updike – while affording plenty of scope – is also something of a commitment, for he seems to publish on average a couple of books a year. In terms of money and space, this can mount up – but when did a collector ever pause to consider trifles such as these?

1	**The Carpentered Hen and Other Tame Creatures** (verse)	Harper 1958	G
2	**Hoping for a Hoopoe** English edition of 1.	Gollancz 1959	E
3	**The Poorhouse Fair** (novel)	Knopf 1959 Gollancz 1959	G E
4	**The Same Door** (stories)	Knopf 1959 Deutsch 1962	G E
5	**Rabbit, Run** (novel)	Knopf 1960 Deutsch 1961	D C
6	**Pigeon Feathers** (stories)	Knopf 1962 Deutsch 1962	D C
7	**The Magic Flute** (juvenile)	Knopf 1962	C
8	**Telephone Poles** (verse)	Knopf 1963 Deutsch 1963	D C
9	**The Centaur** (novel)	Knopf 1963 Deutsch 1963	C B
10	**The Ring** (miscellany)	Knopf 1964	C
11	**Of the Farm** (novel)	Knopf 1965 Deutsch 1973	C B
12	**Assorted Prose**	Knopf 1965 Deutsch 1965	C B
13	**The Music School** (stories)	Knopf 1966 Deutsch 1973	C B
14	**A Child's Calendar** (prose)	Knopf 1966	C
15	**Couples** (novel)	Knopf 1968 Deutsch 1968	C B
16	**Bath After Sailing** (verse)	Pendulum Press 1968	C
17	**Bottom's Dream: Adapted from William Shakespeare's 'A Midsummer Night's Dream'**	Knopf 1969	C
18	**Midpoint and Other Poems**	Knopf 1969 Deutsch 1969	C B
19	**Bech: A Book** (stories)	Knopf 1970 Deutsch 1970	C B
20	**Rabbit Redux** (novel)	Knopf 1971 Deutsch 1972	C C
21	**Seventy Poems**	Penguin 1972	A
22	**Museums and Women and Other Stories**	Knopf 1972 Deutsch 1973	B A
23	**Warm Wine: An Idyll** (story)	Albodocani Press 1973	E
24	**Six Poems**	Aloe Editions 1973	E
25	**Cunts** (verse)	Hallman 1974	F
26	**Buchanan Dying** (play)	Knopf 1974 Deutsch 1974	C B
27	**A Month of Sundays** (novel)	Knopf 1975 Deutsch 1975	C B

28 **Picked-Up Pieces** (essays)	Knopf 1975	C
	Deutsch 1976	B
29 **Marry Me** (novel)	Knopf 1976	C
	Deutsch 1977	B
30 **Tossing and Turning** (verse)	Knopf 1977	C
	Deutsch 1977	B
31 **The Coup** (novel)	Knopf 1978	C
	Deutsch 1979	B
32 **From the Journal of a Leper** (verse)	Lord John Press 1978	E
33 **16 Sonnets**	Ferguson 1979	E
34 **Three Illuminations in the Life of an American Author** (prose)	Targ Editions 1979	C
35 **Problems and Other Stories**	Knopf 1979	C
	Deutsch 1980	B
36 **Too Far to Go: The Maples Stories**	Fawcett 1979	B
37 **Rabbit is Rich** (novel)	Knopf 1981	B
	Deutsch 1982	B
38 **Bech is Back** (novel)	Knopf 1982	B
	Deutsch 1983	B
39 **The Beloved** (verse) A signed edition.	Lord John Press 1983	F
40 **Hugging the Shore** (essays, reviews)	Knopf 1983	C
	Deutsch 1984	C
41 **The Witches of Eastwick** (novel)	Knopf 1984	B
	Deutsch 1984	B

Film:
Rabbit, Run Warner Bros 1969

Upward, Edward Born in Essex, 1903.

A singular literary career, and a very small output. Upward should not be underrated, however, for his little-known trilogy is very fine indeed, and quite on a par with Henry Green or Christopher Isherwood. Isherwood, indeed, was a friend of Upward's in the thirties, and glowed throughout a review of Upward's second published novel, and first of the trilogy, entitled – appropriately enough – *In the Thirties*. 'I believe,' said Isherwood, 'we are being introduced to a masterpiece.' The completed trilogy was published fifteen years later in 1977, and I should not be at all surprised to learn that it is now out of print. It is, as I say, severely underrated.

A curious bit of publishing, the handling of the trilogy. The first volume was published in 1962 and the second in 1969, quite in the normal way. Then in 1977 came the complete trilogy under the blanket title *The Spiral Ascent*, containing the first two novels as well as the newly-published third and final volume. If you come across first editions of volumes one and two, therefore, you are forced to juxtapose them with the complete trilogy in order to complete the trilogy, if you follow me.

Prices can – and should – only go, well – upward.

1	**Buddha** (verse)	Cambridge 1924	G
2	**Journey to the Border** (novel)	Hogarth Press 1938	E
3	**In the Thirties** (novel)	Heinemann 1962	C
4	**The Rotten Elements** (novel)	Heinemann 1969	C
5	**The Railway Accident and Other Stories**	Heinemann 1969	C
6	**The Spiral Ascent**	Heinemann 1977	C

6 Contains 3 and 4 as well as *No Home But the Struggle*, published for the first time, which completes the trilogy.

Vidal, Gore   Born in New York, 1925.

Still very popular and very much read, Vidal is not as eagerly collected in this country as one might expect, and values – even for the early and scarce titles – are holding.

1	**Williwaw** (novel)	Dutton 1946	H
		Heinemann 1970	B
2	**In a Yellow Wood** (novel)	Dutton 1947	G
3	**The City and the Pillar** (novel)	Dutton 1948	F
		Lehmann 1949	D
	A revised edition was published by Dutton in 1965 (**B**), and by Heinemann in 1966 (**B**).		
4	**The Season of Comfort** (novel)	Dutton 1949	E
5	**A Search for the King** (novel)	Dutton 1950	E
6	**Dark Green, Bright Red** (novel)	Dutton 1950	E
		Lehmann 1950	D
7	**The Judgement of Paris** (novel)	Dutton 1952	E
		Heinemann 1953	D
8	**Death in the Fifth Position** (novel) Pseud. Edgar Box.	Dutton 1952	G
		Heinemann 1954	F
9	**Death Before Bedtime** (novel) Pseud. Edgar Box.	Dutton 1953	G
		Heinemann 1954	F
		Dutton 1954	G
10	**Death Likes It Hot** (novel) Pseud. Edgar Box.	Heinemann 1955	F
11	**Messiah** (novel)	Dutton 1954	D
		Heinemann 1955	C
12	**A Thirsty Evil: 7 Short Stories**	Zero Press (NY) 1956	D
		Heinemann 1958	C

13	**Visit to a Small Planet and Other Television Plays** Incl. *Barn Burning, Dark Possession, The Death of Billy the Kid, A Sense of Justice, Smoke, Summer Pavilion* and *The Turn of the Screw.*	Little Brown 1957	C
14	**The Best Man** (play)	Little Brown 1960	B
15	**Three Plays** Cont. *Visit to a Small Planet, The Best Man, On the March to the Sea.*	Heinemann 1962	B
16	**Romulus: A New Comedy**	Dramatists Play Service 1962	B
17	**Three: Williwaw, A Thirsty Evil, Julian the Apostate** (novels)	NAL 1962	B
18	**Rocking the Boat** (essays)	Little Brown 1962 Heinemann 1963	C B
19	**Julian** (novel)	Little Brown 1964 Heinemann 1964	C B
20	**Washington DC** (novel)	Little Brown 1967 Heinemann 1967	C B
21	**Myra Breckinridge** (novel)	Little Brown 1968 Blond 1968	C B
22	**Weekend** (play)	Dramatists Play Service 1968	B
23	**Reflections Upon a Sinking Ship** (essays)	Little Brown 1969 Heinemann 1969	B B
24	**Two Sisters** (novel)	Little Brown 1970 Heinemann 1970	B B
25	**An Evening with Richard Nixon** (play)	Random House 1972	B
26	**Homage to Daniel Shays: Collected Essays 1952–1972** **Collected Essays 1952–1972**	Random House 1972 Heinemann 1974	B B
27	**Burr** (novel)	Random House 1973 Heinemann 1974	B B
28	**Myron** (novel)	Random House 1974 Heinemann 1975	B B
29	**1876** (novel)	Random House 1976 Heinemann 1976	B B
30	**Matters of Fact and Fiction: Essays 1973–1976**	Random House 1977 Heinemann 1977	B B
31	**Great American Families and Others** (non-fiction)	Norton 1977 Times 1977	B B
32	**Kalki** (novel)	Random House 1978 Heinemann 1978	B B
33	**In a Yellow Wood** (novel)	Random House 1979 Heinemann 1979	B B

34 **Creation** (novel)	Random House 1981	B
	Heinemann 1981	B
35 **Duluth** (novel)	Random House 1983	B
	Heinemann 1983	B

Films:
The Left-Handed Gun Warner Bros 1958 (*The Death of Billy the Kid*) **Visit to a Small Planet** Paramount 1959 **The Best Man** United Artists 1968 **Myra Breckinridge** 20th Century Fox 1969 Vidal worked on the screenplays of **The Best Man** and (in collaboration) **Myra Breckinridge**; also on several other films, including **Suddenly, Last Summer**.

Bibliography:
Robert J. Stanton **Gore Vidal: A Primary and Secondary Bibliography** Hall 1978

Vonnegut, Kurt Jnr   Born in Indianapolis, 1922.

Vonnegut appealed very strongly to the young in the sixties, and, while retaining that following, he seems to be appealing to the next generation in quite the same way – and, it must be said, with quite the same books, for *Slaughterhouse-Five* remains the highlight, and is the sort of thing people *mean* when they talk about Vonnegut; they do *not* mean *Slapstick* and *Deadeye Dick*, jolly though these are, in their way. Prices for English editions remain quite low, but he is very much collected in America.

1 **Player Piano** (novel)	Scribner 1952	I
	Macmillan 1953	G
2 **The Sirens of Titan** (novel)	Fawcett 1959	F
	Gollancz 1962	D
3 **Canary in a Cathouse** (stories)	Fawcett 1961	F
4 **Mother Night** (novel)	Fawcett 1961	E
	Cape 1968	B
5 **Cat's Cradle** (novel)	Holt Rinehart 1963	E
	Gollancz 1963	C
6 **God Bless You, Mr Rosewater** (novel)	Holt Rinehart 1965	E
	Cape 1965	C
7 **Welcome to the Monkey House** (pieces)	Delacorte 1968	D
8 **Slaughterhouse-Five** (novel)	Delacorte 1969	E
	Cape 1970	C
9 **Happy Birthday, Wanda June** (play)	Delacorte 1971	B
	Cape 1973	B
10 **Between Time and Timbuctoo** (play)	Delacorte 1972	B
11 **Breakfast of Champions** (novel)	Delacorte 1973	C
	Cape 1973	B

Vonnegut

12	**Wampeters, Foma, and**	Delacorte 1974	C
	Granfalloons: Opinions	Cape 1975	B
13	**Slapstick** (novel)	Delacorte 1976	B
		Cape 1976	A
14	**The Eden Express** (novel)	Delacorte 1976	B
		Cape 1976	A
15	**Jailbird** (novel)	Delacorte 1979	B
		Cape 1979	A
16	**Sun Moon Star** (juvenile)	Harper 1980	C
	With Ivan Chermayeff.	Hutchinson 1980	B
17	**Palm Sunday** (autobiog. fragments)	Delacorte 1981	B
		Cape 1981	B
18	**Deadeye Dick** (novel)	Delacorte 1982	B
		Cape 1983	A

Films:
Slaughterhouse-Five Universal 1972   **Slapstick** International 1981.

Bibliography:
Asa B. Pieratt Jnr and Jerome Klinkowitz **Kurt Vonnegut Jnr: A Descriptive Bibliography and Annotated Secondary Checklist** Shoe String Press 1974.

Wallace, Edgar   Born at Greenwich, 1875. Died 1932.

Apart from stories and plays, Wallace wrote an estimated 150 novels in twenty-seven years. Mercifully, there is a bibliography, which ought to be acquired if one is considering collecting the entire *œuvre* of this phenomenon. It is confined to British editions only, however. Of all his well-known books, I shall confine myself to recording just one – the most desirable, although not the most rare, for those wanting merely a representation of his work.

The Four Just Men	Tallis Press 1905	F

The true 1st has the £500 reward advert printed on the front of its yellow cover, and not the later coloured illustration. A fold-out frontis. should be present, as well as the all-important competition slip – situated at the back of the book. It is a perforated form intended to be removed, filled in, and sent up by the hopeful owner of the volume. Collectors, therefore, seek copies from the libraries of singularly uncompetitive people.

Films:
The Secret Four Ealing 1939 (**The Four Just Men**)
In addition to this, nearly forty other Wallace novels have been filmed.

Waterhouse, Keith   Born in Yorkshire, 1929.

Although his name is a known one, and his work terribly successful, I believe Waterhouse to be very underrated as an English humorist, a novelist of great skill and subtlety. I suppose, though, because he does so much journalism – he does so much *everything*, actually – he is primarily known for it, along with his many stage collaborations with Willis Hall. Indeed, were it not for the great Billy Liar, Waterhouse would not be known for fiction at all. This, though, is excusable, for he is nothing if not diverse, as will be seen from the ensuing checklist of his works. His first book was a non-fictional study of the Café Royal, of all things, and was followed by a clutch of pseudonymous funny books. Now he slips in TV adaptations of Worzel Gummidge between plays, journalism, essays and a novel or two.

1	**The Café Royal:** **90 Years of Bohemia** (non-fiction) With Guy Deghy.	Hutchinson 1955	C
2	**How to Avoid Matrimony** (humour) Pseud. Herald Froy.	Muller 1957 Day 1959	A A
3	**There is a Happy Land** (novel)	Joseph 1957	D
4	**Britain's Voice Abroad** (essay)	Daily Mirror 1957	A
5	**The Future of Television** (essay)	Daily Mirror 1958	A
6	**How to Survive Matrimony** (humour) Pseud. Herald Froy.	Muller 1958	A
7	**The Joneses: How to Keep Up with Them** (humour) Pseud. Lee Gibb.	Muller 1959	A
8	**Billy Liar** (novel)	Joseph 1959 Norton 1960	G E
9	**Billy Liar** (play) With Willis Hall.	Joseph 1960 Norton 1960	B B
10	**Can This be Love?** (humour) Pseud. Herald Froy.	Muller 1960	A
11	**The Higher Jones** (humour) Pseud. Lee Gibb.	Muller 1961	A
12	**Maybe You're Just Inferior** (humour) Pseud. Herald Froy.	Muller 1961	A
13	**Celebration** (play) With Willis Hall.	Joseph 1961	B
14	**Jubb** (novel)	Joseph 1963 Putnam 1964	C B

Waterhouse

15	**All Things Bright and Beautiful** (play) With Willis Hall.	Joseph 1963	B
16	**The Sponge Room and Squat Betty** (plays) With Willis Hall	Evans 1963	A
17	**England, Our England** (play) With Willis Hall.	Evans 1964	A
18	**Come Laughing Home** (play) With Willis Hall.	Evans 1965	A
19	**Help Stamp Out Marriage** (play) With Willis Hall.	French (US) 1966	A
	Say Who You Are	Evans 1967	A
20	**The Bucket Shop** (novel)	Joseph 1968	C
	Everything Must Go	Putnam 1969	C
21	**The Passing of the Third-Floor Buck** (*Punch* pieces)	Joseph 1974	A
22	**Saturday, Sunday, Monday** (play) Adaptation, with Willis Hall, from the play by Eduardo de Filippo.	Heinemann 1974	B
23	**Who's Who** (play) With Willis Hall.	French 1974	A
24	**Children's Day** (play) With Willis Hall.	French 1975	A
25	**Billy Liar on the Moon** (novel)	Joseph 1975 Putnam 1976	B B
26	**Mondays, Thursdays** (*Daily Mirror* pieces)	Joseph 1976	A
27	**Office Life** (novel)	Joseph 1978	A
28	**Whoops-A-Daisy** (play) With Willis Hall.	Evans 1978	A
29	**Filumena** (play) With Willis Hall.	French 1978	A
30	**The Television Adventures of Worzel Gummidge** With Willis Hall.	Puffin 1979	A
31	**Rhubarb, Rhubarb and Other Noises** (journalism)	Joseph 1979	A
32	**More Television Adventures of Worzel Gummidge** With Willis Hall.	Puffin 1980	A
33	**Worzel Gummidge at the Fair** With Willis Hall.	Puffin 1980	A
34	**Worzel Gummidge Goes to the Seaside** With Willis Hall.	Puffin 1980	A

35	**The Trials of Worzel Gummidge** With Willis Hall.	Puffin 1981	A
36	**Maggie Muggins: Or Spring in Earl's Court** (novel)	Joseph 1981	A
37	**Daily Mirror Style** (essay)	Daily Mirror 1981	A
38	**Worzel's Birthday** With Willis Hall.	Puffin 1981	A
39	**Worzel Gummidge and Aunt Sally** With Willis Hall.	Severn House 1982	A
40	**Fanny Peculiar** (*Punch* pieces)	Joseph 1983	A
41	**In the Mood** (novel)	Joseph 1983	A
42	**Mrs Pooter's Diary** (fiction)	Joseph 1983	A
43	**Thinks** (novel)	Joseph 1984	A

Film:
Billy Liar Warner Bros 1962.

Waugh, Evelyn   Born in London, 1903. Died 1966.

Still one of the most respected and collected authors of all. This state I see to be permanent. Every time you read Waugh, he seems to get better and better – there is *always* more to be got from the book than the last time you read it. Similarly, a Waugh first edition seems always to be more expensive than the last time one saw a copy in a shop. There is no possibility that this trend will reverse.

Many of the following were preceded by limited, signed editions.

1	**The World to Come: A Poem in Three Cantos**	privately printed 1916	T
2	**PRB: An Essay on the Pre-Raphaelite Brotherhood**	privately printed 1926	R
3	**Decline and Fall** (novel)	Chapman & Hall 1928	L
		Farrar 1929	J
4	**Rossetti** (biog.)	Duckworth 1928	K
		Dodd 1928	J
5	**Labels** (travel)	Duckworth 1930	K
	A Bachelor Abroad	Farrar 1932	I
6	**Vile Bodies** (novel)	Chapman & Hall 1930	J
		Farrar 1930	H
7	**Remote People** (travel)	Duckworth 1931	J
	They Were Still Dancing	Farrar 1932	I

Waugh

8	**Black Mischief** (novel)	Chapman & Hall 1932	I
		Farrar 1932	G
9	**A Handful of Dust** (novel)	Chapman & Hall 1934	H
		Farrar 1934	G
10	**Ninety-Two Days** (travel)	Duckworth 1934	I
		Farrar 1934	H
11	**Edmund Campion** (biog.)	Longman 1935	H
		Sheed 1935	G
12	**Mr Loveday's Little Outing** (stories)	Chapman & Hall 1936	L
		Little Brown 1936	J
13	**Waugh in Abyssinia** (travel)	Longman 1936	I
		Farrar 1936	H
14	**Scoop** (novel)	Chapman & Hall 1938	G
		Little Brown 1938	F
15	**Robbery Under Law** (travel) **Mexico: An Object Lesson**	Chapman & Hall 1939 Little Brown 1939	L J
16	**Put Out More Flags** (novel)	Chapman & Hall 1942	F
		Little Brown 1942	E
17	**Work Suspended** (unfinished novel)	Chapman & Hall 1942	G
18	**Brideshead Revisited** (novel)	Chapman & Hall 1945	G
		Little Brown 1945	F
19	**When the Going Was Good** (travel) Selection from 5, 7, 10 and 13.	Duckworth 1946 Little Brown 1947	E D
20	**Wine in Peace and War**	Saccone & Speed n.d. (1947)	H
21	**Scott-King's Modern Europe** (novel)	Chapman & Hall 1947 Little Brown 1949	C C
22	**The Loved One** (novel) Preceded by publication in *Horizon*.	Chapman & Hall 1948 Little Brown 1948	C C
23	**Helena** (novel)	Chapman & Hall 1950	C
		Little Brown 1950	C
24	**Men at Arms** (novel)	Chapman & Hall 1952	D
		Little Brown 1952	C
25	**The Holy Places** (essays) This was published in an ordinary edition at fifteen shillings, and in a limited, signed edition at three guineas (**O**).	Queen Anne Press 1952	I
26	**Love Among the Ruins** (novel)	Chapman & Hall 1953	C
27	**Officers and Gentlemen** (novel)	Chapman & Hall 1955	C
		Little Brown 1955	C
28	**The Ordeal of Gilbert Pinfold** (novel)	Chapman & Hall 1957 Little Brown 1957	C C
29	**Ronald Knox** (biog.)	Chapman & Hall 1959	C
		Little Brown 1960	C
30	**A Tourist in Africa** (travel)	Chapman & Hall 1960	C
		Little Brown 1960	C

31 **Unconditional Surrender** (novel)	Chapman & Hall 1961	C
The End of the Battle	Little Brown 1961	C
Together with 24 and 27 it forms		
the War trilogy.		
32 **Basil Seal Rides Again** (novel)	Chapman & Hall 1963	G
	Little Brown 1963	F
33 **A Little Learning** (autobiog.)	Chapman & Hall 1964	C
	Little Brown 1964	C
34 **Diaries**	Weidenfeld 1976	C
Large parts of this first appeared in the	Little Brown 1976	C
Observer Colour Magazine for 25 March		
1973, and for the succeeding seven		
issues. *The Sunday Times* published two		
more extracts immediately prior to		
book publication.		
35 **A Little Order** (journalism)	Methuen 1977	B
	Little Brown 1981	B
36 **The Letters of Evelyn Waugh**	Weidenfeld 1980	C
	Ticknor & Fields 1980	C
37 **Charles Ryder's Schooldays**	Little Brown 1982	C
and Other Stories		
This recently discovered story, relating		
to the narrator in **Brideshead**		
Revisited, was originally published in		
the *Times Literary Supplement*, but was		
not published in book form in the UK.		
38 **The Essays, Articles and**	Methuen 1983	C
Reviews of Evelyn Waugh	Little Brown 1984	C

Films:
The Loved One MGM 1965 **Decline and Fall of a Birdwatcher**
20th Century Fox 1968 (**Decline and Fall**)

Biography:
Christopher Sykes **Evelyn Waugh** Collins 1975.

Wesker, Arnold   Born in London, 1932.

Still a fairly prolific playwright, but notable only for the following clutch of
highlights, the title of one of which (*Chips With Everything*) very quickly
entered the language. In this new era of the microcomputer, the phrase
might be ripe for reprogramming.

1 **Chicken Soup with Barley** (play)	Penguin 1959	B

2	**Roots** (play)	Penguin 1959	B
	This was contained in **New English Dramatists**.		
3	**I'm Talking about Jerusalem** (play)	Penguin 1960	B
	1, 2 and 3 form the Wesker trilogy.		
4	**The Wesker Trilogy** (plays)	Cape 1960	C
	Contains 1, 2 and 3, for the first time in hardback.	Random House 1961	B
5	**The Kitchen** (play)	Penguin 1960	A
	This was contained in **New English Dramatists** 2. An expanded edition was published in 1962 by Cape, and by Random House.		
6	**Chips with Everything** (play)	Cape 1962	B
		Random House 1963	B

Film:
The Kitchen British Lion 1961.

Wheatley, Dennis   Born in 1897. Died 1977.

Wheatley did not publish a book until 1933, and although today his Black Magic novels are of interest – particularly the earlier ones – prime interest is reserved for the Dossiers. In collaboration with J.G. Links, Wheatley published four of these, beginning with *Murder off Miami* in 1936. They were, quite simply, a totally new and appealing way of presenting a crime story – as a police dossier, complete with typescript pages, facsimile telegrams, notes, postcards, and clues – such as strands of hair, fingerprints, and spent matches; all this was bound in wrapps, and tied with red ribbon. A sealed compartment at the rear could be slit open to reveal the solution to the crime – and, not unnaturally, very few survive with the seal intact! They were published, unbelievably, at 3/6d – or $17\frac{1}{2}$p. Today fine copies are Grade E, and hard to find. Wheatley himself foresaw this, for the rear cover of *Murder off Miami* reads: '*Keep this carefully*. It is a First Edition of the first Crime Story ever presented in this way. Should others follow, it is possible that an undamaged copy of "Murder off Miami" may be of considerable interest one day.' They are undated, but later impressions announce '*N*th Thousand' on the cover.

	The Dossiers:		
1	**Murder off Miami**	Hutchinson 1936	F
	File on Bolitho Lane	Morrow 1936	F
2	**Who Killed Robert Prentice?**	Hutchinson 1937	F
	File on Robert Prentice	Greenberg 1937	F
3	**The Mallinsay Massacre**	Hutchinson 1938	E
4	**Herewith the Clues**	Hutchinson 1939	E
	Below is a short selection of Wheatley's Black Magic novels.		

5 **The Devil Rides Out**   Hutchinson 1934   C
6 **To the Devil – a Daughter**   Hutchinson 1953   B
7 **The Satanist**   Hutchinson 1960   B

Films:
The Devil Rides Out Associated British 1971   **To the Devil, a Daughter** EMI 1976.

In addition to these, three further Wheatley novels have been filmed.

White, Patrick   Born in London, 1912. Australian.

Although White is read and collected in his own right as a very considerable author, there is no doubt that there is great nationalistic feeling, in that many Australians collect him simply because he is *their* Nobel prize-winner. Nothing wrong with that – except that very often they appear to be interested in no one else at all.

1 **The Ploughman and Other Poems**	Beacon Press (Australia) 1935	L
2 **Happy Valley** (novel)	Harrap 1939	I
	Viking 1940	H
3 **The Living and the Dead** (novel)	Routledge 1941	H
	Viking 1941	H
4 **The Aunt's Story** (novel)	Routledge 1948	G
	Viking 1948	G
5 **The Tree of Man** (novel)	Viking 1955	D
	Eyre & Spottiswoode 1956	D
6 **Voss** (novel)	Viking 1957	D
	Eyre & Spottiswoode 1957	D
7 **Riders in the Chariot** (novel)	Viking 1961	D
	Eyre & Spottiswoode 1961	C
8 **The Burnt Ones** (stories)	Viking 1964	D
	Eyre & Spottiswoode 1964	C
9 **Four Plays** Cont. **The Ham Funeral, The Season at Sarsparilla, A Cheery Soul** and **Night on Bald Mountain**.	Eyre & Spottiswoode 1965 Viking 1966	C C
10 **The Solid Mandala** (novel)	Viking 1966	D
	Eyre & Spottiswoode 1966	C
11 **The Vivisector** (novel)	Viking 1970	C
	Cape 1970	B

White, P.

12	**The Eye of the Storm** (novel)	Cape 1973	B
		Viking 1974	B
13	**The Cockatoos:**	Cape 1974	B
	Short Novels and Stories	Viking 1975	B
14	**A Fringe of Leaves** (novel)	Cape 1976	B
		Viking 1976	B
15	**Big Toys** (play)	Currency Press (Australia) 1978	C
16	**The Twyborn Affair** (novel)	Cape 1979	B
		Viking 1980	B
17	**The Night the Prowler** (play)	Penguin (Australia) 1979	B
18	**Flaws in the Glass:**	Cape 1981	B
	A Self-Portrait	Viking 1982	B

Bibliography:
Jannette Finch **A Bibliography of Patrick White** Libraries Board (Australia) 1966.

White, T.H.   Born in India, 1906. Died 1964.

There is a great deal of collectors' interest in T.H. White, and for this reason I have now replaced the brief selection of his works that I provided in *Collecting Modern First Editions* with a complete listing.

1	**Loved Helen and Other Poems**	Chatto & Windus 1929	L
		Viking 1929	K
2	**The Green Bay Tree** (verse)	Heffer 1929	K
3	**Dead Mr Nixon** (novel)	Cassell 1931	K
	With R. McNair Scott.		
4	**Darkness at Pemberley** (novel)	Gollancz 1932	I
		Century 1933	G
5	**They Winter Abroad** (novel)	Chatto & Windus 1932	I
	Under the pseudonym James Aston.		
		Viking 1932	H
6	**First Lesson** (novel)	Chatto & Windus 1932	H
	Under the pseudonym James Aston.		
		Knopf 1933	G
7	**Farewell Victoria** (novel)	Collins 1933	G
		Smith & Haas 1934	F
8	**Earth Stopped: Or Mr Marx's Sporting Tour** (novel)	Collins 1934	G
		Putnam 1935	F
9	**Gone to Ground** (novel)	Collins 1935	F
		Putnam 1935	F
10	**England Have My Bones** (non-fiction)	Collins 1936	E
		Macmillan 1936	E
11	**Burke's Steerage: Or, the Amateur**	Collins 1938	D

Gentleman's Introduction to Noble Sports and Pastimes	Putnam 1939	C
12 The Sword in the Stone	Collins 1938	L
(juvenile)	Putnam 1939	K
13 The Witch in the Wood	Putnam 1939	J
(juvenile)	Collins 1940	I
14 The Ill-Made Knight	Putnam 1940	I
(juvenile)	Collins 1941	H
12, 13 and 14 are illustrated by the author.		
15 Mistress Masham's Repose	Putnam 1946	D
(juvenile)	Cape 1947	C
16 The Elephant and the Kangaroo (novel)	Putnam 1947	D
	Cape 1948	C
17 The Age of Scandal	Cape 1950	D
(non-fiction)	Putnam 1950	D
18 The Goshawk (non-fiction)	Cape 1951	D
	Putnam 1952	C
19 The Scandalmonger (non-fiction)	Cape 1952	D
	Putnam 1952	C
20 The Book of Beasts	Cape 1954	D
Edited and translated by T.H.W.	Putnam 1955	D
21 The Master: An Adventure Story	Cape 1957	D
(juvenile)	Putnam 1957	C
22 The Once and Future King	Collins 1958	D
This, the complete Arthurian epic,	Putnam 1958	D
comprises 12 with two new chapters, 13 rewritten and bearing the title The Queen of Air and Darkness, 14, largely unaltered, and The Candle in the Wind, published for the first time.		
23 The Godstone and the Blackymor (non-fiction)	Cape 1959	C
	Putnam 1959	C
24 America at Last: The American Journal of T.H. White	Putnam 1965	C
25 The White/Garnett Letters	Cape 1968	C
Correspondence edited by David Garnett.	Viking 1968	C
26 The Book of Merlyn (novel)	University of Texas	C
This concludes 22.	Press 1977	
27 The Maharajah and Other Stories	Putnam 1981	B
28 Letters to a Friend: The Correspondence Between T.H. White and L.J. Potts	Putnam 1982	B

Biography:
Sylvia Townsend Warner **T.H. White: A Biography** Cape/Chatto 1967.
This includes a bibliography of unpublished writings.

Williams, Tennessee Born in Columbus, Mississippi, 1911.
Pseudonym for Thomas Williams.

Author of over seventy books, ninety per cent of them plays, the highlights of which are listed below. A unique writer who brought us a new form of language – the inarticulacy of the misfit, this catching the feel of the fifties very well, and often memorably played by Brando in the moody black-and-white films.

1	**The Glass Menagerie** (play)	Random House 1945	E
		Lehmann 1948	D
2	**A Streetcar Named Desire** (play)	New Directions 1947	E
		Lehmann 1949	D
3	**The Roman Spring of Mrs Stone** (novel)	New Directions 1950	D
		Lehmann 1950	C
4	**Cat on a Hot Tin Roof** (play)	New Directions 1955	D
		Secker 1956	C
5	**Sweet Bird of Youth** (play)	New Directions 1959	D
		Secker 1961	C
6	**The Milk Train Doesn't Stop Here Anymore** (play)	New Directions 1964	D
		Secker 1964	C

Films:
The Glass Menagerie Warner Bros 1950　**A Streetcar Named Desire** Warner Bros 1951　**Cat on a Hot Tin Roof** MGM 1958
The Roman Spring of Mrs Stone Warner Bros 1961　**Sweet Bird of Youth** MGM 1962　**Boom** Universal 1968 (*The Milk Train Doesn't Stop Here Anymore*)

Williams wrote the screenplays for **The Glass Menagerie** (with Peter Berneis), **A Streetcar Named Desire** (with Oscar Saul) and **Boom**. In addition to these, eight other Williams plays have been filmed.
In 1976, Tennessee Williams's **Memoirs** were published by Doubleday and in England by W.H. Allen.

Wilson, A.N.　Born in Staffordshire, 1950.

Wilson seems set to stay. He has published nine books in seven years, three of them scholarly biographies and the remainder very well received literary novels. Until recently he was also literary editor of the *Spectator*, and he is not yet thirty-five, which must annoy some people to blazes. If you are going to collect him, now is very much the time, for I feel that Wilson is going to be quite prolific and the whole thing could get out of hand. None of them should be *too* difficult – at the moment.

1	**The Sweets of Pimlico** (novel)	Secker 1977	D
2	**Unguarded Hours** (novel)	Secker 1978	C
3	**Kindly Light** (novel)	Secker 1979	C
4	**The Healing Art** (novel)	Secker 1980	C
5	**The Laird of Abbotsford:** **A View of Walter Scott** (biography)	OUP 1980	B
6	**Who was Oswald Fish?** (novel)	Secker 1981	B
7	**The Life of John Milton** (biography)	OUP 1983	B
8	**Scandal** (novel)	Hamilton 1983	B
9	**Hilaire Belloc** (biography)	Hamilton 1984	B
		Atheneum 1984	B

Wilson, Angus   Born in Sussex, 1913.

Still a very popular author with both young and old collectors, and now a grand old man of letters – to say nothing of a knight. His pastiches and satires on middle-class Englishness are always appreciated, though perhaps some fail to recognize a lot of the subtlety that is always there amid the traditional narrative of the story. In this way, I think it is true to say that Wilson may be read on more than one level, and yet be enjoyed. His books are undervalued and surprisingly easy to gather (bar the early stubborn ones) despite being sought after. This apparent dichotomy is rare in the book collecting world, but it does happen; another such case is C.P. Snow and possibly V.S. Pritchett as well (although collectors' interest in the latter has markedly declined, and hence his – maybe temporary – exclusion from this volume). With Angus Wilson, though, I detect a reversal of this trend, and I think a collector would be wise to gather up all he can now, if he wants them, before the dealers start putting up prices.

1	**The Wrong Set and Other Stories**	Secker 1949	E
		Morrow 1950	D
2	**Such Darling Dodos and Other Stories**	Secker 1950	D
		Morrow 1951	C
3	**Emile Zola** (non-fiction)	Secker 1952	C
		Morrow 1952	C
4	**Hemlock and After** (novel)	Secker 1952	C
		Viking 1952	C
5	**For Whom the Cloche Tolls** (essay) With Philippe Jullian.	Methuen 1953	C
6	**The Mulberry Bush** (play)	Secker 1956	B
7	**Anglo-Saxon Attitudes** (novel)	Secker 1956	C
		Viking 1956	B
8	**A Bit Off the Map and Other Stories**	Secker 1957	C
		Viking 1957	B
9	**The Middle Age of Mrs Eliot** (novel)	Secker 1958	C
		Viking 1959	B

Wilson, A.

10 **The Old Men at the Zoo** (novel)	Secker 1961	B
	Viking 1961	B
11 **The Wild Garden: or, Speaking of Writing** (non-fiction)	University of California Press 1963	B
	Secker 1963	B
12 **Tempo: The Impact of Television on the Arts** (non-fiction)	Studio Vista 1964	C
	Dufour 1966	B
13 **Late Call** (novel)	Secker 1964	C
	Viking 1965	B
14 **No Laughing Matter** (novel)	Secker 1967	B
	Viking 1967	B
15 **Death Dance: 25 Stories**	Viking 1969	B
16 **The World of Charles Dickens** (non-fiction)	Secker 1970	B
	Viking 1970	B
17 **As If by Magic** (novel)	Secker 1973	B
	Viking 1973	A
18 **The Strange Ride of Rudyard Kipling** (biography)	Secker 1977	B
	Viking 1978	B
19 **Setting the World on Fire** (novel)	Secker 1980	B
	Viking 1980	B
20 **Diversity and Depth in Fiction: Selected Critical Writings**	Secker 1983	B
	Viking 1983	B

Wilson, Colin   Born in Leicester, 1931.

It seems scarcely believable, but these are the facts: between 1956 and 1976, Wilson published forty books. Since then (the last time I listed him) he has added another fifteen. Little wonder he seems so consumed by phenomena. He is still very popular and collected, particularly by the younger set, which gives the lie to the critics' opinion that *The Outsider* was the only decent book he ever wrote; they even changed their minds about *that*, later on. How these collectors keep up with Wilson's output, however, God alone knows.

1 **The Outsider** (philosophy)	Gollancz 1956	E
	Houghton Mifflin 1956	D
2 **Religion and the Rebel** (non-fiction)	Gollancz 1957	C
	Houghton Mifflin 1957	C
3 **The Age of Defeat** (non-fiction) **The Stature of Man**	Gollancz 1959	C
	Houghton Mifflin 1959	C
4 **Ritual in the Dark** (novel)	Gollancz 1960	C
	Houghton Mifflin 1960	C

5 **Adrift in Soho** (novel)	Gollancz 1961	D
	Houghton Mifflin 1961	C
6 **Encyclopedia of Murder** (non-fiction)	Barker 1961	E
	Putnam 1962	D
With Patricia Pitman.		
7 **The Strength to Dream:** **Literature and the Imagination** (non-fiction)	Gollancz 1962	C
	Houghton Mifflin 1962	C
8 **Origins of the Sexual Impulse** (non-fiction)	Barker 1963	C
	Putnam 1963	C
9 **The World of Violence** (novel)	Gollancz 1963	C
The Violent World of Hugh Green	Houghton Mifflin 1963	C
10 **Man Without a Shadow** (novel)	Barker 1963	C
The Sex Diary of Gerard Sorme	Dial Press 1963	C
11 **Necessary Doubt** (novel)	Barker 1964	C
	Simon & Schuster 1964	C
12 **Rasputin and the Fall of the** **Romanovs** (non-fiction)	Barker 1964	D
	Farrar Straus 1964	C
13 **Brandy of the Damned:** **Discoveries of a Musical Eclectic** **Chords and Discords: Purely** **Personal Opinions on Music** A supplemented edition, entitled **Colin Wilson on Music**, was published by Pan in 1967 (**B**).	Baker 1964	C
	Atheneum 1966	C
14 **Beyond the Outsider: The** **Philosophy of the Future**	Barker 1965	B
	Houghton Mifflin 1965	B
15 **Eagle and Earwig** (essay)	Barker 1965	B
16 **The Glass Cage** (novel)	Barker 1966	C
	Random House 1967	C
17 **Introduction to the New** **Existentialism**	Hutchinson 1966	B
	Houghton Mifflin 1967	B
18 **Sex and the Intelligent** **Teenager** (non-fiction)	Arrow 1966	B
19 **Voyage to a Beginning** (autobiog.)	Woolf 1966	B
	Crown 1969	B
20 **The Mind Parasites** (novel)	Barker 1967	C
	Arkham House 1967	C
21 **The Philosopher's Stone** (novel)	Barker 1969	B
	Crown 1971	B
22 **Bernard Shaw: A Reassessment** (non-fiction)	Hutchinson 1969	B
	Atheneum 1969	B
23 **A Casebook of Murder** (non-fiction)	Frewin 1969	B
	Cowles 1970	B

Wilson, C.

24	**The Killer** (novel)	NEL 1970	C
	Lingard	Crown 1970	B
25	**The God of the Labyrinth** (novel)	Hart-Davis 1970	B
	The Hedonists	NAL 1971	B
26	**Strindberg** (play)	Calder 1970	B
		Random House 1971	B
27	**Poetry and Mysticism** (non-fiction)	Hutchinson 1970	B
		City Lights 1970	B
28	**The Strange Genius of David Lindsay** (non-fiction) With E.H. Visiak and J.B. Pick.	Barker 1970	B
29	**The Black Room** (novel)	Weidenfeld 1971	C
30	**The Occult: A History**	Hodder & Stoughton 1971	B
		Random House 1971	B
31	**New Pathways in Psychology**	Gollancz 1972	B
		Taplinger 1972	B
32	**Order of Assassins: The Psychology of Murder** (non-fiction)	Hart-Davis 1972	B
33	**L'Amour: The Way of Love** (non-fiction)	Crown (NY) 1972	B
34	**Strange Powers** (non-fiction)	Latimer 1973	B
		Random House 1975	B
35	**Tree by Tolkien** (essay)	Covent Garden Press 1973	C
		Capra Press 1974	B
36	**Hermann Hesse** (essay)	Village Press (UK) 1974	B
		Leaves of Grass Press 1974	B
37	**William Reich** (essay)	Village Press 1974	B
		Leaves of Grass Press 1974	B
38	**Jorge Luis Borges** (essay)	Village Press 1974	B
		Leaves of Grass Press 1974	B
39	**The Schoolgirl Murder Case** (novel)	Granada 1974	C
		Crown 1974	C
40	**A Book of Booze** (non-fiction)	Gollancz 1974	B
41	**Mysterious Powers** (non-fiction) This was republished in America by Doubleday in the same year as **They Had Strange Powers** (B).	Aldus 1975	B
		Danbury Press 1975	B
42	**The Craft of the Novel** (non-fiction)	Gollancz 1975	C
43	**The Space Vampires** (novel)	Granada 1976	B
		Random House 1976	B

44 **Enigmas and Mysteries** (non-fiction)	Aldus 1976	B
	Doubleday 1976	B
45 **The Geller Phenomenon** (non-fiction)	Aldus 1976	B
46 **Mysteries: An Investigation into the Occult, the Paranormal and the Supernatural**	Hodder & Stoughton 1978	B
	Putnam 1978	B
47 **Science Fiction as Existentialism** (essay)	Bran's Head Press 1978	C
48 **The Search for the Real Arthur** (essay)	Bossiney 1979	B
49 **Starseekers** (non-fiction)	Hodder & Stoughton 1980	B
	Doubleday 1981	B
50 **Anti-Sartre, With an Essay on Camus**	Borgo Press (US) 1980	C
51 **The War against Sleep: The Philosophy of Gurdjieff**	Aquarian Press 1980	C
52 **Frankenstein's Castle** (story)	Ashgrove Press 1980	C
53 **The Quest for Wilhelm Reich** (non-fiction)	Granada 1981	B
	Doubleday 1981	B
54 **Poltergeist** (novel)	NEL 1981	B
	Putnam 1982	B
55 **Witches** (non-fiction) Illustrated by Una Woodruff.	Dragon's World 1982	B
56 **Access to Inner Worlds** (non-fiction)	Hutchinson 1983	B
57 **Encyclopedia of Modern Murder** With D. Seaman.	Barker 1983	B
58 **A Criminal History of Mankind** (non-fiction)	Granada 1984	B
	Putnam 1984	B

Film:
Space Vampires Canon 1981.

Bibliography:
John A. Weigel **Colin Wilson** Twayne (US) 1975.
A critical work, containing a bibliography.

Wodehouse, P.G.   Born in Guildford, 1881. Died 1975.

From the collector's point of view, Plum has now become one of the most expensive twentieth-century authors of all – and although this is suitable (the whole world *should* be clamouring for him) it is rather hard on the younger collector who might have come to Wodehouse as a result of all the razzmatazz surrounding the centenary in 1981, only to discover that he has no hope whatever of competing in what has become a world of rather big money. What a change in ten short years. When I started collecting P.G. (I wasn't yet a bookseller) every shop one entered had shelves of the things – firsts and reprints all jumbled up, for it made no difference as Wodehouse was known to write funny books, which were intended to be read, enjoyed, lent, borrowed and discarded. A fine copy in a dust-wrapper might have commanded a slightly higher price than one without – say, twenty-five shillings instead of a pound. No prestigious West End dealer would touch Wodehouse at all, reminding you rather sniffily that they were *serious* dealers in lasting literature. There were no auction records because no book by Wodehouse had ever been sent to auction. By the time I published *Collecting Modern First Editions* (1977) Plum was fairly enthusiastically collected, but even then the elusive early boys' books were in the fifty-pound category. When my *P. G. Wodehouse: An Illustrated Biography* came out (1979) prices had roughly doubled, but the real boom has taken place since then. *Every* dealer now lists and recognizes Wodehouse, and very high prices are achieved at auction, the rarer items usually going to the West End dealers, who then resell them (often to America) at God alone knows what. There are people now collecting Wodehouse who five years ago had never *heard* of Wodehouse, and even now show little inclination to read him; they have heard, however, that he has become a sound investment. All this, of course, would have amused Plum himself, but not angered him; *nothing* angered Plum. Not long ago I was asked to contribute an entry on him for *The Fontana Dictionary of Modern Thought*, of all things. Wodehouse has truly become all things to all men. I managed to condense his life into the 100 required words with remarkable ease; it was not a terribly *eventful* life for he spent the greater part of it writing books. Since then we have had the centenary which brought forth a welter of books (my own was paperbacked) the very fine Pierpont Morgan exhibition, and critical reappraisals galore. I arranged a season of Wodehouse films at The National Film Theatre, which was fun, and even since then we have had Frances Donaldson's authorized biography, a Companion from Richard Usborne, and quite a few anthologies and reissues. Plum, then, it will be seen, is rather popular.

I sometimes get asked whether collectors' interest in Plum has peaked. This feeling might arise from the fact that some titles do hang fire on the shelves. I think the truth is that most collectors have now assembled a goodly pile, but everyone is chasing those elusive titles which, by definition, rarely come up, while new collectors are rather deterred by the current level of prices; there sometimes appears to be something of a lull, therefore, but interest remains at fever pitch among the fanatics, of whom there is a growing number.

1	**The Pothunters** (novel) This first book is bound in blue, with silver ornament, and not the later pictorial cover. No adverts. Very, very scarce.	Black 1902 Macmillan (US) 1924	O G
2	**A Prefect's Uncle** (novel)	Black 1903 Macmillan 1924	N G
3	**Tales of St Austin's** (stories)	Black 1903 Macmillan 1923	N G
4	**The Gold Bat** (novel)	Black 1904 Macmillan 1923	N G
5	**William Tell Told Again** This retelling of the classic tale is scarce in any edition, but the 1st may be recognized by the date on the t/p, and the absence of the publisher's address.	Black 1904	K
6	**The Head of Kay's** (novel)	Black 1905 Macmillan 1922	N G
7	**Love Among the Chickens** (novel) A 'Popular Edition' revised and entirely rewritten by the author was reissued by Jenkins in 1921 (**C**).	Newnes 1906 Circle Publishing Co. 1909	P M
8	**The White Feather** (novel)	Black 1907 Macmillan 1922	N G
9	**Not George Washington** (novel) With Herbert Westbrook.	Cassell 1907	O
10	**The Globe By the Way Book** Again written with Herbert Westbrook, this paperback was a compilation of the 'By the Way' columns from the **Globe** Paper.	Globe 1908	Q
11	**The Swoop** (novel) A pictorially wrapped paperback.	Alston Rivers 1909	N
12	**Mike** (novel) The second part of this novel was reissued as **Enter Psmith** Black 1935 (**E**); the whole novel was then revised and reissued in two volumes – **Mike at Wrykyn** (**E**) and **Mike and Psmith** (**E**) Jenkins 1953.	Black 1909 Macmillan 1924	M G
13	**The Intrusion of Jimmy** (novel) **A Gentleman of Leisure** Not to be confused with the Newnes reissue of 1911.	Watt (US) 1910 Alston Rivers 1910	M K
14	**Psmith in the City** (novel)	Black 1910	L
15	**The Prince and Betty** (novel)	Watt 1912	M

16	**The Prince and Betty** (novel) An almost entirely different book to 15.	Mills & Boon 1912	L
17	**The Little Nugget** (novel)	Methuen 1913	K
		Watt 1914	K
18	**The Man Upstairs** (stories)	Methuen 1914	K
19	**Something New** (novel)	Appleton (US) 1915	K
	Something Fresh	Methuen 1915	J
20	**Psmith Journalist** (novel) Another version of 15.	Black 1915	L
21	**Uneasy Money** (novel)	Appleton 1916	K
		Methuen 1917	J
22	**Piccadilly Jim** (novel) Wodehouse's first book with Jenkins.	Dodd Mead 1917 Jenkins 1918	H G
23	**The Man with Two Left Feet** (stories)	Methuen 1917 Burt 1933	I D
24	**My Man Jeeves** (stories) The first Jeeves title. This small red volume was issued in Newnes 1/9d Novel Series.	Newnes 1919	M
25	**Their Mutual Child** (novel) **The Coming of Bill**	Boni & Liveright 1919 Jenkins 1920	G E
26	**A Damsel in Distress** (novel)	Doran 1919 Jenkins 1919	I I
27	**The Little Warrior** (novel) **Jill the Reckless**	Doran 1920 Jenkins 1921	I H
28	**Indiscretions of Archie** (stories)	Jenkins 1921 Doran 1921	H H
29	**The Clicking of Cuthbert** (stories) The 1st lists only eight titles on the verso of the half-title.	Jenkins 1922	G
	Golf Without Tears	Doran 1924	F
30	**Three Men and a Maid** (novel) **The Girl on the Boat** English edition revised from original American	Doran 1922 Jenkins 1922	I H
31	**The Adventures of Sally** (novel) Dated 1923.	Jenkins 1922	H
	Mostly Sally	Doran 1923	G
32	**The Inimitable Jeeves** (stories) This must list ten titles on the verso of the half-title.	Jenkins 1923	H
	Jeeves	Doran 1923	G
33	**Leave it to Psmith** (novel)	Jenkins 1923 Doran 1924	F E
34	**Ukridge** (stories) Thirteen titles must appear on the verso of the half-title.	Jenkins 1924	G
	He Rather Enjoyed It	Doran 1926	F

35	**Bill the Conqueror** (novel)	Methuen 1924	F
		Doran 1925	E
36	**Carry On, Jeeves** (stories)	Jenkins 1925	H
		Doran 1927	G
37	**Sam the Sudden** (novel)	Methuen 1925	F
	Sam in the Suburbs	Doran 1925	F
38	**The Heart of a Goof** (stories)	Jenkins 1926	F
	Divots	Doran 1927	F
39	**Hearts and Diamonds** (play adapt.)	Prowse 1926	D
	With Laurie Wylie.		
40	**The Play's the Thing** (play adapt.)	Brentano's (US) 1927	D
41	**The Small Bachelor** (novel)	Methuen 1927	F
		Doran 1927	F
42	**Meet Mr Mulliner** (stories)	Jenkins 1927	G
		Doran 1928	F
43	**Good Morning, Bill** (play)	Methuen 1928	F
44	**Money for Nothing** (novel)	Jenkins 1928	G
		Doran 1928	F
45	**Mr. Mulliner Speaking** (stories)	Jenkins 1929	G
		Doubleday 1930	F
46	**Fish Preferred** (novel)	Doubleday 1929	G
	Summer Lightning	Jenkins 1929	G
47	**A Damsel in Distress** (play)	French 1930	D
	With Ian Hay.		
48	**Baa, Baa, Black Sheep** (play)	French 1930	D
	With Ian Hay.		
49	**Very Good, Jeeves** (stories)	Doubleday 1930	G
		Jenkins 1930	G
50	**Big Money** (novel)	Doubleday 1931	G
		Jenkins 1931	G
51	**If I Were You** (novel)	Doubleday 1931	G
		Jenkins 1931	G
52	**Jeeves Omnibus** (anthol.)	Jenkins 1931	F
53	**Leave It to Psmith** (play)	French 1932	D
	With Ian Hay.		
54	**Louder and Funnier** (essays)	Faber 1932	L
	Wodehouse's only book of humorous essays, and his only book from Faber. Only those copies in yellow cloth, with the Rex Whistler d/w, are the first issue. Sheets were later bound in green for the Faber Library series. (E)		
55	**Doctor Sally** (novel)	Methuen 1932	G
56	**Hot Water** (novel)	Jenkins 1932	G
		Doubleday 1932	F
57	**Nothing but Wodehouse** (anthol.)	Doubleday 1932	D

58	**Mulliner Nights** (stories)	Jenkins 1933	G
		Doubleday 1933	F
59	**Heavy Weather** (novel)	Little Brown 1933	G
		Jenkins 1933	G
60	**Candlelight** (play adapt.)	French 1934	D
61	**A Century of Humour** (ed. P.G.W.)	Hutchinson 1934	C
62	**Library of Humour:**	Methuen 1934	C
	P. G. Wodehouse (anthol.)		
63	**Right Ho, Jeeves** (novel)	Jenkins 1934	F
	Brinkley Manor	Little Brown 1934	F
64	**Thank You, Jeeves** (novel)	Jenkins 1934	F
		Little Brown 1934	F
65	**Enter Psmith** (novel)	Black 1935 (see 12)	E
66	**Mulliner Omnibus** (anthol.)	Jenkins 1935	D
67	**Blandings Castle** (stories)	Jenkins 1935	F
		Doubleday 1935	E
68	**The Luck of the Bodkins** (novel)	Jenkins 1935	F
		Little Brown 1936	E
69	**Anything Goes** (play)	French 1936	C
70	**Young Men in Spats** (stories)	Jenkins 1936	F
		Doubleday 1936	E
71	**Laughing Gas** (novel)	Jenkins 1936	E
		Doubleday 1936	D
72	**The Three Musketeers** (play)	Chappell 1937	C
	With Gifford Grey and George	Harms 1937	C
	Grossmith.		
73	**Lord Emsworth and Others**	Jenkins 1937	E
	(stories)		
	Crime Wave at Blandings	Doubleday 1937	E
74	**Summer Moonshine** (novel)	Doubleday 1937	F
		Jenkins 1938	F
75	**The Code of the Woosters** (novel)	Doubleday 1938	G
		Jenkins 1938	G
76	**Weekend Wodehouse** (anthol.)	Jenkins 1939	D
		Doubleday 1939	C
77	**Uncle Fred in the Springtime**	Doubleday 1939	F
	(novel)	Jenkins 1939	F
78	**Wodehouse on Golf** (anthol.)	Doubleday 1940	C
79	**Eggs, Beans and Crumpets**	Jenkins 1940	F
	(stories)	Doubleday 1940	F
80	**Quick Service** (novel)	Jenkins 1940	E
		Doubleday 1940	E
81	**Money in the Bank** (novel)	Doubleday 1942	D
		Jenkins 1946	D
82	**Joy in the Morning** (novel)	Doubleday 1946	D
		Jenkins 1947	D
83	**Full Moon** (novel)	Doubleday 1947	D
		Jenkins 1947	D

84	**Spring Fever** (novel)	Doubleday 1948	D
		Jenkins 1948	D
85	**Uncle Dynamite** (novel)	Jenkins 1948	D
		Didier 1948	D
86	**The Best of Wodehouse** (anthol.)	Pocket Books (US) 1949	C
87	**The Mating Season** (novel)	Jenkins 1949	D
		Didier 1949	D
88	**Nothing Serious** (stories)	Jenkins 1950	E
		Doubleday 1951	D
89	**The Old Reliable** (novel)	Jenkins 1951	E
		Doubleday 1951	D
90	**Best of Modern Humor** (ed. P.G.W.)	McBride (US) 1952	C
91	**The Week-End Book of Humo(u)r** (ed. P.G.W.)	Washburn (US) 1952	C
		Jenkins 1954	C
92	**Barmy in Wonderland** (novel)	Jenkins 1952	F
	Angel Cake	Doubleday 1952	E
93	**Pigs Have Wings** (novel)	Doubleday 1952	C
		Jenkins 1952	C
94	**Mike at Wrykyn** (novel)	Jenkins 1953	E
95	**Mike and Psmith** (novel) For 94 and 95, see 12.	Jenkins 1953	E
96	**Ring for Jeeves** (novel)	Jenkins 1953	E
	The Return of Jeeves	Simon & Schuster 1954	E
97	**Bring on the Girls** (autobiog.) Written with Guy Bolton. The English edition was rewritten from the original American, and has a different selection of photographs.	Simon & Schuster 1953 Jenkins 1954	F E
98	**Performing Flea** (letters) An extensively revised edition, entitled **Author! Author!**, was published in America	Jenkins 1953 Simon & Schuster 1962	E E
99	**Jeeves and the Feudal Spirit** (novel)	Jenkins 1954	E
	Bertie Wooster Sees It Through	Simon & Schuster 1955	E
100	**Carry on Jeeves** (play) With Guy Bolton.	Evans 1956	C
101	**French Leave** (novel)	Jenkins 1956	D
		Simon & Schuster 1959	D
102	**America, I Like You** (autobiog.)	Simon & Schuster 1956	E
103	**Over Seventy** (autobiog.) A revised edition of 102.	Jenkins 1957	E

Wodehouse

104	**Something Fishy** (novel)	Jenkins 1957	D
	The Butler Did It	Simon & Schuster 1957	D
105	**Selected Stories by P. G. Wodehouse**	Modern Library 1958	C
106	**Cocktail Time** (novel)	Jenkins 1958	D
		Simon & Schuster 1958	D
107	**A Few Quick Ones** (stories)	Simon & Schuster 1959	D
		Jenkins 1959	D
108	**The Most of P. G. Wodehouse** (anthol.)	Simon & Schuster 1960	C
109	**How Right You are, Jeeves** (novel)	Simon & Schuster 1960	D
	Jeeves in the Offing	Jenkins 1960	D
110	**The Ice in the Bedroom** (novel) The English edition lacks the word 'The' in the title.	Simon & Schuster 1961	C
		Jenkins 1961	C
111	**Service with a Smile** (novel)	Simon & Schuster 1961	D
		Jenkins 1962	D
112	**Stiff Upper Lip, Jeeves** (novel)	Simon & Schuster 1963	D
		Jenkins 1963	D
113	**Biffen's Millions** (novel)	Simon & Schuster 1964	C
	Frozen Assets	Jenkins 1964	C
114	**The Brinkmanship of Galahad Threepwood** (novel)	Simon & Schuster 1965	C
	Galahad at Blandings	Jenkins 1965	C
115	**Plum Pie** (stories)	Jenkins 1966	C
		Simon & Schuster 1967	C
116	**A Carnival of Modern Humo(u)r** (ed. P.G.W.) This, along with 90 and 91, was edited in association with Scott Meredith.	Delacorte 1967	C
		Jenkins 1968	C
117	**The World of Jeeves** (anthol.)	Jenkins 1967	C
118	**The Purloined Paperweight** (novel)	Simon & Schuster 1967	C
	Company for Henry	Jenkins 1967	C
119	**Do Butlers Burgle Banks?** (novel)	Simon & Schuster 1968	C
		Jenkins 1968	C
120	**A Pelican at Blandings** (novel)	Jenkins 1969	C
	No Nudes is Good Nudes	Simon & Schuster 1970	C
121	**The Girl in Blue** (novel)	Barrie & Jenkins 1970	C
		Simon & Schuster 1971	C

122	**Much Obliged, Jeeves** (novel)	Barrie & Jenkins 1971	C
	Jeeves and the Tie That Binds	Simon & Schuster 1971	C
	This novel was published to coincide with P.G.W.'s ninetieth birthday.		
123	**The World of Mr Mulliner**	Barrie & Jenkins 1972	C
	(anthol.)	Taplinger 1974	C
124	**Pearls, Girls, and Monty Bodkin** (novel)	Barrie & Jenkins 1972	B
	The Plot That Thickened	Simon & Schuster 1973	B
125	**The Golf Omnibus** (anthol.)	Barrie & Jenkins 1973	B
		Simon & Schuster 1974	B
126	**Bachelors Anonymous** (novel)	Barrie & Jenkins 1973	B
		Simon & Schuster 1974	B
127	**The World of Psmith** (anthol.)	Barrie & Jenkins 1974	B
128	**Aunts Aren't Gentlemen** (novel)	Barrie & Jenkins 1974	B
	The Cat-Nappers	Simon & Schuster 1974	B
129	**The World of Ukridge** (anthol.)	Barrie & Jenkins 1975	B
130	**The World of Blandings** (anthol.)	Barrie & Jenkins 1976	B
131	**The Uncollected Wodehouse** (stories and articles) Edited by David Jasen, introduced by Malcolm Muggeridge.	Seabury Press (US) 1976	C
132	**Vintage Wodehouse** (anthology) Edited by Richard Usborne.	Barrie & Jenkins 1977	B
133	**Sunset at Blandings** (novel) Unfinished, posthumous novel, edited by Richard Usborne.	Chatto & Windus 1977	B
		Simon & Schuster 1977	B
134	**Wodehouse on Wodehouse** Contains his three autobiographical works: **Bring on the Girls**, **Performing Flea**, and **Over Seventy**.	Hutchinson 1980	B
135	**Tales from the Drones Club** (anthology)	Hutchinson 1982	B
136	**Wodehouse Nuggets** (anthology) Chosen by Richard Usborne.	Hutchinson 1983	B
137	**The World of Uncle Fred** (anthology)	Hutchinson 1983	B
138	**Four Plays** Contains **The Play's the Thing**, **Good Morning Bill**, **Leave it to Psmith** and **Come on Jeeves**.	Methuen 1983	B

Films:
Gentleman of Leisure Lasky 1915   **Uneasy Money** Essanay 1917   **Oh Boy!** Pathe 1919   **Piccadilly Jim** Selznick 1919

Wodehouse

The Prince and Betty Pathe 1920   **Damsel in Distress** Pathe
1920   **Oh Lady! Lady!** Realart 1920   **Their Mutual Child** American
Film Co. 1920   **A Gentleman of Leisure** Lasky 1923   **The Clicking
of Cuthbert** Stoll 1924   **Sally** First National 1925   **The Small
Bachelor** Universal 1927   **Oh Kay!** First National 1928   **Sally**
(remake) First National 1930   **Summer Lightning** British &
Dominions 1933   **Leave it to Me** British International 1933   (*Leave it to
Psmith*)   **Have a Heart** MGM 1934   **Piccadilly Jim** MGM
1936   **Anything Goes** Paramount 1936   **Thank You, Jeeves** Fox
1936   **A Damsel in Distress** RKO 1937   **Step Lively, Jeeves** Fox
1937   **Anything Goes** Paramount 1956   **The Girl on the Boat** United
Artists 1961

There are now about two dozen works on Wodehouse, including:

Biography/Bibliography:
David A. Jasen **A Bibliography and Reader's Guide to the First
Editions of P. G. Wodehouse** Barrie & Jenkins 1971
Joseph Connolly **P. G. Wodehouse: An Illustrated Biography** Orbis
1979   Frances Donaldson **P. G. Wodehouse: The Authorized
Biography** Weidenfeld 1982

Criticism, etc.:
Richard Usborne **Wodehouse at Work to the End** Barrie & Jenkins
1976   Richard Usborne **A Wodehouse Companion** Elm Tree
1981   ed. James A. Heineman and Donald R. Bensen **P. G.
Wodehouse: A Centenary Celebration 1881–1981** Pierpont Morgan
Library (US) 1981. This is a truly magnificent confection. It contains
essays on just about every single aspect of Plum, and the most detailed
bibliography to date, by Eileen McIlvaine. The book was softbacked, but
a hardcover edition came out in the UK from the Oxford University Press
in 1982.

Woolf, Leonard   Born in London, 1880. Died 1969.

Not just the Brian Epstein of the Bloomsbury Group, but himself the author
of a large number of books – many of a political nature – the highlights of
which are listed below. As founder of The Hogarth Press, he would no doubt
be gratified by the fact that there are many collectors around eager for
anything in first edition that was issued by the press, and not just the
undisputed highlights from Virginia. This is a very rare distinction for a
publisher, for despite the name, the Hogarth Press was not a press in the
sense of Golden Cockerel or Nonesuch; the Press was a trade and commercial
publisher, by far the greatest part of its output being ordinary productions at
ordinary prices. Hogarth Press books, then, are not collected for their
intrinsic beauty, but because of their importance in the history of publishing.
The only other house that I can think of that shares this distinction is

Penguin: I have yet to hear of a Cape collector, or a Faber collector – or indeed any other trade publisher.

Stories about the primitive workings of the Press abound, the most droll centring around Leonard's thriftiness. If it is true, though, that he hung Hogarth Press galley and page proofs in the lavatory in place of something more customary, today's collector thinks not 'how mean!' but only of Leonard's consummate extravagance!

1	**The Village in the Jungle** (novel)	Arnold 1913	J
		Harcourt Brace 1926	D
2	**The Hotel** (play)	Hogarth Press 1939	E
		Dial Press 1963	C
3	**Sowing** (autobiog.)	Hogarth Press 1960	D
		Harcourt Brace 1960	C
4	**Growing** (autobiog.)	Hogarth Press 1961	C
		Harcourt Brace 1962	B
5	**Beginning Again** (autobiog.)	Hogarth Press 1964	C
		Harcourt Brace 1964	B
6	**Downhill All the Way** (autobiog.)	Hogarth Press 1967	C
		Harcourt Brace 1967	B
7	**The Journey Not the Arrival Matters** (autobiog.)	Hogarth Press 1969	C
		Harcourt Brace 1970	B

Woolf, Virginia   Born in London, 1882. Died 1941.

Who was or is the greatest female English novelist? Many people would come up with Jane Austen, or a Bronte. Many more, I think, would go for Virginia Woolf. Her reputation is mighty, and the vast amount of posthumously published material has – far from having had a diminishing effect – enhanced it still further, for with her letters, and most particularly with her diary, we have master works of the first order; the five-volume diary really could come to be ranked amongst her finest works. The young seem to approach the lady with trepidation, and are very often surprised to find how very much at one with her they are. Within a traditional framework, she comes across as intensely modern and unforgettable; it is difficult to read *The Waves* and remain indifferent.

To many, Virginia Woolf *is* the Bloomsbury Group. She is certainly the greatest talent to have emerged from this singular circle. The Bloomsbury gravy train steams on for ever, though, for the public (and the review pages) seem never to tire of the latest discoveries about Lytton and Duncan and Vanessa and Carrington and Vita and Ottoline and all.

1	**The Voyage Out** (novel)	Duckworth 1915	M
		Doran 1920	I

Woolf, V.

2	**Two Stories** Cont. **The Mark on the Wall** by Virginia, and **The Three Jews** by Leonard. It is notable for being the very first Hogarth Press publication, printed in an edition of 150 wrappered copies.	Hogarth Press 1917	N
3	**Kew Gardens** (story) 150 copies printed, in wrpps.	Hogarth Press 1919	K
4	**Night and Day** (novel)	Duckworth 1919 Doran 1920	J I
5	**Monday or Tuesday** (stories) Woodcuts and cover design by Vanessa Bell.	Hogarth Press 1921 Harcourt Brace 1921	J I
6	**Jacob's Room** (novel)	Hogarth Press 1922 Harcourt Brace 1923	I H
7	**Mr Bennett and Mrs Brown** (essay) No. 1 in the Hogarth Essays series.	Hogarth Press 1924	G
8	**The Common Reader** (essays)	Hogarth Press 1925 Harcourt Brace 1925	H G
9	**Mrs Dalloway** (novel)	Hogarth Press 1925 Harcourt Brace 1925	I H
10	**To the Lighthouse** (novel)	Hogarth Press 1927 Harcourt Brace 1927	I H
11	**Orlando: A Biography** (novel) The Gaige edition was limited to 861 copies, 800 numbered and signed for sale at $15.	Crosby Gaige (NY) 1928 Hogarth Press 1928 Harcourt Brace	L H G
12	**A Room of One's Own** (essay) The 1st joint American-English edition was limited to 492 copies, 450 for sale, and each signed.	Fountain Press/ Hogarth Press 1929 Hogarth Press 1929 Harcourt Brace 1929	L H F
13	**Street Haunting** (essay) Limited to 500 signed copies.	Westgate Press (San Francisco) 1930	K
14	**On Being Ill** (essay) Limited to 250 signed copies.	Hogarth Press 1930	L
15	**Beau Brummell** (essay) Limited to 550 signed copies.	Rimington & Hooper (NY) 1930	K
16	**The Waves** (novel)	Hogarth Press 1931 Harcourt Brace 1931	J I
17	**A Letter to a Young Poet** (essay) No. 8 in the Hogarth Letters series.	Hogarth Press 1932	D
18	**The Common Reader: Second Series** (essays)	Hogarth Press 1932 Harcourt Brace 1932	G F
19	**Flush: A Biography**	Hogarth Press 1933 Harcourt Brace 1933	D D
20	**Walter Sickert: A Conversation** (essay)	Hogarth Press 1934	E

21 **The Roger Fry Memorial Exhibition** (address) Only 125 copies printed, and none for sale.	Bristol 1935	J
22 **The Years** (novel)	Hogarth Press 1937 Harcourt Brace 1937	H G
23 **Three Guineas** (essay)	Hogarth Press 1938 Harcourt Brace 1938	E D
24 **Reviewing** (essay) No. 4 in the Hogarth Sixpenny Pamphlets series.	Hogarth Press 1939	D
25 **Roger Fry: A Biography**	Hogarth Press 1940 Harcourt Brace 1940	F E
26 **Between the Acts** (novel)	Hogarth Press 1941 Harcourt Brace 1941	E D
27 **The Death of the Moth** (essays)	Hogarth Press 1942 Harcourt Brace 1942	E D
28 **A Haunted House** (stories)	Hogarth Press 1943 Harcourt Brace 1944	D C
29 **The Moment and Other Essays**	Hogarth Press 1947 Harcourt Brace 1948	C B
30 **The Captain's Death Bed** (essays) The American edition actually preceded by one week.	Hogarth Press 1950 Harcourt Brace 1950	D D
31 **A Writer's Diary**	Hogarth Press 1953 Harcourt Brace 1954	D C
32 **Virginia Wolf & Lytton Strachey: Letters**	Hogarth Press 1956 Harcourt Brace 1956	C B
33 **Granite and Rainbow** (essays)	Hogarth Press 1958 Harcourt Brace 1958	D C
34 **Contemporary Writers** (essays)	Hogarth Press 1965 Harcourt Brace 1966	C B
35 **Nurse Lugton's Golden Thimble** (story) With pictures by Duncan Grant.	Hogarth Press 1966	E
36 **Mrs Dalloway's Party** (story)	Hogarth Press 1973	B
37 **The Flight of the Mind: The Letters of Virginia Woolf 1888–1912**	Hogarth Press 1975 Harcourt Brace 1975	C C
38 **Moments of Being** (autobiog.)	Sussex University Press 1976	B
39 **The Question of Things Happening: The Letters of Virginia Woolf 1912–1922**	Hogarth Press 1976 Harcourt Brace 1976	C C
40 **Freshwater** (comedy)	Hogarth Press 1976	B
41 **The Diary of Virginia Woolf Volume I: 1915–1919**	Hogarth Press 1977 Harcourt Brace 1977	C C
42 **Books and Portraits** (essays)	Hogarth Press 1977 Harcourt Brace 1977	B B

43 **A Change of Perspective:**	Hogarth Press 1977	C
The Letters of Virginia Woolf	Harcourt Brace 1977	C
1923–1928		
44 **The Pargiters** (fiction)	Hogarth Press 1977	B
	Harcourt Brace 1977	B
45 **The Diary of Virginia Woolf**	Hogarth Press 1978	C
Volume II: 1920–1924	Harcourt Brace 1978	C
46 **A Reflection of the Other**	Hogarth Press 1978	C
Person: The Letters of	Harcourt Brace 1978	C
Virginia Woolf 1929–1931		
47 **The Sickle Side of the Moon**	Hogarth Press 1979	C
The Letters of Virginia	Harcourt Brace 1979	C
Woolf 1932–1935		
48 **The Diary of Virginia Woolf**	Hogarth Press 1980	C
Volume III: 1925–1930	Harcourt Brace 1980	C
49 **Leave the Letters Till We're**	Hogarth Press 1980	C
Dead: The Letters of Virginia	Harcourt Brace 1980	C
Woolf 1936–1941		
50 **The Diary of Virginia Woolf**	Hogarth Press 1982	C
Volume IV: 1931–1935	Harcourt Brace 1982	C
51 **The London Scene** (essay)	Hogarth Press 1982	A
	Random House 1982	A
52 **The Diary of Virginia Woolf**	Chatto & Windus 1984	C
Volume V: 1936–1941	Harcourt Brace 1984	C

Biography:
Quentin Bell **Virginia Woolf** (2 vols) Hogarth Press 1972; Harcourt Brace 1972.

Bibliography:
B.J. Kirkpatrick **A Bibliography of Virginia Woolf** Hart-Davis 1957.

Wyndham, John   Born in Birmingham, England, 1903.
Died 1969.
Pseudonym of John Beynon Harris.

The early books are scarce, and quite avidly collected. Wyndham will always be known for his *Day of the Triffids*, though – a cautionary tale for gardeners everywhere.

1 **Foul Play Suspected** (novel)	Newnes 1935	I
Pseud. John Beynon.		
2 **The Secret People** (novel)	Newnes 1935	H
Pseud. John Beynon.		
3 **Planet Plane** (novel)	Newnes 1935	H
Pseud. John Beynon.		
Reissued by Michael Joseph in 1972 as		
Stowaway to Mars (**B**).		

4 **The Day of the Triffids** (novel)	Joseph 1951	G
	Doubleday 1951	F
5 **The Kraken Wakes** (novel)	Joseph 1953	E
Out of the Deeps	Ballantine 1953	C
6 **Jizzle** (stories)	Dobson 1954	C
7 **The Chrysalids** (novel)	Joseph 1955	D
8 **Re-Birth** (stories)	Ballantine (NY) 1955	C
9 **The Seeds of Time** (stories)	Joseph 1956	C
10 **The Midwich Cuckoos** (novel)	Joseph 1957	D
	Ballantine 1957	C
11 **The Outward Urge** (stories) 'With L. Parkes'. Lucas Parkes is another of Wyndham's pseudonyms, apparently used because the author considered the stories to be unlike his usual style.	Joseph 1959	C
12 **Trouble with Lichen** (novel)	Joseph 1960	C
13 **Consider her Ways and Others** (stories) The title story first appeared in **Sometime, Never** Eyre & Spottiswoode 1956; Ballantine 1956.	Joseph 1961	C
14 **The John Wyndham Omnibus** Con. 4, 5 and 7, the last two appearing in America for the first time.	Joseph 1964 Simon & Schuster 1966	B B
15 **Chocky** (novel)	Joseph 1968	B
16 **The Man from Beyond** (stories)	Joseph 1975	B

Films:
The Village of the Damned MGM 1960 (*The Midwich Cuckoos*) **The Day of the Triffids** Rank 1962.

ACKNOWLEDGEMENTS

I am indebted to the following publishers for permission to reproduce dust-wrapper designs for use as illustration within this book: Associated Book Publishers, John Calder, Jonathan Cape, Cassell, Chatto & Windus, William Collins, Faber & Faber, Samuel French, Victor Gollancz, Granada Publishing, Hamish Hamilton, William Heinemann, Hodder & Stoughton, Hutchinson, Michael Joseph, Longman, Macmillan Publishers, John Murray, Martin Secker & Warburg, Weidenfeld & Nicolson.

I should also like to thank Anthony Buckeridge for permission to quote from *Jennings and Darbishire* (Collins); Patricia, for her indefatigable telephoning, verification, and patience; Alexander Walker, for the sub-title; Stephen Adamson, for his Draconian editing; Godfrey Smith, for his faith and encouragement; Miss Olwyn Hughes, for biographical information; and – as usual – the London Library, for their coolness, calmness and (more to the point) collectedness. The rest is all my fault.